# Hands-On Microservices with Node.js

Build, test, and deploy robust microservices in JavaScript

**Diogo Resende**

Packt

BIRMINGHAM - MUMBAI

# Hands-On Microservices with Node.js



**Commissioning Editor:** Kunal Chaudhari
**Acquisition Editor:** Nigel Fernandes
**Content Development Editor**: Arun Nadar
**Technical Editor:** Leena Patil
**Copy Editor:** Safis Editing
**Project Coordinator:** Sheejal Shah
**Proofreader:** Safis Editing
**Indexer:** Tejal Daruwale Soni
**Graphics:** Jason Monteiro
**Production Coordinator:** Deepika Naik

First published: June 2018

Production reference: 1270618

Published by Packt Publishing Ltd.
Livery Place
35 Livery Street
Birmingham
B3 2PB, UK.

ISBN 978-1-78862-021-5

www.packtpub.com

# Contributors

## About the author

**Diogo Resende** is a developer with more than 15 years of experience. He has worked with Node.js almost from the beginning. His computer education and experience in many industries and telecommunication projects have given him a wide background knowledge of other architecture components and approaches that influence the overall performance of an application.

# About the reviewer

**Bruno Joseph D'mello** works at Accion labs as a senior software developer. He has 6 years of experience in web application development, in domains such as entertainment, social media, enterprise, and IT services. Bruno follows Kaizen and enjoys the freedom of architecting new things on the web. He has also contributed some of his knowledge by authoring books such as *Web Development in Node.js and MongoDB - Second Edition, What You Need to Know about Node.js*, and *JavaScript and JSON Essentials*.

*Thanks to my family for their patience and encouragement.*

# Packt is searching for authors like you

If you're interested in becoming an author for Packt, please visit `authors.packtpub.com` and apply today. We have worked with thousands of developers and tech professionals, just like you, to help them share their insight with the global tech community. You can make a general application, apply for a specific hot topic that we are recruiting an author for, or submit your own idea.

# Table of Contents

# Preface

This book is an end-to-end guide on how to split your monolithic Node.js application into several microservices. We'll cover some of the toolkits available, such as Express, Hydra, and Seneca, and create a simple microservice. We'll introduce you to continuous integration using Mocha to add a test suite, we'll use chai to test the HTTP interface, and we'll use nyc to see the test coverage.

We'll cover the concept of containers and use Docker to make our first deployment. We'll then use other tools, such as Docker Swarm, to help us to scale our service. We'll see how to do the same using Kubernetes, both locally and be using Google Cloud Platform, always using the same minimal microservice architecture and with minimal changes to the code.

## Who this book is for

The book is targeted at people who know the basics of Node.js and want to enter the world of microservices, get to know its advantages and techniques, and understand why it's so popular. It can also be useful for developers in other similar programming languages, such as Java or C#.

## What this book covers

`Chapter 1`, *Age of Microservices*, covers the evolution of computing and how development has changed and shifted from paradigm to paradigm depending on processing capacity and user demand, ultimately resulting in the age of microservices.

`Chapter 2`, *Modules and Toolkits*, introduces you to some modules that help you create a microservice, detailing different approaches: from very raw and simple modules, such as Micro and Express, to full toolkits, such as Hydra and Seneca.

`Chapter 3`, *Building a Microservice*, covers the development of a simple microservice using the most common module, Express, with a very simple HTTP interface.

`Chapter 4`, *State and Security*, covers the development of our microservice: from using the server filesystem to moving to a more structured database service, such as MySQL.

`Chapter 5`, *Testing*, shows how to use Mocha and chai to add test coverage to our previous microservice.

`Chapter 6`, *Deploying Microservices*, introduces you to Docker and helps you create a container image to use to run our microservice.

`Chapter 7`, *Scaling, Sharding, and Replicating*, covers the concept of replication when using Docker Swarm and Kubernetes locally to scale our microservice.

`Chapter 8`, *Cloud-Native Microservices*, shows how to migrate our microservice from the local Kubernetes to Google Cloud Platform, as an example of a fully cloud-native microservice.

`Chapter 9`, *Design Patterns*, enumerates some of the most common architectural design patterns and reviews the continuous integration and deployment loop used throughout the book.

# To get the most out of this book

You should have basic Node.js skills and be somewhat comfortable with the language. We will cover Docker and Kubernetes, and it can be helpful to know the concepts of containers—but it's not mandatory.

You need to have Node.js (and npm) installed. We recommend using the current stable version, but you're free to use a previous version if it's an LTS one, with possible adaptions. If you want to deploy Kubernetes locally, you'll need to install it later on.

## Download the example code files

You can download the example code files for this book from your account at `www.packtpub.com`. If you purchased this book elsewhere, you can visit `www.packtpub.com/support` and register to have the files emailed directly to you.

You can download the code files by following these steps:

1. Log in or register at `www.packtpub.com`.
2. Select the **SUPPORT** tab.
3. Click on **Code Downloads & Errata**.
4. Enter the name of the book in the **Search** box and follow the onscreen instructions.

Once the file is downloaded, please make sure that you unzip or extract the folder using the latest version of:

- WinRAR/7-Zip for Windows
- Zipeg/iZip/UnRarX for Mac
- 7-Zip/PeaZip for Linux

The code bundle for the book is also hosted on GitHub at `https://github.com/PacktPublishing/Hands-On-Microservices-with-Node.js`. In case there's an update to the code, it will be updated on the existing GitHub repository.

We also have other code bundles from our rich catalog of books and videos available at `https://github.com/PacktPublishing/`. Check them out!

# Conventions used

There are a number of text conventions used throughout this book.

`CodeInText`: Indicates code words in the text, database table names, folder names, filenames, file extensions, pathnames, dummy URLs, user input, and Twitter handles. Here is an example: "Arrow functions are a shorter expression function syntax without their own function scope, meaning `this` reference will point to the parent scope."

A block of code is set as follows:

```
function start() {
  this.uptime = process.uptime();
  setTimeout(() => {
    console.log(this.uptime);
  }, 5000);
}
start();
```

Any command-line input or output is written as follows:

```
npm init -y
npm install express -save
```

**Bold**: Indicates a new term, an important word, or words that you see onscreen. For example, words in menus or dialog boxes appear in the text like this. Here is an example: "Go to the **Tables** section on top to see the databases."

Warnings or important notes appear like this.

Tips and tricks appear like this.

# Get in touch

Feedback from our readers is always welcome.

**General feedback**: Email `feedback@packtpub.com` and mention the book title in the subject of your message. If you have questions about any aspect of this book, please email us at `questions@packtpub.com`.

**Errata**: Although we have taken every care to ensure the accuracy of our content, mistakes do happen. If you have found a mistake in this book, we would be grateful if you would report this to us. Please visit `www.packtpub.com/submit-errata`, selecting your book, clicking on the Errata Submission Form link, and entering the details.

**Piracy**: If you come across any illegal copies of our works in any form on the Internet, we would be grateful if you would provide us with the location address or website name. Please contact us at `copyright@packtpub.com` with a link to the material.

**If you are interested in becoming an author**: If there is a topic that you have expertise in and you are interested in either writing or contributing to a book, please visit `authors.packtpub.com`.

# Reviews

Please leave a review. Once you have read and used this book, why not leave a review on the site that you purchased it from? Potential readers can then see and use your unbiased opinion to make purchase decisions, we at Packt can understand what you think about our products, and our authors can see your feedback on their book. Thank you!

For more information about Packt, please visit `packtpub.com`.

# 1
# The Age of Microservices

Decades ago, more specifically in 1974, Intel introduced 8080 to the world, which is an 8-bit processor with a 2 MHz clock speed and 64 KB of memory. This processor was used in Altair and began the revolution in personal computers.

It was sold pre-assembled or as a kit for hobbyists. It was the first computer to have enough power to actually be used for calculations. Even though it had some poor design choices and needed an engineering major to be able to use and program it, it started the spread of personal computers to the general public.

The technology evolved rapidly and the processor industry followed Moore's law, almost doubling speed every two years. Processors were still single core, with a low-efficiency ratio (power consumption per clock cycle). Because of this, servers usually did one specific job, called a service, like serving HTTP pages or managing a **Lightweight Directory Access Protocol** (**LDAP**) directory. Services were the monolith, with very few components, and were compiled altogether to be able to take the most out of the hardware processor and memory.

In the 90s, the internet was still only available for the few. Hypertext, based on HTML and HTTP, was in its infancy. Documents were simple and browsers developed language and protocol as they pleased. Competition for market share was ferocious between Internet Explorer and Netscape. The latter introduced JavaScript, which Microsoft copied as JScript:

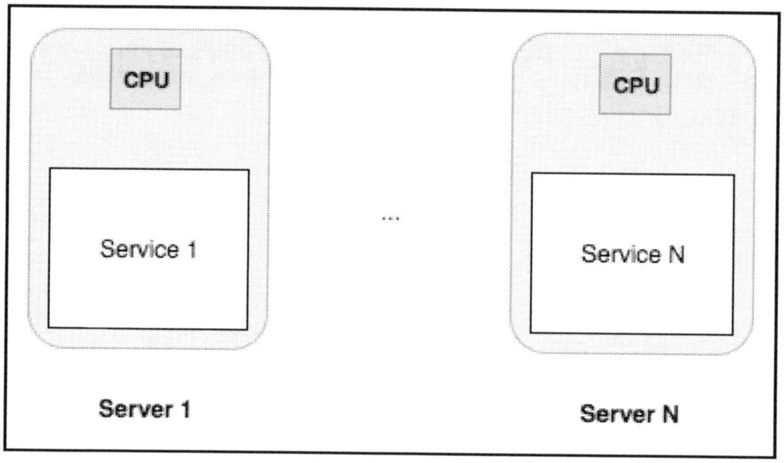


Simple single-core servers

After the turn of the century, processor speed continued to increase, memory grew to generous sizes, and 32-bit became insufficient for allocating memory addresses. The all-new 64-bit architecture appeared and personal computer processors hit the 100 W consumption mark. Servers gained muscle and were able to handle different services. Developers still avoided breaking the service into parts. Interprocess communication was considered slow and services were kept in threads, inside a single process.

The internet was starting to become largely available. Telcos started offering triple play, which included the internet bundled with television and phone services. Cellphones became part of the revolution and the age of the smartphone began.

JSON appeared as a subset of the JavaScript language, although it's considered a language-independent data format. Some web services began to support the format.

The following is an example of servers with a couple of services running, but still having only one processor.

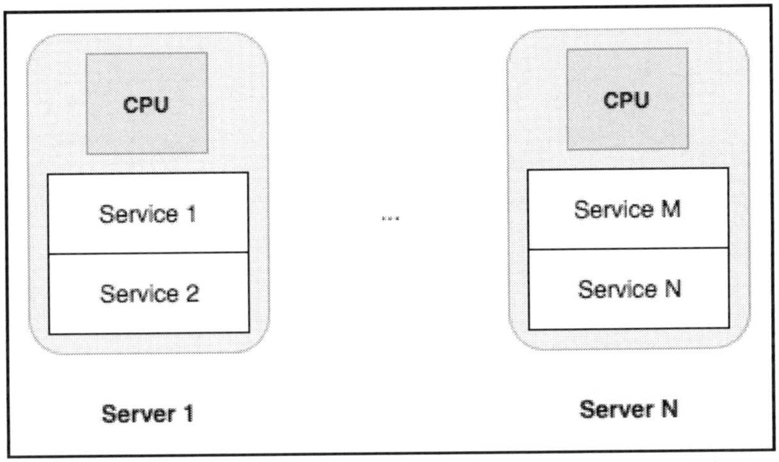


Powerful but single-core servers

Processor evolution then shifted. Instead of the increased speed that we were used to, processors started to appear with two cores, and then four cores. Eight cores followed, and it seemed the evolution of the computer would follow this path for some time.

This also meant a shift in architecture in the development paradigms. Relying on the system to take advantage of all processors is unwise. Services started to take advantage of this new layout and now it's common to see services having at least one processor per core. Just look at any web server or proxy, such as Apache or Nginx.

The internet is now widely available. Mobile access to the internet and its information corresponds to more or less half of all internet access.

In 2012, the **Internet Engineering Task Force** (**IETF**) began its first drafts for the second version of HTTP or HTTP/2, and **World Wide Web Consortium** (**W3C**) did the same for HTML/HTML5, as both standards were old and needed a remake. Thankfully, browsers agreed on merging new features and specifications and developers no longer have the burden of developing and testing their ideas on the different browser edge cases.

The following is an example of servers with more services running as we reach a point where each server has more than one processor:

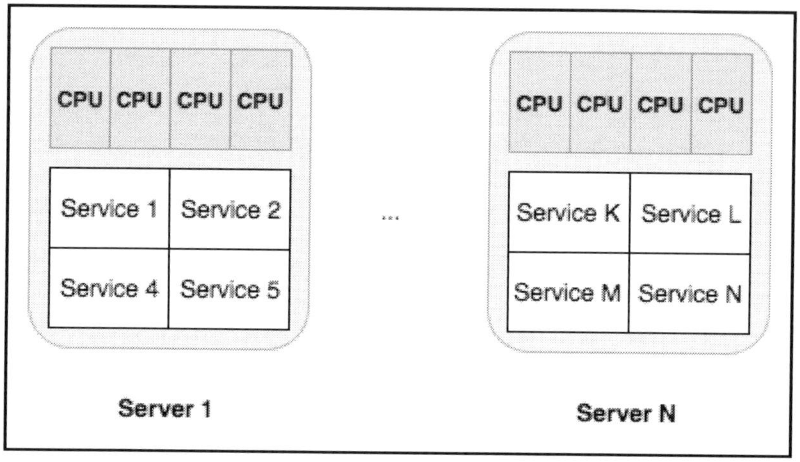


Powerful multi-core servers

Access to information in real time is a growing demand. The **Internet of Things (IoT)** multiplies the number of devices connected to the internet. People now have a couple of devices at home, and the number will just keep rising. Applications need to be able to handle this growth.

On the internet, HTTP is the standard protocol for communication. Routers usually do not block it, as it is considered a low traffic protocol (in contrast with video streams). This is actually not true nowadays, but it's now so widely used that changing this behavior would probably cause trouble.

Nowadays, it's actually so common to have the HTTP serving developer API working with JSON that most programming languages that release any version after 2015 probably support this data format natively.

As a consequence of processor evolution, and because of the data-demanding internet we now have, it's important to not only be able to scale a service or application to the several available cores, but also to scale outside a single hardware machine.

Many developers started using and following the **Service-Oriented Architecture (SOA)** principle. It's a principle where the architecture is focused on services, and each service presents itself to others as an application component and provides information to other application components, passing messages over some standard communication protocol.

# Introducing microservices

Microservices, which are a variation of SOA, have become more and more appealing. Many projects have embraced this architecture, and it's not difficult to understand why. With the constant increase in demand for information, applications become more complex, especially with more information being transferred from new data sources to new data visualization devices.

New communication technologies have emerged, social communities spring up like mushrooms, and people expect an application to be able to merge into today's cyber lifestyle.

Microservices come to the rescue by defining a simple strategy: break every complex service into a small, simpler service that is aiming for common functionality. The idea is that services should be small and lightweight - so small that they can be easily maintained, developed, and tested, and so lightweight that they can be responsive and scale more easily:

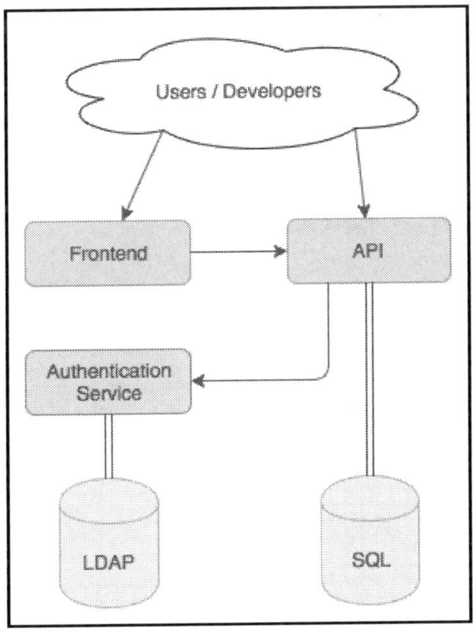


Example of a simple microservices architecture

The preceding diagram is an example of an application that has been split into small microservices (marked as green and blue), with one for the frontend interface, another one for the API, and one just for authentication.

The idea is to decompose the business logic into small and reusable parts, easily understandable in separate chunks, enabling parallel development by different teams or groups. This way, people can develop parts without being worried about breaking an other's code. Each part should be considered a black box to other parts.

It is only important that communication is well-described. It's common for microservices to communicate over HTTP and use JSON as the data format. There are other formats available, such as XML, but they have fallen into desuetude. It's also common to use AMQP as an inter-service communication, but usually not as a public API service.

To summarize, there are several advantages of using this architecture:

- **Maintenance**: Services, when separate, become easier to develop, test, and deploy because they should be simpler and small
- **Design enforcement**: A proper and good design is enforced on the application being developed
- **Knowledge encapsulation**: Services will have specific objectives, such as delivering emails, which will lead to service re-usage and knowledge about specific tasks being grouped together in services
- **Replaceable**: Services become easier to swap because their functionality and communication is well-known
- **Technology agnostic**: Each service can be developed using the best tools and languages to build it correctly
- **Performant**: Services are small and lightweight, and, as mentioned previously, use the best tools available
- **Upgradable**: Services should be interchangeable and upgradable separately
- **Productivity**: When complexity starts to grow, productivity will be better than in a monolith application

There are also costs associated with this architecture, namely:

- **Dependencies**: Because of this architecture being technology agnostic, different dependencies for different services may arise

- **Complexity**: For small applications, the bootstrap complexity is bigger compared to the monolith
- **End-to-end testing**: It becomes more complex to test the application from end to end as the number of services to inter-connect is definitely bigger than in a monolith application

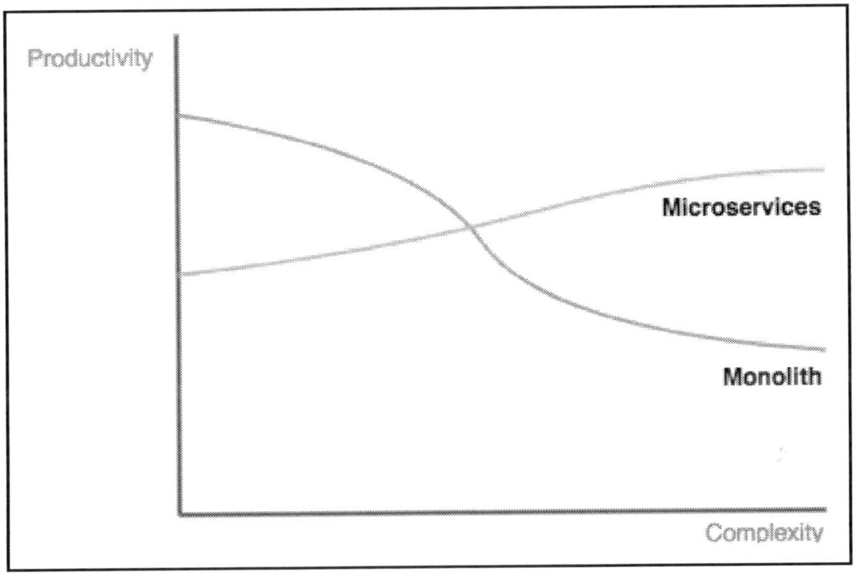


Variation in productivity as complexity grows for both monolith and microservices architecture

The graph is not to be taken very seriously; it's just an approximation of the difference between monolith and microservice architectures. In the beginning, when complexity was just beginning, productivity for microservices was poor as the architecture bootstrap demanded more work and thought.

As complexity started to increase, monolith applications became more difficult to manage and productivity began to decrease. On the other hand, as the microservices architecture started to separate services, productivity increased as the bootstrap already passed and each service was easier to manage.

Some may argue that microservices productivity will not grow as complexity will eventually also hit every service, but that's not true if a team follows the number one rule: if the complexity of a service is too much, split the service into smaller ones.

This architecture design brings long-term advantages if used correctly and across several applications. Services can be reused, which can potentially lead to more intensive usage, which will eventually lead to a more resilient and better-tested service.

Also, future applications can bootstrap faster if a development team has already bootstrapped one before. Previous services can also be integrated, which might lead to gaining an initial application testbed faster.

Using a microservices approach also helps to eliminate any long-term commitment to a technology stack. In the near future, when a team feels the need to change the stack, they can start new services using the new stack, and upgrade the old services one by one if they want to, without compromising the entire application.

# Introducing Node.js

Node.js has become a very popular language, so to speak. It's not actually a language, it's a wraparound language, like JavaScript, or ECMAScript. JavaScript was developed for the browser and it is actually small by definition. Then, browsers created a layer of access to the page elements and events, called DOM. That's one of the reasons why people hate the language so much. Node.js takes only the base language and adds an API so that developers have access to I/O, namely, the filesystem and network.

Ryan Dahl started developing Node.js back in 2009. He felt the need for a performant and less blocking program than the ones that were available. Node.js used Google's V8 JavaScript engine from the beginning and was first introduced at the JSConf in Berlin in 2009.

Looking just at the language, it's actually a sound and small, functional, object-oriented, prototype-based language. Everything is an object or inherits from it. Even numbers and functions inherit from an object. The good parts are as follows:

- Functions are first-class objects
- Functions and block-scoped variables
- Closures and anonymous functions
- Loose typing (can be seen as a bad aspect)

Node.js introduced JavaScript to a group of API modules that enable developers to access the filesystem, run and manage processes, and communicate over the network. Since it was first designed to replace a traditional web server, it also has HTTP and HTTPS modules to perform the roles of the client or server. Some other modules exist around these ones, which can be built as separate modules from the core (like DNS or URL), but live and are maintained inside the core.

At first, Node.js was very unstable, and not only the code's stability, but also the API's stability. Methods could change between versions dramatically. Modules got deprecated and replaced by others rapidly (search for the sys module for more information). Only brave developers would use it in production.

By the time it hit version 0.8, it became more reliable and the API had been stabilized. Large companies started supporting it and the community grew. Although there was a fork in 2014 because of internal conflicts, the community survived and the two code trees merged back in 2015:

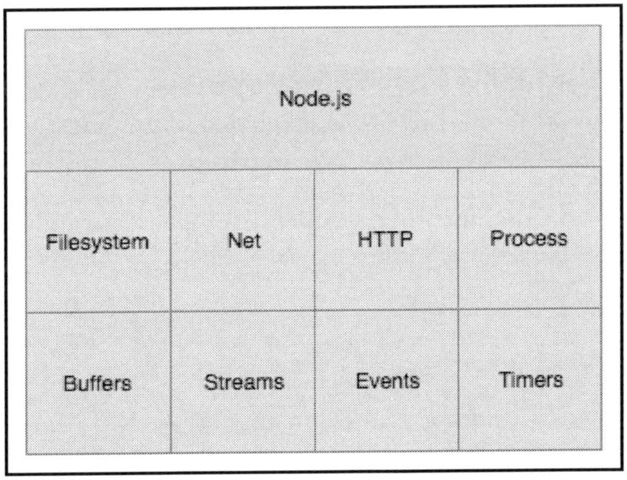


Some of the most frequently used Node.js modules

Because of its use of Google's V8, and because it has a small and stable API, it's very fast and reliable. The reason for having a small API is that one of the guidelines of the community is to only have core functionality in the core API since everything else should go into a module. This has also become a major advantage of Node.js. It has a huge community with hundreds of thousands of modules available.

If you stop and think about it, this is the microservices approach – having separate modules to do one job and one job only, and do it well. You can easily find good, stable, and mature modules for specific needs, which are used by thousands of developers. These mature modules are all easy to deploy and have test suites to ensure they keep stable and functional.

But Node.js is not only about the modules. JavaScript has also evolved in the last couple of years and Google's V8 has always been an early adopter, so Node.js developers get access to the latest new features. Some of them have given developers new ways of simplifying code and removing some of the so-called **callback hell**.

Node.js's **Long Term Support** (**LTS**) version already has stable support for many new language features. Let's see some of them and how they're useful.

# Modules

You develop Node.js code in separate files, called modules. There are three module types:

- Core modules, which you can load anywhere
- Dependency modules, which you can also load anywhere
- Local modules, which you need to load based on the relative path

Modules are loaded synchronously and cached. So, a repeated load will actually not be a load; instead, Node.js will pass you a reference to the already loaded module. This is true for all three types of modules:

```
# loading a JSON file with settings from same path as module
const settings = require("./settings");
```

Local modules are simple files where you need to know the relative or full path. You can also load a path and Node.js will look up the `index.js` file inside it. You can also load JSON files. You don't need to specify the file extension since Node.js will look for `.js` and `.json` files.

A module is nothing more than an object. The module developers decide what to expose and what not to. When you load a module, the code inside can have timers and I/O operations just like your own code. Even without you initializing it, it can run immediately after you load it.

There are hundreds of thousands of modules available. Take some time to search for something you need instead of writing one of your own. Some modules are structured so you can load parts of it (like async and lodash), thereby avoiding the memory footprint of loading everything when you just need a function or two.

# Arrow functions

Arrow functions are a shorter expression function syntax without their own function scope, meaning `this` reference will point to the parent scope. This helps developers avoid saving a reference to the parent scope so they are able to reach it later on.

```
function start() {
  this.uptime = process.uptime();
  setTimeout(() => {
    console.log(this.uptime);
  }, 5000);
}
start();
```

It also helps to write less code for simple operation functions, for example, on array methods. Arrow functions are quite useful when it comes to manipulating arrays of information, whether for filtering, transforming, or reducing them to single values:

```
let double = function (value) {
    return value * 2;
};

[ 1, 2, 3 ].map(double);      // [ 2, 4, 6 ]
[ 1, 2, 3 ].map(v => v * 2); // [ 2, 4, 6 ]
```

# Classes

JavaScript's classes are syntactic sugar over the inheritance model. They introduced a new way of defining object-oriented inheritance that existed in JavaScript but that new developers were not used to. They also introduced a simpler way of extending and defining an object prototype:

```
class Rectangle {
    constructor (w, h) {
        this.w = w;
        this.h = h;
    }
    get area () {
```

```
        return this.w * this.h;
    }
    static clone(r) {
        return new Rectangle(r.w, r.h);
    }
}
```

We just created a `Rectangle` class, with a constructor to specify dimensions and an area method, too. We also added a static method to clone a `Rectangle` instance.

Unlike the previous, and still possible, prototype definition, using this syntax will force a stricter development. More specifically:

- There's no hoisting, which means the class must be defined before usage
- There's no prototype redefinition

# Promises and async/await

A `Promise` is an object that represents the completion or failure of an asynchronous operation. The `Promise` can be chained to perform serial operations, run in parallel until all operations execute, or even race operations and wait only for the first completion or failure:

```
Promise.race([
    new Promise((resolve, reject) => {
        // some possibly long operation
    }),
    new Promise((resolve, reject) => {
        setTimeout(reject, 5000);
    })
]).then(() => {
    console.log("success!");
}, () => {
    console.log("failed");
});
```

More recently, a syntactic sugar was created around `Promise` to mimic synchronous code syntax. Basically, you can indicate that a function is asynchronously using the `async` keyword. The function will then return a `Promise` when called. When the function returns a value, the `Promise` is resolved with that value. If the function throws an error, the `Promise` is rejected.

You can then use asynchronous functions inside other asynchronous functions, as follows:

```
function delay(timeout) {
  return new Promise((resolve) => {
    setTimeout(resolve, timeout);
  });
}
async function run() {
  await delay(1000);
  console.log("done");
}
run();
```

# Spread and rest syntax

The spread syntax allows an iterable to be expanded in places where arguments (in functions) or elements (in arrays) are expected. It's very useful when, for example, a function accepts an initial set of arguments and then an unlimited one:

```
const concat = (separator, ...parts) => (parts.join(separator));

concat(", ", 1, 2, 3); // "1, 2, 3"
```

This example is especially important in arrow functions since you don't have access to the arguments object. It's also quite useful to merge arrays, as in the following example:

```
const a = [ 1, 2, 3 ];
const b = [ 4, 5, 6 ];

[ ...a, ...b ]; // [ 1, 2, 3, 4, 5, 6 ]
```

# Default function parameters

There's no longer the need to use logical operators or check argument types to define default argument values. They can be defined directly in the prototype:

```
function pad(text, len, char = " ") {
    return text.substr(0, len) +
           (text.length < len ? char.repeat(text.length - len) : "");
}
pad("John", 10, "=");
```

If you've developed in languages like Python before, remember default arguments in JavaScript are evaluated at call time, not when defining the function. This means a new object is created every time:

```
function add(value, list = []) {
    list.push(value);
    return list;
}

add(1); // [ 1 ]
add(2); // [ 2 ] , not [ 1, 2 ]
```

# Destructuring

Destructuring is the convenient method of constructing (target) or extracting (source) properties from an object. It gives the developer the ability to pick specific object properties from arguments or swap variable values, for example:

```
// head = 1, tail = [ 2, 3, 4]
let [ head, ...tail ] = [ 1, 2, 3, 4 ];

// list = [ "john", "jane" ]
let { users: list } = { users: [ "john", "jane" ] };
```

You can also have more complex destructuring in assignments and function arguments. You can also assign default values:

```
class Rectangle {
    constructor({ width = 100, height = 50 } = {}) {
        this.width = width;
        this.height = height;
    }
}
```

# Template literals

Template literals are string literals that allow embedded expressions. Another advantage of these literals is that they can be written in multiple lines:

```
function hello(name) {
    console.log(`Hello ${name}`);
}
```

It's not a simple variable substitution, since it evaluates expressions of any kind:

```
function hello(name, age) {
    console.log(`hi ${name}, you were born in ${(new Date).getFullYear() -
age}`);
}
```

# Advantages of using Node.js

Node.js has become a very strong competitor for building all kinds of applications. Large companies use it nowadays to deliver frontend interfaces and information, but also for specific backend services and developer API interfaces. Twitter, LinkedIn, and eBay are examples of these companies.

Let's go through all of the advantages of using Node.js one by one.

## Node.js Package Manager

The huge number of modules available today makes it easy to start developing any kind of application or service, and npm ensures you're able to deploy your code in other servers easily. In fact, npm is also one of the advantages of Node.js and is also responsible for its spread.

```
# look how fast it checks dependencies (infinite levels), downloads them
# and installs them locally

$ npm i express
+ express@4.16.2
added 48 packages in 3.129s
```

There has always been some criticism about using Node.js, with people considering it slow and inefficient for some tasks. Some usually point to the fact that the code is single-threaded, but forget that the core API, which is your only way of communicating over the network or with the filesystem, uses a thread pool of workers to handle your actions:

```
const http = require("http");

// request is done in a separate thread, code execution continues
http
.request("http://www.google.com")
.once("response", (res) => {
    console.log(res.headers);
```

```
})
.end();

console.log("getting google.com headers..");
```

# Asynchronous I/O

The main purpose and the initial idea behind Node.js was to be able to handle asynchronous I/O effectively. To achieve that goal, Node.js has a very good toolkit. It's built around libuv, which empowers the JavaScript language to do asynchronous I/O.

This means that it's kind of a silver bullet in this field. As long as your application is slim, not very CPU intensive, and is able to handle I/O efficiently, Node.js is the right tool for you.

Although it's true that your code runs in a single thread, as soon as your code needs to open a file or make an HTTP request, it uses other threads to do so. So, to really take advantage of the Node.js architecture, you should use it for writing code that actually needs the core API.

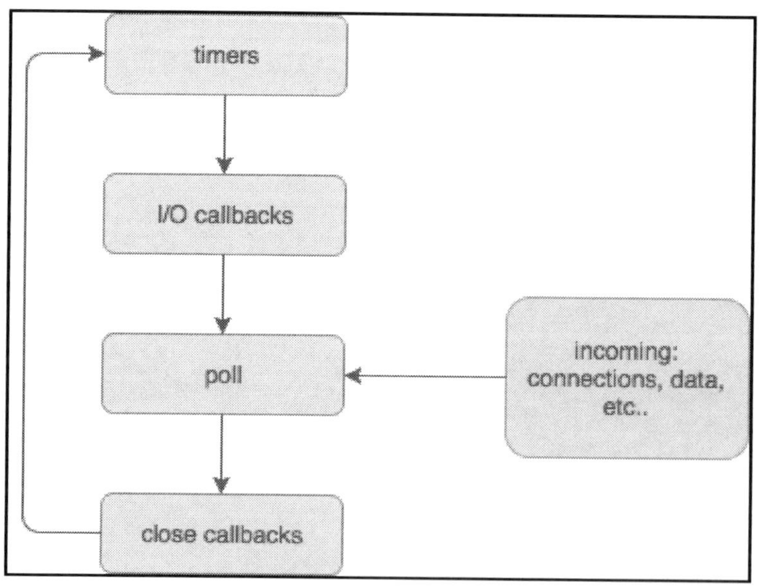


The simplified version of the Node.js Event Loop

The Event Loop is a loop mechanism that is responsible for handling asynchronous I/O code. The code you write synchronously runs immediately. The rest, like connecting to a third-party API, a database, or opening a file, will be queued in the poll. After that, if any timeout occurs (by a `setTimeout` or `setInterval`), they run. After that, run the I/O callbacks, if any. This is data from a file or a socket, for example. Finally, the close callbacks are executed. This is an over-simplified idea of the loop. There are several other tasks in-between (such as `setImmediate` before the close callbacks).

If you're writing code to perform some processor-intensive calculations, with big number manipulation or with fraction precision, Node.js will perform poorly. You may need to find modules to help you address these disadvantages by moving its weak points out of the JavaScript context.

> TIP: If you still want to use Node.js for performance tasks, try creating a C++ module and use that instead. You can then pass the calculations to this module and still be able to use Node.js for other tasks that you would normally need more code for in C++.

# Community

People around the language can also influence it, and in this case positively. There were some strange moments in the past, more specifically, sometime before the `io.js` fork. But the community didn't give up and the commitment to the language has brought it to what it is now.

It's a strong community around a structured language that has gained traction like no other. Developers know what to expect and there's an effort to keep it stable and secure, which, for me, is one of the fundamental principles for a developer to even consider using a language.

Summing up, the advantages of Node.js are as follows:

- A stable and mature language, used and known by web developers for years
- A performant core, based on Google's V8 engine
- A huge community and large module base, with dozens of modules for each task that you can choose from
- An active and maintained core, with a focus on stability and security

# From monolith to microservices

As we described previously, a microservices architecture is based on a loosely coupled set of services that work together to achieve a specific target application. At the end of the spectrum, there are monolith applications.

A monolith application is composed of a set of components that are tightly coupled. These components are usually developed using the same language and the application runs as a whole. The first noticeable difference is probably the slow start. Deploying might also be slow since you might need a couple of dependencies before having anything up and running.

Let's imagine an event application, a simple one, an application that lets users define events and be notified when those events are about to start.

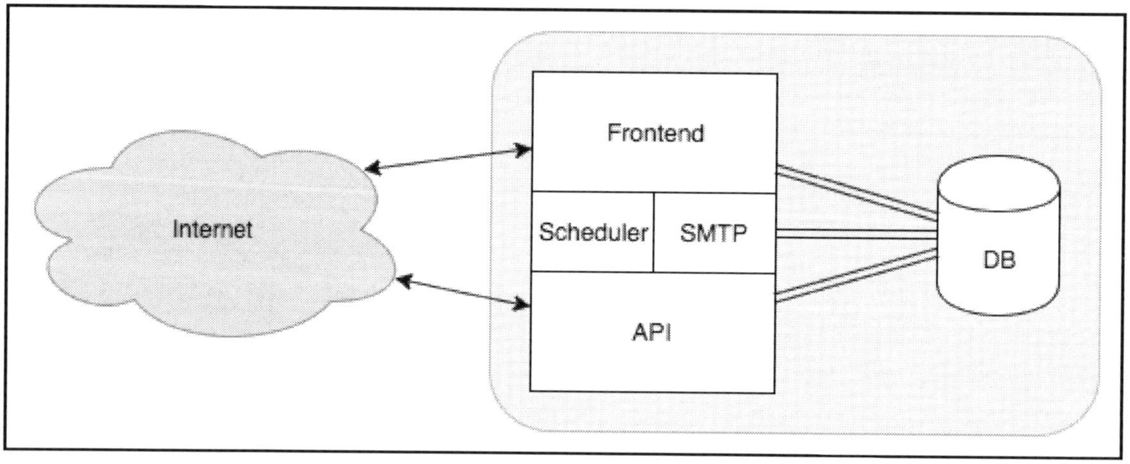


A monolith event application

Let's describe what the event application does:

- It allows users to register themselves and add events to a calendar
- A few minutes before the event starts (that's what the **Scheduler** component is for), the users receive an email with the event information (that's the **SMTP** component)
- Users can use the frontend interface or the **API** interface

Imagine the preceding application as being a monolith (the greyed out area on the right). Imagine that all four parts are part of the same process, even though they could be in separate threads. Imagine that the database is accessed directly across the application. Sound good?

Well, it sounds terrible, perhaps not for a small application, but for a medium one, this would be a representation of chaos. Having a group of developers making new features or improvements would be a nightmare, and for new developers entering the group, it would take some time before having the base knowledge to make some changes.

The first principle that you should follow is the **Don't Repeat Yourself** (**DRY**) principle. Avoiding multiple components from accessing a data source helps developers in the future. Later on, if there's a need to change the data source or part of its structure, it will be easier if only one component manipulates it. This is not always possible, but if it is possible, you should keep the data source access to a minimum.

In our example, the API should probably have access, and all others should use the API.

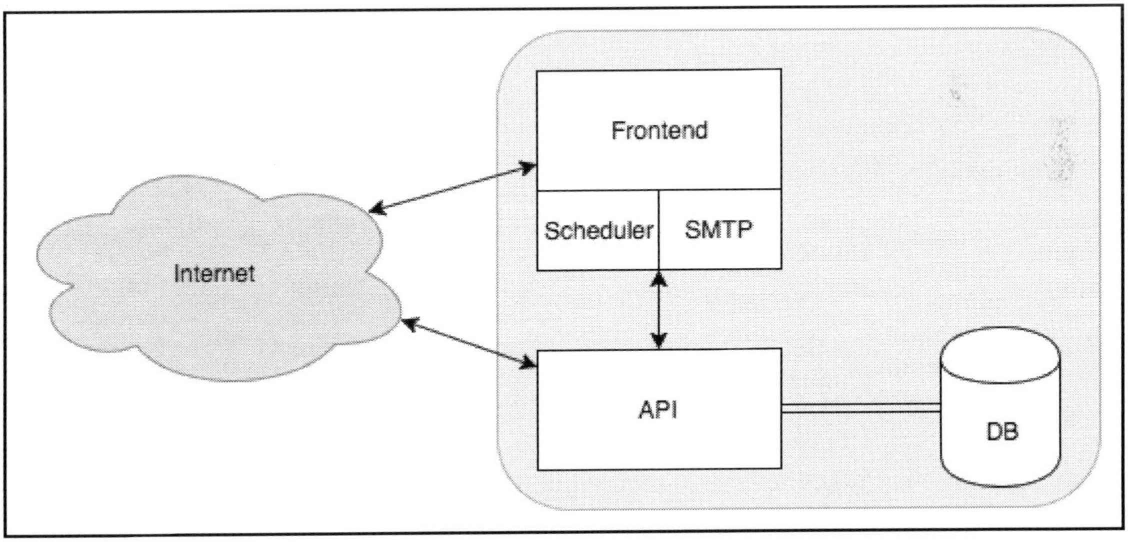


A single service accessing a data source

We now have two services:

- The API, which is the only service accessing the data source
- The frontend, which is the user's interface to change the data source

Although the frontend is used to manage events, it uses the API service to manipulate data sources. Besides having only one service managing data sources, it forces you to think of the API for external developers. It's a win-win.

There is still room for improvement. The **Frontend** could be in a separate service, allowing you to scale the interface according to user traffic, and have the other parts on separate services. **Scheduler** and **SMTP** are both candidates for separate services. **SMTP** should be thought of as a reusable service for other applications you might develop later on.

Let's take a look at how we could build the same application using the microservices approach:

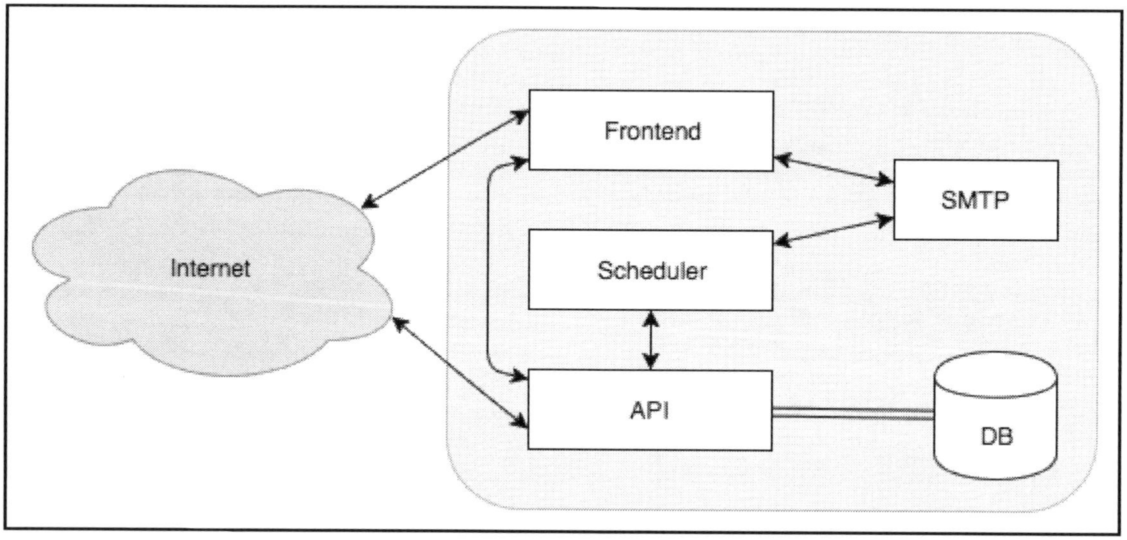


A microservices event application

It looks more complex. Well, the architecture is more complex. The difference is that now, we have loosely coupled components, and each one of them is easily understandable and maintainable. Summing up the changes and advantages:

- The **API** is the only one accessing the database so it can change from SQLite, MongoDB, MySQL, or anything else, and no other component is affected
- **SMTP** can be used from the **Frontend** and **Scheduler**, and if you decide to change it from using a local service to using a third-party email sending **API**, you can make the change easily

- **SMTP** is a candidate for being a reusable service in other applications, meaning you can use it in other applications or event share the same service between multiple applications

You can think of these components as capabilities of your application. They can be swapped, upgraded, maintained, and scaled, all without affecting other components or your application.

A commonly underestimated advantage of using this approach is that your application is much more resilient to failures. In a monolith application, any part can bring your application offline. In this microservices approach, this application might not send emails but can still be running and accessible. Add caching into the mixture and the API can restart in moments.

# Patterns of microservices

Microservices architecture, like other archicectures, has a set of patterns that are easily identifiable and form the basis for this application development approach.

Some of these patterns can make the initial bootstrap a burden and can eventually be postponed. Others are essential from the beginning or you will have difficulty, later on, in migrating to a full microservice approach.

The following patterns are not an extensive list but they represent a solid foundation:

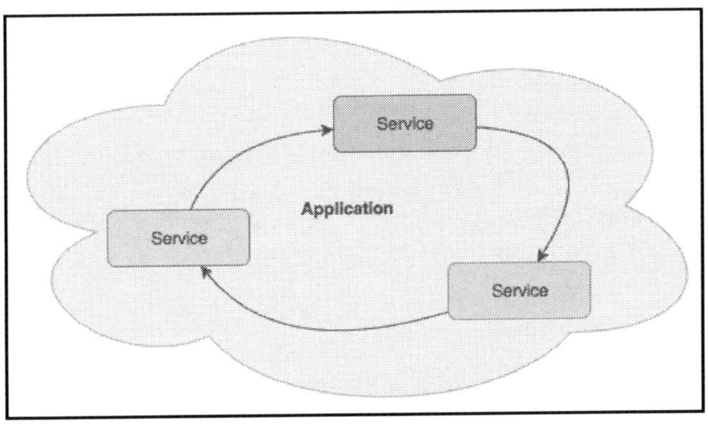


An example of services working together to form an application

# Decomposable

The main pattern behind a microservice architecture is the ability to have loosely coupled services. These services are decomposed, separated into smaller parts. This decomposition should create a set of services that implement a set of strongly related functions.

Each service should be small but complete, meaning it should run a set of functions in a given context. Those functions should represent all the functions you need or need to support for that context. What this means is that if you have a service that handles meeting events, all meeting event functions should be done using that service, whether it's creating an event, changing, removing, or getting information about a specific event. This ensures that an implementation change to events will affect that service only.

Decomposing an application can take one of two main approaches:

- By capability, when a service has a specific power or set of powers, such as sending emails, regardless of its content
- By subdomain, when a service has the complete knowledge of a subdomain or module of your application domain

In our previous event application, a service that was decomposed by capability is, for example, the SMTP service. A service decomposed by the domain could be the API service, assuming the application only manages events:

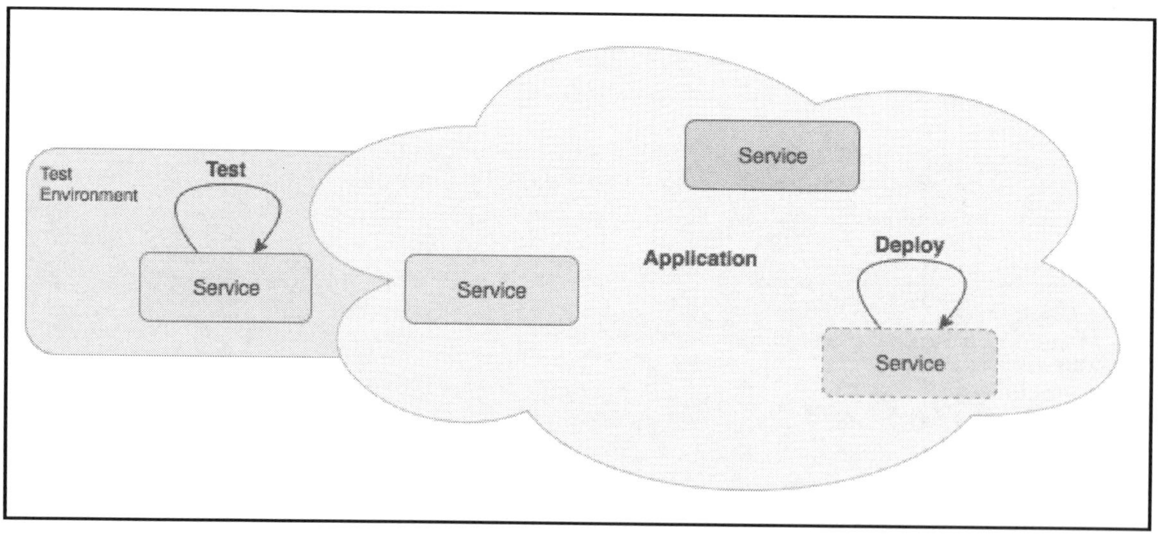


An example of services being tested and deployed autonomously, instead of the whole application

# Autonomous

In a microservice architecture, each service should be autonomous. A small team should be able to run it without the other services that make your application. That team should also be able to develop autonomously and make changes to implementation without affecting the application.

The development team should be able to:

- Test, creating business logic and unit tests to ensure the service functions work as expected
- Deploy, upgrading functionality, without restarting other services in the process

Services should be able to evolve regardless of others, keeping backward compatibility, adding new functions, and scaling to several locations, with minimal changes to the architecture:

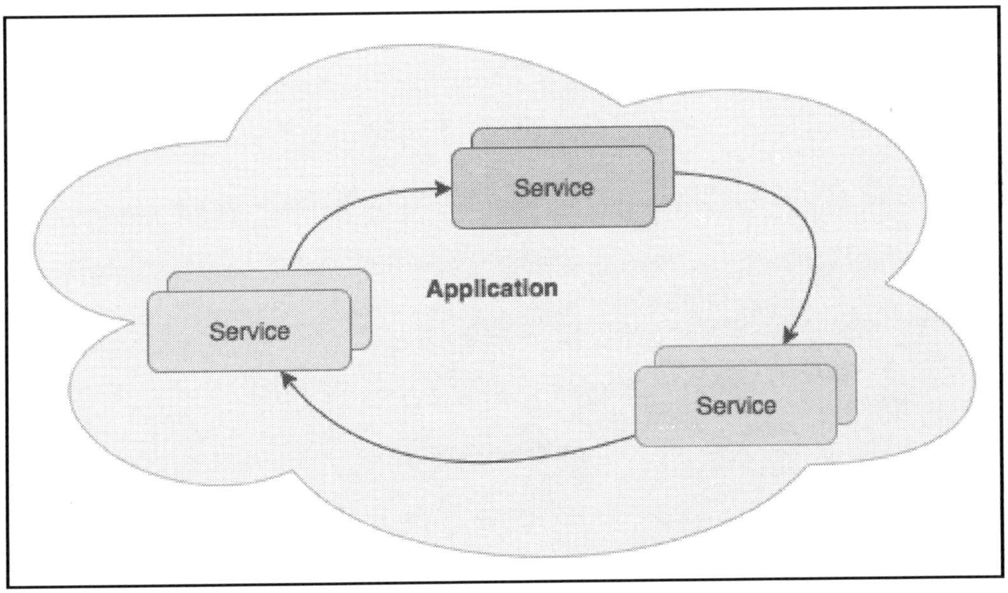


An example of an application with two instances per service, making it fault-tolerant

## Scalable

A service should be scalable. At least two instances should be able to run in parallel, enabling failure tolerance and maintenance downtime. A service can also, later on, scale geographically, be near your customers, and improve apparent performance and application response.

For this scaling to be effective, the application platform will need service discovery and routing, a service that could be used by other services to register themselves and expose their capabilities. Other services could, later on, inquire this service directory and know how to reach these capabilities.

To reduce complexity for other services, a service router can redirect requests to service instances. For example, to send emails, you could have three instances and one central router that would redirect requests in a round-robin manner. If any of those instances go offline, the router will stop redirecting to it and the rest of the application doesn't need to care about it.

Another approach could be to use a DNS approach. The name service is capable of handling registrations to a subdomain, and then, when another service makes simple requests, it will receive one or all of the addresses and connect it as if there was only one service operating:

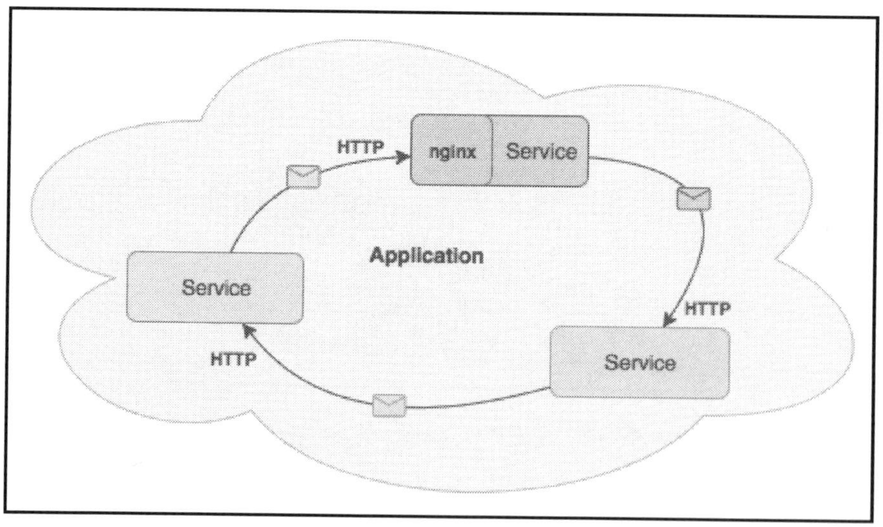


An example of communication between services of an application

## Communicable

Usually, services communicate over HTTP using a REST-compliant API. This is not a pattern that you must follow, but it's something that comes naturally based on how common HTTP is nowadays, making it an obvious choice.

There are plenty of HTTP servers out there, making it easy to expose a non-HTTP service with minimum effort.

HTTP is also a mature communication transport layer. It's a stateless protocol, giving developers and operations many features, such as:

- Caching commonly used and often updated resources
- Proxying and routing requests
- Securing communication over TLS

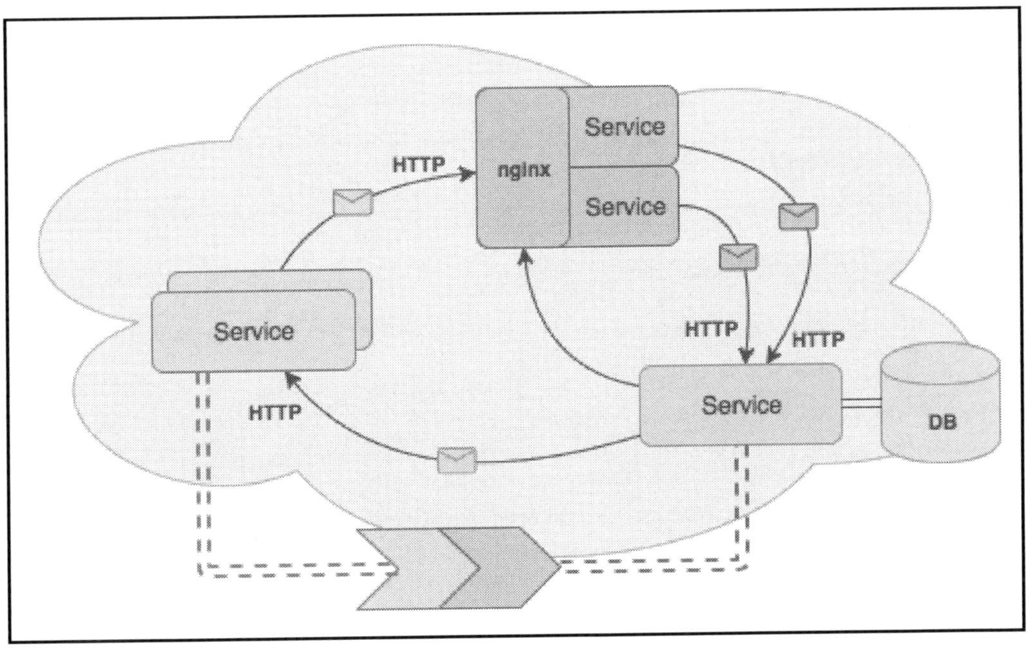


A complex application with several services and streams of communication

# Disadvantages of microservices

Microservices have a lot of advantages, and they become more evident in the long term when the application becomes more complex. The microservice patterns primarily introduce complexity and enforce you to be very strict around development in order to avoid losing track of the entire application.

To start with, developers add to the complexity of the distributed system. This distributed system enforces a network communication -- not only do the services need to communicate with each other; they also need to find one another using some kind of service discovery technique.

This adds the need for a stable network to exchange requests. It adds layers of complexity just to exchange a simple request. It will also add an extra layer of security, both for development that needs to support it and for the operations that need to address it. As has been said previously, using bootstrap is harder than using a monolith application.

The operations team can also see some complexity in deployment. It's better to look at several services as separate components for deployment. This is actually as they should look for this architecture. They can, in the long term, even use some of the deployed architecture for new applications. Still, complexity for operations deployment and monitoring is even bigger.

Although not a direct disadvantage, because the architecture is loosely coupled and each service can be built using the best tools for the job, this can increase the heterogeneous environment, which will require operations to have knowledge of a broader technology scope. This can potentially lead to mistakes. Try to look for the second-best tool for the job if that tool is already used in operations.

The operations team will also have to possibly manage more third-party services, such as message queues, as they're commonly used to enable service communication. Other added services that might be added for scalability are service discovery. In a fully scalable application, operations just deploy new services and they register themselves and get used by all of your application's ecosystem.

As you can see, although development might get easier and you'll be able to parallel the application development across teams, there's also an added complexity if you intend to fully scale your application.

As a recommendation, do not plan your application to scale to millions of requests unless you really know it will handle that amount in the near future. Plan your application to have small and lightweight services to start with. It will be easier to do than upgrade the services to scale.

As a possible macro strategy, split your application using these three guidelines:

- Split services by capabilities
- Try to keep subdomains on a single service
- Prepare for scale, but don't scale while there's no need to

# Summary

In conclusion, microservices architecture is a good, clear pattern that helps tackle more complex projects. In the long term, it reduces the complexity associated with new projects by appealing to service reuse. It helps to structure an application into loosely coupled services that can be independently developed and tested by small, different teams. It comes at the cost of initial proper planning and a more complex deployment.

Before creating your first microservice, let's look at some Node.js tools that could eventually help you leverage your next big project. This is what we'll be covering in the next chapter.

# 2
# Modules and Toolkits

Now that we have reviewed what Node.js's new features are, and now that we know what a microservice is, it's time to see what tools or modules we can we to create one. We'll review a couple of options and build a more or less simple microservice so that we can point out advantages and disadvantages for each approach.

We'll look at four different modules:

- **Express**: One of the most commonly used modules in the Node.js ecosystem
- **Micro**: A very minimalistic microservices approach
- **Seneca**: A microservice toolkit based on property matching
- **Hydra**: A package that bundles a couple of modules to help you resolve many microservices concerns, such as distribution and monitoring

## Express

If you're familiar with Node.js, you probably know of one module that is the core for most Node.js platforms and applications that are around. You have probably heard of Express, and it's not by accident. It's eight years old and it's been there since the beginning of Node.js.

Express is a rock-solid layer that helps you create applications faster. As it states on its website, it's a *fast, unopinionated,* and *minimalist web framework*.

Node.js has an HTTP module that you can use to create a simple HTTP server. The problem is that it's too raw and you'll have to do a ton of work so that you can make it usable and modular. Instead of you creating that layer, you can use Express.

To install Express, create a folder and run the following command:

```
npm init -y
npm install express —save
```

Then, create a file called `app.js` and place the following code inside it:

```
let express = require("express");
let app     = express();

app.get("/", (req, res) => {
    res.send("Hello World");
});

app.listen(80);
```

Then, run your code using the following command:

```
node app
```

Go to your browser and type the address `http://localhost:3000/`. You should see something like the following:

With Express, you can associate functions to routes. A route is a URL with a specific HTTP verb, but it doesn't necessarily have to. You can have automatic parameters parsing inside routes. You can even associate more functions to the same route and have them be called sequentially. You can also stop the sequence at any time. It's up to you; remember, Express is not opinionated.

Change your `app.js` to the following code and run it again:

```
let express = require("express");
let app     = express();
let stack   = [];

app.post("/stack", (req, res, next) => {
    let buffer = "";

    req.on("data", (data) => {
        buffer += data;
    });
    req.on("end", () => {
        stack.push(buffer);
        return next();
    });
});

app.delete("/stack", (req, res, next) => {
    stack.pop();
    return next();
});

app.get("/stack/:index", (req, res) => {
    if (req.params.index >= 0 && req.params.index < stack.length) {
        return res.end("" + stack[req.params.index]);
    }
    res.status(404).end();
});

app.use("/stack", (req, res) => {
    res.send(stack);
});

app.listen(3000);
```

You'll have trouble testing it in the browser because we're using `POST` and `DELETE` verbs. Instead, let's use `curl` and make requests in the command line. Follow this sequence and see if you understood the preceding code:

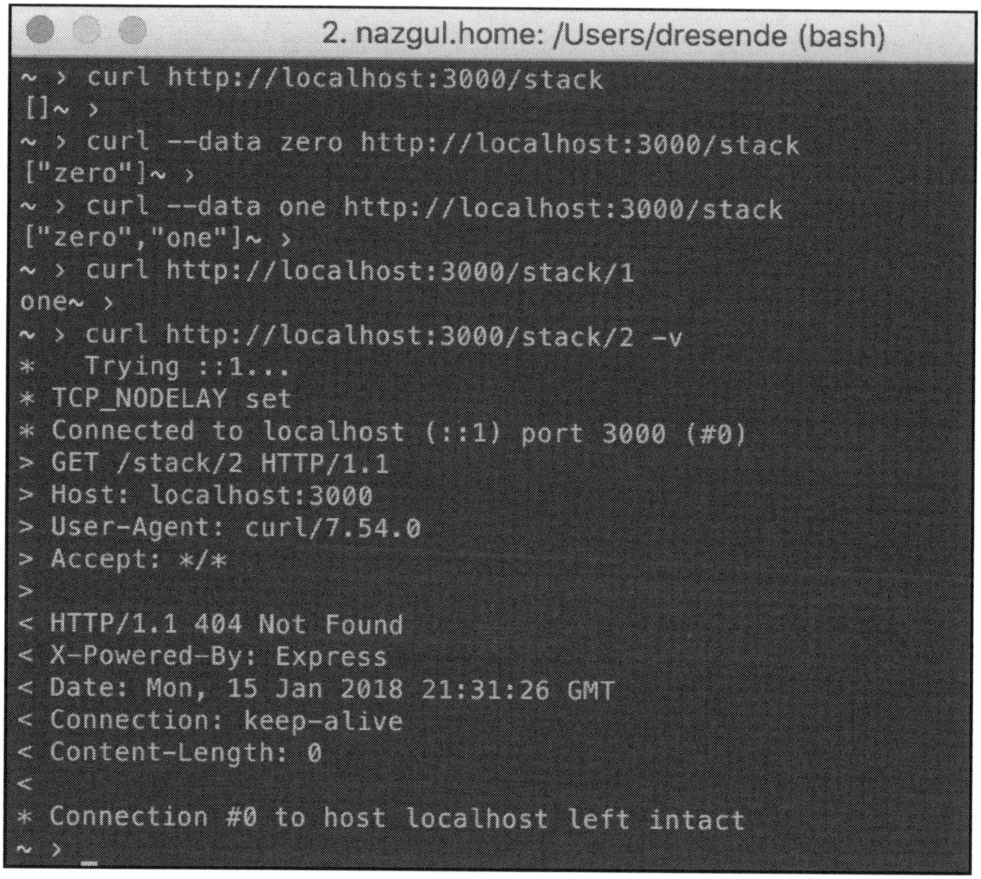


We first make a request to `/stack` just to see if it will return an empty array. Then, we use `--data` to pass `zero` as the HTTP request body and `curl` assumes it's a `POST`. We do it again, this time, with body `one`. For both requests, we get the final stack result. We then request stack index 1 and it returns `one`. We then request index 2 and, as you can see by the `-v` parameter, our code returns a proper `404 Not Found` error.

You might have wondered how the stack is returned on both GET and POST requests and that's the reason for calling next(), which tells Express to pass to the next route (if there are any) available. In our case, it's the route that's been defined that's using the use method. This is a catch all for all HTTP verbs. Remember: route definition order is important and that's why the catch all is done at the end.

As you can see, we can scale pretty fast to complex logic. It's important to note that although Express really helps you create an HTTP service easier, it's still just an improved layer over the http and https modules that are available.

To help you even more, it has an integrated modular system, called middleware, and hundreds of compatible published modules that help you create services even faster, such as session handling, templating, caching, and security modules.

Let's make our example a little bit more complex so that you can see what I mean. First, install some middleware:

```
npm i body-parser --save
```

Now, change your code to this:

```
let express = require("express");
let body    = require("body-parser");
let route   = express.Router();
let app     = express();
let stack   = [];

app.use(body.text({ type: "*/*" }));

route.post("/", (req, res, next) => {
    stack.push(req.body);

    return next();
});

route.delete("/", (req, res, next) => {
    stack.pop();

    return next();
});

route.get("/:index", (req, res) => {
    if (req.params.index >= 0 && req.params.index < stack.length) {
        return res.end("" + stack[req.params.index]);
    }
    res.status(404).end();
```

```
});

route.use((req, res) => {
    res.send(stack);
});

app.use("/stack", route);
app.listen(3000);
```

It has the same number of lines, but we improved our code by making two important changes:

- Instead of reading the request body, we now use a middleware, `body-parser`, which handles it for us and supports several body types and compression.
- We created an `express.Route` and attached it to our service at the last but one line. We can use this to move our route definition to a separate file and make it URL agnostic (see how we only mention `/stack` once, when attaching).

# Micro

Let's look at another interesting tool. This module is called micro and was created by ZEIT, a team of some of the most influential Node.js developers. It is meant to be a minimalistic framework to create slim and fast microservices.

Let's repeat our first example. Create a folder and run the following command:

```
npm init -y
npm install --save micro
```

Now, create a file called `app.js` and write the following code inside it:

```
module.exports = (req, res) => {
    res.end("Hello World");
};
```

Change your `scripts` property in `package.json` to this:

```
"scripts": {
    "start": "micro"
},
```

Now, just run this:

```
npm start
```

You'll see something like this, which indicates that a micro is running on its default port, 3000:

```
micro: Accepting connections on port 3000
```

You can now refresh your browser and you will get the same page you saw earlier. But now, you have it with only three lines of code (and some configuration).

That's it. Micro is very minimalistic. You'll have to declare and install all your dependencies as it won't do anything other than enable you to write very slim microservices. This is handy if you don't want to carry the 2.3 MB of dependencies from our first Express example.

# Seneca

Now it's time for a completely different approach. Let's look at another framework called Seneca. This framework was designed to help you develop message-based microservices. It has two distinct characteristics:

- **Transport agnostic**: Communication and message transport is separated from your service logic and it's easy to swap transports
- **Pattern matching**: Messages are JSON objects and each function exposes what sort of messages they can handle based on object properties

Being able to change transports is not a big deal; many tools allow you to do so. What is really interesting about this framework is its ability to expose functions based on object patterns. Let's start by installing Seneca:

```
npm install seneca
```

For now, let's forget the transport and create a producer and consumer in the same file. Let's look at an example:

```
const seneca  = require("seneca");
const service = seneca();

service.add({ math: "sum" }, (msg, next) => {
    next(null, {
        sum : msg.values.reduce((total, value) => (total + value), 0)
    });
});

service.act({ math: "sum", values: [ 1, 2, 3 ] }, (err, msg) => {
```

```
        if (err) return console.error(err);

        console.log("sum = %s", msg.sum);
    });
```

There's a lot to absorb. The easy part comes first as we include the `seneca` module and create a new service.

We then expose a producer function that matches an object that has `math` equal to `sum`. This means that any request object to the service that has the property `math` and that is equal to `sum` will be passed to this function. This function accepts two arguments. The first, which we called `msg`, is the request object (the one with the `math` property and anything else the object might have). The second argument, `next`, is the callback that the function should invoke when finished or in case of an error. In this particular case, we're expecting an object that also has a `values` list and we're returning the sum of all values by using the `reduce` method that's available in arrays.

Finally, we invoke `act`, expecting it to consume our producer. We pass an object with the `math` equal to `sum` and a list of `values`. Our producer should be invoked and should return the sum.

Assuming you have this code in `app.js`, if you run this in the command line, you should see something like this:

```
$ node app
sum = 6
```

Let's try and replicate our previous stack example. This time, instead of having the consumer and producer in the code, we'll use `curl` as the consumer, just like we did previously.

First, we need to create our `service`. We do that, as we've seen before, by loading Seneca and creating an instance:

```
const seneca  = require("seneca");
const service = seneca({ log: "silent" });
```

We explicitly tell it that we don't care about logging for now. Now, let's create a variable to hold our stack:

```
const stack = [];
```

We then create our producers. We'll create three of them: one for adding an element to the stack, called push; one to remove the last element from the stack, called pop; and one to see the stack, called get. Both push and pop will return the final stack result. The third producer is just a helper function so that we can see the stack without performing any operations.

To add elements to the stack, we define:

```
service.add("stack:push,value:*", (msg, next) => {
    stack.push(msg.value);

    next(null, stack);
});
```

There are a few new things to see here:

- We defined our pattern as a string instead of an object. This action string is a shortcut to the extended object definition.
- We explicitly indicate that we need a value.
- We also indicate that we don't care what the value is (remember, this is pattern matching).

We now define a simpler function to remove the last element of the `stack`:

```
service.add("stack:pop", (msg, next) => {
    stack.pop();

    next(null, stack);
});
```

This one is simpler as we don't need a value, we're just removing the last one. We're not addressing the case where the stack is empty already. An empty array won't throw an exception, but perhaps, in a real scenario, you would want another response.

Our third function is even simpler as we just return the `stack`:

```
service.add("stack:get", (msg, next) => {
    next(null, stack);
});
```

Finally, we need to tell our `service` to listen for messages. The default transport is HTTP and we just indicate port `3000` as we did in our previous examples:

```
service.listen(3000);
```

Wrap all this code in a file and try it out. You can use curl or just try it in your browser. Seneca won't differentiate between HTTP verbs in this case. Let's begin by checking our `stack`. The URL describes an action (`/act`) we want to perform and the query parameter gets converted to our pattern:

We can then try adding the value `one` to our `stack` and see the final `stack`:

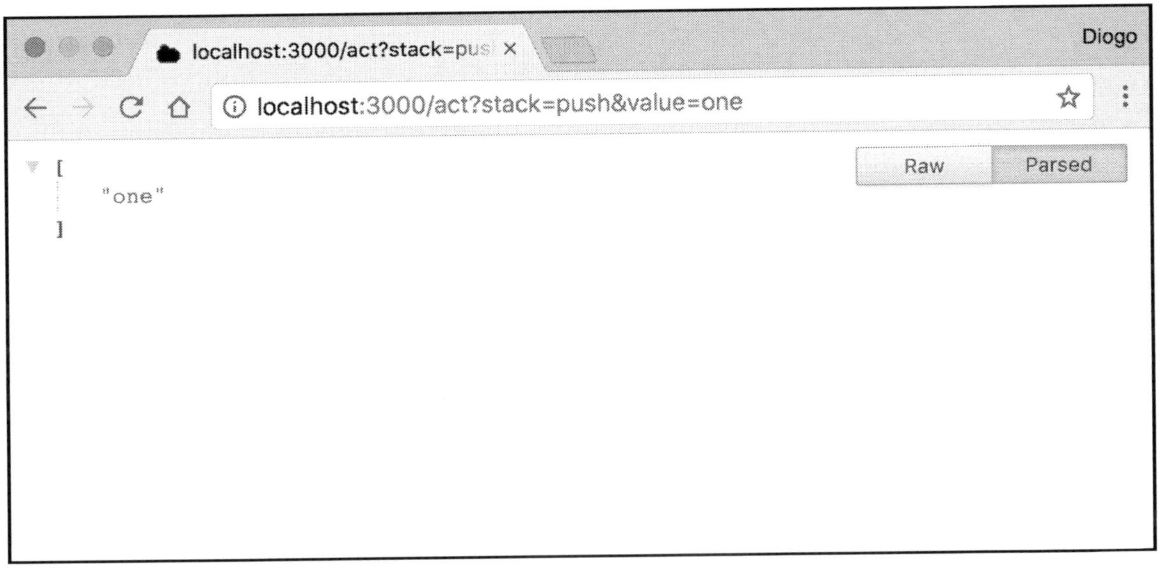


We can continue and add the value `two` and see how the `stack` grows:

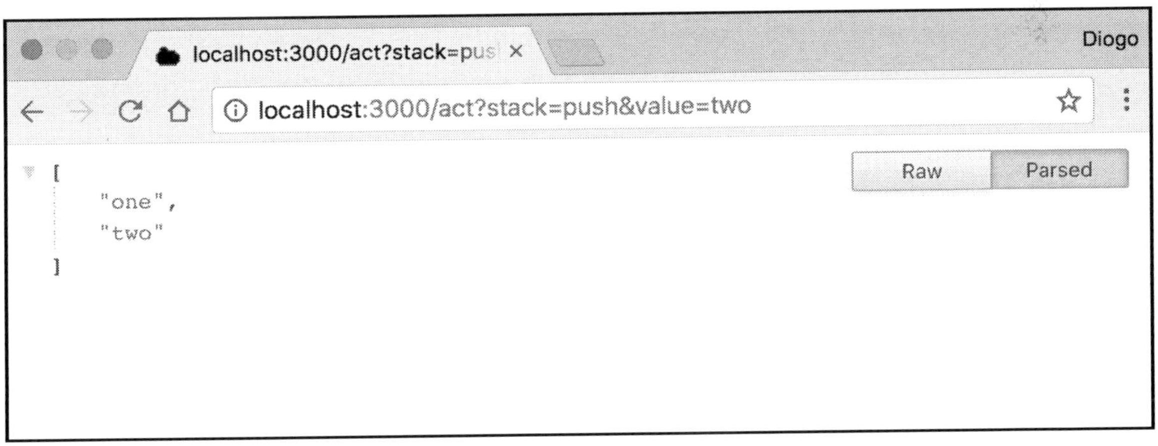

If we then try to remove the last element, we'll see the `stack` shrinking:

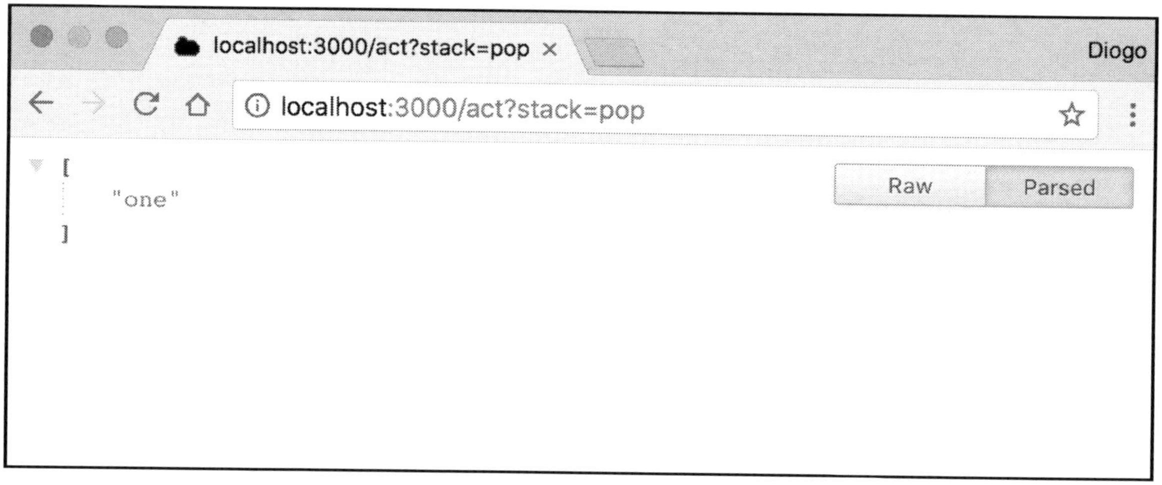


As in Express, Seneca also has middleware that you can install and use. In this case, the middleware is called plugins. By default, Seneca includes a number of core plugins for transport, and both HTTP and TCP transports are supported. There are more transports available, such as **Advanced Message Queuing Protocol** (**AMQP**) and Redis.

There are also storage plugins for persistent data and there's support for several database servers, both relational and non-relational. Seneca exposes an **object-relational mapping** (**ORM**)-like interface to manage data entities. You can manipulate entities and use a simple storage in development and then move to production storage later on. Let's see a more complex example of this:

```
const async   = require("async");
const seneca  = require("seneca");
const service = seneca();

service.use("basic");
service.use("entity");
service.use("jsonfile-store", { folder : "data" });

const stack = service.make$("stack");

stack.load$((err) => {
    if (err) throw err;

    service.add("stack:push,value:*", (msg, next) => {
        stack.make$().save$({ value: msg.value }, (err) => {
            return next(err, { value: msg.value });
```

```
        });
    });

    service.add("stack:pop,value:*", (msg, next) => {
        stack.list$({ value: msg.value }, (err, items) => {
            async.each(items, (item, next) => {
                item.remove$(next);
            }, (err) => {
                if (err) return next(err);

                return next(err, { remove: items.length });
            });
        });
    });

    service.add("stack:get", (msg, next) => {
        stack.list$((err, items) => {
            if (err) return next(err);

            return next(null, items.map((item) => (item.value)));
        });
    });

    service.listen(3000);
});
```

Just run this new code and we'll see how this code behaves by making some requests to test it. First, let's see how our `stack` is by requesting it:

Nothing different. Now, let's add the value `one` to the `stack`:

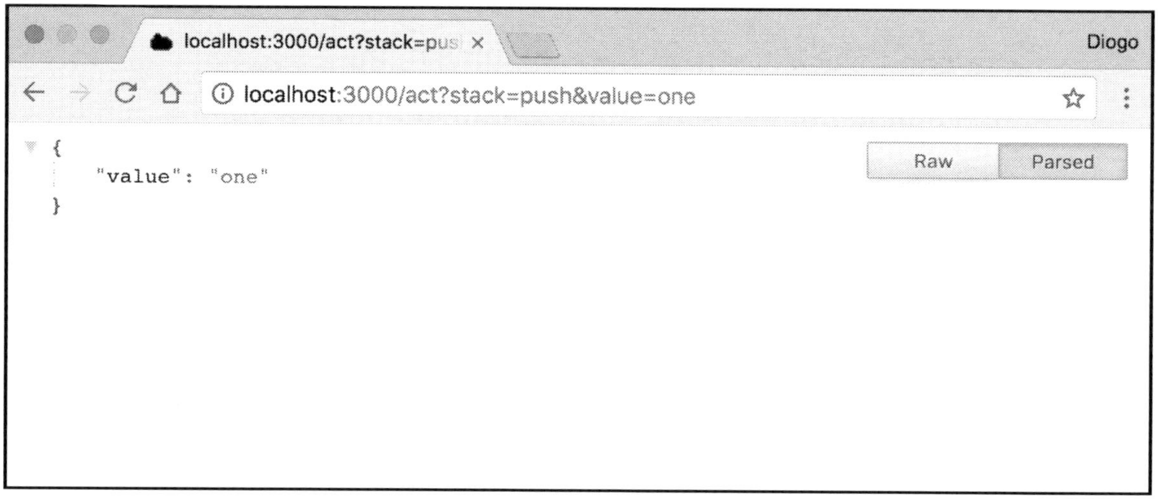


Well, we haven't received the final `stack`. We could, but instead we changed the service to return the exact item that was added. It's actually a good way to confirm what we just did. Let's add another one:

Again, it returns the value we just added. Now, let's see how our stack is:

Our `stack` now has our two values. Now comes one big difference compared with the previous code. We're using *entities*, an API exposed by Seneca, which helps you store and manipulate data objects using a simple abstraction layer similar to an ORM, or to people who are familiar with Ruby, an `ActiveRecord`.

Our new code, instead of just popping out the last value, removes a value we indicate. So, let's remove the value `one` instead of `two`:

Success! We removed exactly one item. Our code will remove all items from the `stack` that match the value (it has no duplication check so you can have repeated items). Let's try to remove the same item again:

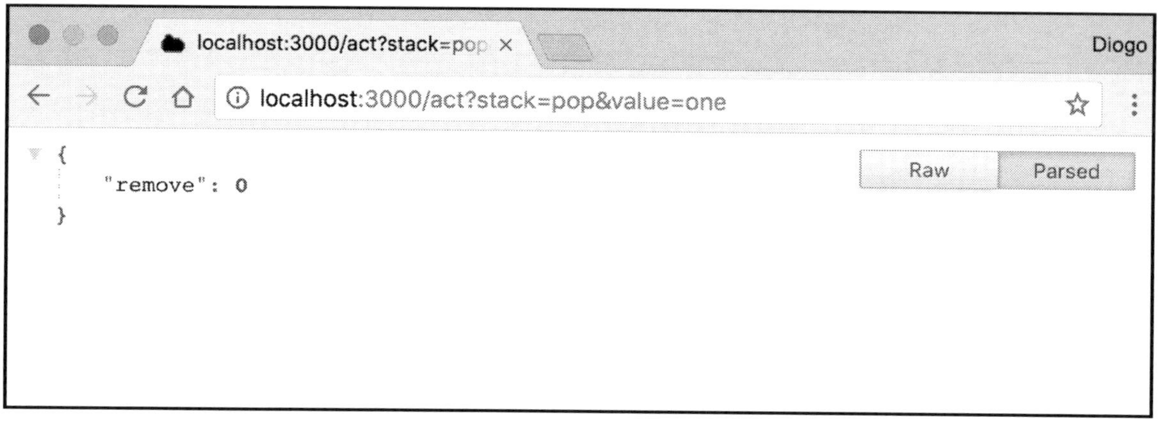


No more items match `one`, so it didn't remove anything. We can now check our `stack` and confirm that we still have the value `two`:

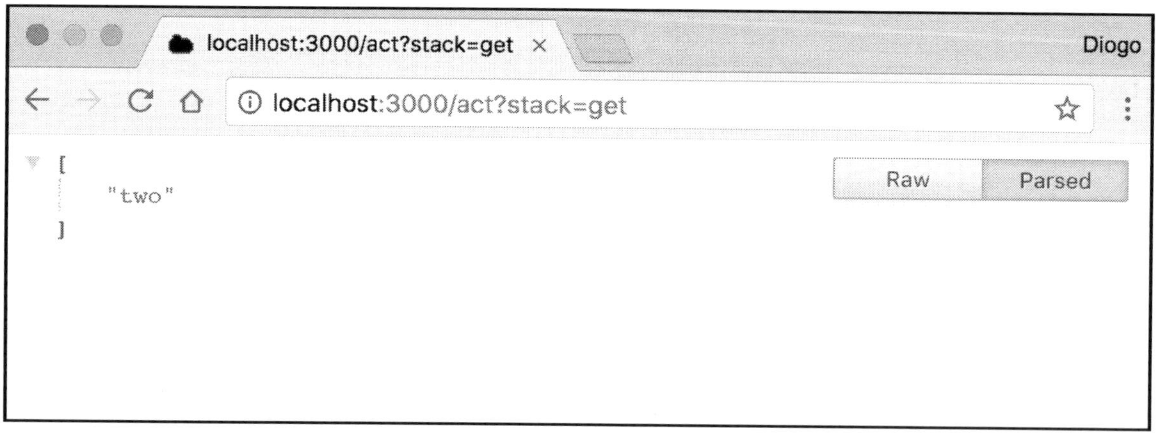


Correct! And, as a bonus, you can stop and restart the code and your stack will still have the value `two`. That's because we're using the JSON file store plugin.

When testing using Chrome or any other browser, be aware that sometimes, browsers make requests in advance while you're typing. Because we already tested our first code, which had the same URL addresses, the browser might duplicate requests and you might get a stack with duplicated values without knowing why. This is why.

# Hydra

Let's get back to Express. As you've seen before, it's a rock-solid layer on top of the `http` module. Although it adds an important base layer in the somewhat raw module, it still lacks many features you need to make a good microservice.

As there are lots of plugins out there to extend Express, it can be hard to pick a useful list for us to use.

After picking the right list, you'll still need to make other decisions:

- How can I distribute my service with multiple instances?
- How can the service be discovered?
- How can I monitor whether my service is running properly?

Enter Hydra, a framework that facilitates building distributed microservices. Hydra leverages the power of Express and helps you create microservices or communicate with microservices.

It will, out of the box, enable you to:

- Do service registration and service discovery, allowing your microservices to discover and be discoverable
- Communicate with microservices and load balance communication between multiple instances, taking care of failed instances and automatically rerouting requests to other running instances
- Monitor instances, checking whether the microservice is available and operating normally

Unlike the other modules we've reviewed so far, Hydra has a dependency that is not installable directly using the NPM. Hydra uses Redis to accomplish its goal. Look for information on the Redis website at `https://redis.io/` to install it on your operating system before continuing. If you have macOS and use Homebrew, type the following to install `redis`:

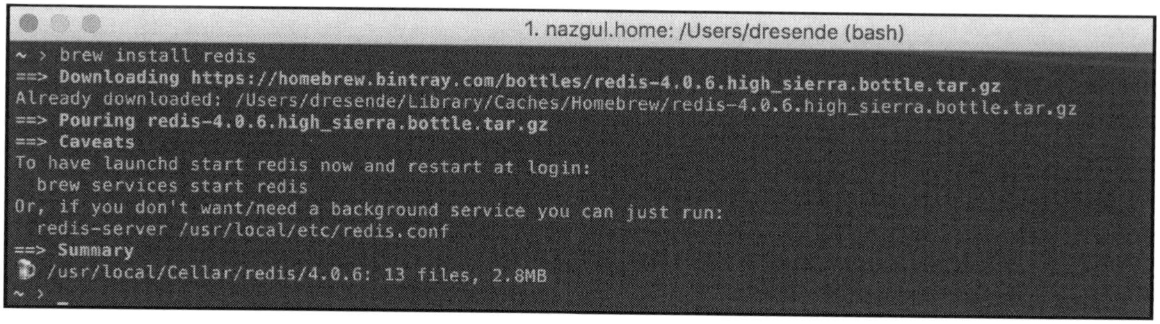


Now, let's make sure `redis` has successfully started:

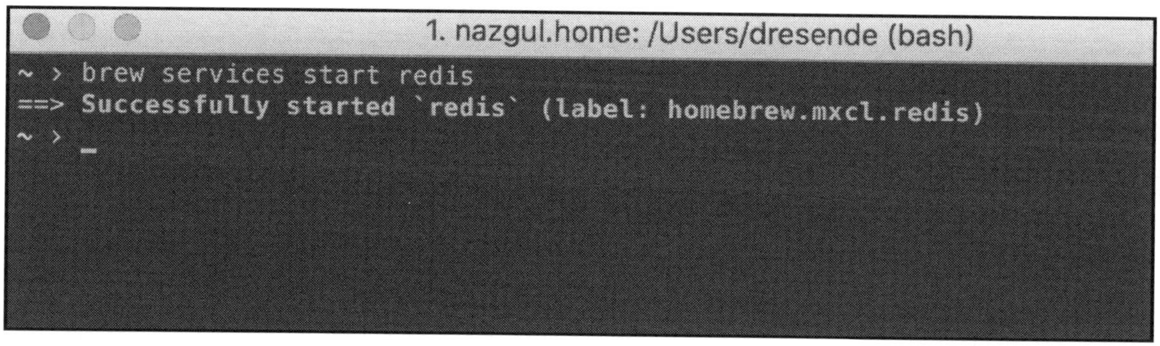


After that, we need to install Hydra command-line tools:

```
sudo npm install -g yo generator-fwsp-hydra hydra-cli
```

We now need to configure the connection to Redis. We do this by creating a configuration. Type in the command and follow the instructions. If you installed it locally (or used the preceding instructions), you should answer something similar to the following screenshot:

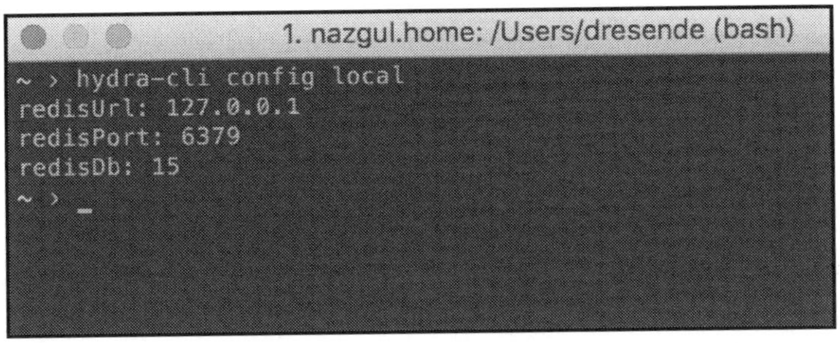


Now, let's create a very simple microservice, just to see what the workflow is like. Hydra has a scaffolding tool using `yeoman`. To create a service, type the following command and follow the instructions:

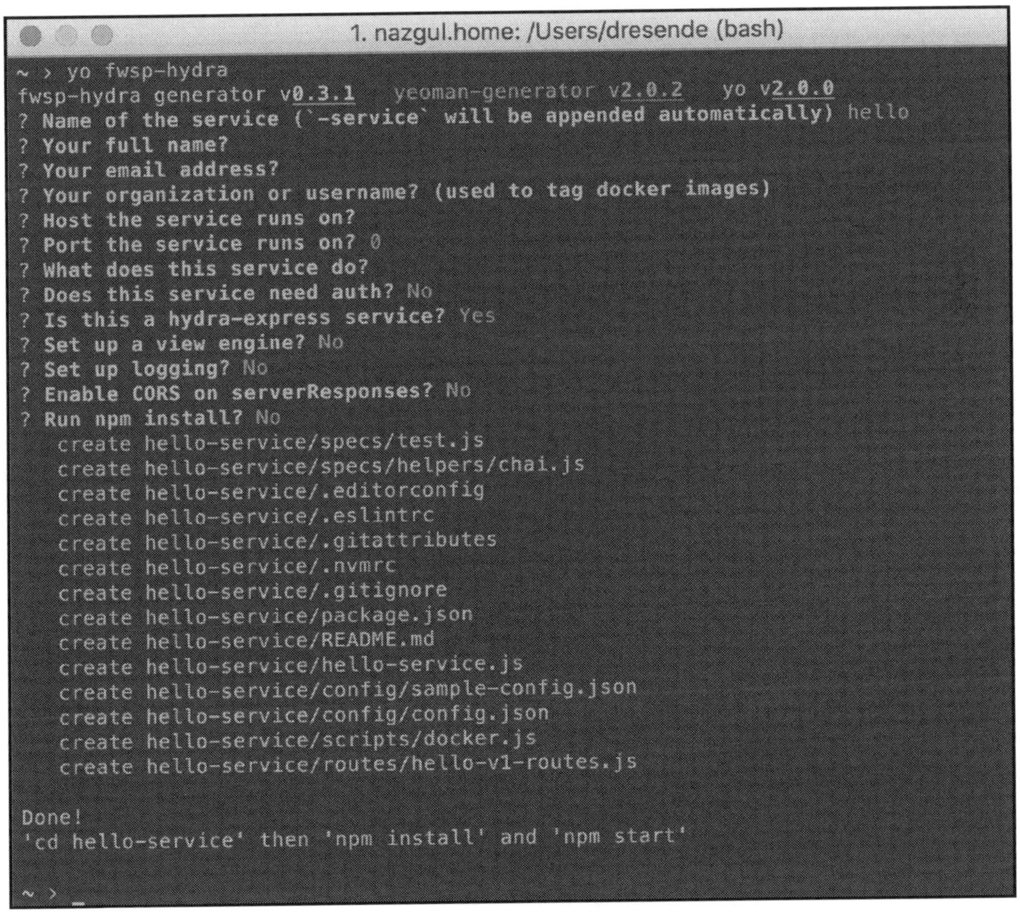

On the name of the service, just type **hello**. Just hit *Enter* to the rest of the questions to use the defaults. In the end, enter the folder that was created and install the dependencies:

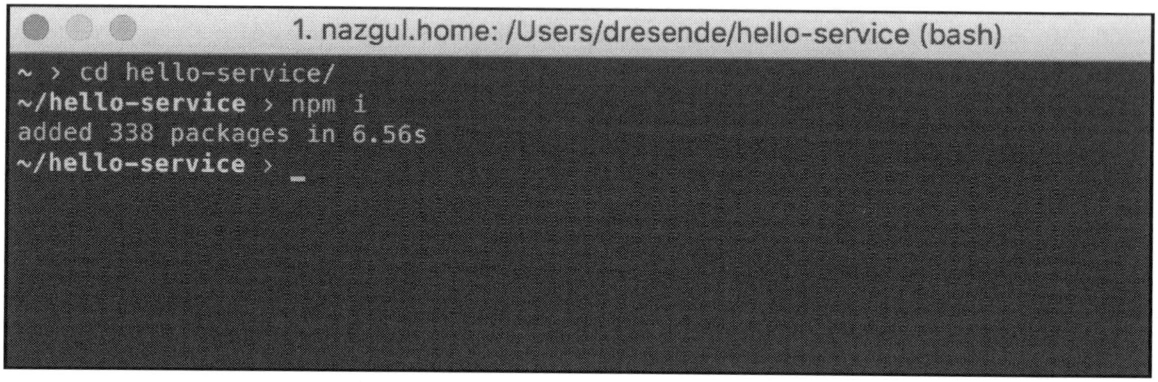


The service is now ready to start. You might have already seen the instructions when scaffolding the service. Let's start the service:

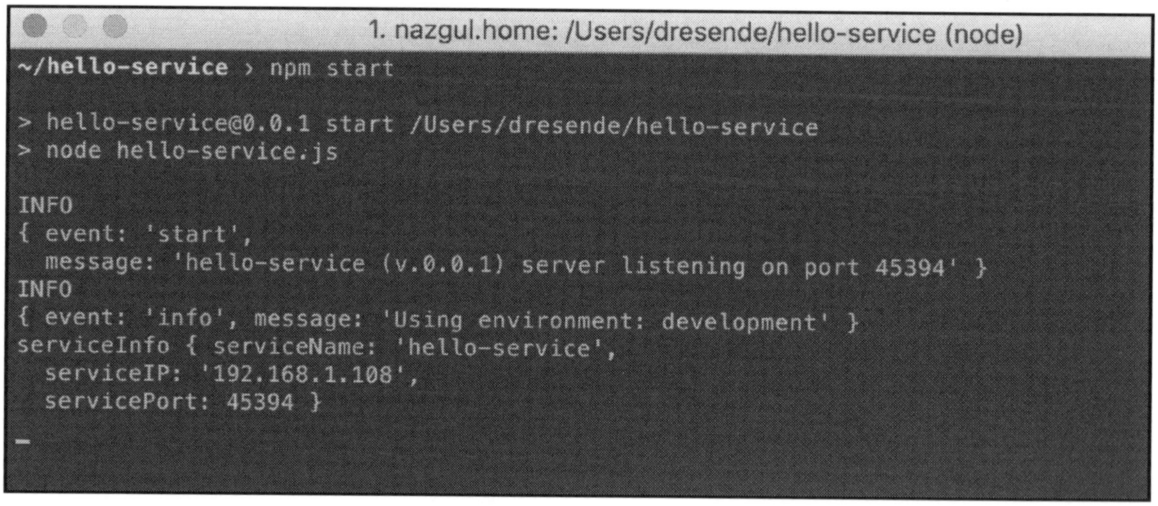

As we can see from the preceding screenshot, the service has started and has been attached to a local IP (**192.168.1.108**) and port (**45394**). Open up the folder in your code editor:

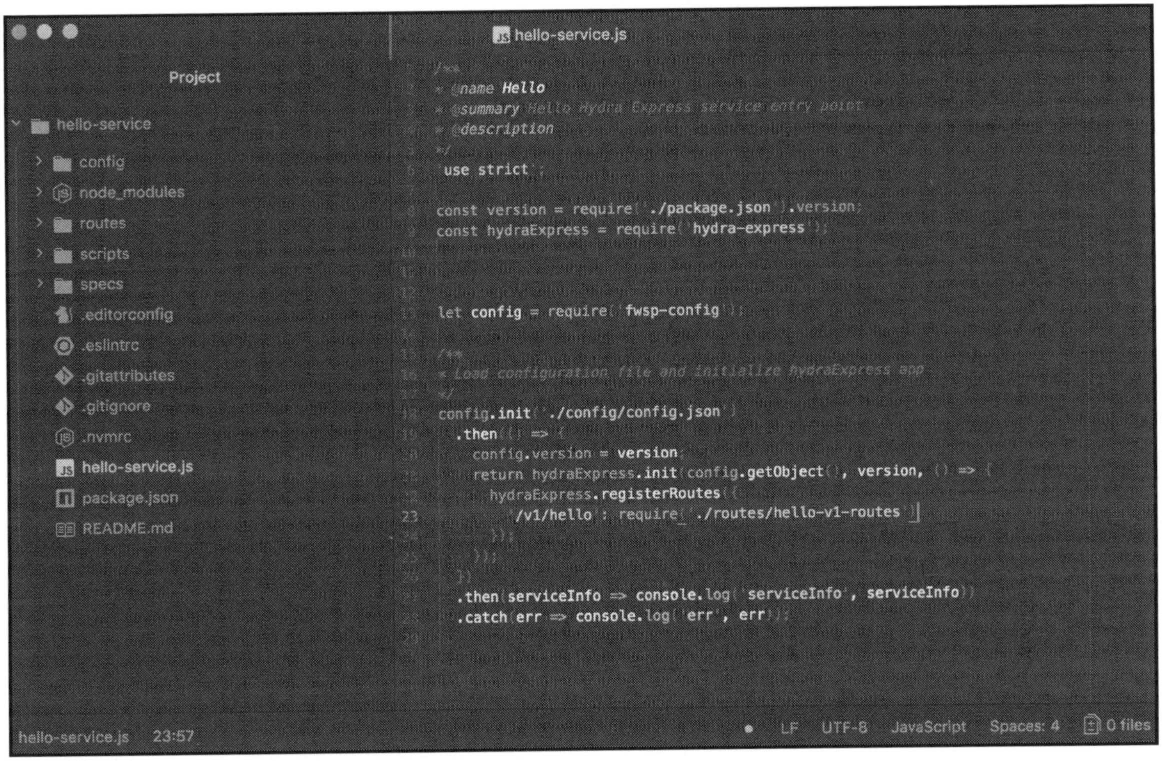

You'll see a file in the base folder called `hello-service.js`, which has the service routes inside it. You'll find the `/v1/hello` route, which points to another file in `routes/hello-v1-routes.js`:

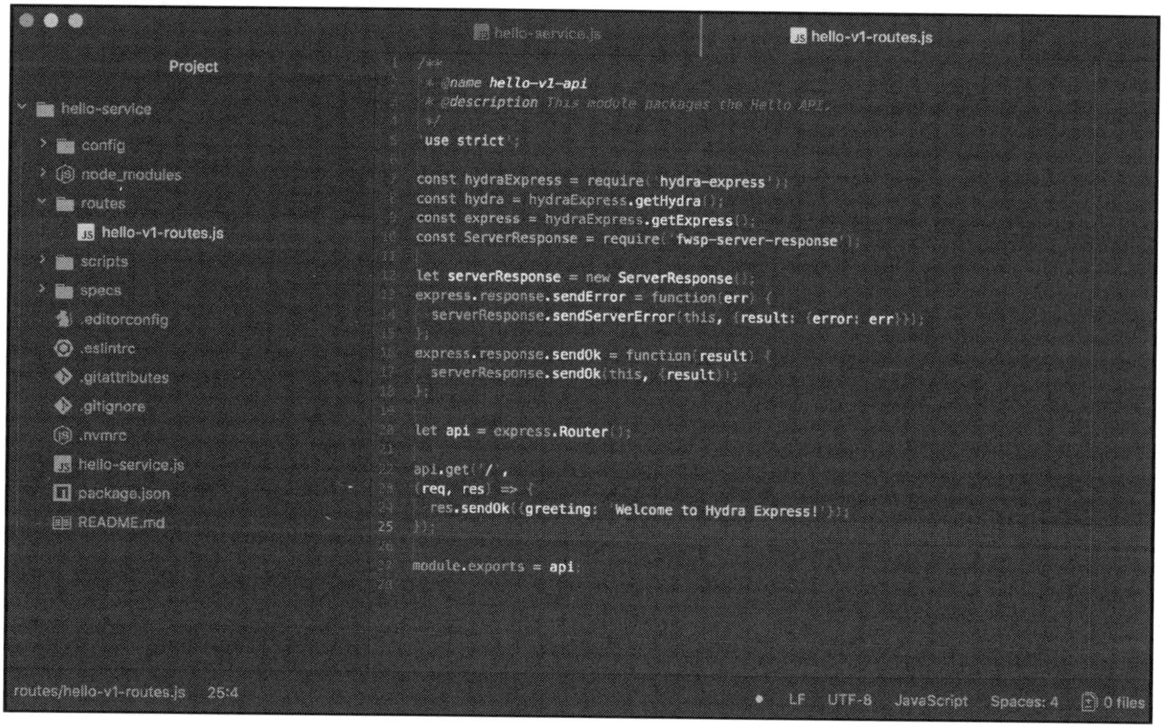


Inside that file, you'll see the response to that route. Now, let's jump to a web browser and see if it's up and running:

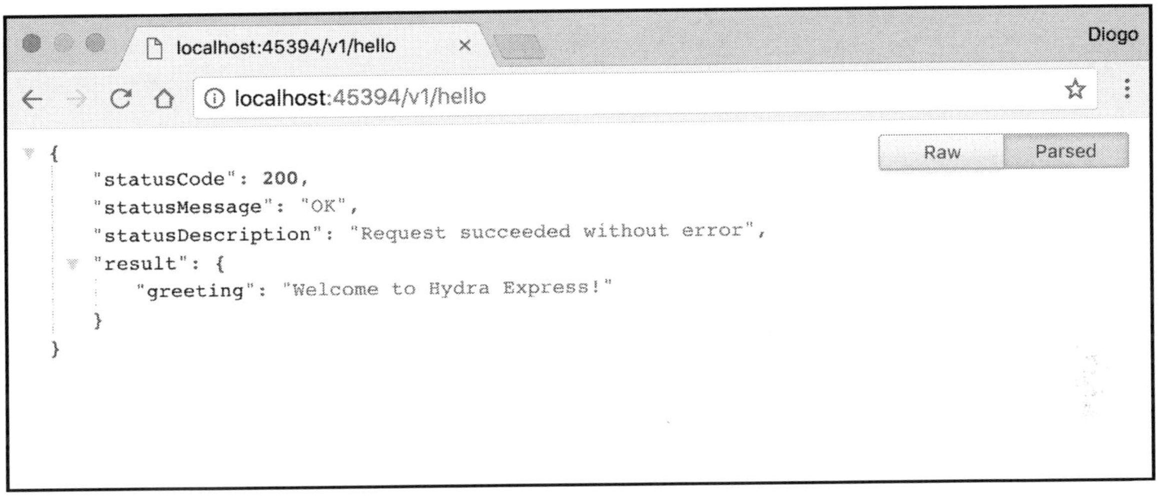


What we saw in the file is inside the result property of the JSON response. We just deployed our first Hydra microservice without writing a single line of code!

# Summary

We've just covered a range of different modules and toolkits to help develop microservices. From the tiny Micro, through patterns in Seneca, to the Hydra bundle, many approaches are available.

They all target different audiences and fill different needs. I would advise you to experiment with some of them to help you make a better choice instead of just picking one.

Let's dig into some of these tools and start creating a more complete microservice. In the next chapter, we'll be making a useful microservice, covering different use cases, while we develop a fully functional and distributed microservice.

# 3
# Building a Microservice

Now that we've seen some examples of building microservices using some tools, let's dig deeper and create a microservice from scratch using these tools. To accomplish our goal, we'll first use Express, then see how we could refactor it using Hydra, and finally, we'll create our microservice using the Seneca approach.

There are many microservices we could create, but some are more interesting than others. More specifically, a microservice that you can use in several applications is obviously more useful.

Let's create an image processing microservice. We'll start with a simple thumbnail service, and then we'll evolve to make some simple image transformations. We'll be covering how to:

- Build a microservice using Express
- Use external modules to manipulate images
- Build our previous microservice in Hydra and Seneca

The microservice name is very important, as it gives identity. Let's name it *imagini*, the Latin name for image.

## Using Express

As we've seen before, Express gives us a very simple but very useful layer on top of the default Node.js HTTP module. Let's create an empty folder, initialize our `package.json` file, and install Express:

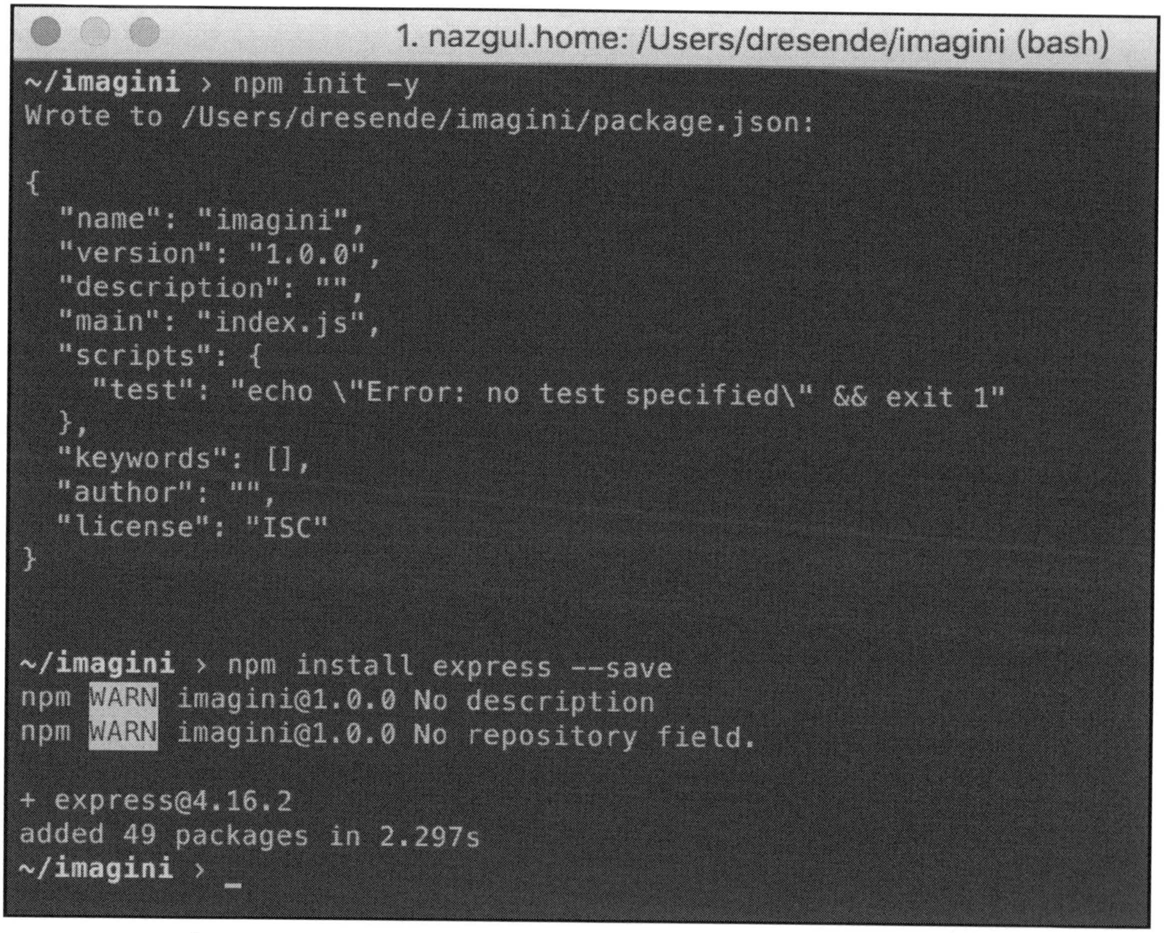

To help us get around images, we'll use the `sharp` module, a very fast image manipulation tool for the modern web. It will allow us to easily transform and resize images in a simple serial interface. Let's just install it now:

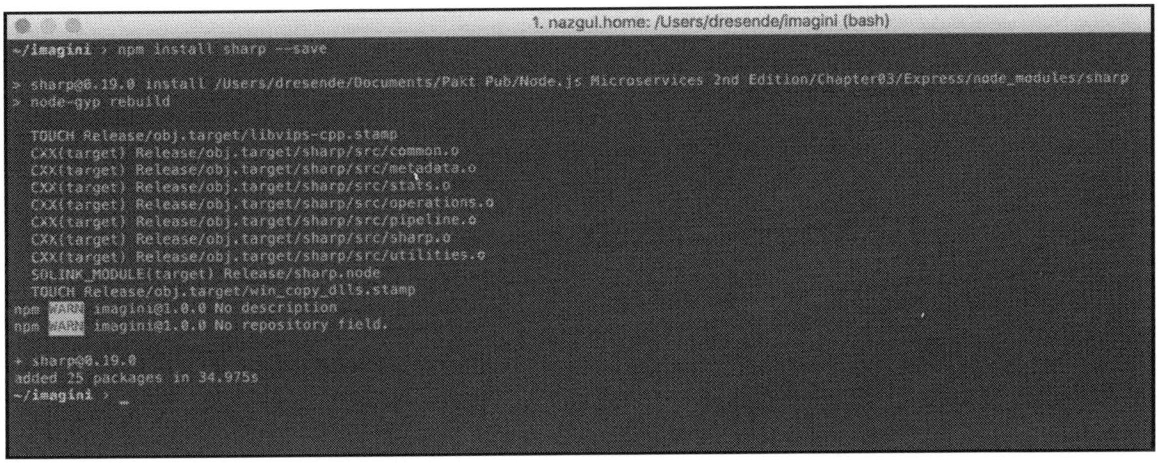


Let's start by exposing an address to return thumbnails. We'll need to first define our default parameters. Later on, we'll allow the user to change the default values. Our service will run on port `3000` and will accept thumbnail requests on both PNG and JPEG formats. Here's our not-so-simple service:

```
const express = require("express");
const sharp   = require("sharp");
const app     = express();

app.get(/\/thumbnail\.(jpg|png)/, (req, res, next) => {
    let format    = (req.params[0] == "png" ? "png" : "jpeg");
    let width     = 300;
    let height    = 200;
    let border    = 5;
    let bgcolor   = "#fcfcfc";
    let fgcolor   = "#ddd";
    let textcolor = "#aaa";
    let textsize  = 24;
    let image     = sharp({
        create : {
            width      : width,
            height     : height,
            channels   : 4,
            background : { r: 0, g: 0, b: 0 },
    }
```

```
    });

    const thumbnail = new Buffer(
`<svg width="${width}" height="${height}">
    <rect
        x="0" y="0"
        width="${width}" height="${height}"
        fill="${fgcolor}" />
    <rect
        x="${border}" y="${border}"
        width="${width - border * 2}" height="${height - border * 2}"
        fill="${bgcolor}" />
    <line
        x1="${border * 2}" y1="${border * 2}"
        x2="${width - border * 2}" y2="${height - border * 2}"
        stroke-width="${border}" stroke="${fgcolor}" />
    <line
        x1="${width - border * 2}" y1="${border * 2}"
        x2="${border * 2}" y2="${height - border * 2}"
        stroke-width="${border}" stroke="${fgcolor}" />
    <rect
        x="${border}" y="${(height - textsize) / 2}"
        width="${width - border * 2}" height="${textsize}"
        fill="${bgcolor}" />
    <text
        x="${width / 2}" y="${height / 2}" dy="8"
        font-family="Helvetica" font-size="${textsize}"
        fill="${textcolor}" text-anchor="middle">${width} x
${height}</text>
</svg>`
    );

    image.overlayWith(thumbnail)[format]().pipe(res);
});

app.listen(3000, () => {
    console.log("ready");
});
```

We start by getting access to both `express` and `sharp` modules. We then initialize our Express application:

```
const express = require("express");
const sharp   = require("sharp");
const app     = express();
```

We then create a route to get an image, with a regular expression that will catch the address `/thumbnail.png` and `/thumbnail.jpg`. We'll use the extension to ascertain what image type the user wants. We define some default parameters, such as sizes and colors:

```
let format    = (req.params[0] == "png" ? "png" : "jpeg");
let width     = 300;
let height    = 200;
let border    = 5;
let bgcolor   = "#fcfcfc";
let fgcolor   = "#ddd";
let textcolor = "#aaa";
let textsize  = 24;
```

We then create an empty image using `sharp`:

```
let image = sharp({
    create : {
        width      : width,
        height     : height,
        channels   : 4,
        background : { r: 0, g: 0, b: 0 },
    }
});
```

We then create an SVG file with an outer border, two crossing lines, and a text in the middle with the size of the image. Next, we overlay the SVG on our empty image, and output the result to the user:

```
image.overlayWith(thumbnail)[format]().pipe(res);
```

Finally, we initialize our service on port `3000`:

```
app.listen(3000, () => {
    console.log("ready");
});
```

Save the full code shown previously as `imagini.js`, and run it on the console:

You can now head to your web browser and just type the address of our service, and you'll see something like the following image:

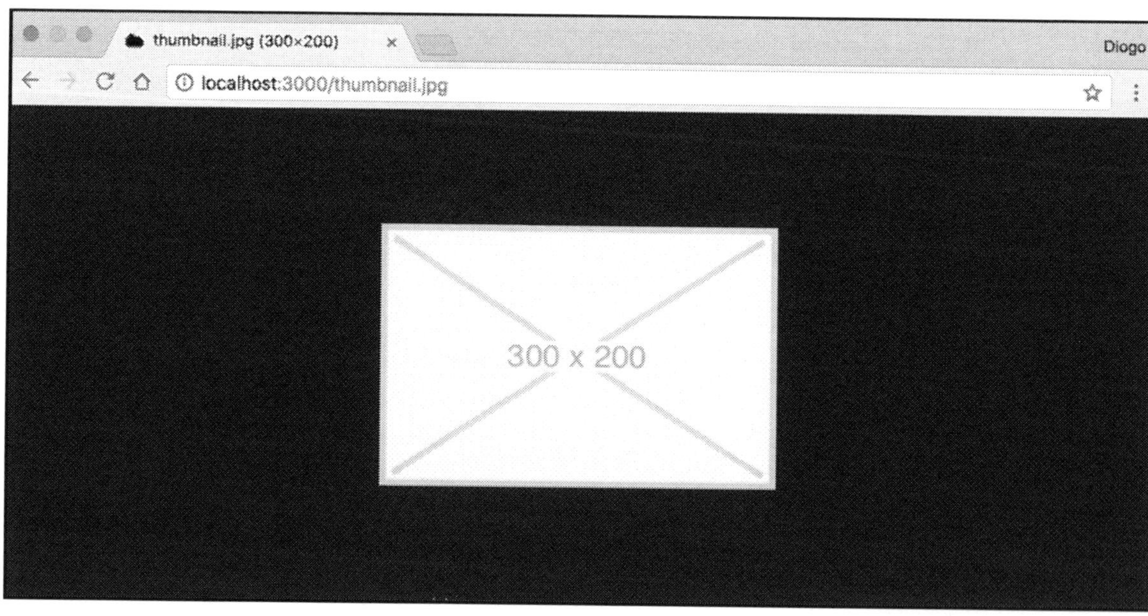


We can now start accepting some changes. Let's change our default variables to something like this:

```
let width     = +req.query.width || 300;
let height    = +req.query.height || 200;
```

```
let border    = +req.query.border || 5;
let bgcolor   = req.query.bgcolor || "#fcfcfc";
let fgcolor   = req.query.fgcolor || "#ddd";
let textcolor = req.query.textcolor || "#aaa";
let textsize  = +req.query.textsize || 24;
```

The preceding code is not safe for production. Use it only for demonstration purposes. We'll take a look at security in the next chapter.

Restart our service and play with query parameters to see the result. Here's an example of changing the width to 500 px, the border to 2 px, and the foreground color to cyan:

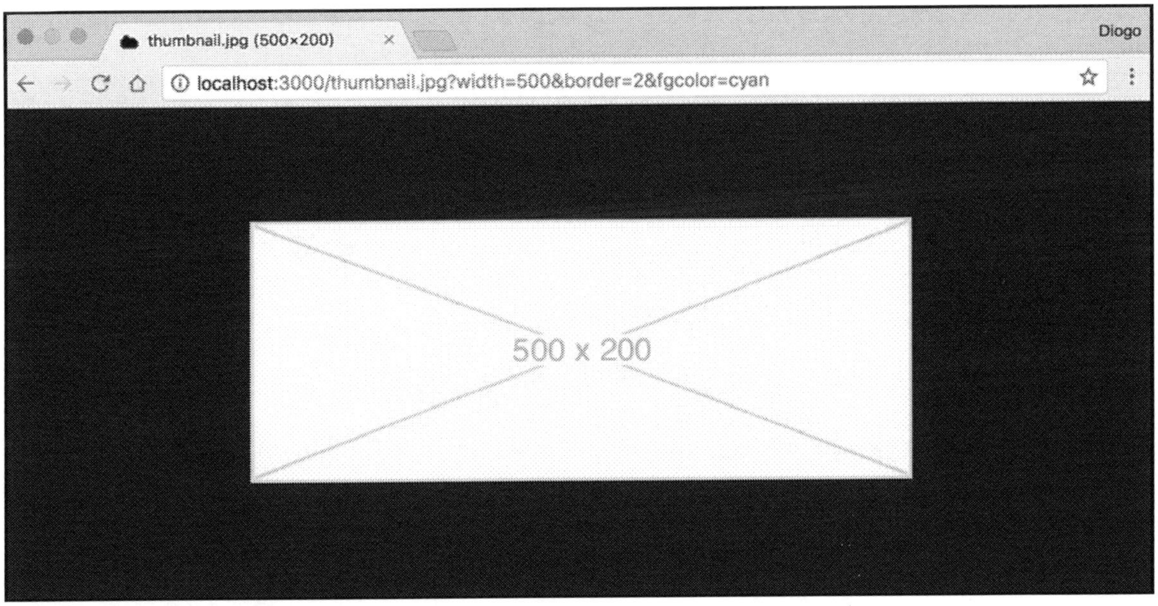


Well, it looks awesome, but it's not very useful as it is, as it just shows the same empty image. Though perhaps more applicable for prototyping, in the real world, it would be more useful if it could create thumbnails from images we upload. Let's do that.

To do so, we need to be able to:

- Upload images, which should be stored somewhere
- Check whether an image exists
- Download an image thumbnail

To simplify, we'll create dynamic routes in a specific path, and we'll use HTTP verbs (`GET`, `POST`, `DELETE`, and so on) to distinguish the actions. When uploading images, we'll use `POST` and the body should have the image data. To check if an image exists, we'll use `HEAD`. To download an image thumbnail, we'll use `GET`.

# Uploading images

Let's first add our route to handle uploading images. We'll use a body parser module that will handle compressed requests automatically for us.

```
npm install body-parser --save
```

We'll include it along with other core modules that we'll need. Add these lines on the top of our `service` file:

```
const bodyparser = require("body-parser");
const path       = require("path");
const fs         = require("fs");
```

We can now create the function that will handle our upload:

```
app.post("/uploads/:image", bodyparser.raw({
    limit : "10mb",
    type  : "image/*"
}), (req, res) => {
    let image = req.params.image.toLowerCase();

    if (!image.match(/\.(png|jpg)$/)) {
        return res.status(403).end();
    }

    let len = req.body.length;
    let fd  = fs.createWriteStream(path.join(__dirname, "uploads",
    image), {
        flags    : "w+",
        encoding : "binary"
    });

    fd.write(req.body);
    fd.end();

    fd.on("close", () => {
        res.send({ status : "ok", size: len });
    });
});
```

We're expecting an HTTP POST on the /uploads path. It must be an image with a maximum size of 10 MB. Let's analyze the code in detail.

```
let image = req.params.image.toLowerCase();

if (!image.match(/\.(png|jpg)$/)) {
    return res.status(403).end();
}
```

We start by checking whether the image name passed ends with .png or .jpg. If not, we reply with an HTTP 403 response code, which means **forbidden**, as we're just accepting those types of images:

```
let len = req.body.length;
let fd  = fs.createWriteStream(path.join(__dirname, "uploads", image), {
    flags    : "w+",
    encoding : "binary"
});
```

We then create a stream to the local file where we'll save our image. The name of the file will be the name of the image. We also store the image size so we can return that to the user when we finish saving. This enables the microservice user to check if we received all the data.

```
fd.write(req.body);
fd.end();

fd.on("close", () => {
    res.send({ status : "ok", size: len });
});
```

Lastly, we write the image to file and, after properly closing the stream, we reply to the user with a JSON response with a status and a size property.

Don't forget to create the uploads folder inside the microservice folder. Then, restart the service. We'll continue to use curl to test our services. We'll need an image to try it out. I searched for a Google image and saved it locally. I then uploaded it to our service using this command:

```
curl -X POST -H 'Content-Type: image/png' \
    --data-binary @example.png \
    http://localhost:3000/uploads/example.png
```

We're telling `curl` that we want to:

- Send a `POST` request
- Define the `Content-Type` header saying it's a PNG image
- Add the content of the `example.png` file (I downloaded) inside the request body
- Send the request to the `/upload/example.png` path of our microservice

After executing the command, I received a JSON response. The size matches my file:

```
{ "status" : "ok", "size" : 55543 }
```

We can't see the image using our microservice just yet, but we can check it locally. You should have a copy of the file in the `uploads` folder. For reference, here's the image I'm using:

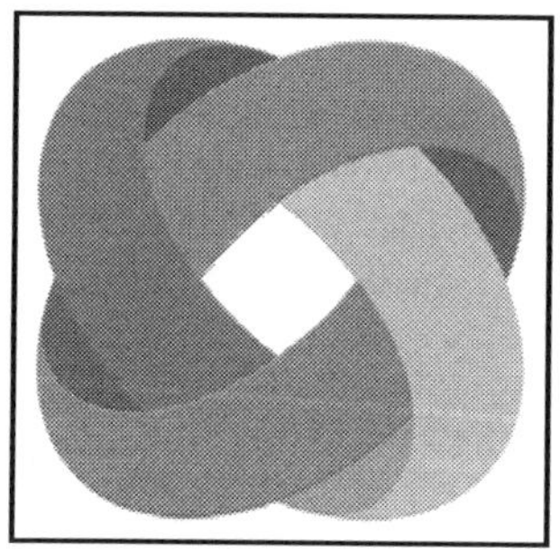

# Checking an image exists in the folder

We can now create a route to check whether an image exists in our `uploads` folder. We'll use the HEAD verb. If you're not familiar with it, it's just like a `GET` request, but without a body (no content). It's used to request only information (headers) from a path.

```
app.head("/uploads/:image", (req, res) => {
    fs.access(
        path.join(__dirname, "uploads", req.params.image),
        fs.constants.R_OK ,
        (err) => {
            res.status(err ? 404 : 200);
            res.end();
        }
    );
});
```

We'll look for a similar route, but this time we're only handling HEAD requests. This is a simple check. We just question if the current process has read access to the local file.

```
fs.access(path, mode, callback);
```

If so, we'll reply with HTTP response code `200`, which means *Found*. If not, we'll reply with HTTP response code `404`, which means *Not Found*:

```
res.status(err ? 404 : 200);
```

Add the preceding code and restart the service.

If you use `curl` to check for our previously uploaded file, you'll receive something like this:

```
curl --head 'http://localhost:3000/uploads/example.png'

HTTP/1.1 200 OK
X-Powered-By: Express
Content-Length: 0
Connection: keep-alive
```

If you change the path to something else, you should receive something like this:

```
curl --head 'http://localhost:3000/uploads/other.png'

HTTP/1.1 404 Not Found
X-Powered-By: Express
Connection: keep-alive
```

# Downloading images

Now that we have uploaded our file and checked whether it's stored on the server, we want to be able to download it anytime. Let's create a route to download it. It will be just like the HEAD route we created, but now using the `GET` verb. Here's an example of how we can implement the route:

```
app.get("/uploads/:image", (req, res) => {
    let ext = path.extname(req.params.image);

    if (!ext.match(/^\.(png|jpg)$/)) {
        return res.status(404).end()
    }

    let fd = fs.createReadStream(path.join(__dirname, "uploads",
    req.params.image));
```

```
        fd.on("error", (e) => {
            if (e.code == "ENOENT") {
                return res.status(404).end()
            }

            res.status(500).end();
        });

        res.setHeader("Content-Type", "image/" + ext.substr(1));

        fd.pipe(res);
    });
```

We first start by checking the image extension:

```
    let ext = path.extname(req.params.image);
```

If the extension is not `.png` or `.jpg`, we immediately return an HTTP response code `404`, which means *Not Found*:

```
    if (!ext.match(/^\.(png|jpg)$/)) {
        return res.status(404).end();
    }
```

If the extension is acceptable, we create a readable stream to the image file path:

```
    let fd = fs.createReadStream(path.join(__dirname, "uploads",
    req.params.image));
```

We then attach an error handler that will catch errors when reading the local file. If the error code is `ENOENT`, it means the file does not exist, so we again return an HTTP response code `404`. For any other error codes, we return an HTTP response code `500`, which means *Internal Server Error*:

```
    fd.on("error", (e) => {
        if (e.code == "ENOENT") {
            return res.status(404).end()
        }

        res.status(500).end();
    });
```

Returning code `500` is up to you. Perhaps you prefer to always return a `404` and hide the error differences from the user. That's a design decision; it depends on how you want your users to see your microservice and what target users will use it.

Then, we use the previously stored extension to set the content type returned to the user, in order to identify the image type we're sending. The content type should be in the format image/extension (without a dot):

```
res.setHeader("Content-Type", "image/" + ext.substr(1));
```

Finally, we pipe the file content to the response. This is a helper method that will trigger reads from the file stream and write them to the response. When the whole file has been read, the response is ended automatically:

```
fd.pipe(res);
```

Let's try it out. Restart our service and open your web browser. If you point to the previously uploaded image, you should get a copy of it:

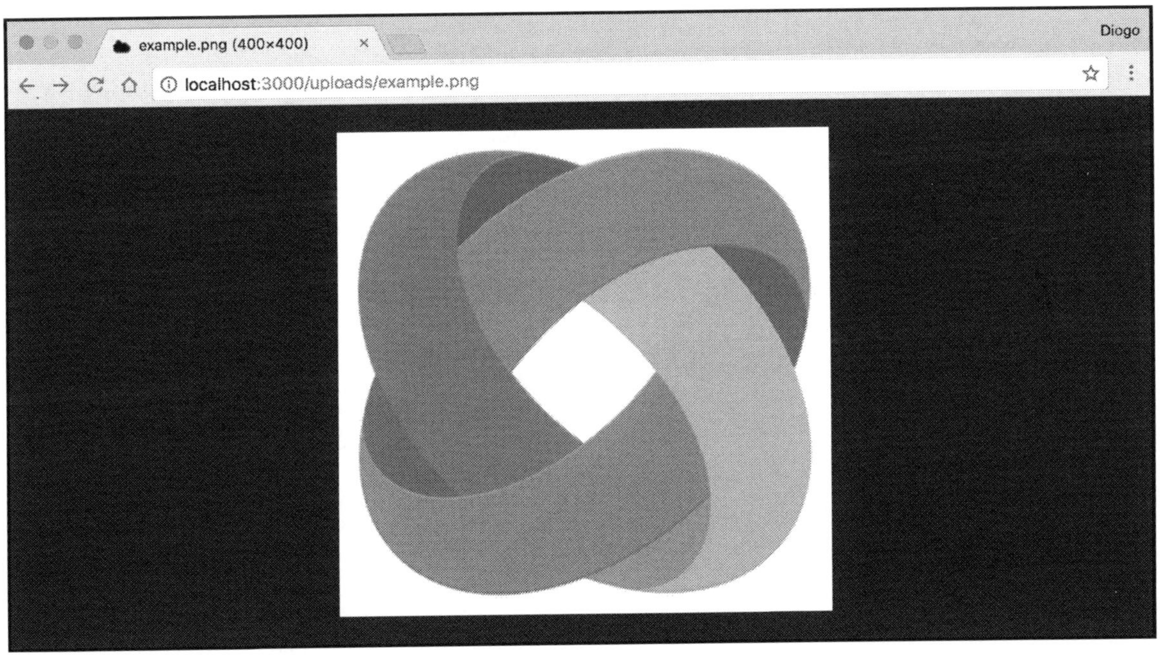

If you change the path to something that you haven't uploaded, you should get an **HTTP ERROR 404**:

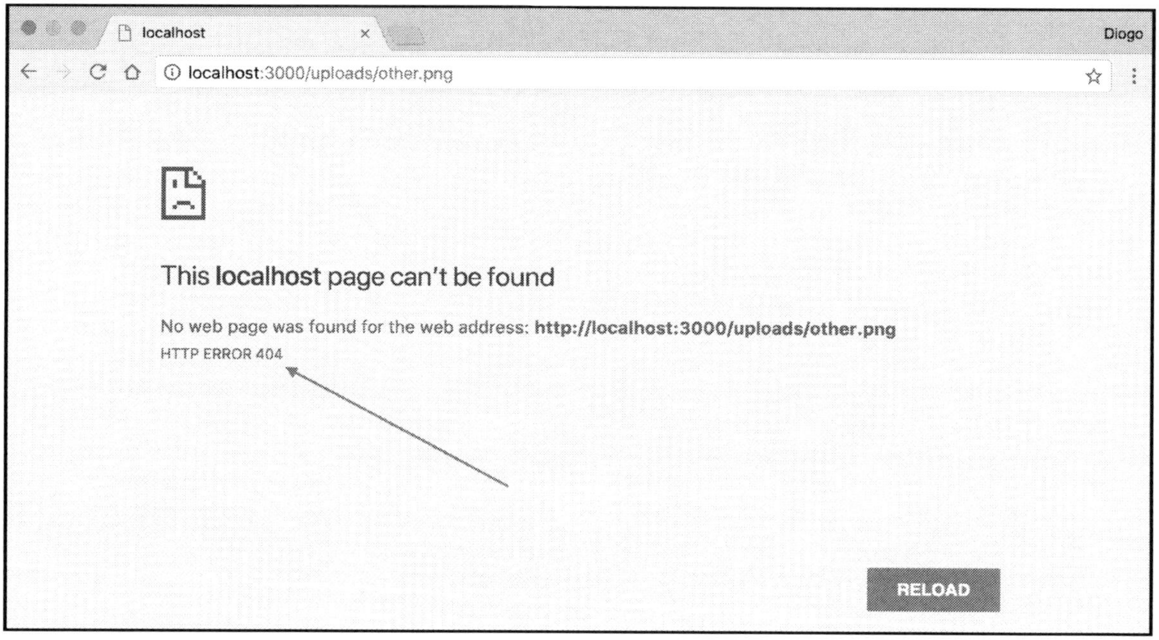


This is not very appealing. We can change our error handler to check whether the request might accept HTML content and return a custom message:

```
fd.on("error", (e) => {
    if (e.code == "ENOENT") {
        res.status(404);

        if (req.accepts('html')) {
            res.setHeader("Content-Type", "text/html");

            res.write("<strong>Error:</strong> image not found");
        }

        return res.end();
    }

    res.status(500).end();
});
```

You should now receive a nicer response:

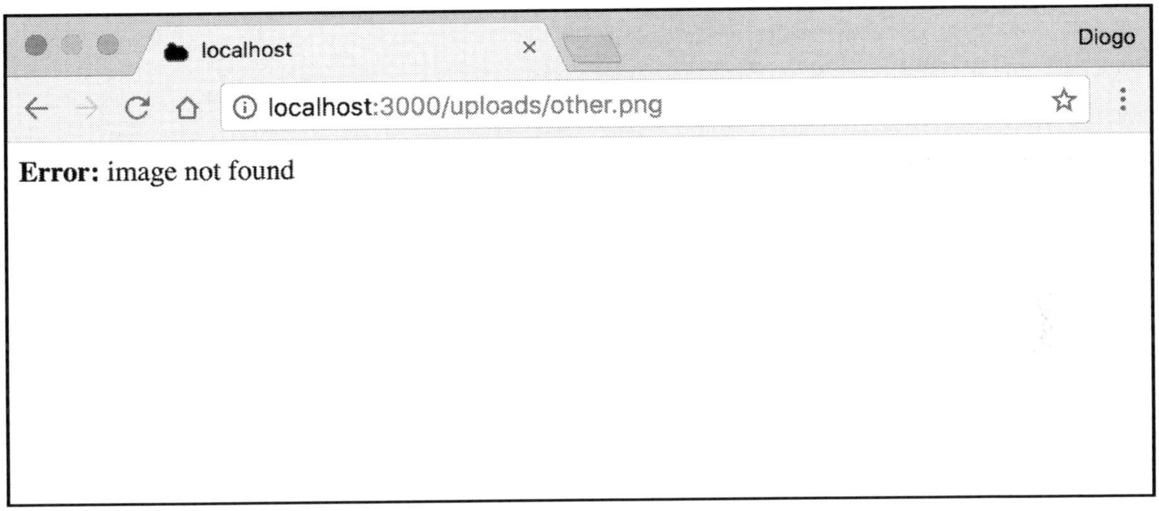


If you're familiar with Express, you could instead use a render engine and define a custom error template, or look for error handler modules that generate beautiful error pages.

# Using route parameters

Now that we've written more than 100 lines of code, let's take a step back and look at it. There's certainly space for optimizations. Let's use another awesome feature of Express – route parameters. They allow you to preprocess any route that uses a parameter and check whether it's valid, and do all kinds of stuff such as fetching additional information from a database or another server.

We'll use it to validate our image name for now:

```
app.param("image", (req, res, next, image) => {
    if (!image.match(/\.(png|jpg)$/i)) {
        return res.status(req.method == "POST" ? 403 : 404).end();
    }

    req.image     = image;
    req.localpath = path.join(__dirname, "uploads", req.image);

    return next();
});
```

We start by checking whether the name matches a PNG or JPG image and, if not, we immediately reply with a `403` (for `POST` requests) or `404` error code (for anything else). If the name is acceptable, we store the image and the expected local path in the request object, for consulting it later.

We can now rewrite our routes, so let's start with our upload route:

```
app.post("/uploads/:image", bodyparser.raw({
    limit : "10mb",
    type  : "image/*"
}), (req, res) => {
    let fd  = fs.createWriteStream(req.localpath, {
        flags    : "w+",
        encoding : "binary"
    });

    fd.end(req.body);

    fd.on("close", () => {
        res.send({ status : "ok", size: req.body.length });
    });
});
```

Our initial check was completely removed since the parameter was pre-validated. Also, we can now use `req.localpath`. I also optimized code by removing an unnecessary variable allocation (`len`) and just using `.end()` by avoiding `.write()`.

```
app.head("/uploads/:image", (req, res) => {
    fs.access(req.localpath, fs.constants.R_OK , (err) => {
        res.status(err ? 404 : 200).end();
    });
});
```

Our image check route looks almost exactly the same. This route had no security, so at least we introduced the pre-validation automatically. It's still far from acceptable for production, but it's a good start:

```
app.get("/uploads/:image", (req, res) => {
    let fd = fs.createReadStream(req.localpath);

    fd.on("error", (e) => {
        res.status(e.code == "ENOENT" ? 404 : 500).end();
    });

    res.setHeader("Content-Type", "image/" +
path.extname(req.image).substr(1));
```

```
        fd.pipe(res);
    });
```

Our image download route got a bit smaller. I removed the fancy error to keep the service clean as it will most probably be used by other services and programs, not users directly.

The change we introduced centralizes the image parameter check. We can go a little further and see if the name has special characters that would allow a malicious user to fetch a file from a location other than our local uploads folder. Let's save that for the next chapter.

# Generating thumbnails

We created upload and download routes, but they do nothing to the image other than storing it locally. Picking on our first thumbnail route, let's change our download route to be able to tell us the size we want for the image:

```
app.param("width", (req, res, next, width) => {
    req.width = +width;

    return next();
});

app.param("height", (req, res, next, height) => {
    req.height = +height;

    return next();
});
```

We start by defining two parameters, width, and height. These are numbers, so we'll assume they can be casted to a number type and stored in the request object.

Since we want to be able to specify sizes, let's create different routes using the route parameters we just introduced. To keep our code DRY, let's create a function to download the image and enable us to avoid repeating a very similar code. Our function will be able to handle optional resize:

```
function download_image(req, res) {
    fs.access(req.localpath, fs.constants.R_OK , (err) => {
        if (err) return res.status(404).end();

        let image = sharp(req.localpath);

        if (req.width && req.height) {
            image.ignoreAspectRatio();
        }
```

```
        if (req.width || req.height) {
            image.resize(req.width, req.height);
        }

        res.setHeader("Content-Type", "image/" +
        path.extname(req.image).substr(1));

        image.pipe(res);
    });
}
```

Our function first starts by checking whether the image exists. This will avoid the `sharp` module from throwing for non-existent images. We then initialize the image processing by passing its local path. We then do something interesting:

```
if (req.width && req.height) {
    image.ignoreAspectRatio();
}
```

First, if we receive both width and height, we tell `sharp` to ignore aspect ratio and resize as we tell it. Otherwise, it would maintain aspect ratio and center the image in the final size. You can check the difference by commenting out those first three lines:

```
if (req.width || req.height) {
    image.resize(req.width, req.height);
}
```

Second, if we receive one of the `width` or `height` parameters, we resize the image. We can resize with only one of the parameters. The `sharp` module is also able to resize using only one of the parameters if the other is undefined, so the line just works and will maintain aspect ratio.

We then just do what we did before: set the content type response header and send the image to the user. Now, we can create multiple routes for this function.

We'll allow three different download scenarios:

- A particular fixed-size image
- An aspect ratio resize by passing only width or height
- A full-size image

For the first scenario, we'll use our previous `width` and `height` parameters:

```
app.get("/uploads/:width(\\d+)x:height(\\d+)-:image", download_image);
```

This will allow a route address similar to the following:

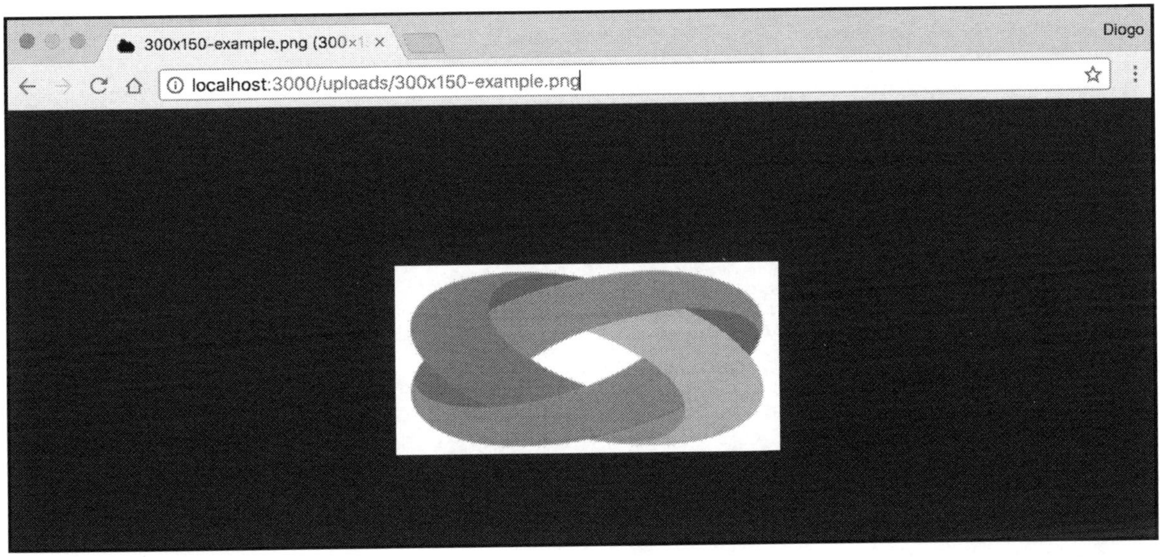


For the second scenario, we'll use similar routes, where the missing parameter is replaced by an underscore:

```
app.get("/uploads/_x:height(\\d+)-:image", download_image);
app.get("/uploads/:width(\\d+)x_-:image", download_image);
```

These will allow routes similar to the one as follows:

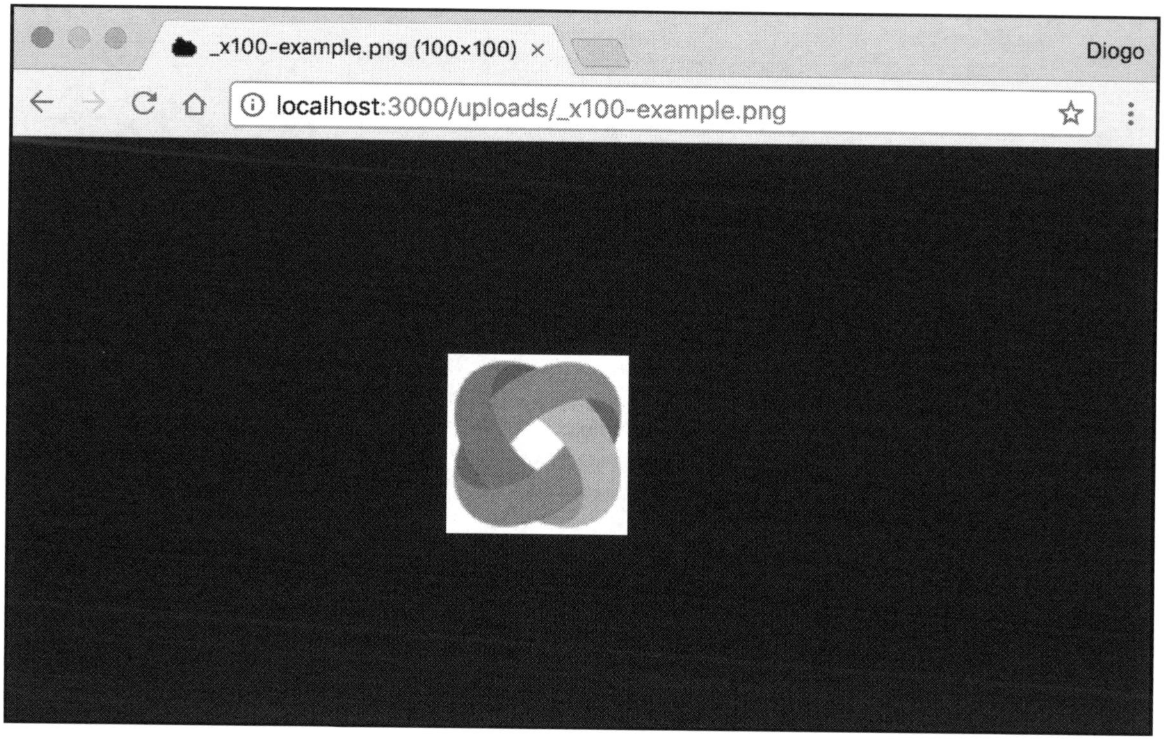


For the third and final scenario, we'll keep the same route:

```
app.get("/uploads/:image", download_image);
```

These four routes must be defined in this order. This is important because route parameters are based on regular expressions and they're greedy, so we need to define our more complicated routes first, and then the simpler ones.

# Playing around with colors

Let's have some more fun and add a simple effect: `greyscale`. Let's add a parameter that will indicate to our service that the user wants the image in shades of grey:

```
app.param("greyscale", (req, res, next, greyscale) => {
    if (greyscale != "bw") return next("route");

    req.greyscale = true;
```

```
        return next();
    });
```

Our parameter will only match the `bw` string. If it matches, it will mark a flag in the request object.

We can now change our image download function to handle this parameter, if defined:

```
    function download_image(req, res) {
        fs.access(req.localpath, fs.constants.R_OK , (err) => {
            if (err) return res.status(404).end();

            let image = sharp(req.localpath);

            if (req.width && req.height) {
                image.ignoreAspectRatio();
            }

            if (req.width || req.height) {
                image.resize(req.width, req.height);
            }

            if (req.greyscale) {
                image.greyscale();
            }

            res.setHeader("Content-Type", "image/" +
            path.extname(req.image).substr(1));

            image.pipe(res);
        });
    }
```

Finally, for every one of our four download routes, we need to add another one to enable grey scaling. This means our user can take advantage of our resizing options and can `greyscale` the image if he prefers:

```
    app.get("/uploads/:width(\\d+)x:height(\\d+)-:greyscale-:image",
    download_image);
    app.get("/uploads/:width(\\d+)x:height(\\d+)-:image", download_image);
    app.get("/uploads/_x:height(\\d+)-:greyscale-:image", download_image);
    app.get("/uploads/_x:height(\\d+)-:image", download_image);
    app.get("/uploads/:width(\\d+)x_-:greyscale-:image", download_image);
    app.get("/uploads/:width(\\d+)x_-:image", download_image);
    app.get("/uploads/:greyscale-:image", download_image);
    app.get("/uploads/:image", download_image);
```

For every one of our initial four routes, we added a similar route before that, with the greyscale parameter. The user just has to prefix the image name with `bw-` to automatically enable `greyscale`.

In the end, excluding our first generated thumbnail, you should have something similar to the following code. I removed the code blocks inside the routes and our download function, so you're able to see the base structure:

```
const bodyparser = require("body-parser");
const path       = require("path");
const fs         = require("fs");
const express    = require("express");
const sharp      = require("sharp");
const app        = express();

app.param("image", (req, res, next, image) => { ... });
app.param("width", (req, res, next, width) => { ... });
app.param("height", (req, res, next, height) => { ... });
app.param("greyscale", (req, res, next, greyscale) => { ... });

app.post("/uploads/:image", bodyparser.raw({ limit: "10mb", type: "image/*"
}), (req, res) => { ... });

app.head("/uploads/:image", (req, res) => { ... });

app.get("/uploads/:width(\\d+)x:height(\\d+)-:greyscale-:image",
download_image);
app.get("/uploads/:width(\\d+)x:height(\\d+)-:image", download_image);
app.get("/uploads/_x:height(\\d+)-:greyscale-:image", download_image);
app.get("/uploads/_x:height(\\d+)-:image", download_image);
app.get("/uploads/:width(\\d+)x_-:greyscale-:image", download_image);
app.get("/uploads/:width(\\d+)x_-:image", download_image);
app.get("/uploads/:greyscale-:image", download_image);
app.get("/uploads/:image", download_image);

app.listen(3000, () => {
    console.log("ready");
});

function download_image(req, res) {
    ...
}
```

You can now restart our service and make some tests. Taking our first image as an example, we can request a `greyscale` version:

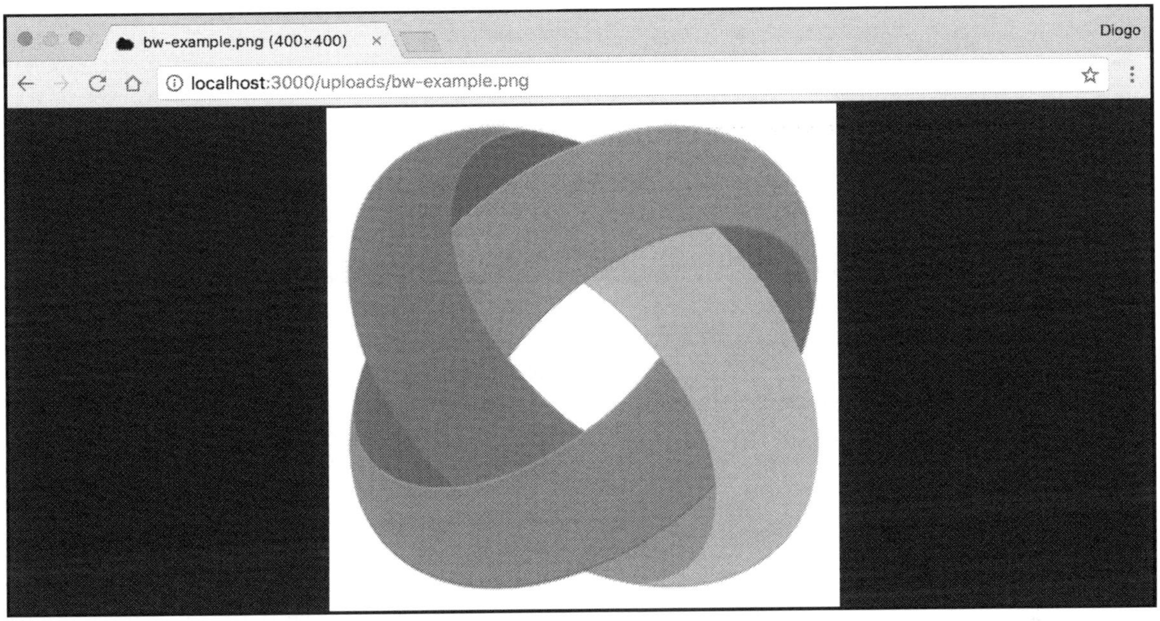

You can still resize the image as we did before, with the optional `greyscale` filter:

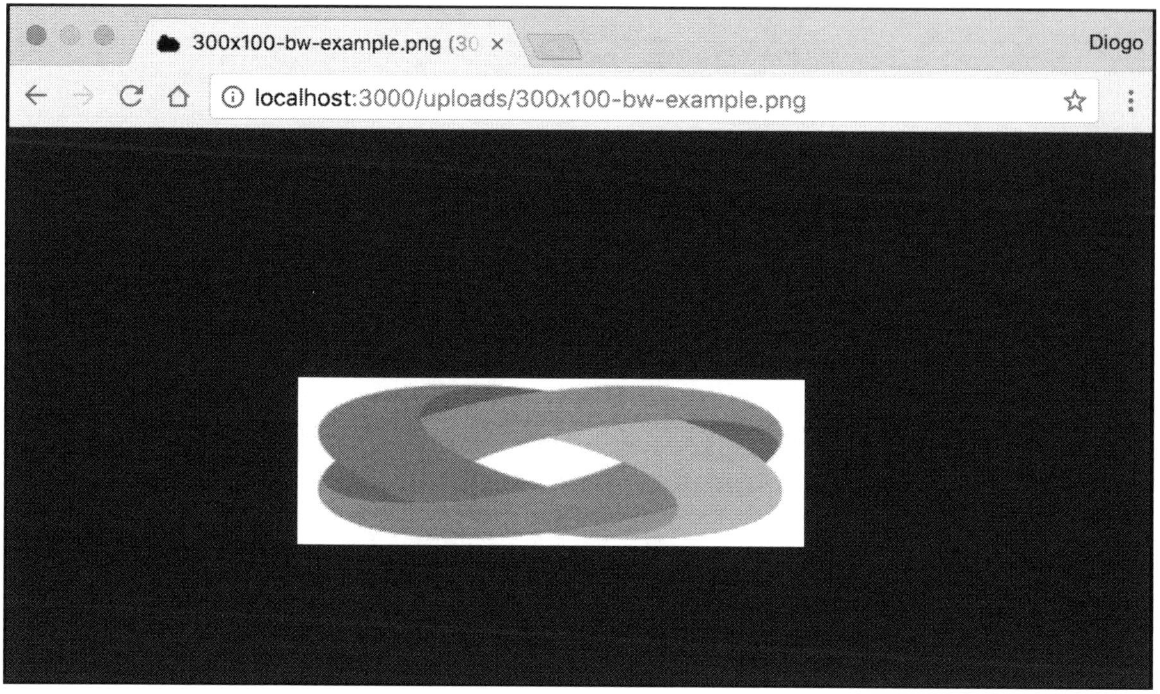


We can take advantage of the `sharp` module and add some more interesting image manipulations for our service. This way, we can use it in more projects as it evolves to a full-featured image manipulation service.

We can start by adding a blurring option, something that will make the image seem unfocused. We can also do the opposite, and make the image sharper. We can also flip the image horizontally and vertically.

# Refactor routes

These options look neat but, following the route we're doing, it will probably be a mess to create all the path possibilities. We're also narrowing on the image names as we're creating virtual prefixes for these image manipulations options.

Let's make a change while we're at the beginning. Instead of using route parameters, let's use query parameters. They can be added in the order we want, and don't affect the path. We could also use request headers, but these would be harder to test both on the browser and using fetching modules such as request.

So, before we add our neat image manipulations, let's refactor our code to use query parameters. Express handles and decodes query parameters automatically, so we just need to change our download `image` function:

```
function download_image(req, res) {
    fs.access(req.localpath, fs.constants.R_OK , (err) => {
        if (err) return res.status(404).end();

        let image     = sharp(req.localpath);
        let width     = +req.query.width;
        let height    = +req.query.height;
        let greyscale = (req.query.greyscale == "y");

        if (width > 0 && height > 0) {
            image.ignoreAspectRatio();
        }

        if (width > 0 || height > 0) {
            image.resize(width || null, height || null);
        }

        if (greyscale) {
            image.greyscale();
        }

        res.setHeader("Content-Type", "image/" +
        path.extname(req.image).substr(1));

        image.pipe(res);
    });
}
```

We're not validating as we probably should, but we're ensuring the width and height are positive numbers. For greyscaling, we're checking whether the query parameter equals `y`. If you prefer to support more options on greyscaling such as `yes` or `true`, change the line to something like the following:

```
let greyscale = [ "y", "yes", "1", "on"].includes(req.query.greyscale);
```

Now, we can drop the `width`, `height`, and `greyscale` route parameters we added before, and just keep the `image` parameter. Also, all our download routes can be removed, and we just keep the simpler one. In the end, we'll have something like this:

```
const bodyparser = require("body-parser");
const path       = require("path");
const fs         = require("fs");
const express    = require("express");
const sharp      = require("sharp");
const app        = express();

app.param("image", (req, res, next, image) => {
    if (!image.match(/\.(png|jpg)$/i)) {
        return res.status(req.method == "POST" ? 403 : 404).end();
    }

    req.image     = image;
    req.localpath = path.join(__dirname, "uploads", req.image);

    return next();
});

app.post("/uploads/:image", bodyparser.raw({
    limit : "10mb",
    type  : "image/*"
}), (req, res) => {
    let fd  = fs.createWriteStream(req.localpath, {
        flags    : "w+",
        encoding : "binary"
    });

    fd.end(req.body);

    fd.on("close", () => {
        res.send({ status : "ok", size: req.body.length });
    });
});

app.head("/uploads/:image", (req, res) => {
    fs.access(req.localpath, fs.constants.R_OK , (err) => {
        res.status(err ? 404 : 200).end();
    });
});

app.get("/uploads/:image", download_image);

app.listen(3000, () => {
```

```
        console.log("ready");
    });
```

Let's try it out now. You should be able to do a resize like we did before, but with a different address:

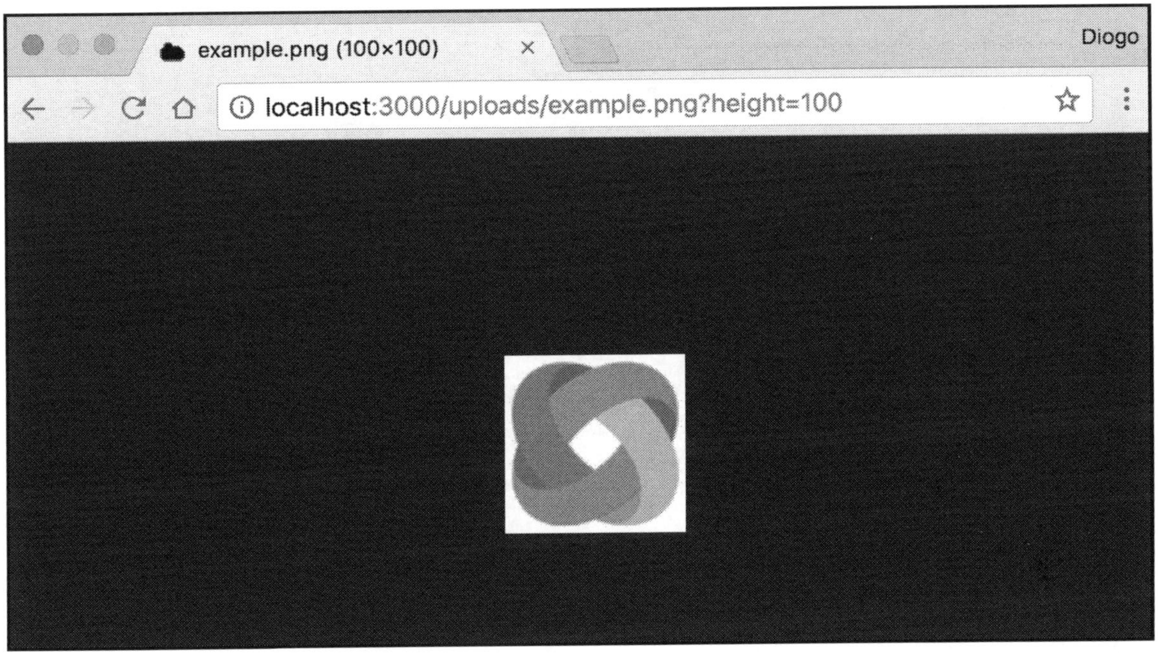

We can also add the `greyscale` function to it:

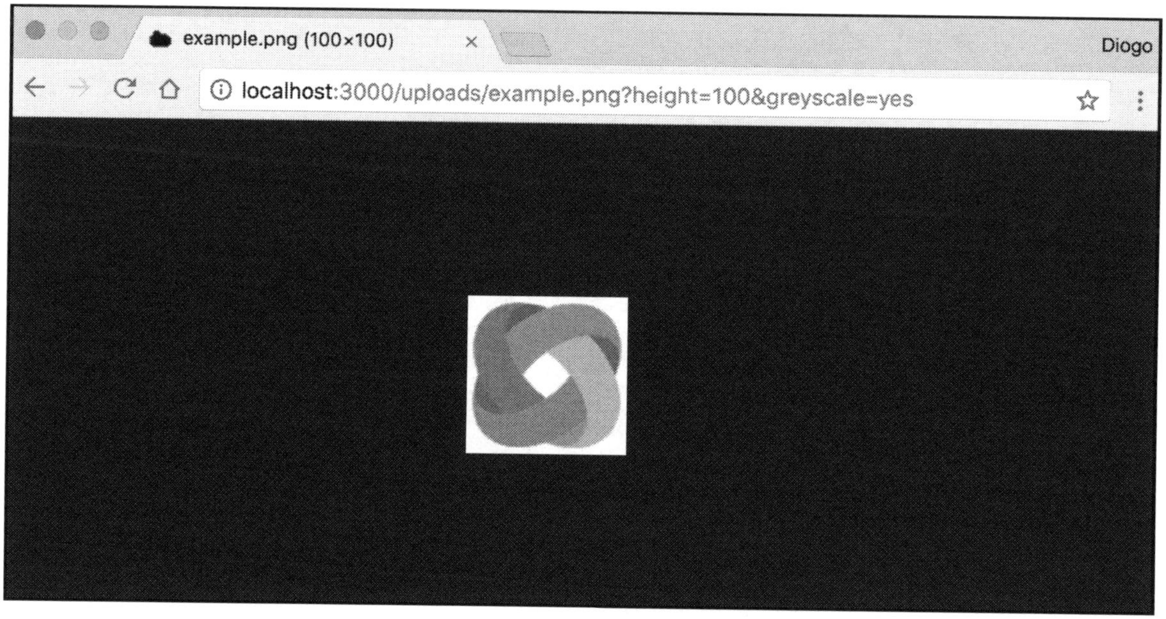


# Manipulating images

Let's add the other image manipulation options we mentioned before. Let's use the Sharp naming for flipping. We'll use the query parameter `flip` to flip the image vertically, and the query parameter `flop` to flip it horizontally. We'll also add the optional query parameters `blur` and `sharpen`, which should be positive numbers.

Our image download function can be reintegrated directly in our download route, since we only have one route now. In the end, we would end up with something like this:

```
app.get("/uploads/:image", (req, res) => {
    fs.access(req.localpath, fs.constants.R_OK , (err) => {
        if (err) return res.status(404).end();

        let image     = sharp(req.localpath);
        let width     = +req.query.width;
        let height    = +req.query.height;
        let blur      = +req.query.blur;
        let sharpen   = +req.query.sharpen;
        let greyscale = [ "y", "yes", "1",

       "on"].includes(req.query.greyscale);
        let flip      = [ "y", "yes", "1",
        "on"].includes(req.query.flip);
        let flop      = [ "y", "yes", "1",
        "on"].includes(req.query.flop);

        if (width > 0 && height > 0) {
            image.ignoreAspectRatio();
        }

        if (width > 0 || height > 0) {
            image.resize(width || null, height || null);
        }

        if (flip)        image.flip();
        if (flop)        image.flop();
        if (blur > 0)    image.blur(blur);
        if (sharpen > 0) image.sharpen(sharpen);
        if (greyscale)   image.greyscale();

        res.setHeader("Content-Type", "image/" +
        path.extname(req.image).substr(1));

        image.pipe(res);
    });
});
```

We should be able to play with it now; flipping and sharpening the image leads to something like this:

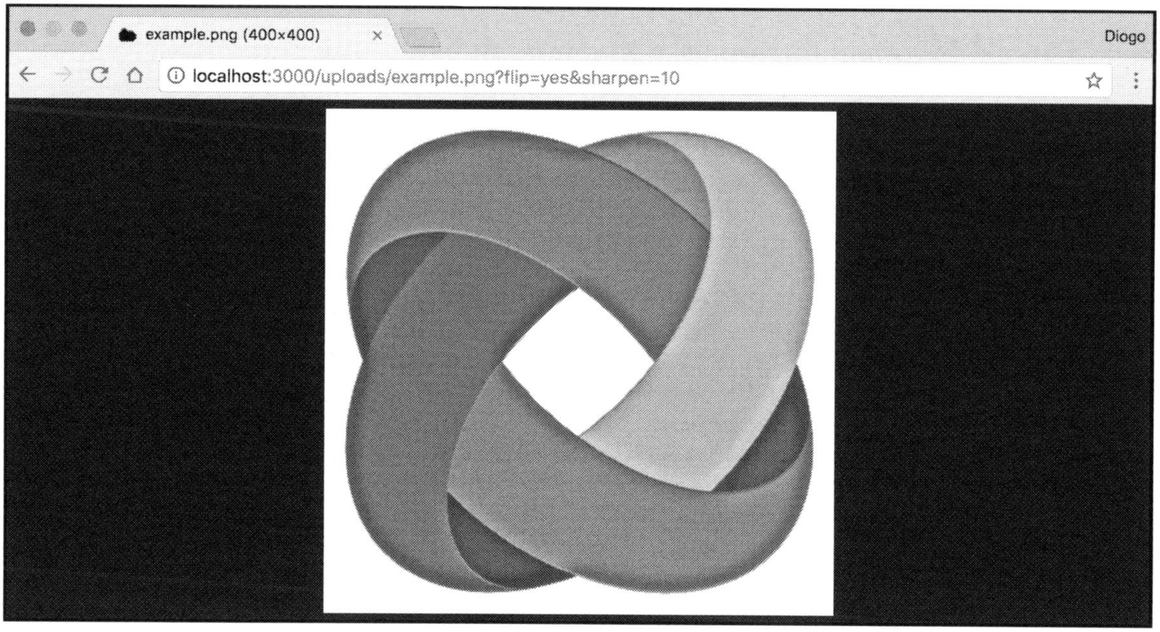

Blurring the image leads to something similar to this:

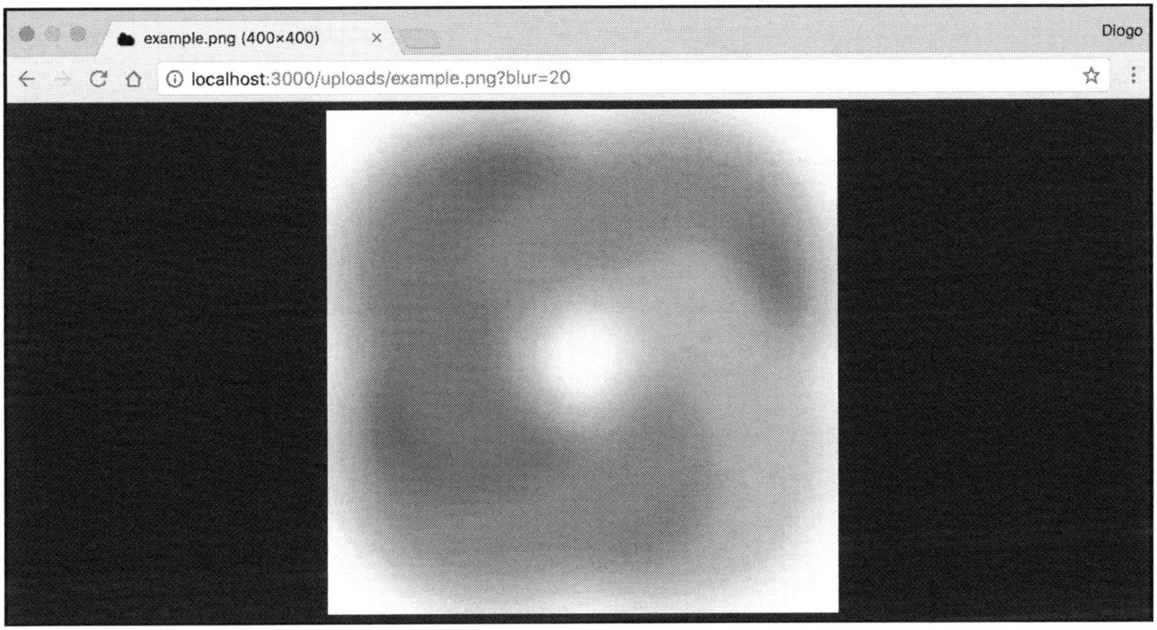

Well, that looks awesome for a first iteration. Let's see what it would look like if we use Hydra instead.

# Using Hydra

As you may remember, Hydra has a scaffolding command that helps to bootstrap our service quickly. Let's use it, and prepare our base layout. Run `yo fwsp-hydra` and answer the questions. You can leave most of them as default. Depending on the versions you'll use, you should get something similar to the lines shown here:

```
fwsp-hydra generator v0.3.1   yeoman-generator v2.0.2   yo v2.0.1
? Name of the service (`-service` will be appended automatically) imagini
? Your full name? Diogo Resende
? Your email address? dresende@thinkdigital.pt
? Your organization or username? (used to tag docker images) dresende
? Host the service runs on?
? Port the service runs on? 3000
? What does this service do? Image thumbnail and manipulation
? Does this service need auth? No
? Is this a hydra-express service? Yes
? Set up a view engine? No
? Set up logging? No
? Enable CORS on serverResponses? No
? Run npm install? No
   create imagini-service/specs/test.js
   create imagini-service/specs/helpers/chai.js
   create imagini-service/.editorconfig
   create imagini-service/.eslintrc
   create imagini-service/.gitattributes
   create imagini-service/.nvmrc
   create imagini-service/.gitignore
   create imagini-service/package.json
   create imagini-service/README.md
   create imagini-service/imagini-service.js
   create imagini-service/config/sample-config.json
   create imagini-service/config/config.json
   create imagini-service/scripts/docker.js
   create imagini-service/routes/imagini-v1-routes.js

Done!

'cd imagini-service' then 'npm install' and 'npm start'
```

Well, let's do just that. Let's enter our service folder and install dependencies. If you then start it using `npm start`, and open the browser and point it to our service, you should get something like this:

Not surprising, because Hydra created a different base route. To enable versioning and having different services running on the same HTTP backend, Hydra scaffolding created a route under the `/v1/imagini` prefix. Remember, we scaffolded Hydra with Express integration, so many of the terms we discussed earlier will be the same here:

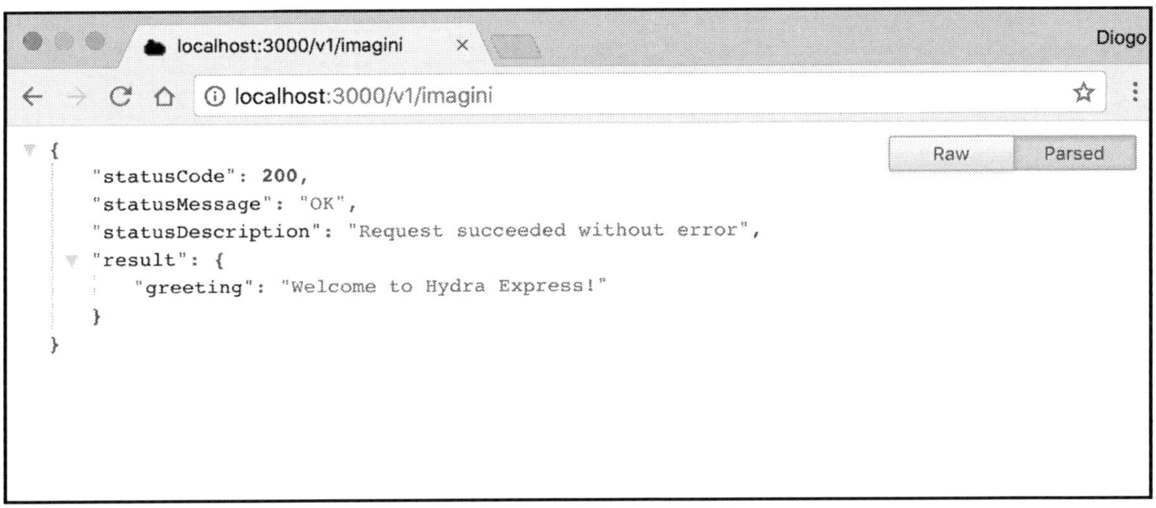

Before we pick our previous code and integrate into Hydra, we need to add our Sharp dependency to `package.json`. Look up the `dependencies` property and add `sharp`. You should end up with something along these lines:

```
(...)
"dependencies": {
    "sharp"                : "^0.19.0",
    "body-parser"          : "^1.18.2",
    "fwsp-config"          : "1.1.5",
    "hydra-express"        : "1.5.5",
    "fwsp-server-response" : "2.2.6"
},
(...)
```

Now, run `npm install` to install Sharp. Then, open the `imagini-v1-routes.js` file, which is under the `routes` folder. Basically, what it does is get a handler for Hydra and Express, prepare a generic JSON server response (that's what the `fwsp-server-response` module is), create an Express router, attach the / route, and then export it.

We'll keep this structure for now. I refactored the file as I'm a bit picky about indentation and quotes. I added our image route parameter and added the image upload route. I changed our previous route code to drop the `/uploads` route prefix, and use the new `sendOk` and `sendError` functions you see in the preceding code:

```
/**
 * @name          imagini-v1-api
 * @description   This module packages the Imagini API.
 */
"use strict";

const fs             = require("fs");
const path           = require("path");
const sharp          = require("sharp");
const bodyparser     = require("body-parser");
const hydraExpress   = require("hydra-express");
const ServerResponse = require("fwsp-server-response");
const hydra          = hydraExpress.getHydra();
const express        = hydraExpress.getExpress();

let serverResponse = new ServerResponse();

express.response.sendError = function (err) {
    serverResponse.sendServerError(this, { result : { error : err }});
};

express.response.sendOk = function (result) {
```

```
    serverResponse.sendOk(this, { result });
};

let api = express.Router();

api.param("image", (req, res, next, image) => {
    if (!image.match(/\.(png|jpg)$/i)) {
        return res.sendError("invalid image type/extension");
    }

    req.image     = image;
    req.localpath = path.join(__dirname, "../uploads", req.image);

    return next();
});

api.post("/:image", bodyparser.raw({
    limit : "10mb",
    type  : "image/*"
}), (req, res) => {
    let fd  = fs.createWriteStream(req.localpath, {
        flags    : "w+",
        encoding : "binary"
    });

    fd.end(req.body);

    fd.on("close", () => {
        res.sendOk({ size: req.body.length });
    });
});

module.exports = api;
```

Then, we restart our microservice, create the `uploads` folder under the `imagini-service` folder, and try to upload an image. Like before, I used `curl` to test it:

```
curl -X POST -H 'Content-Type: image/png' \
    --data-binary @example.png \
    http://localhost:3000/v1/imagini/example.png
```

As expected, I received a JSON response with our `size` property:

```
{
    "statusCode"        : 200,
    "statusMessage"     : "OK",
    "statusDescription" : "Request succeeded without error",
```

```
        "result" : {
            "size" : 55543
        }
    }
```

We can have our uploaded file in our `uploads` folder. We're getting there; just two more routes:

```
api.head("/:image", (req, res) => {
    fs.access(req.localpath, fs.constants.R_OK , (err) => {
        if (err) {
            return res.sendError("image not found");
        }

        return res.sendOk();
    });
});
```

Our check route is very similar. We just changed the return methods to use the methods defined previously:

```
api.get("/:image", (req, res) => {
    fs.access(req.localpath, fs.constants.R_OK , (err) => {
        if (err) {
            return res.sendError("image not found");
        }

        let image     = sharp(req.localpath);
        let width     = +req.query.width;
        let height    = +req.query.height;
        let blur      = +req.query.blur;
        let sharpen   = +req.query.sharpen;
        let greyscale = [ "y", "yes", "true", "1",
        "on"].includes(req.query.greyscale);
        let flip      = [ "y", "yes", "true", "1",
        "on"].includes(req.query.flip);
        let flop      = [ "y", "yes", "true", "1",
        "on"].includes(req.query.flop);

        if (width > 0 && height > 0) {
            image.ignoreAspectRatio();
        }

        if (width > 0 || height > 0) {
            image.resize(width || null, height || null);
        }
```

```
            if (flip)          image.flip();
            if (flop)          image.flop();
            if (blur > 0)      image.blur(blur);
            if (sharpen > 0) image.sharpen(sharpen);
            if (greyscale)     image.greyscale();

            res.setHeader("Content-Type", "image/" +
            path.extname(req.image).substr(1));

            image.pipe(res);
        });
    });
```

Our image download method is equally similar. For this route, we're not using the JSON responses, and instead just return our image directly. This allows us to try it out on our browser:

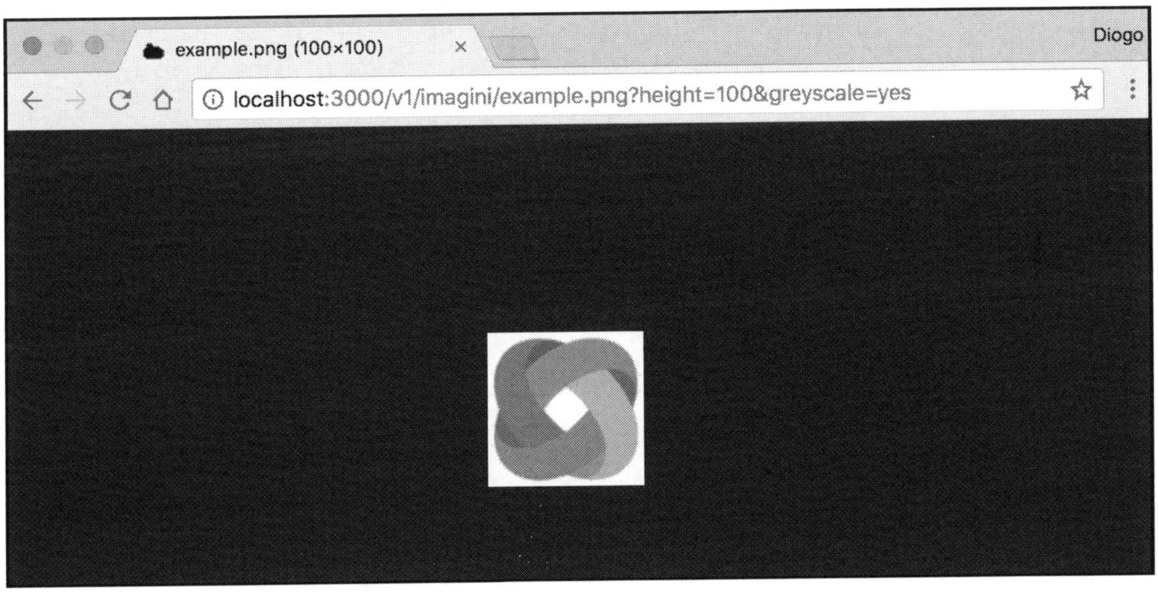


We just migrated our service from Express to Hydra. Not much of a difference, but Hydra gives you a more robust layout, about which we'll find out more later on. Let's take a look at our third framework: Seneca.

# Using Seneca

Remember that routing on this framework is all about patterns. Let's keep it simple for now and use a role property to indicate what we want to do (upload, check, or download).

By default, every message should be JSON-encoded, so we'll encode the image in `base64` to pass it as a string inside the JSON messages to upload and download.

Create a folder for our Seneca service, and then create a child folder called `uploads`. Then, install `seneca` and `sharp` on that folder by running the following command:

```
npm install seneca sharp --save
```

Then, create a file called `imagini.js` with the following content:

```
const seneca  = require("seneca");
const sharp   = require("sharp");
const path    = require("path");
const fs      = require("fs");
const service = seneca();

service.add("role:upload,image:*,data:*", function (msg, next) {
    let filename = path.join(__dirname, "uploads", msg.image);
    let data = Buffer.from(msg.data, "base64");

    fs.writeFile(filename, data, (err) => {
        if (err) return next(err);

        return next(null, { size : data.length });
    });
});

service.listen(3000);
```

What this does is initiate a simple service with a route for uploading. Since we're receiving all the image content directly on an object property, I used `fs.writeFile`. It's a simpler method and gives me an error whether something incorrect happens, which we can pass on to the route response.

I also used `Buffer.from` to convert our image data, which we'll be uploading in `base64`.

So, let's just start it as we did with the others. I included the same `example.png` image and used `curl` to test this out.

```
curl -H "Content-Type: application/json" \
--data '{"role":"upload","image":"example.png","data":"'"$( base64
```

```
example.png)"'"}' \
http://localhost:3000/act
```

Seneca promptly replied with the following:

```
{"size":55543}
```

This is the image size. Notice I'm taking advantage of bash interpolation (variable substitution) to directly convert the image file to `base64` and pass it to `curl`, which then sends that JSON piece of data to our service:

```
service.add("role:check,image:*", function (msg, next) {
    let filename = path.join(__dirname, "uploads", msg.image);

    fs.access(filename, fs.constants.R_OK , (err) => {
        return next(null, { exists : !err });
    });
});
```

Our check route is very similar. Instead of just replying with an HTTP 404 response code, we reply with a stringified JSON object with a boolean property exists, which will indicate if the image was found.

Here, we are checking for our image using `curl`:

```
curl -H "Content-Type: application/json" \
    --data '{"role":"check","image":"example.png"}' \
    http://localhost:3000/act
```

We will respond with the following:

```
{"exists":true}
```

If you change the image name, it will respond with `false`:

```
service.add("role:download,image:*", function (msg, next) {
    let filename = path.join(__dirname, "uploads", msg.image);

    fs.access(filename, fs.constants.R_OK , (err) => {
        if (err) return next(err);

        let image     = sharp(filename);
        let width     = +msg.width;
        let height    = +msg.height;
        let blur      = +msg.blur;
        let sharpen   = +msg.sharpen;
        let greyscale = !!msg.greyscale;
```

```
            let flip       = !!msg.flip;
            let flop       = !!msg.flop;

            if (width > 0 && height > 0) {
                image.ignoreAspectRatio();
            }

            if (width > 0 || height > 0) {
                image.resize(width || null, height || null);
            }

            if (flip)          image.flip();
            if (flop)          image.flop();
            if (blur > 0)      image.blur(blur);
            if (sharpen > 0) image.sharpen(sharpen);
            if (greyscale)     image.greyscale();

            image.toBuffer().then((data) => {
                return next(null, { data: data.toString("base64") });
            });
        });
    });
```

Our downloaded route has some changes:

- Instead of query parameters, we check directly on `msg`. One noticeable advantage is that we have types and not just strings, so we can use Boolean and numbers directly.
- Instead of returning the image in binary, so that we could just open in the browser, we convert it to `base64` and pass it on the JSON response.

We need some tools to test this on the command line. Since I use JSON a lot, I have `jq` installed. I strongly recommend you install it too and take a look at the tutorials. It will make your life easier. Using the `base64` command we previously used to encode, we can decode the content and pipe the data to a local file:

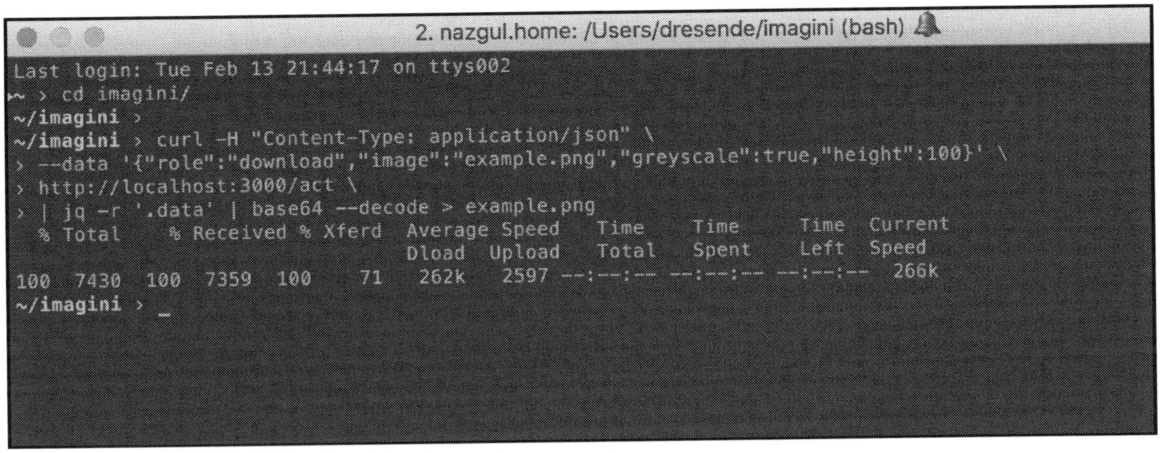


We can then open the folder and see the image is there. Notice I added `greyscale` and resized the image just by passing two more JSON parameters:

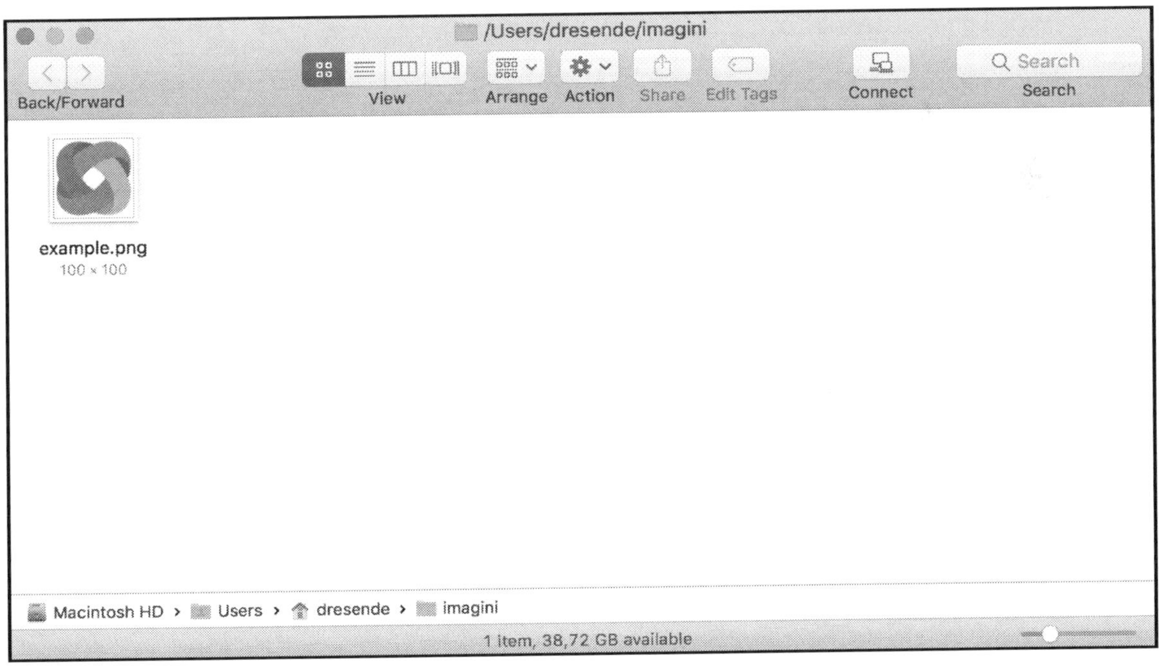

# Plugins

In the spirit of Seneca, we should make a plugin for our `imagini` service. Let's split our code into two parts:

- The `imagini` plugin, a service that manipulates images
- A Seneca microservice, which exposes the `imagini` plugin, and possibly others later on

There's lot of room for improvement on our code, starting with code we repeated constantly. It's important to detect repetitions while our service is still very small.

The most repeated part is the local filename. This is actually something you might want to configure when starting the service, so let's change that to a function. Start by changing our `imagini.js` file to be a plugin. Clear all content and write this code:

```
const sharp   = require("sharp");
const path    = require("path");
const fs      = require("fs");

module.exports = function (settings = { path: "uploads" }) {
    // plugin code goes here
};
```

This is the basis of our plugin. We're loading the modules we need, but not Seneca, because our plugin will have access to the service directly. Seneca itself will load the plugin by calling our exported function. Following the idea of being able to configure the local image folder, we define an optional `settings` parameter, which will default to an object with the property `path` equal to `uploads`, which is the folder we've been using so far.

Now, let's add the content of our plugin, inside the preceding function:

```
const localpath = (image) => {
    return path.join(settings.path, image);
}
```

We start by defining a function that will convert our image parameter to the local path. We can actually reduce the function to be written in one single line:

```
const localpath = (image) => (path.join(settings.path, image));
```

Then, let's create another function that will check whether we have access to a local file, and return a Boolean (if it exists or not) and the filename we provided:

```
const access = (filename, next) => {
    fs.access(filename, fs.constants.R_OK , (err) => {
        return next(!err, filename);
    });
};
```

We can use this for our image check, and for our image download. This way, we can improve or even cache the results for greater performance, avoiding excessive filesystem hits. Our image check route can now be written in a very concise way:

```
this.add("role:check,image:*", (msg, next) => {
    access(localpath(msg.image), (exists) => {
        return next(null, { exists : exists });
    });
});
```

Notice that we're referring to the `this` object. Our Seneca service will call our plugin function and reference itself to `this`. Again, we can write it in a more concise way:

```
this.add("role:check,image:*", (msg, next) => {
    access(localpath(msg.image), (exists) => (next(null, { exists })));
});
```

Our upload route is fairly simple and has no changes:

```
this.add("role:upload,image:*,data:*", (msg, next) => {
    let data = Buffer.from(msg.data, "base64");

    fs.writeFile(localpath(msg.image), data, (err) => {
        return next(err, { size : data.length });
    });
});
```

The download route uses our previously created helper functions to avoid storing our local filename. We also made some tweaks to how `width` and `height` were treated:

```
this.add("role:download,image:*", (msg, next) => {
    access(localpath(msg.image), (exists, filename) => {
        if (!exists) return next(new Error("image not found"));

        let image     = sharp(filename);
        let width     = +msg.width || null;
        let height    = +msg.height || null;
        let blur      = +msg.blur;
```

```
        let sharpen   = +msg.sharpen;
        let greyscale = !!msg.greyscale;
        let flip      = !!msg.flip;
        let flop      = !!msg.flop;

        if (width && height) image.ignoreAspectRatio();
        if (width || height) image.resize(width, height);
        if (flip)            image.flip();
        if (flop)            image.flop();
        if (blur > 0)        image.blur(blur);
        if (sharpen > 0)     image.sharpen(sharpen);
        if (greyscale)       image.greyscale();

        image.toBuffer().then((data) => {
            return next(null, { data: data.toString("base64") });
        });
    });
});
```

There are actually a lot of variables we're using where we could just check the message parameter instead. We can rewrite our download function and get one-third reduction:

```
this.add("role:download,image:*", (msg, next) => {
    access(localpath(msg.image), (exists, filename) => {
        if (!exists) return next(new Error("image not found"));

        let image     = sharp(filename);
        let width     = +msg.width || null;
        let height    = +msg.height || null;

        if (width && height) image.ignoreAspectRatio();
        if (width || height) image.resize(width, height);
        if (msg.flip)        image.flip();
        if (msg.flop)        image.flop();
        if (msg.blur > 0)    image.blur(blur);
        if (msg.sharpen > 0) image.sharpen(sharpen);
        if (msg.greyscale)   image.greyscale();

        image.toBuffer().then((data) => {
            return next(null, { data: data.toString("base64") });
        });
    });
});
```

In the end, you should have an `imagini.js` file with the following content:

```
const sharp   = require("sharp");
const path    = require("path");
```

```
const fs       = require("fs");

module.exports = function (settings = { path: "uploads" }) {
    const localpath = (image) => (path.join(settings.path, image));
    const access    = (filename, next) => {
        fs.access(filename, fs.constants.R_OK , (err) => {
            return next(!err, filename);
        });
    };

    this.add("role:check,image:*", (msg, next) => {
        access(localpath(msg.image), (exists) => (next(null, { exists })));
    });

    this.add("role:upload,image:*,data:*", (msg, next) => {
        let data = Buffer.from(msg.data, "base64");

        fs.writeFile(localpath(msg.image), data, (err) => {
            return next(err, { size : data.length });
        });
    });

    this.add("role:download,image:*", (msg, next) => {
        access(localpath(msg.image), (exists, filename) => {
            if (!exists) return next(new Error("image not found"));

            let image     = sharp(filename);
            let width     = +msg.width || null;
            let height    = +msg.height || null;

            if (width && height) image.ignoreAspectRatio();
            if (width || height) image.resize(width, height);
            if (msg.flip)        image.flip();
            if (msg.flop)        image.flop();
            if (msg.blur > 0)    image.blur(blur);
            if (msg.sharpen > 0) image.sharpen(sharpen);
            if (msg.greyscale)   image.greyscale();

            image.toBuffer().then((data) => {
                return next(null, { data: data.toString("base64") });
            });
        });
    });
};
```

We just need to create our Seneca service and use our plugin. This is actually very straightforward. Create a file called `seneca.js`, and add the following:

```
const seneca  = require("seneca");
const service = seneca();

service.use("./imagini.js", { path: __dirname + "/uploads" });

service.listen(3000);
```

What the code does, line by line, is as follows:

1. Loads the `seneca` module
2. Creates a Seneca `service`
3. Loads the `imagini.js` plugin and passes our desired path
4. Starts `service` on port `3000`

That's it, our service is now a plugin and could be used by any Seneca service! You should now start our `service` by running the new file and not `imagini.js` directly:

```
node seneca
```

# Summary

As you can see, writing a service does not change much between frameworks. Our code is very similar, with minor changes. Seneca is stricter about message format and content, so we used `base64` to encode our image inside the JSON message. Other than that, everything is the same.

For tools such as Express, which is a broader tool in terms of doing everything you might need, and not just microservices, you'll need to find the right plugins, and perhaps write several more plugins, in order to help you reach a production-ready microservice. You get the advantage of being able to choose everything about the service, but you need to write a lot of code. To facilitate the task, Hydra might be a good start for an initial set of plugins.

For other tools such as Seneca, some aspects of the microservice (for instance, the communication using JSON messages and service composition) are already packed. This comes at the price of a stricter service definition.

In the next chapter, we will discuss the security of our three service versions, and how we can store state.

# 4
# State and Security

Now that we have created our microservice base layout on different frameworks, it's time to read our code more carefully and see if everything looks good. It's easy to just keep writing code and stop thinking about what we're doing, but later on, when we do stop for a while, we'll be wasting time deleting repeated code and reorganizing our service.

It's always better to think before we code. This is something you'll learn with time, to value the time you dedicate to plan your service or think about a new feature. It's never a good idea to just start coding. In theory, your **Service** should be inside a **Security** layer, with a good and stable connection to **State**:

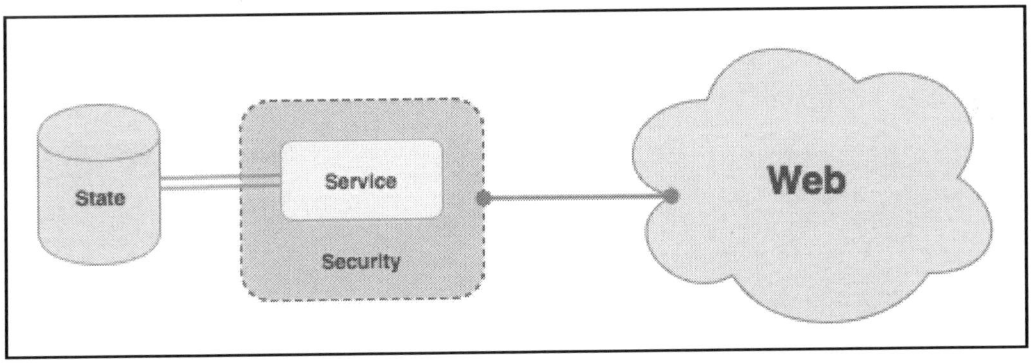


## State

Think of state as a person's memory. Usually, a service has state, which means it has memory of actions and information it's serving. The idea is that our service will run indefinitely, but sometimes we're forced to restart it or even stop it for some time because of maintenance or an upgrade.

Ideally, a service should resume without losing state, giving its users the perception that it never stopped. This is achieved by doing one of two things:

- Having state stored in a persistent storage
- Saving state in a persistent storage before stopping and loading that state after restarting

The first option will make your service a bit slower (nothing is faster than state in system memory) but should give you a more consistent state across restarts.

The second option is trickier, because sometimes our service might stop abruptly and be unable to save that state, but for those use cases, you may not care about the state. It's up to you.

There are a lot of options to store state; it will depend on what you want to store. For a microservice, you should avoid the filesystem so as to make your service more compatible with multiple operating systems.

# Storing state

Depending on your service, you can store state using:

- A **relational database management system (RDBMS)**, such as MySQL or PostgreSQL
- A **non-relational database management system**, or NoSQL, such as MongoDB or RethinkDB
- An **in-memory database (IMDB)**, such as Redis or Memcached

The first option is still the most commonly used one. You'll rely on stable and more than proven database systems that run in multiple systems and that you can find on any cloud service where you might want to deploy your microservice. Apart from the maturity of most solutions, a relational database, if properly set up, should give you consistency.

The second option is more recent compared to the first one. Usually, there are no fixed tables as in RDBMS, and you normally work with collections of documents that are just common JSON structures. It's more agile as there are usually no restrictions, and each document might have a different structure. The more agile, the less consistent.

All three options, depending on the specific system you choose, support replication, which should enable fault tolerance and improve speed in geographically spaced instances.

Let's try each of the three options using one of the suggested systems. Let's begin with the relational database, and use MySQL.

# MySQL

Installing MySQL is very simple. Just head to the official website and follow the instructions. You'll usually be asked for a password for the root user, which you can use later on to manage the server settings and user accounts.

There are some options to connect to a MySQL server using Node.js, but the best tools are the `mysql` and `mysql2` modules. They both serve the required purpose, and neither is the next version of the other, they're just a bit different in design and supported features.

First, let's add the dependency to our service. On the terminal, go to our service folder and type:

```
npm install mysql --save
```

We can now include our dependency and configure a connection to the database. To avoid having the credentials in our code, we can create a separate file and put settings there that we may change in the future, and that shouldn't belong in the code. We can take advantage of Node.js being able to include JSON files, and just write our settings in JSON.

Create a file called `settings.json`, and add the following content:

```
{
    "db": "mysql://root:test@localhost/imagini"
}
```

We defined a setting called `db` that has a database URI, which is a handy way of defining our database access and credentials using an address similar to any website address. Our database uses `mysql`; it's at `localhost` (using the default port), which can be accessed using the username `root` and the password `test`, and our database name is called `imagini`. We can now include the module and settings, and create the connection:

```
const settings = require("./settings");
const mysql    = require("mysql");
const db       = mysql.createConnection(settings.db);
```

This module only connects to the database when you make a query. This means the service would start and you wouldn't know whether your connection settings are correct until you make the first query. We don't want to figure out we can't connect to the database only when the service is used later on, so let's force a connection and check if the server is running and accepts our connection:

```
db.connect((err) => {
    if (err) throw err;

    console.log("db: ready");

    // ...
    // the rest of our service code
    // ...

    app.listen(3000, () => {
        console.log("app: ready");
    });
});
```

This way, if anything is wrong with the database, the service won't start and will throw an exception, which will notify you to check what's wrong. Here's an example of a possible error:

```
Error: ER_ACCESS_DENIED_ERROR: Access denied for user 'root'@'localhost'
(using password: YES)
```

This indicates you probably typed the password incorrectly, or the user doesn't match, or even the hostname or database may be wrong. Ensuring you connect to the database before setting up the service means your service won't be exposed to the public without a proper state.

Our microservice has a very simple state, so to speak. Our state is the images previously uploaded. Instead of using the filesystem, we can now use the database and create a table to store them all:

```
db.query(
    `CREATE TABLE IF NOT EXISTS images
    (
        id INT(11) UNSIGNED NOT NULL AUTO_INCREMENT,
        date_created TIMESTAMP NOT NULL DEFAULT CURRENT_TIMESTAMP,
        date_used TIMESTAMP NULL DEFAULT NULL,
        name VARCHAR(300) NOT NULL,
        size INT(11) UNSIGNED NOT NULL,
        data LONGBLOB NOT NULL,
```

```
        PRIMARY KEY (id),
        UNIQUE KEY name (name)
    )
    ENGINE=InnoDB DEFAULT CHARSET=utf8`
);
```

We can issue this query every time the service starts because it will create the images table only if it doesn't exist already. If we don't change its structure, it's fine to always do this.

You can see we're creating a table with a unique identification number (`id`), a creation date (`date_created`), a date to know when our image has been used(`date_used`), the `name` of the image, the `size` of it in bytes, and the image `data`. The size is a little redundant here as we could just check the data length, but bear with me, this is just an example.

We also defined our name as a unique key, meaning it has an index for quickly finding images by name, and also ensures our name does not repeat and that no one can overwrite an image (without removing it first).

Having the images stored this way on a database table gives you several advantages, such as regarding:

- How many images you have
- The size of every image and the total size
- When the images were created and last used

It also enables you to improve your service; for example, you can delete images that are not used for longer than a specific time period. You can also make this dependent on the image sizes. Later, you can add authentication (mandatory or not) and have user-specific rules.

It's also easy to back up and replicate the state to another site. There are plenty of tools for backing up databases, and you can have another MySQL server acting as a slave to this one and have your images replicated in real time to another geographical location.

Let's change our service from the previous chapter to use our table instead of the previously used folder on our filesystem. We can remove our `fs` module dependency (don't remove the path dependency for now):

```
app.param("image", (req, res, next, image) => {
    if (!image.match(/\.(png|jpg)$/i)) {
        return res.status(403).end();
    }

    db.query("SELECT * FROM images WHERE name = ?", [ image ], (err,
    images) => {
```

```
        if (err || !images.length) {
            return res.status(404).end();
        }

        req.image = images[0];

        return next();
    });
});
```

Our `app.param` is completely different. We now validate the `image` against our `image` table. If it doesn't find it, it returns code `404`. If it does find it, it stores the `image` information in `req.image`. We can now change our `image` upload to store the `image` on our table:

```
app.post("/uploads/:name", bodyparser.raw({
    limit : "10mb",
    type : "image/*"
}), (req, res) => {
    db.query("INSERT INTO images SET ?", {
        name : req.params.name,
        size : req.body.length,
        data : req.body,
    }, (err) => {
        if (err) {
            return res.send({ status : "error", code: err.code });
        }

        res.send({ status : "ok", size: req.body.length });
    });
});
```

Uploading images no longer use the filesystem and instead creates a new row on our table. We don't need to specify the `id` as it's automatic. Our creation date is also automatic as it defaults to the current timestamp. Our use date defaults to `NULL`, which means we haven't used the `image` yet:

```
app.head("/uploads/:image", (req, res) => {
    return res.status(200).end();
});
```

Our `image` check method now gets extremely simple as it relies on the previous `app.param` to check whether the `image` exists, so, if we get to this point, we already know the image exists (it's on `req.image`), so we just need to return the code `200`.

Before updating our image `fetch` method, let's try our service. If you start it on the console, you can immediately open any MySQL administration tool and check our database. I'm using Sequel Pro for macOS. Although there's a Pro in the name, it's free software and it's damn good:

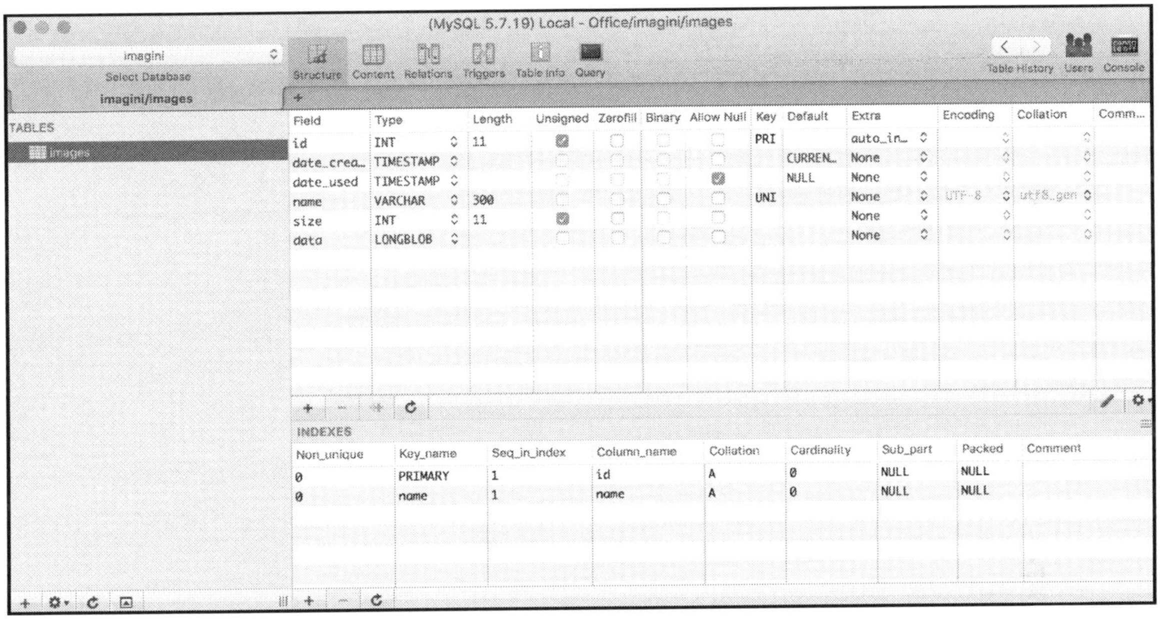


Our table was created, and you can check it has all the properties and indexes we defined. Let's now upload an `image` once again:

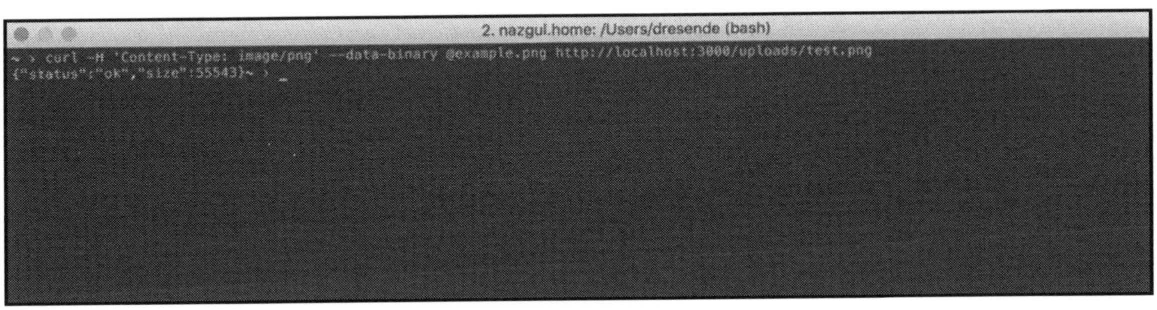

As before, it returns a JSON response with a success status and the size of the `image`. If you look at Sequel again, on the content separator, you'll see our **images** data:

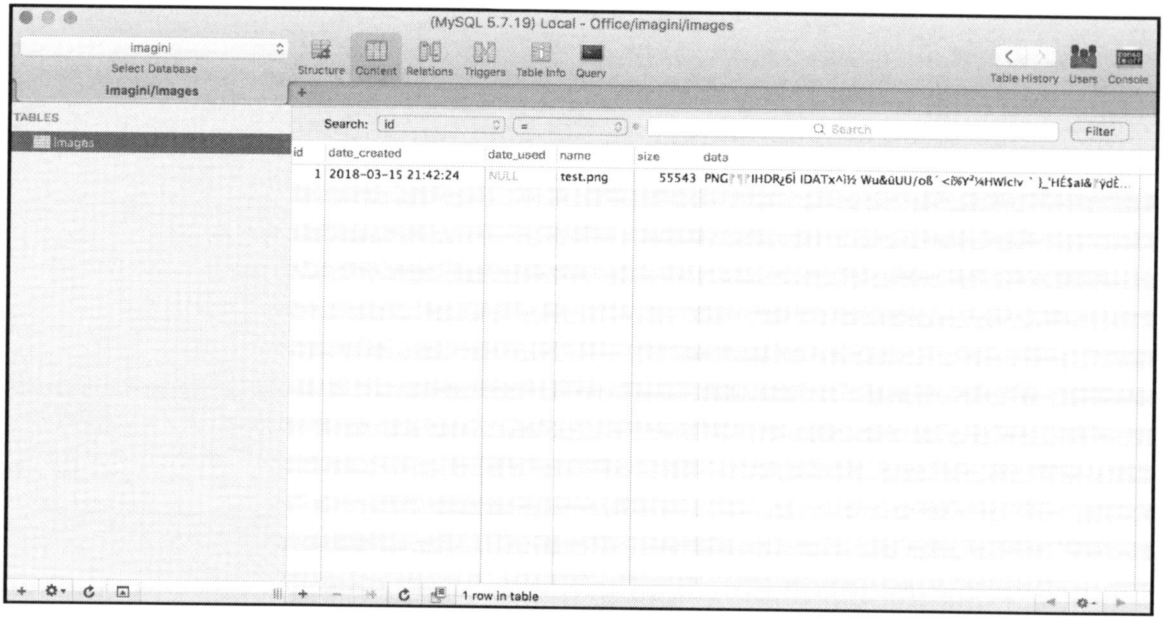

Let's try and upload the `image` again. Previously, our service would just overwrite it. Now, because of our unique index, it should deny an `INSERT` with the same name:

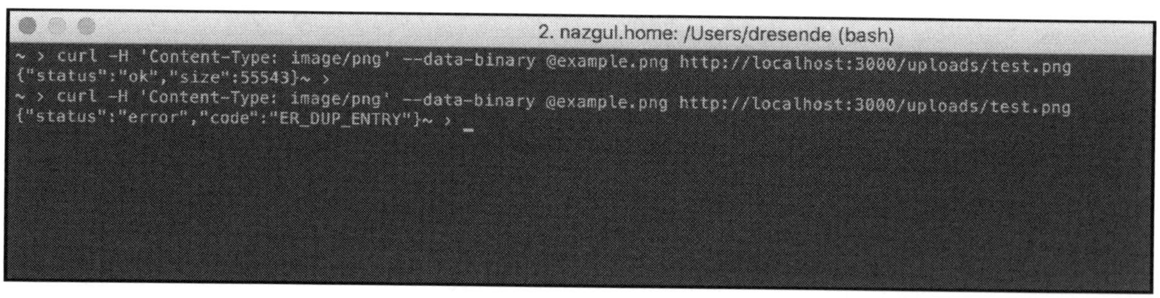


Great! The `ER_DUP_ENTRY` is the MySQL code for duplicate insertion. We can rely on that and deny overwriting images.

We can also check whether our `image` exists using the `check` method:

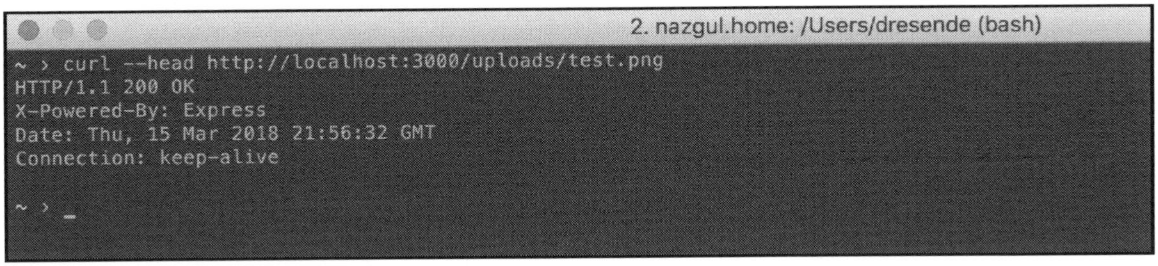


If we use another name, we'll get a code `404`:

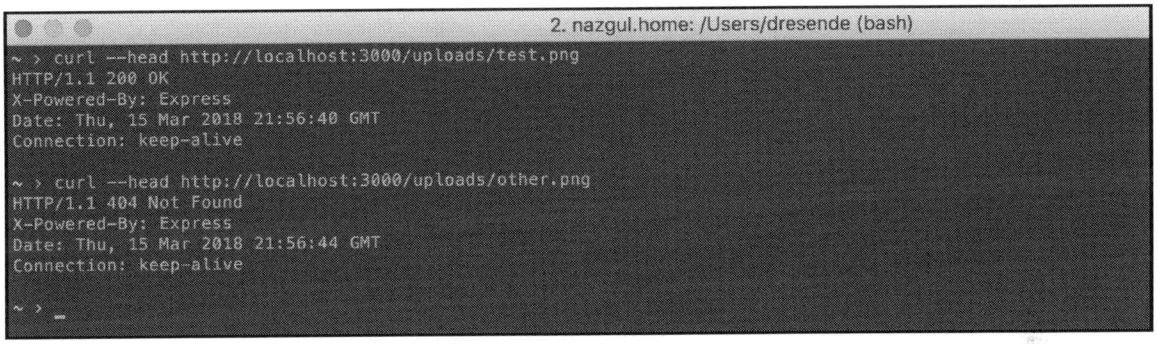


It looks like everything is working great. Let's now change our final method, the `image` manipulation one. This method is almost the same; we just don't have to read the `image` file, as it's already available:

```
app.get("/uploads/:image", (req, res) => {
    let image     = sharp(req.image.data);
    let width     = +req.query.width;
    let height    = +req.query.height;
    let blur      = +req.query.blur;
    let sharpen   = +req.query.sharpen;
    let greyscale = [ "y", "yes", "true", "1",
    "on"].includes(req.query.greyscale);
    let flip      = [ "y", "yes", "true", "1",
    "on"].includes(req.query.flip);
    let flop      = [ "y", "yes", "true", "1",
    "on"].includes(req.query.flop);

    if (width > 0 && height > 0) {
        image.ignoreAspectRatio();
    }
```

```
    if (width > 0 || height > 0) {
        image.resize(width || null, height || null);
    }

    if (flip)        image.flip();
    if (flop)        image.flop();
    if (blur > 0)    image.blur(blur);
    if (sharpen > 0) image.sharpen(sharpen);
    if (greyscale)   image.greyscale();

    db.query("UPDATE images " +
             "SET date_used = UTC_TIMESTAMP " +
             "WHERE id = ?", [ req.image.id ]);

    res.setHeader("Content-Type", "image/" +
path.extname(req.image.name).substr(1));

    image.pipe(res);
});
```

You can see how we used the path dependency to get the extension of the `image` name. The rest is the same. We just add an update to our image every time we request this method.

We can use a web browser to test our method and see our previously uploaded image:

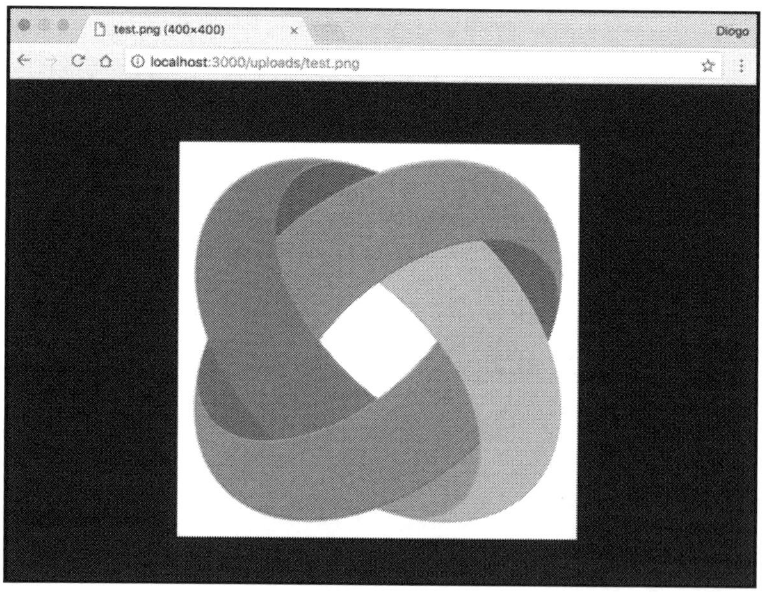

Everything should just work as before because we haven't changed our image manipulation dependency, so blurring and the other actions should work as expected:

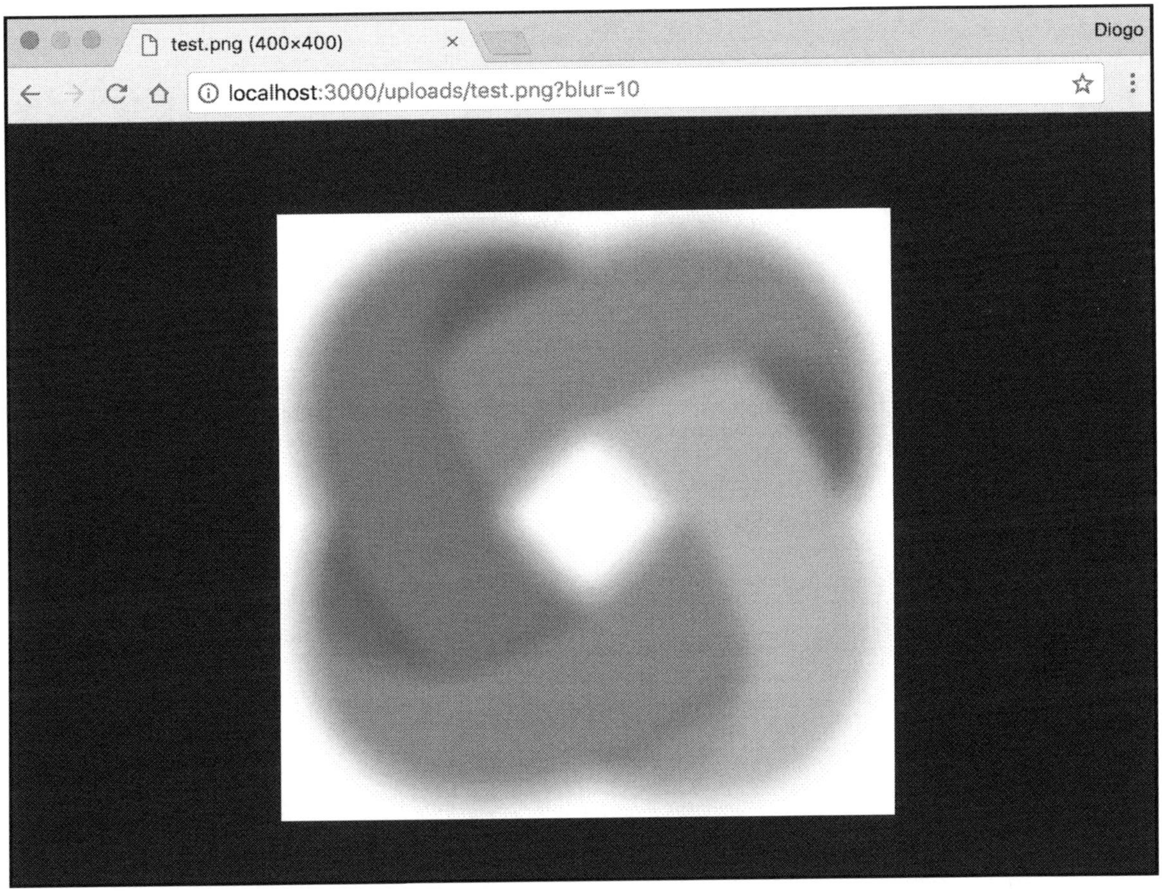


We can now improve our service and add a method we didn't expose before: deleting an `image`. To do that, we can use the `DELETE` verb from HTTP and just remove the `image` from our table:

```
app.delete("/uploads/:image", (req, res) => {
    db.query("DELETE FROM images WHERE id = ?", [ req.image.id ], (err)
    => {
        return res.status(err ? 500 : 200).end();
    });
});
```

We just have to check whether the query resulted in an error. If so, we respond with a code `500` (internal server error). If not, we respond with the usual code `200`.

Let's restart our microservice and try to delete our `image`:

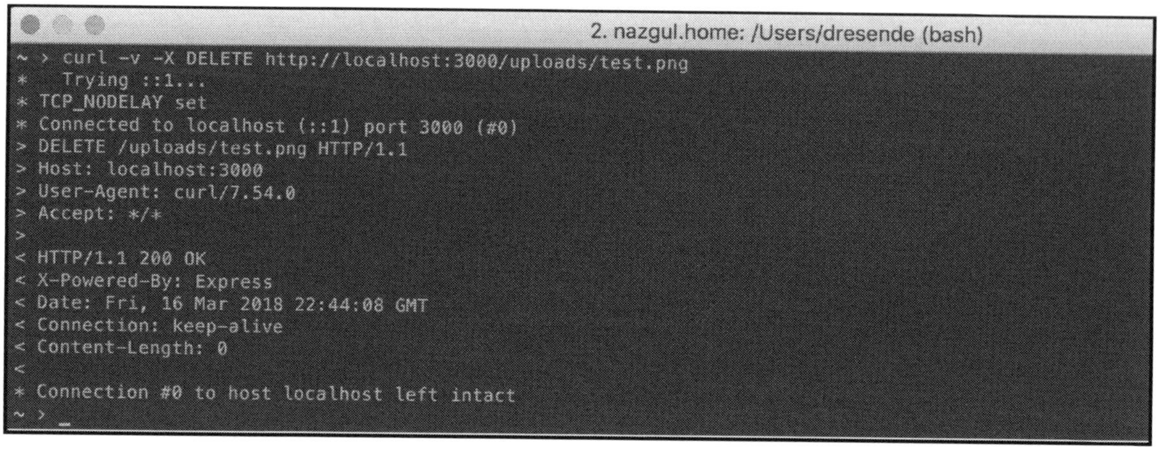

It looks like it worked; it responded with a code `200`. If we try to open our image in the web browser, we should see something like this:

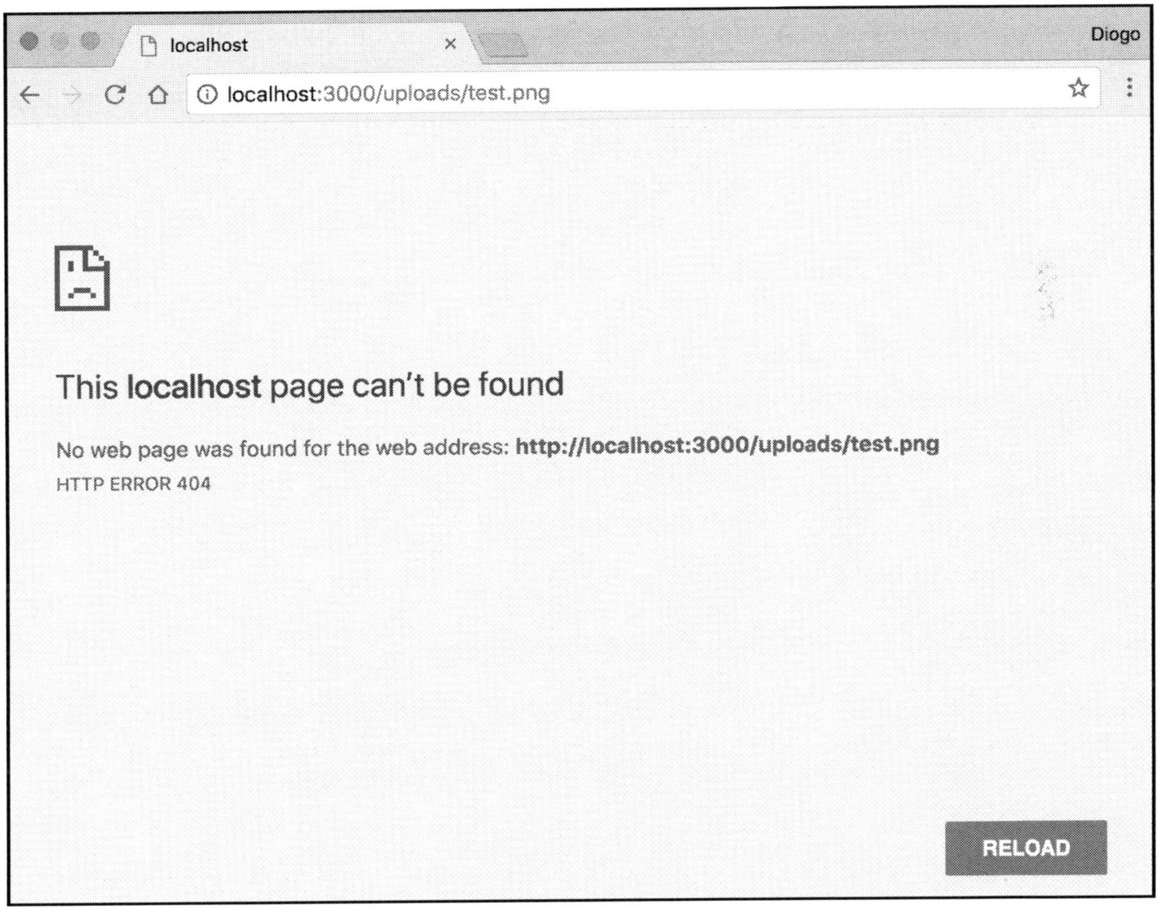

On Sequel, the table should now be empty too:

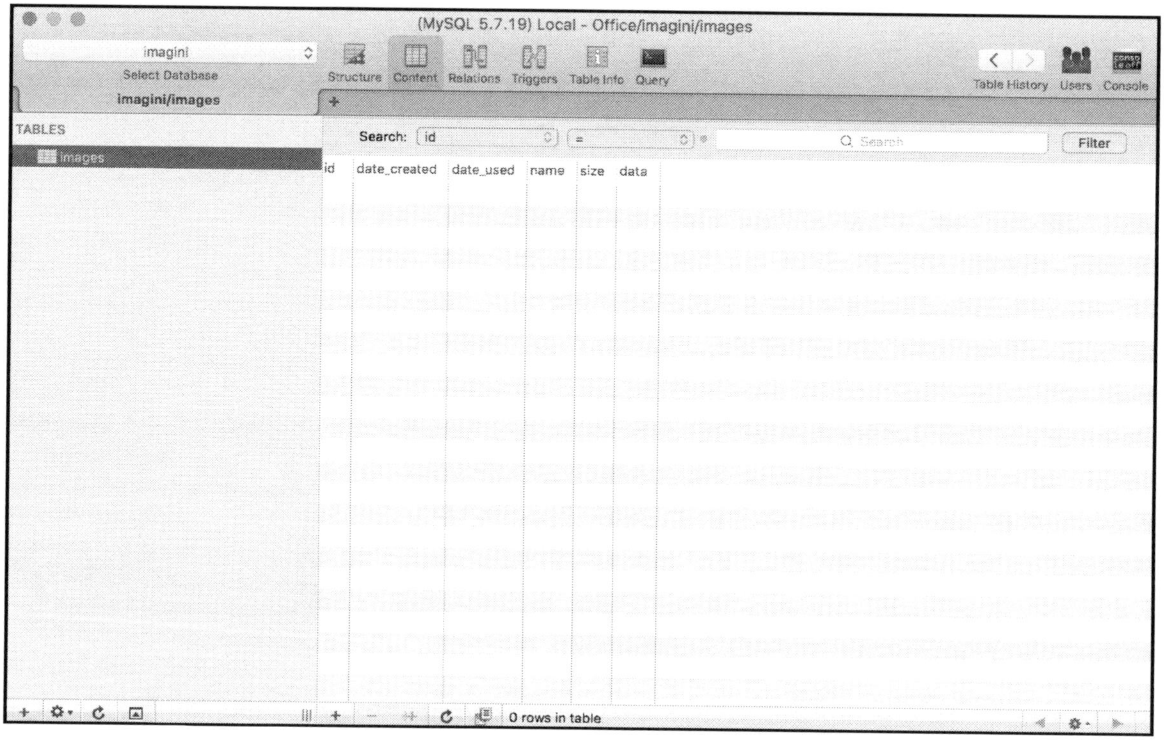


We now have a functional microservice with a state that persists across restarts, as we intended. You can now deploy to any cloud service with no dependency on the filesystem, just a database.

You could easily change MySQL to another database or use an **object relational mapping (ORM)** module to enable you to change database server without changing your code. An ORM is a library that allows you to use a common interface to access different types of databases. Usually, this kind of abstraction involves not using SQL at all and reducing your interaction with the databases to simpler queries (to allow for interoperability between database servers).

Let's take this opportunity to go a little further and add a few methods that got simplified by this migration to the database. Let's create a method that exposes statistics about our database, and let's remove old images.

Our first statistics method should just return a JSON structure with some useful information. Let's expose the following:

- The total number of images
- The total size of the images
- How long our service is running
- When the last time was that we uploaded an image

Here's an example of how our statistics method could look:

```
app.get("/stats", (req, res) => {
    db.query("SELECT COUNT(*) total" +
             ", SUM(size) size " +
             ", MAX(date_created) last_created " +
             "FROM images",
    (err, rows) => {
        if (err) {
            return res.status(500).end();
        }

        rows[0].uptime = process.uptime();

        return res.send(rows[0]);
    });
});
```

Restart the service, and let's try it:

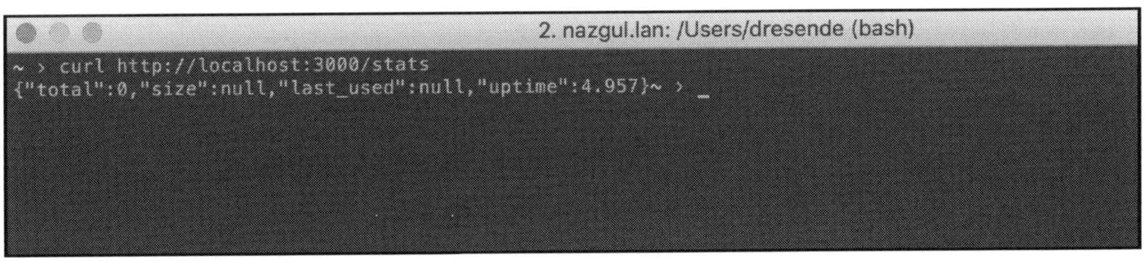


As we can see, we have no images as we just removed our image previously. There's no size because we have no images. There's also no used date, and the service uptime is 5 seconds.

If we upload our previous image, we will get different results, something like the following screenshot:

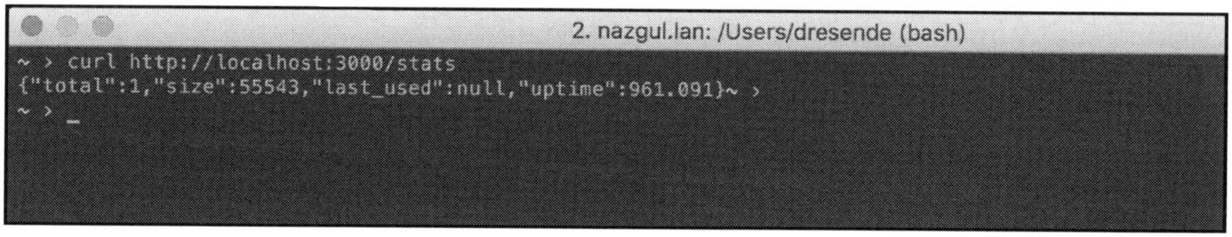


Now, for our second task, deleting old images, we need to check our database periodically. We'll use an interval timer and just run a `DELETE` query. The intervals mentioned in the following query are just an example; you can write the conditions you want.

```
setInterval(() => {
    db.query("DELETE FROM images " +
             "WHERE (date_created < UTC_TIMETSTAMP - INTERVAL 1 WEEK
             AND date_used IS NULL) " +
             " OR (date_used < UTC_TIMETSTAMP - INTERVAL 1 MONTH)");
}, 3600 * 1000);
```

This query deletes `images` that were not used in the past month (but were used before) or images that were not used in the past week (and never used before). This means that images uploaded need to be used at least once or they will get removed quickly.

You can think of a different strategy, or use no strategy and delete manually if you want. Now that we've seen MySQL, let's move on and look at another kind of database server.

# RethinkDB

Let's see the differences for a non-relational database using RethinkDB. If you don't have it, just install it by following the official documentation (`https://www.rethinkdb.com/docs/`). Let's just start the server:

```
rethinkdb
```

This will start the server, which comes with a very nice administration console on port `8080`. You can open it in the web browser:

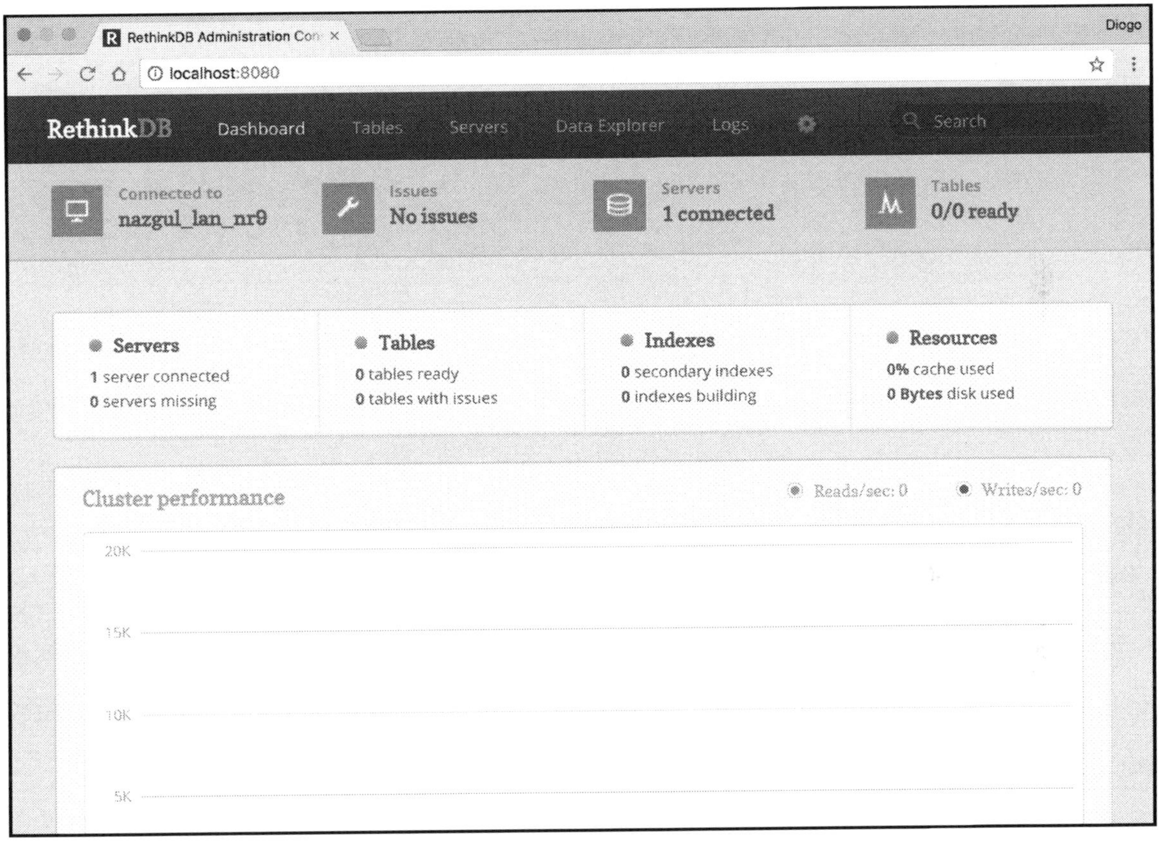

Go to the **Tables** section on top to see the databases:

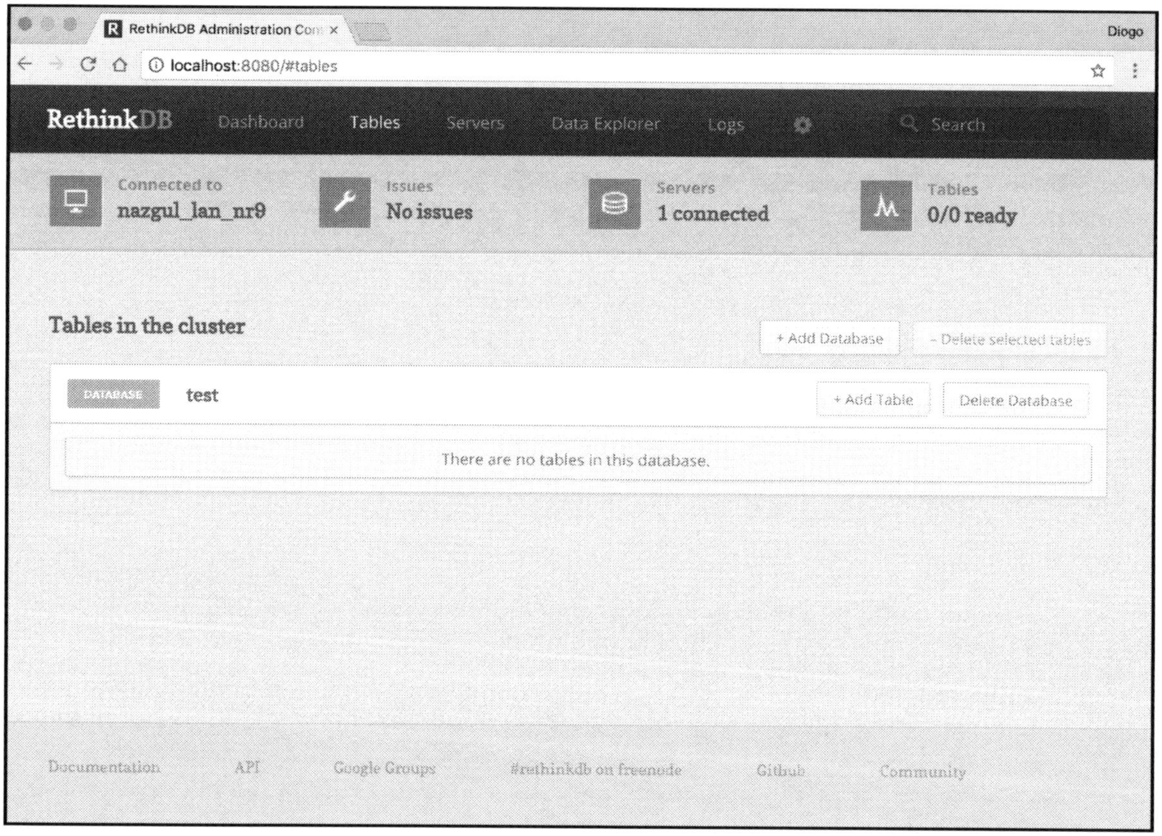

Create a database called `imagini` using the **Add Database** button. You should now have our database ready. You need nothing else here:

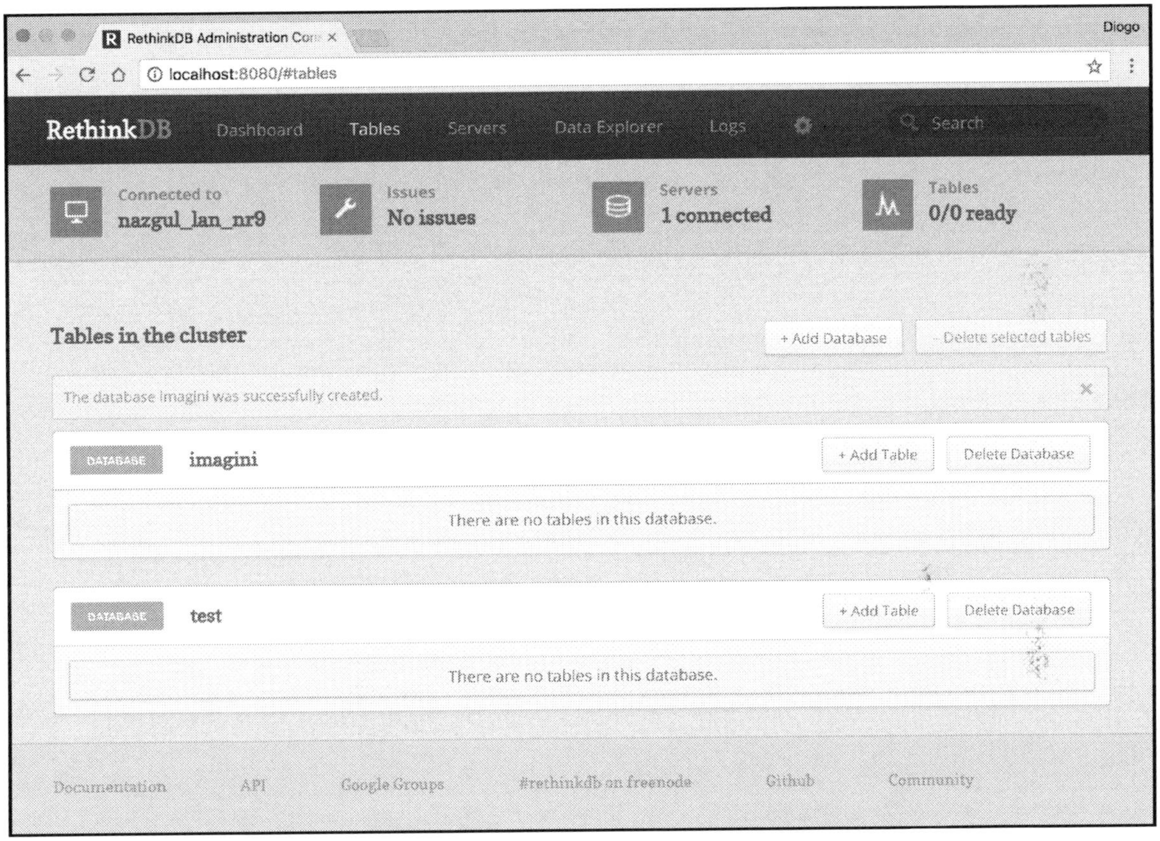


To use our new database, we need to install the `rethinkdb` dependency. You can remove the MySQL dependency:

```
npm uninstall mysql --save
npm install rethinkdb --save
```

Now, let's change our `settings` file. This module doesn't accept a connection string, so we'll use a JSON structure:

```
{
    "db": {
        "host" : "localhost",
        "db" : "imagini"
    }
```

```
}
```

To include our dependency, we just need to include the module:

```
const rethinkdb = require("rethinkdb");
```

Then, use this to connect to our server:

```
rethinkdb.connect(settings.db, (err, db) => {
    if (err) throw err;

    console.log("db: ready");

    // ...
    // the rest of our service code
    // ...

    app.listen(3000, () => {
        console.log("app: ready");
    });
});
```

After connecting, we can create our table as we did before. This time, we don't need to specify any structure:

```
rethinkdb.tableCreate("images").run(db);
```

The `rethinkdb` object is the one we'll use to manipulate our table, and the `db` object is a connection object used to reference the connection and to indicate where to run our manipulations.

If you restart our service just like this, you'll see a new table on our previously created database:

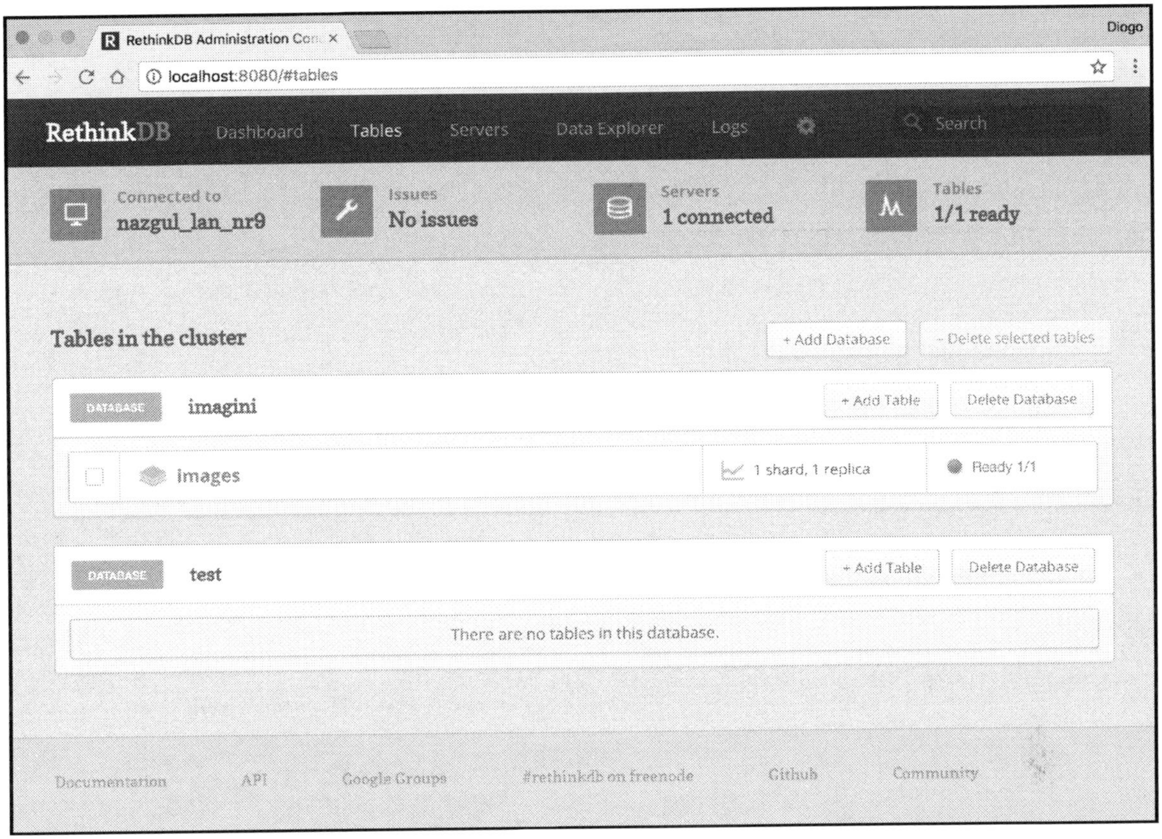


If you restart our service again, you'll get an error trying to create the table that already exists. We need to check whether it already exists, and only issue the command if not:

```
rethinkdb.tableList().run(db, (err, tables) => {
    if (err) throw err;

    if (!tables.includes("images")) {
        rethinkdb.tableCreate("images").run(db);
    }
});
```

Moving on, our upload method should be changed slightly to something like the following:

```
app.post("/uploads/:name", bodyparser.raw({
    limit : "10mb",
    type : "image/*"
}), (req, res) => {
    rethinkdb.table("images").insert({
```

```
            name : req.params.name,
            size : req.body.length,
            data : req.body,
        }).run(db, (err) => {
            if (err) {
                return res.send({ status : "error", code: err.code });
            }

            res.send({ status : "ok", size: req.body.length });
        });
    });
```

If you restart the server just like this, you should be able to upload an `image`:

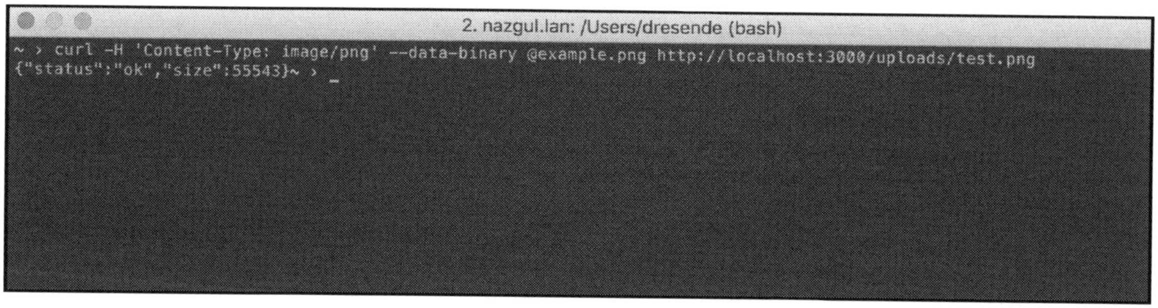


We receive the same response, just like with MySQL. We can go to the **Data Explorer** section in the administration console and get our record to see whether it's there:

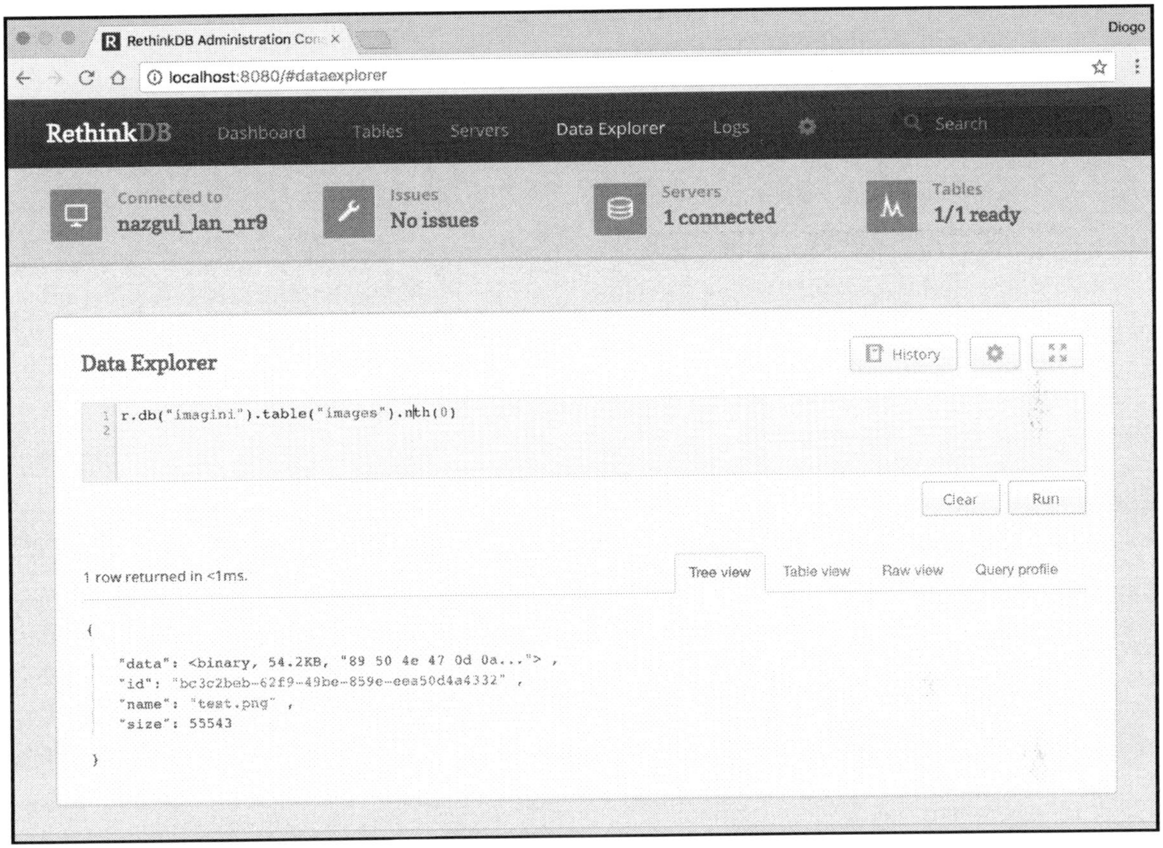


Looks good. Notice our record ID is not a number, it's a **Universally Unique Identifier (UUID)**. This is because RethinkDB has support for sharding (our table is sharded by default if there was more than one server) and it's easier to shard unique identifiers than an incremental number.

Moving on to our Express parameter:

```
app.param("image", (req, res, next, image) => {
    if (!image.match(/\.(png|jpg)$/i)) {
        return res.status(403).end();
    }

    rethinkdb.table("images").filter({
        name : image
    }).limit(1).run(db, (err, images) => {
        if (err) return res.status(404).end();
```

```
            images.toArray((err, images) => {
                if (err) return res.status(500).end();
                if (!images.length) return res.status(404).end();

                req.image = images[0];

                return next();
            });
        });
    });
```

With this change, we can now restart our service and see whether our `image` exists:

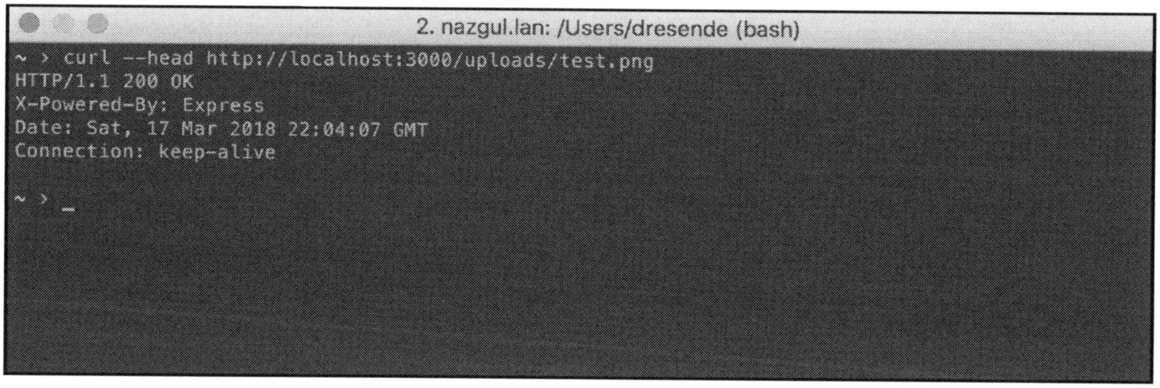


We need to change the download just a little bit. We need to remove the previous query to update our usage date and replace it with a new one:

```
app.get("/uploads/:image", (req, res) => {
    let image     = sharp(req.image.data);
    let width     = +req.query.width;
    let height    = +req.query.height;
    let blur      = +req.query.blur;
    let sharpen   = +req.query.sharpen;
    let greyscale = [ "y", "yes", "true", "1",
    "on"].includes(req.query.greyscale);
    let flip      = [ "y", "yes", "true", "1",
    "on"].includes(req.query.flip);
    let flop      = [ "y", "yes", "true", "1",
    "on"].includes(req.query.flop);

    if (width > 0 && height > 0) {
        image.ignoreAspectRatio();
    }
```

```
    if (width > 0 || height > 0) {
        image.resize(width || null, height || null);
    }

    if (flip)          image.flip();
    if (flop)          image.flop();
    if (blur > 0)      image.blur(blur);
    if (sharpen > 0)   image.sharpen(sharpen);
    if (greyscale)     image.greyscale();

    rethinkdb.table("images").get(req.image.id).update({ date_used :
    Date.now() }).run(db);

    res.setHeader("Content-Type", "image/" +
    path.extname(req.image.name).substr(1));

    image.pipe(res);
});
```

We can now download our image using the web browser:

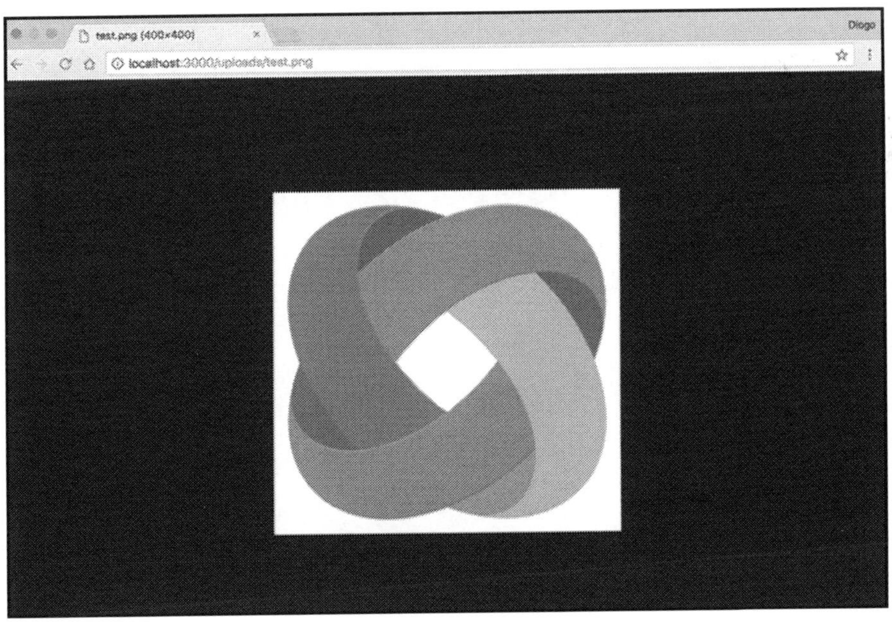

Next, we need to update our image removal method. It's as easy as our upload:

```
app.delete("/uploads/:image", (req, res) => {
    rethinkdb.table("images").get(req.image.id).delete().run(db, (err)
    => {
        return res.status(err ? 500 : 200).end();
    });
});
```

This time, we used the image unique ID to remove it. If we try again using the `curl` command, we'll receive a code `200`:

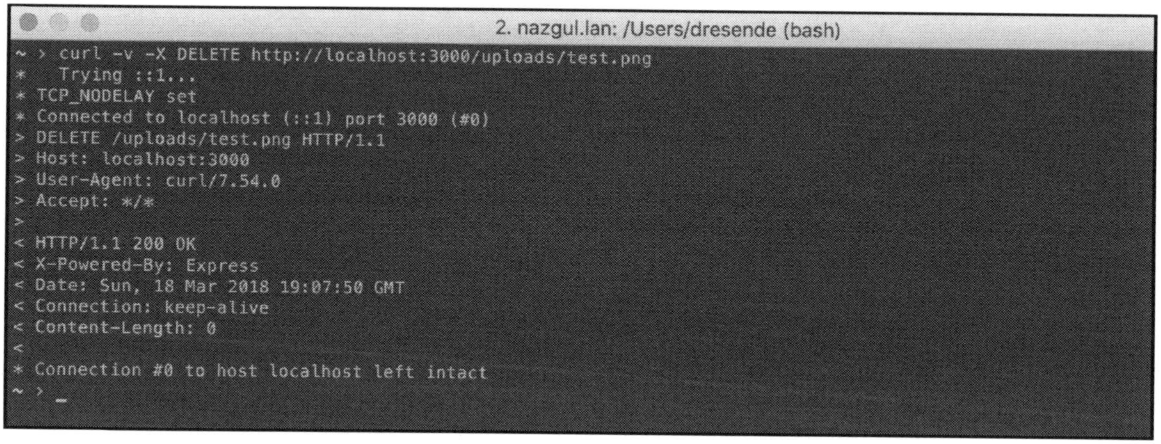


If we try to get the first record of our table, we'll see there's nothing there:

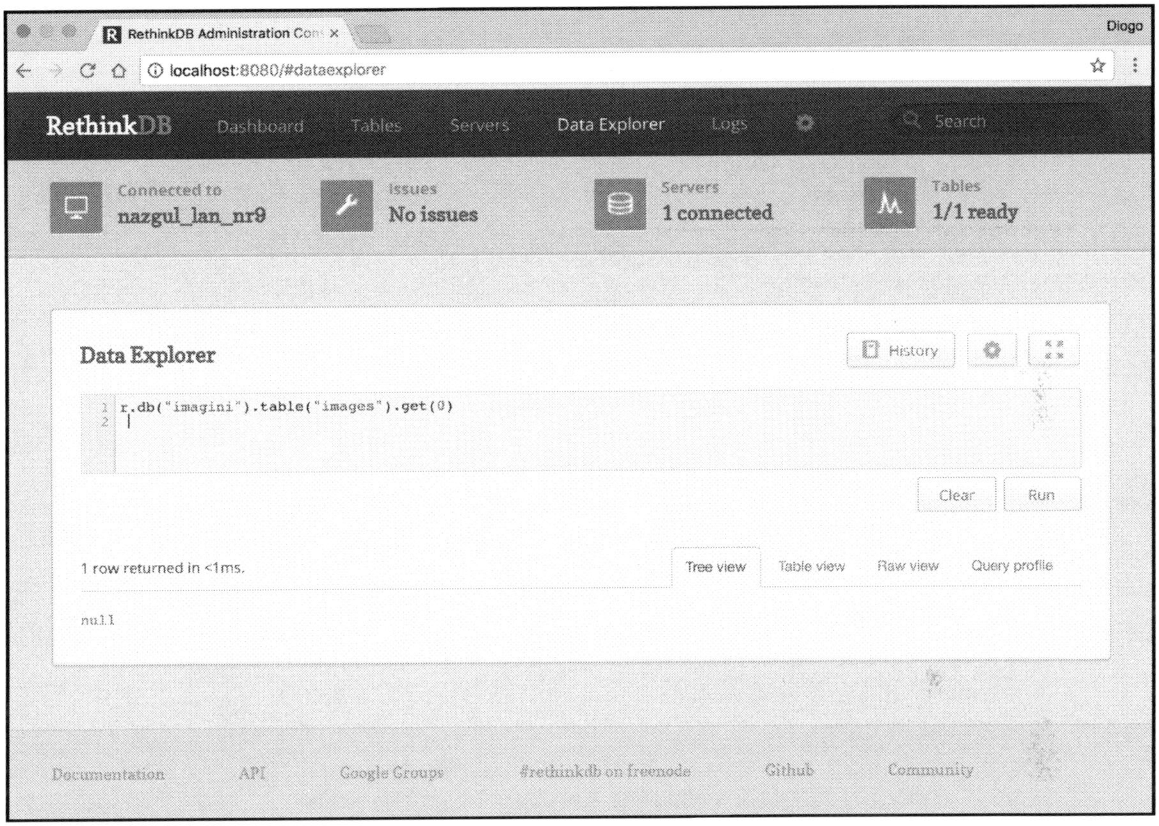


Finally, there are our two extra features that we added after introducing MySQL: the statistics and removing old unused images.

Our statistics method is not so simple as running an SQL query with aggregations. We must calculate each of our statistics:

```
app.get("/stats", (req, res) => {
    let uptime = process.uptime();

    rethinkdb.table("images").count().run(db, (err, total) => {
        if (err) return res.status(500).end();

        rethinkdb.table("images").sum("size").run(db, (err, size) => {
            if (err) return res.status(500).end();

            rethinkdb.table("images").max("date_created").run(db, (err,
            last_created) => {
                if (err) return res.status(500).end();
```

```
                    last_created = (last_created ? new
                    Date(last_created.date_created) : null);

                    return res.send({ total, size, last_created, uptime });
                });
            });
        });
    });
```

We should have a similar result to before:

Removing old images is more or less easy; we just need to filter the images we want to remove, and then remove them:

```
setInterval(() => {
    let expiration = Date.now() - (30 * 86400 * 1000);

    rethinkdb.table("images").filter((image) => {
        return image("date_used").lt(expiration);
    }).delete().run(db);
}, 3600 * 1000);
```

I simplified the previous strategy and am just removing `images` older than 1 month (30 days, times 86,400 seconds a day, times 1,000 milliseconds).

# Redis

In-memory databases are different from the previous two types, as they're usually not structured, which means you have no tables. What you have is normally lists of some kind that you can look up and manipulate, or simple hash tables.

Taking advantage of the Redis instance we installed previously for Hydra, let's see another drawback, or actually feature, of this kind of database. Let's connect to our Redis instance and make the following sequence of instructions:

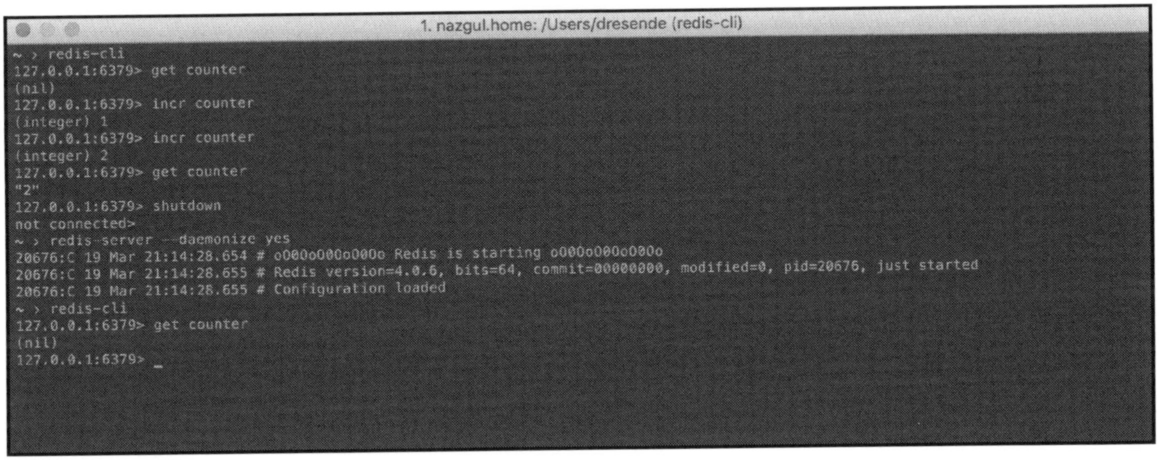


What we did here was to:

1. Connect to the Redis service using `redis-cli`.
2. Get the content of the counter, which is nil (nothing), because we haven't defined it yet.
3. Increment the counter, which is now automatically defined and set to `1`.
4. Increment the counter again, which is now `2`.
5. Get the content of the counter, which is of course `2`.
6. Shut down the Redis service.
7. Start the Redis service.
8. Connect to the Redis service again.
9. Get the content of the counter, which is nil (nothing).

Where's our counter? Well, this is an in-memory database, so everything is gone when we shut down the Redis service. This is the design of almost all kinds of in-memory databases.

They're designed to be fast and in-memory. Their purpose is normally to cache data that is expensive to get, such as some complex calculations, or extensive to download, and we want that to be available faster (in-memory).

I wasn't completely fair with Redis as it actually allows your data to be saved between service restarts. So, let's see how far we can go in using it to save our microservice state.

As before, let's uninstall `rethinkdb` and install the `redis` module:

```
npm uninstall rethinkdb --save
npm install redis --save
```

Let's ignore our `settings.json` file (you can remove it if you prefer) and assume Redis will be on our local machine.

First, we need to include the `redis` module and create a `Client` instance:

```
const redis = require("redis");
const db    = redis.createClient();
```

We then need to wait until it connects:

```
db.on("connect", () => {
    console.log("db: ready");

    // ...
    // the rest of our service code
    // ...

    app.listen(3000, () => {
        console.log("app: ready");
    });
});
```

There are a couple of ways we can use Redis to store our data. To make it simple, as we don't have tables, let's use hashes to store our images. Each image will have a different hash, and the name of the hash will be the name of the image.

As there are no tables in this kind of database, our initialization code can just be removed.

Next, let's change our upload method to store data on Redis. As I mentioned, let's store it in a hash with the name of the `image`:

```
app.post("/uploads/:name", bodyparser.raw({
    limit : "10mb",
    type : "image/*"
}), (req, res) => {
    db.hmset(req.params.name, {
        size : req.body.length,
        data : req.body.toString("base64"),
    }, (err) => {
        if (err) {
            return res.send({ status : "error", code: err.code });
        }

        res.send({ status : "ok", size: req.body.length });
    });
});
```

The `hmset` command lets us set multiple fields of a hash, in our case, `size` and `data`. Notice we're storing our image content in `base64` encoding, otherwise we'll lose data. If we restart our service and try to upload our test `image`, it should work fine:

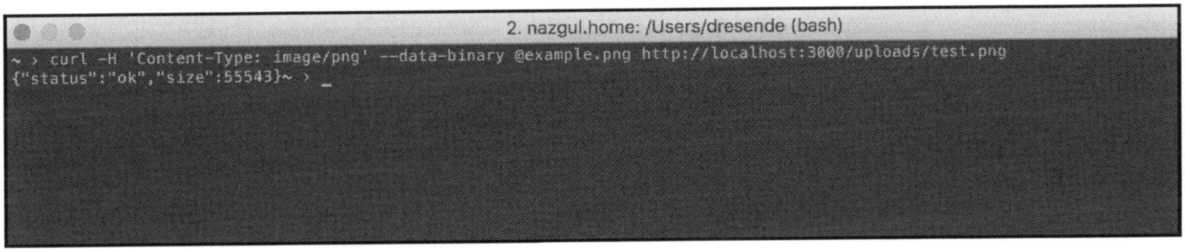


We can then use `redis-cli` and see whether our image is there. Well, we're checking to see whether our hash has the field size and matches our image size:

Great! We can now change our Express parameter to look for the `image` hash:

```
app.param("image", (req, res, next, name) => {
    if (!name.match(/\.(png|jpg)$/i)) {
        return res.status(403).end();
    }
```

```
    db.hgetall(name, (err, image) => {
        if (err || !image) return res.status(404).end();

        req.image      = image;
        req.image.name = name;

        return next();
    });
});
```

Our `image` check method should work now. And, for our download method to work, we just need to change the image loading to decode our previous `base64` encoding:

```
app.get("/uploads/:image", (req, res) => {
    let image     = sharp(Buffer.from(req.image.data, "base64"));
    let width     = +req.query.width;
    let height    = +req.query.height;
    let blur      = +req.query.blur;
    let sharpen   = +req.query.sharpen;
    let greyscale = [ "y", "yes", "true", "1",
"on"].includes(req.query.greyscale);
    let flip      = [ "y", "yes", "true", "1",
"on"].includes(req.query.flip);
    let flop      = [ "y", "yes", "true", "1",
"on"].includes(req.query.flop);

    if (width > 0 && height > 0) {
        image.ignoreAspectRatio();
    }

    if (width > 0 || height > 0) {
        image.resize(width || null, height || null);
    }

    if (flip)        image.flip();
    if (flop)        image.flop();
    if (blur > 0)    image.blur(blur);
    if (sharpen > 0) image.sharpen(sharpen);
    if (greyscale)   image.greyscale();

    db.hset(req.image.name, "date_used", Date.now());

    res.setHeader("Content-Type", "image/" +
path.extname(req.image.name).substr(1));

    image.pipe(res);
});
```

Our images are now being served from Redis. As a bonus, we're adding/updating a `date_used` field in our `image` hash to indicate when it was last used:

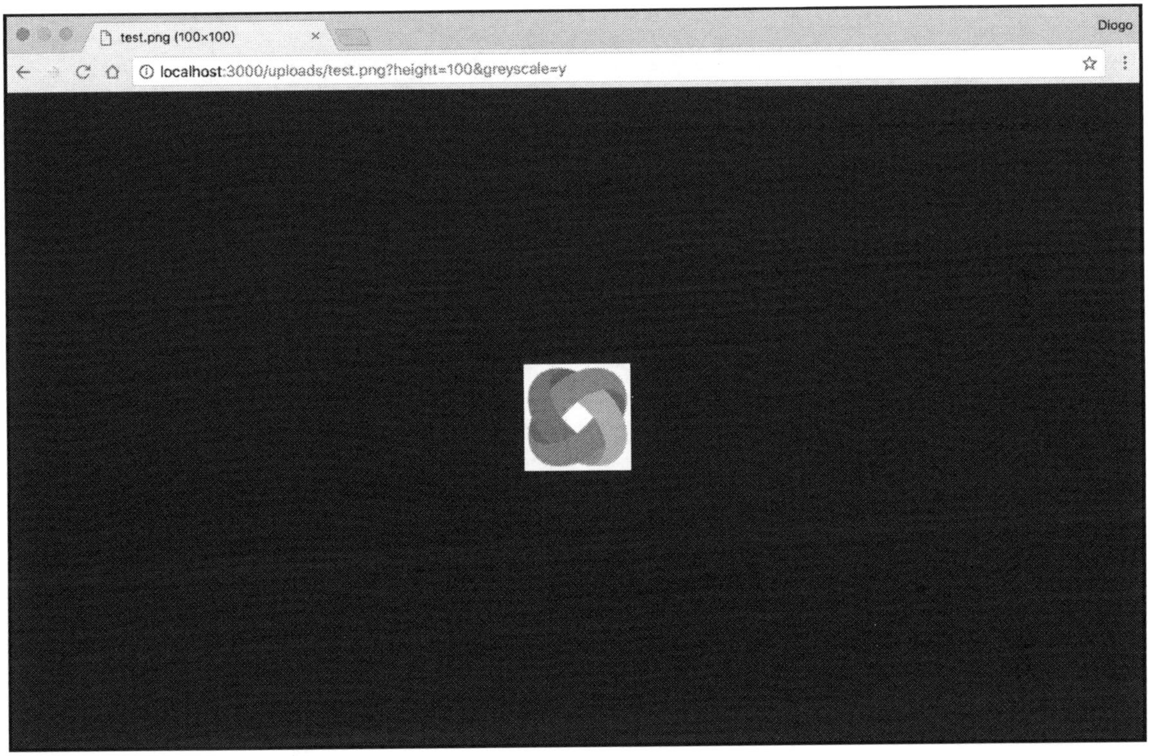


Removing our `image` is as simple as removing our hash:

```
app.delete("/uploads/:image", (req, res) => {
    db.del(req.image.name, (err) => {
        return res.status(err ? 500 : 200).end();
    });
});
```

We can then try to remove our `test` image:

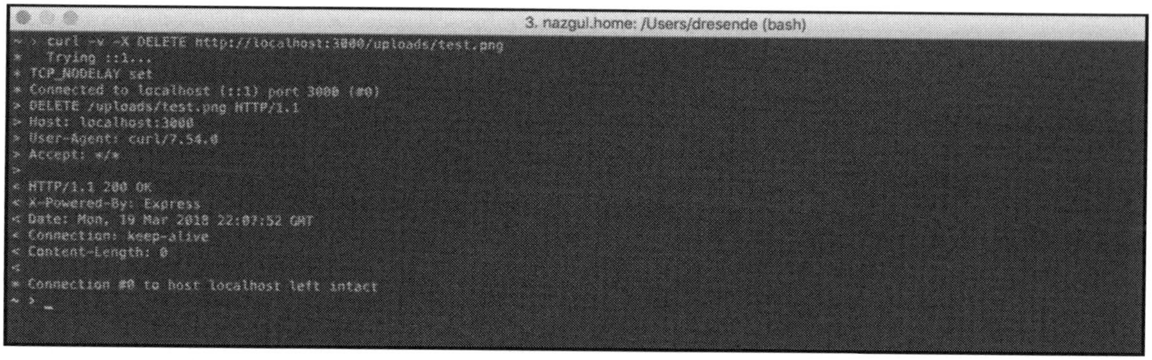


Using `redis-cli` to check whether the hash exists, we see that it's gone:

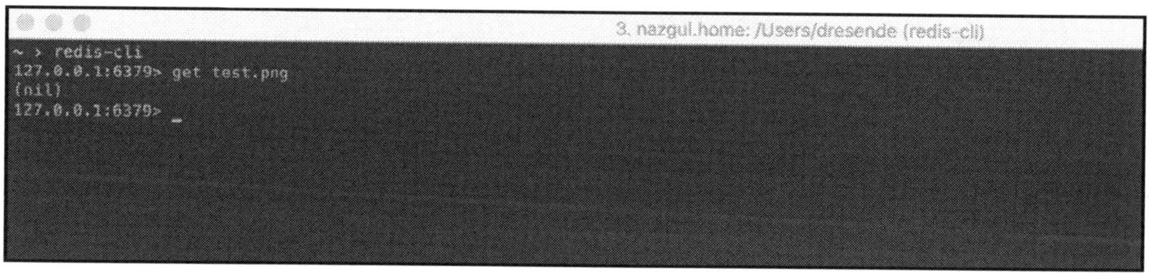


The only two features missing are the statistics and removing old images.

For the statistics, that could be hard as we're using generic hash tables and we can't be sure how many hash tables are defined, and if all or any have image data. We would have to scan all hash tables, which is complex for large sets.

To remove old images, the problem is the same as there's no way of looking for hash tables with a specific condition, such as a field value.

There are still other paths available to tackle this problem. For example, we could have another hash table with just our image names and use dates. But, the complexity would increase, and the integrity could be at risk as we're splitting information through different hash tables with no certainty of making **Atomicity**, **Consistency**, **Isolation**, and **Durability** (**ACID**) operations.

# Conclusion

As we've seen, there are plenty of options to store our microservice state. Depending on the type of information we're manipulating, there are databases better-prepared to handle our data.

It all depends on a few different questions we should ask ourselves:

- Is our data integrity important?
- Is our data structure complex?
- How and what type of information do we need to acquire?

If our data integrity is important or the data structure is complex, do not use in-memory databases. Depending on the complexity, see if you need a non-relational database, or whether you can go with a relational database that can handle more complex manipulation and data aggregation operations, which will help you to achieve the last point.

# Security

One good practice is to write code iteratively, testing every time we make a new small feature or improvement, and always write code thinking of all the features we envision for our service.

Thinking about the service roadmap allows you to prepare the service for future improvements, reducing the amount of code wasted or replaced later on.

For instance, in terms of security:

- Is our service secure? Is it prepared for some types of malicious attacks?
- Is our service private? Should it have some kind of authentication or authorization mechanism?

Luckily, our frameworks allow our code to be composed and allow us to add layers of security later. For example, using Express or Hydra, we can add a precedent routing function that will run before any of our service methods, allowing us to enforce, for example, authentication.

Looking at our service, since it exposes its methods using HTTP, there are a couple of improvements we can add to it, for example:

- **Authentication**: Forcing anyone that uses it to identify themselves. Or, just the upload and removal methods. It's up to you. There could also be user accounts, and each user would see their respective list of images.
- **Authorization**: Restricting, for example, what networks could access the service, independently of having a valid authentication or not.
- **Confidentiality**: Giving your users protection against prying eyes over the network traffic.
- **Availability**: Restricting the maximum usage frequency of the service, per client, to ensure a single client cannot block your entire service.

To introduce these improvements, you may add an authentication module such as the Passport module, and use a certificate to give your users a more secure HTTPS experience.

Other types of insecurity come directly from your code and don't improve by adding a certificate or forcing authentication. I'm referring to:

- Bugs, programming logic flaws, and use cases not properly tested, which can lead to minor or serious problems
- Dependency bugs, which you might not be aware of but can still ruin your service and may force you to look for alternative dependencies, which is never a pleasant task

To minimize these events, you should always keep evolving your test suite, adding use cases as they show up, ensuring a new bug that is solved does not reappear later. Regarding dependency bugs, you can subscribe to the Node Security Project and even integrate it with your code to always know when one of your dependencies is a risk.

If there were source code commandments, the next four would surely be on the list:

- Keep the code simple. If the code is getting complex, stop, look back, and split the code into simpler parts.
- Validate external input, whether it's the user or another service. Never trust data from the outside.
- Deny by default and not the opposite, checking whether someone has access to a resource and denying anyone that is not.
- Add test cases from the beginning of the project.

# Summary

The state is part of any service, and state is built upon data. For a more cloud-native experience, a service cannot depend on a traditional filesystem and needs to use other kinds of storage structures to store data. Databases are a natural progress, and there are some types of databases to choose from, depending on how important and complex our data is.

Assuming our state is securely stored in a database service of some kind, it's also important to ensure our data cannot be corrupted using our service. There can be security flaws and bugs in our service that may put our data at risk, so it's important to write simple code, validate input, and think about security in general when planning the service roadmap.

To progress our service, let's introduce something we haven't done yet, and should, which is a proper test suite. In the next chapter, we'll see some good options and create a test suite, establishing whether anything needs to change in order to make our service as secure as possible.

# 5
# Testing

When you're developing an application, it will eventually form a structure and evolve into a stable product that you can use in production and sell to your customers. In the beginning, everything may seem simple and many tend to postpone the construction of a proper test suite.

> *"Debugging is twice as hard as writing the code in the first place."*
>
> *—Brian W. Kernighan and P. J. Plauger in The Elements of Programming Style*

Later on, the application may become just sufficiently complex for you to hesitate to begin testing. You may eventually give up and never test your application. It may be frustrating, especially if you have never seen or used any test suite before.

Proper testing gives you more than a little bit of quality assurance. Proper testing gives you:

- **Predictability**: This means that your code execution, no matter if it's an application or just a module, will have an expected result. As you evolve the tests and introduce different test cases, you begin to fulfill all the uses for your code, and you ensure its results were as intended.
- **Feature coverage**: This means that you can measure what parts of your code are tested or not. There are plenty of tools to inspect your code and tell you what parts of it haven't been used in your test suite, which helps you create specific tests for specific parts of the code that are not yet covered.
- **Safe evolution**: This is a side effect. When your code gets complex, if your test suite has good code coverage, you can make changes and add features without compromising stability, as you can continuously run the test suite and see if it breaks anything.

There's a developing methodology that involves first creating a test for a new feature and then making sure the test passes. This way, you can focus on how you think your code should be used (in the new test) and then evolve it (actually develop it) so the test stops failing and gives proper results.

So, let's begin by looking at some testing methodologies, and then write our first test. Then, let's see how code coverage can help in the testing process. Finally, we'll look at how you can mock parts of your code.

# Types of testing methodologies

There are several types of testing methodologies. You can have tests to measure performance by stressing your application with specific actions and checking whether it achieves the expected minimum results. Those are important, but not at this stage. We should focus on other kinds of tests.

Our goal is to have a test suite that ensures our code behaves as we designed it. To ensure that, we must have:

- Unit tests, to check individual code units, such as some functions
- Integration tests, to check whether external actions produce the expected results

Using these two types of test, and having a full code coverage, we'll be able to develop new features and run regression tests, which is just a fancy way of saying that our test suite still passes, and our new code does not break (there's no regression).

You may see these regression tests as and when you run the test suite on your laptop and the results are OK, and then you commit your code to GitHub, for example, and Travis runs the same test suite on different environments to see if nothing breaks. If you're pushing to a pull request on GitHub, you'll be unable to merge your changes unless every test result passes.

To achieve full test coverage, you'll necessarily have test cases in the same language as the one used to develop the application, which in our case is Node.js. It's not mandatory, but it simplifies a lot of the tools used to run the test cases use the same language, as this creates a friendlier environment for other developers.

When using open source modules, it's not uncommon for others to find issues and try to fix them. Having test frameworks that involve installing third-party software will lower the interest in helping to fix them. On the other hand, if the user just needs to clone the repository, fix and run the tests, that will be a much more enjoyable experience.

# Using frameworks

There are a couple of test frameworks available for Node.js. What they do is give you an environment where you can focus on the test cases. Some frameworks will even do code coverage more or less automatically.

One of the most commonly used frameworks is `mocha`, which is a simple yet powerful framework. It can be used for general unit testing, but also for performance, as it is able to highlight slow tests.

Let's try it out and prepare our microservice for the tests. You can use any of the previous versions; it should not matter for the storage model we're using, only the microservice interface. First of all, let's install `mocha` as a development dependency. We're also using an assertion library called `chai`, which has a plugin specifically for HTTP testing:

```
npm install -save-dev mocha chai chai-http
```

Then, change your `package.json` file to update the scripts part to something similar to this:

```
"scripts": {
    "test": "node test/run"
},
```

This tells NPM that, to test our microservice, it should run the `node test/run` command. We now need to create this file (`test/run.js`) so it will actually work. Create the `test` folder, add the `run.js` file, and add only this line to it:

```
console.log("ok");
```

Now, go to a console on our microservice folder and run the `test` command:

```
npm test
> imagini@1.0.0 test /Users/dresende/imagini
> node test/run

Ok
```

The first step is complete. This is not actually a test, but we now have the initial structure.

# Integrating tests

We will now create our first integration tests. Each of our tests will run separately, meaning they should not depend on any other test and should follow a predictable workflow. First, we need to change our `run.js` file to run all test files. For that, we'll use `mocha` and add all files found in the `integration` folder:

```
const fs    = require("fs");
const path  = require("path");
const mocha = require("mocha");
const suite = new mocha();

fs.readdir(path.join(__dirname, "integration"), (err, files) => {
    if (err) throw err;

    files.filter((filename) =>
    (filename.match(/\.js$/))).map((filename) => {
        suite.addFile(path.join(__dirname, "integration", filename));
    });

    suite.run((failures) => {
        process.exit(failures);
    });
});
```

Then, let's create the `integration` folder inside our `test` folder, and let's create our first test file, called `image-upload.js`. Add this content to the file:

```
describe("Uploading image", () => {
    it("should accept only images");
});
```

If we now run the tests again, we should see the default `mocha` response with no tests passing and no tests failing:

```
npm test
> imagini@1.0.0 test /Users/dresende/imagini
> node test/run

0 passing (2ms)
```

To avoid repeating code, let's create a `tools.js` file inside the `test` folder, so we can export common tasks that every test file can use. Out of the box, I'm thinking about our microservice location and a sample image:

```
const fs   = require("fs");
```

```
const path = require("path");

exports.service = require("../imagini.js");
exports.sample  = fs.readFileSync(path.join(__dirname, "sample.png"));
```

Create a `sample.png` image in the `test` folder. When a test needs to upload an image, it will use that sample. In the future, we could have different kinds of samples, such as huge images, to test performance and limitations.

# Using chai

We also need to make a little change to our microservice. We need to export its app so that the HTTP plugin from `chai` can load it and were able to test it without the need to run in a separate console. Add this to the end of our microservice file:

```
module.exports = app;
```

You should have a folder hierarchy similar to the following screenshot:

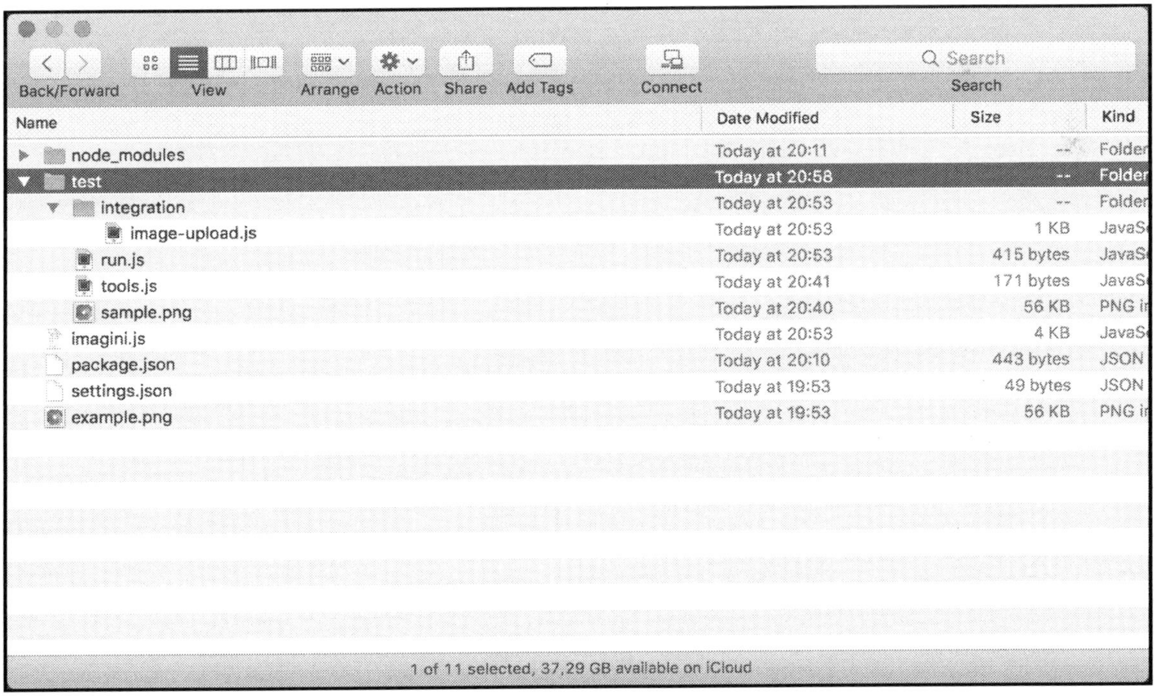

We should now change our `image-upload.js` test file to create our first real test:

```
const chai  = require("chai");
const http  = require("chai-http");
const tools = require("../tools");

chai.use(http);

describe("Uploading image", () => {
    beforeEach((done) => {
        chai
        .request(tools.service)
        .delete("/uploads/test_image_upload.png")
        .end(() => {
            return done();
        });
    });

    it ("should accept a PNG image", function (done) {
        chai
        .request(tools.service)
        .post ("/uploads/test_image_upload.png")
        .set ("Content-Type", "image/png")
        .send(tools.sample)
        .end((err, res) => {
            chai.expect(res).to.have.status(200);
            chai.expect(res.body).to.have.status("ok");

            return done();
        });
    });
});
```

We start by first including the `chai` modules and our `tools` file:

```
const chai  = require("chai");
const http  = require("chai-http");
const tools = require("../tools");

chai.use(http);
```

Then, we describe our test file as `Uploading image`:

```
describe("Uploading image", () => {
```

We'll add the different use cases we can think of, related to the uploading of images.

Inside, we use `beforeEach`, which is a `mocha` method that will be called before every test in this file. Remember, we want our tests to be consistent, so we add this method to remove our image before running every test. We don't care whether the image exists:

```
beforeEach((done) => {
    chai
    .request(tools.service)
    .delete("/uploads/test_image_upload.png")
    .end(() => {
        return done();
    });
});
```

Look how we use the `tools.service`, which points to our microservice. If, later on, we change the name or somehow make it more complex, we just need to change the `tools` file, and everything should work.

Then, we add our first `integration` file's test – a simple image upload:

```
it("should accept a PNG image", (done) => {
    chai
    .request(tools.service)
    .post("/uploads/test_image_upload.png")
    .set("Content-Type", "image/png")
    .send(tools.sample)
    .end((err, res) => {
        chai.expect(res).to.have.status(200);
        chai.expect(res.body).to.have.status("ok");

        return done();
    });
});
```

It checks whether the HTTP response code is `200` and if the response body, which is a JSON structure, has the status property set to `ok`. And we're done!

Let's run our test suite again and see how it goes.

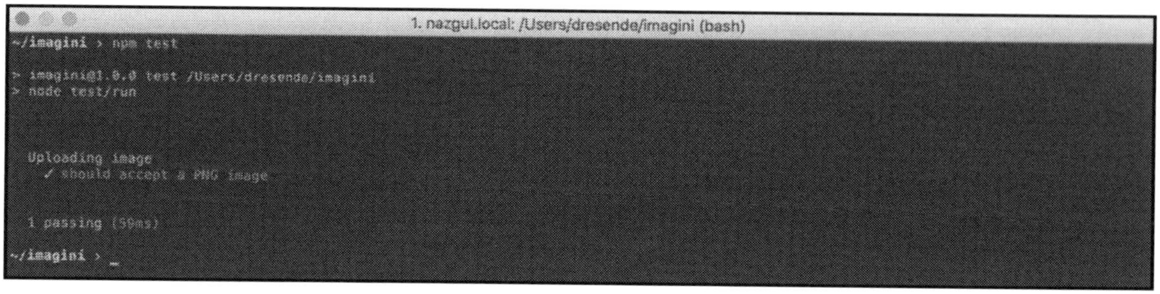


## Adding code coverage

Now that our test suite is working and has one test, let's introduce code coverage. Adding this from the beginning of development is very easy and will help us focus on parts of the code that need to be tested, especially some use cases that involve specific conditions (such as `if-then-else` statements in our code). Having it all set up from the start of development is easy. On the other hand, if you have a fully working code and want to add tests and coverage, it will be harder and will take quite some time.

To add code coverage, we'll introduce another module. We'll install it globally to be able to run the tests with it directly:

```
npm install -g nyc
```

We can now run our tests with the following instrumentation:

```
nyc npm test
```

This should run our tests with the instrumentation installed. In the end, you'll get a nice console report.

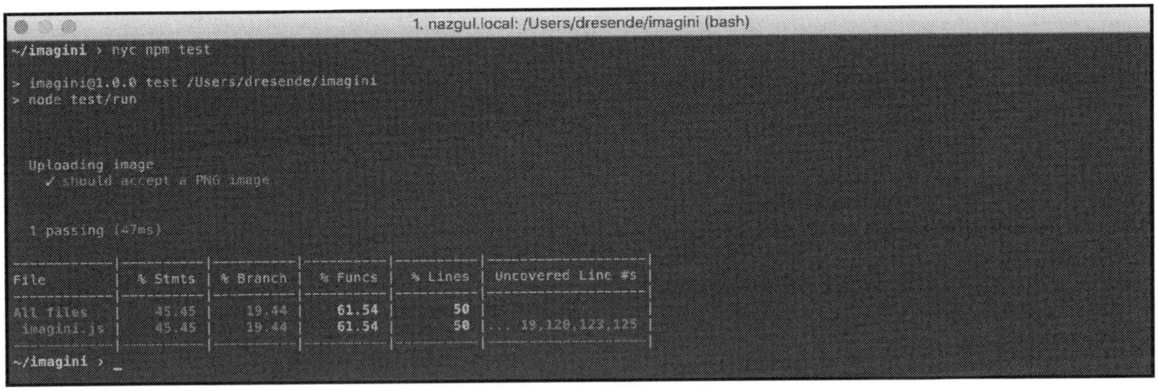


The coverage results are stored inside in a `.nyc_output` folder. This enables you to look at the last test results without running tests again. This is useful if your test suite is big and takes some time to finish.

To see the results, you just run `nyc report`:

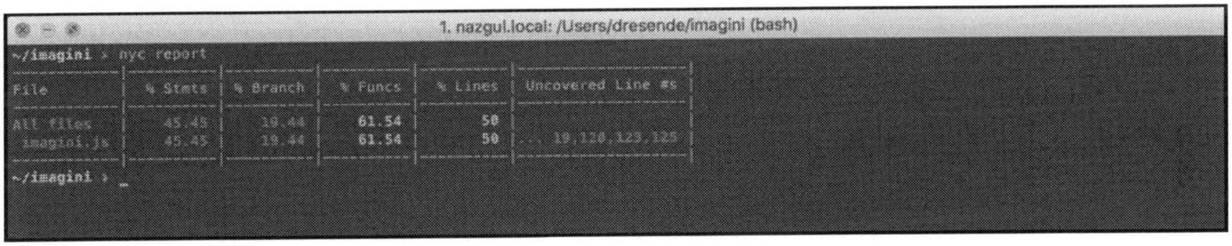


The result is a console report. There are several other styles of reports. One particularly useful one is the `html` report. Let's generate it:

```
nyc report --reporter=html
```

You should now have a `coverage` folder with an `index.html` file. Open that in your browser, and you should see something like the following screenshot:

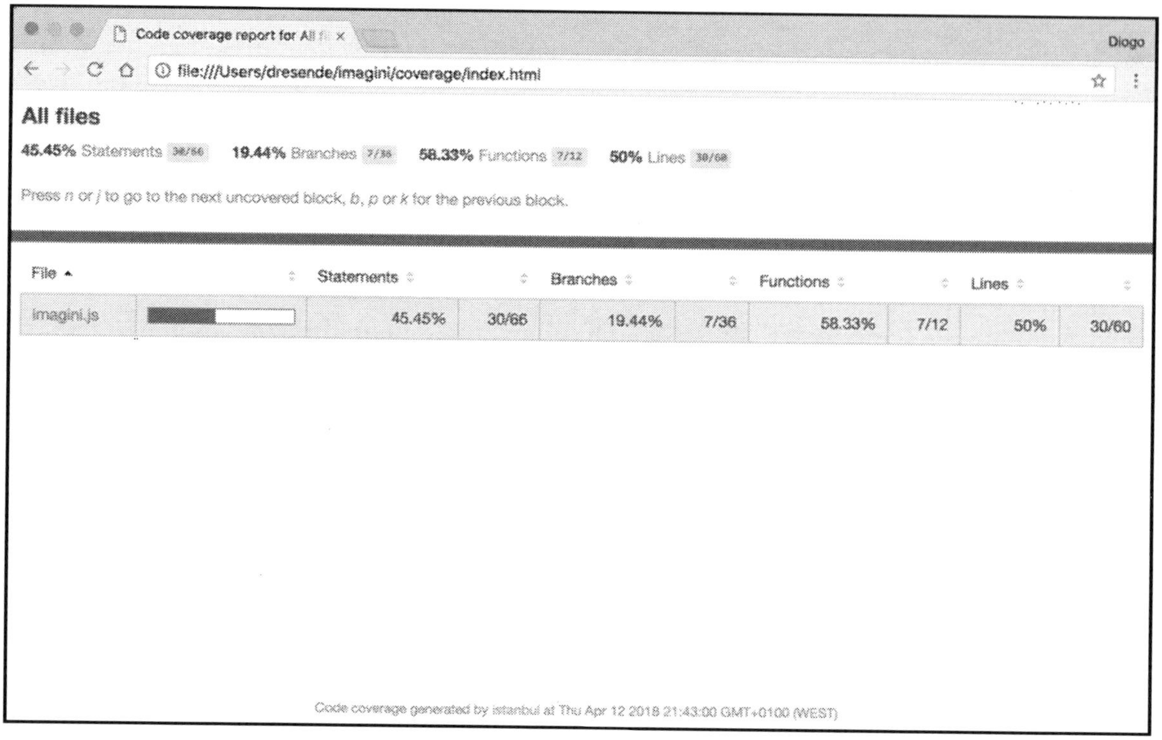


We only have one file that represents our microservice. If we had more, they would be listed hierarchically. There are global average statistics for every file.

There are three important groups of columns:

- **Statements**: Which represent code statements (conditions, assignments, assertions, calls, and so on)
- **Branches**: Which represent possible code control workflows, such as if-then-else or switch-case statement possibilities
- **Functions**: Which represent our actual code functions and callbacks

You can click in our file, look at the specific details of it and, more specifically, see the code and information line by line:

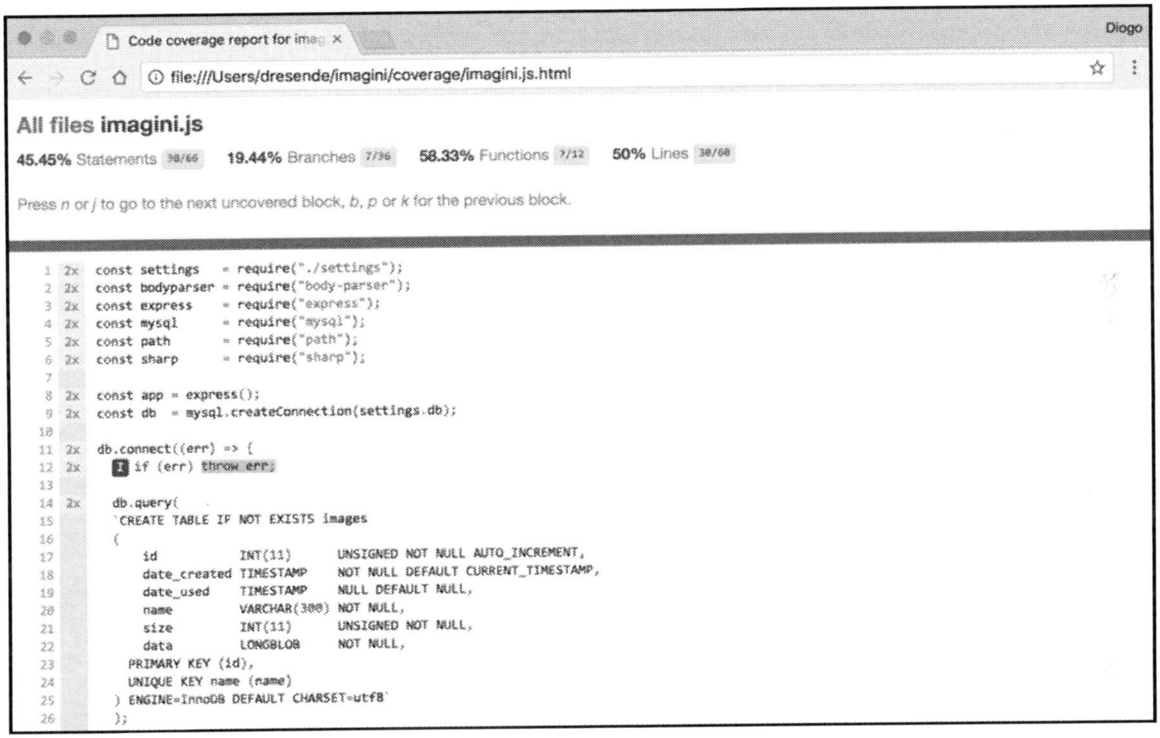


To the right of every line number, you see a gray area and, in this case, you see `2x` in some of the lines. This is the execution count for that line. The execution has passed by that line twice. This is actually not that important, unless you're looking for bits of code that get largely executed and you want to do some kind of optimization.

You can also see that *line 12* has two changes. First, there's a pinkish background in the back of `throw err`. That means that statement never got executed, which is normal for now as we always successfully connected to the database. The mark before the `if` statement means that the condition never got executed:

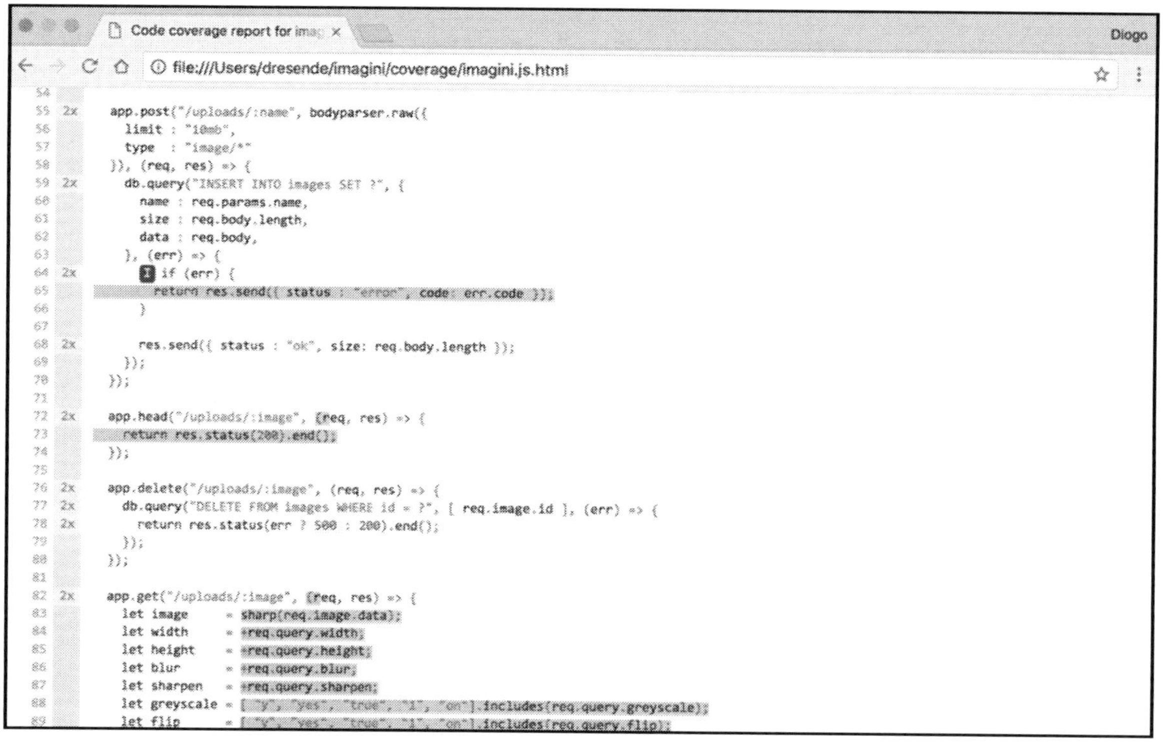

If you scroll a few lines down, we'll see more lines with marks. For example, we can see our image upload method got almost completely covered. The only statement missing is the error handling.

As we delete our test image before running the tests, our image deletion method is also covered. Again, the only missing branch is if the database returns an error to our `DELETE` query.

Before going any further with the image upload, let's add another `integration` test file called `image-parameter.js`, and add some tests to increase our coverage:

```
const chai = require("chai");
const http = require("chai-http");
const tools = require("../tools");

chai.use(http);

describe("The image parameter", () => {
    beforeEach((done) => {
        chai
        .request(tools.service)
        .delete("/uploads/test_image_parameter.png")
        .end(() => {
            return done();
        });
    });

    it("should reply 403 for non image extension", (done) => {
        chai
        .request(tools.service)
        .get("/uploads/test_image_parameter.txt")
        .end((err, res) => {
            chai.expect(res).to.have.status(403);

            return done();
        });
    });

    it("should reply 404 for non image existence", (done) => {
        chai
        .request(tools.service)
        .get("/uploads/test_image_parameter.png")
        .end((err, res) => {
            chai.expect(res).to.have.status(404);

            return done();
        });
    });
});
```

Let's run our test suite and see how it goes:

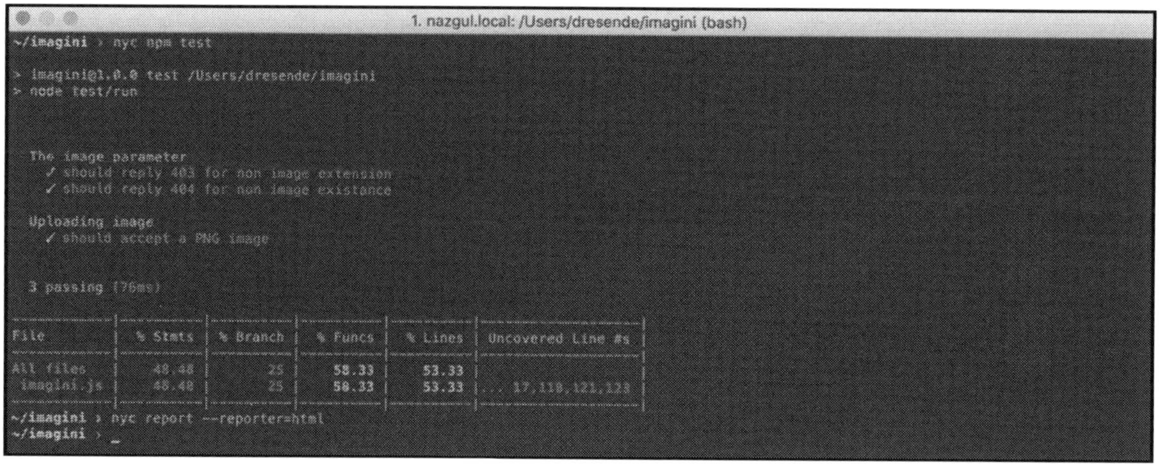


Refresh the HTML report page and look at our parameter method:

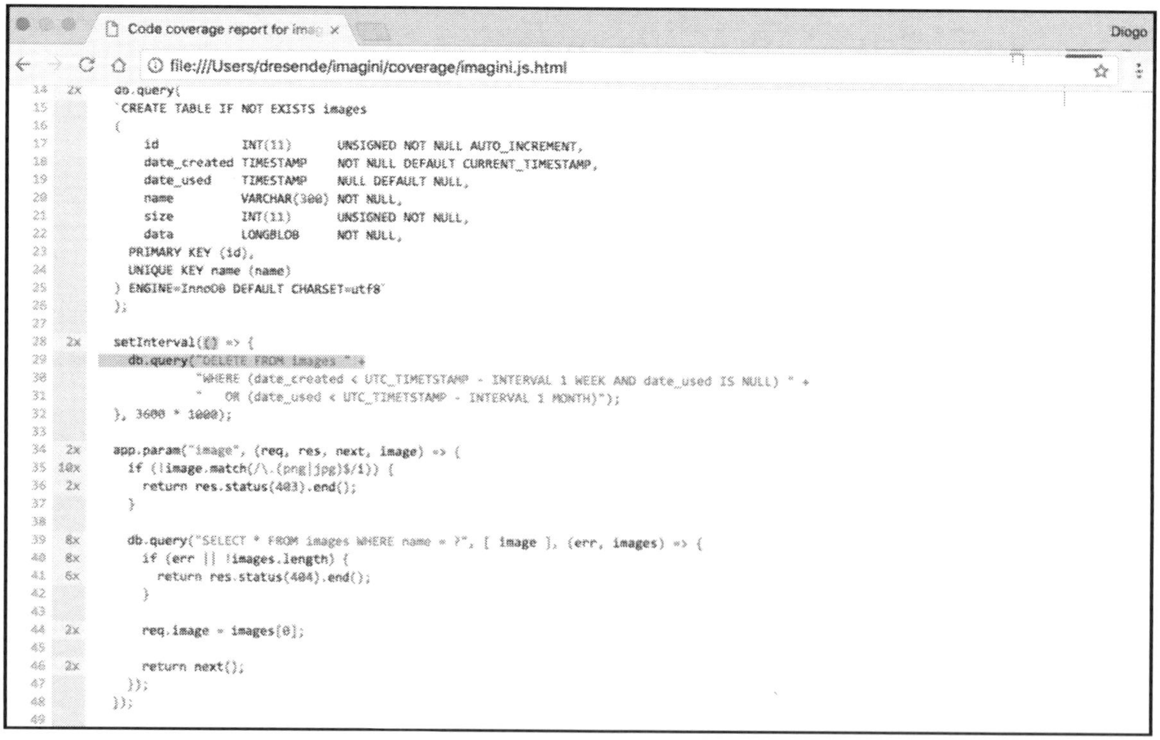

As you can see, we now cover the following condition:

```
if (!image.match(/\.(png|jpg)$/i)) {
```

The following condition:

```
if (err || !images.length) {
```

We now have full coverage on this method.

There are other coverage lines that are harder to test, such as timers (you can see one on *line 28*), `catch` statements, or external errors coming from databases or other storage sources. There are ways of mocking those events, and we'll cover them later on.

# Covering all code

For now, let's focus on adding coverage to our code. It's important to have it covered as much as possible when it's still just a small service. If we start adding tests and coverage when it's already big, you'll be frustrated, and it will be hard to find the motivation to cover it all.

This way, you'll find it rewarding to cover it in the beginning and keep the coverage percentage as high as possible along with code evolution.

Let's get back to our image upload test, and add another test:

```
it("should deny duplicated images", (done) => {
    chai
    .request(tools.service)
    .post("/uploads/test_image_upload.png")
    .set("Content-Type", "image/png")
    .send(tools.sample)
    .end((err, res) => {
        chai.expect(res).to.have.status(200);
        chai.expect(res.body).to.have.status("ok");

        chai
        .request(tools.service)
        .post("/uploads/test_image_upload.png")
        .set("Content-Type", "image/png")
        .send(tools.sample)
        .end((err, res) => {
            chai.expect(res).to.have.status(200);
            chai.expect(res.body).to.have.status("error");
            chai.expect(res.body).to.have.property("code",
```

```
                    "ER_DUP_ENTRY");

                    return done();
                });
            });
        });
```

This will upload the same image twice in a row and we should receive an error from the database saying there's a duplicate. Let's run the tests again:

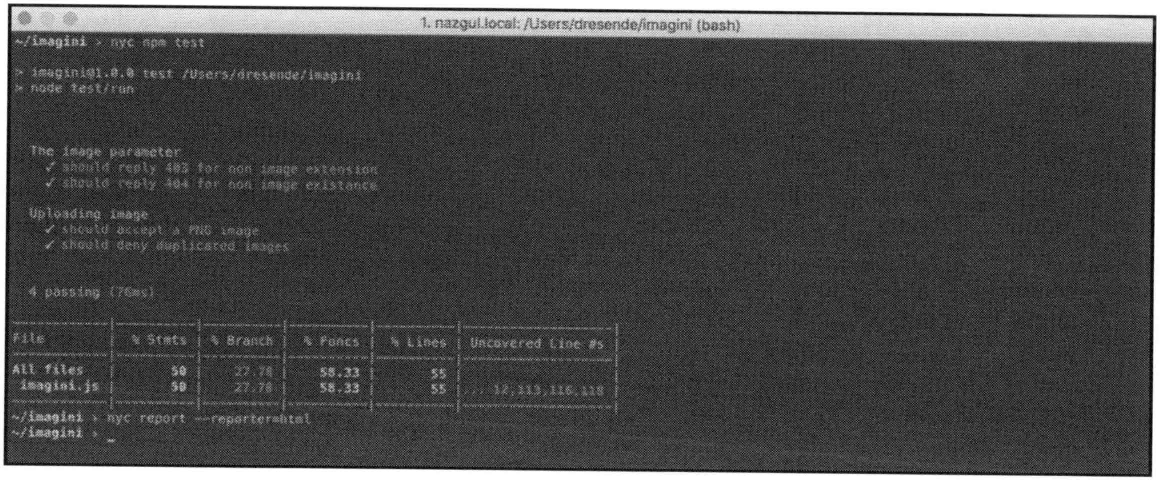

Now, let's open the initial page of the coverage report:

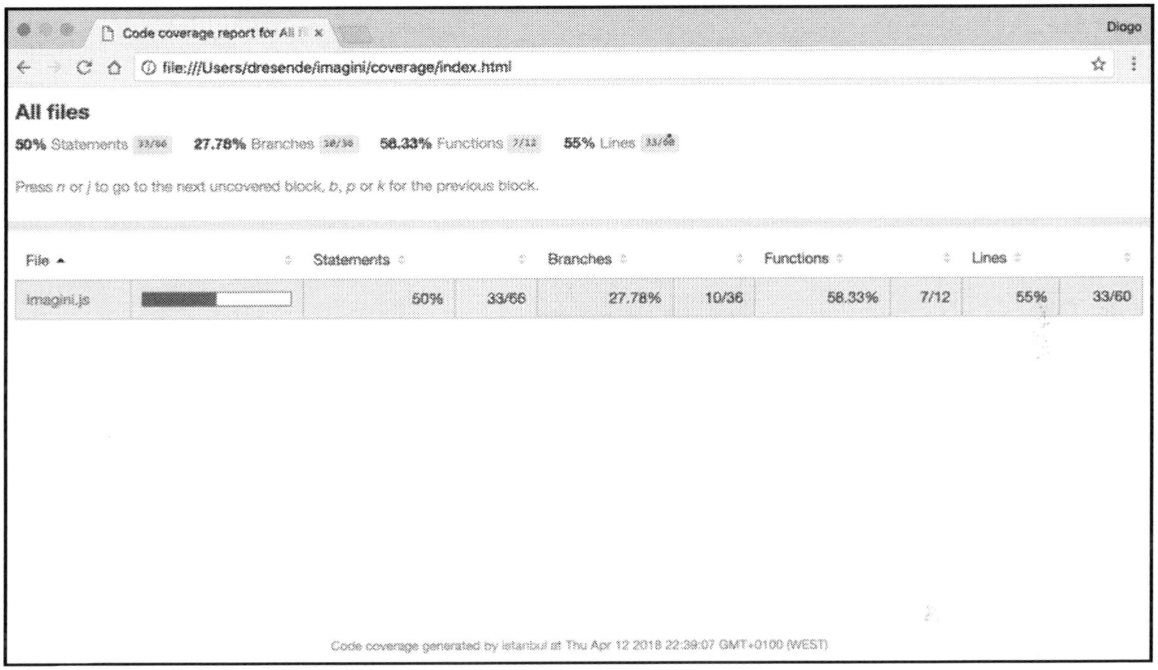

Notice that our file is no longer in a red background. This means the statement coverage has reached *50%*. Let's click on our file and see how our image upload method is covered:

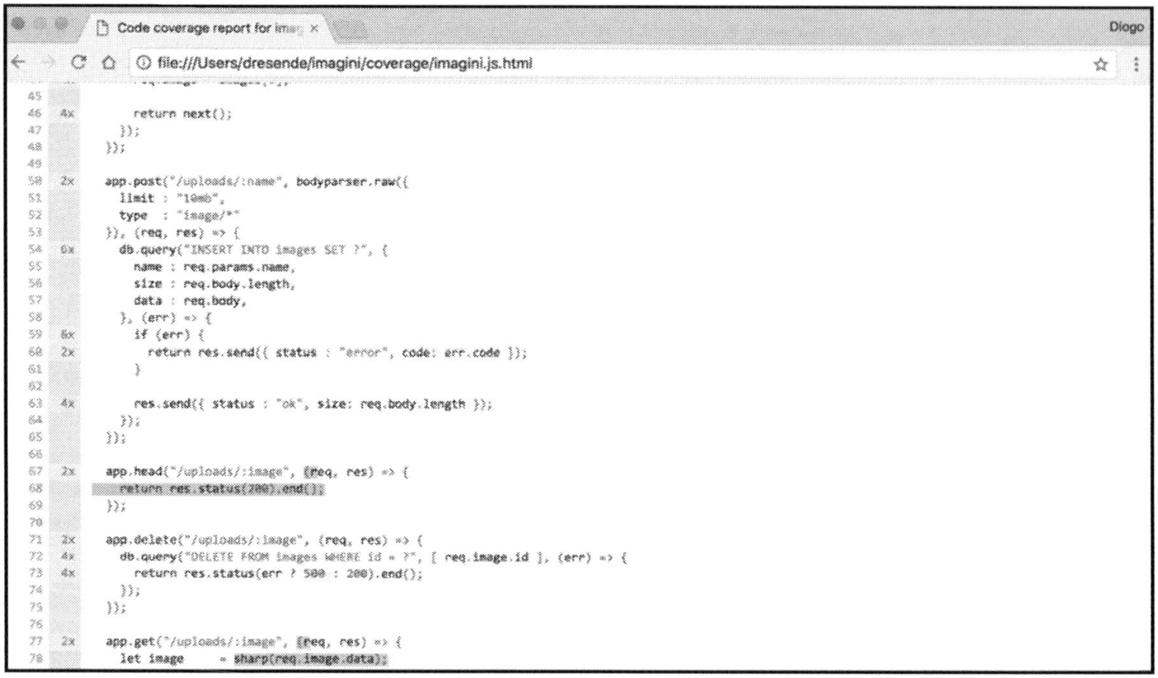


It's complete! We can now move on. Just a reminder before we move to another method: having full coverage does not mean there are no bugs. That's something you need to understand. You might have a use case that you're not expecting, and so, you have no code for it, so there's no obvious coverage.

For example, the `bodyparser` module will not limit the type of content. If we upload a text file with an image name on it, our code will accept it and store it in the database without noticing. Think of this use case as your homework, and try to create a test to cover that use case and then fix the code.

Let's move to the next method we see after our upload method: the image check on *line 67*. Let's create a new integration test file called `image-check.js`, and add a simple test:

```
const chai = require("chai");
const http = require("chai-http");
const tools = require("../tools");

chai.use(http);
```

```
describe("Checking image", () => {
    beforeEach((done) => {
        chai
        .request(tools.service)
        .delete("/uploads/test_image_check.png")
        .end(() => {
            return done();
        });
    });

    it("should return 404 if it doesn't exist", (done) => {
        chai
        .request(tools.service)
        .head("/uploads/test_image_check.png")
        .end((err, res) => {
            chai.expect(res).to.have.status(404);

            return done();
        });
    });

    it("should return 200 if it exists", (done) => {
        chai
        .request(tools.service)
        .post("/uploads/test_image_check.png")
        .set("Content-Type", "image/png")
        .send(tools.sample)
        .end((err, res) => {
            chai.expect(res).to.have.status(200);
            chai.expect(res.body).to.have.status("ok");

            chai
            .request(tools.service)
            .head("/uploads/test_image_check.png")
            .end((err, res) => {
                chai.expect(res).to.have.status(200);

                return done();
            });
        });
    });
});
```

Let's run the test suite:

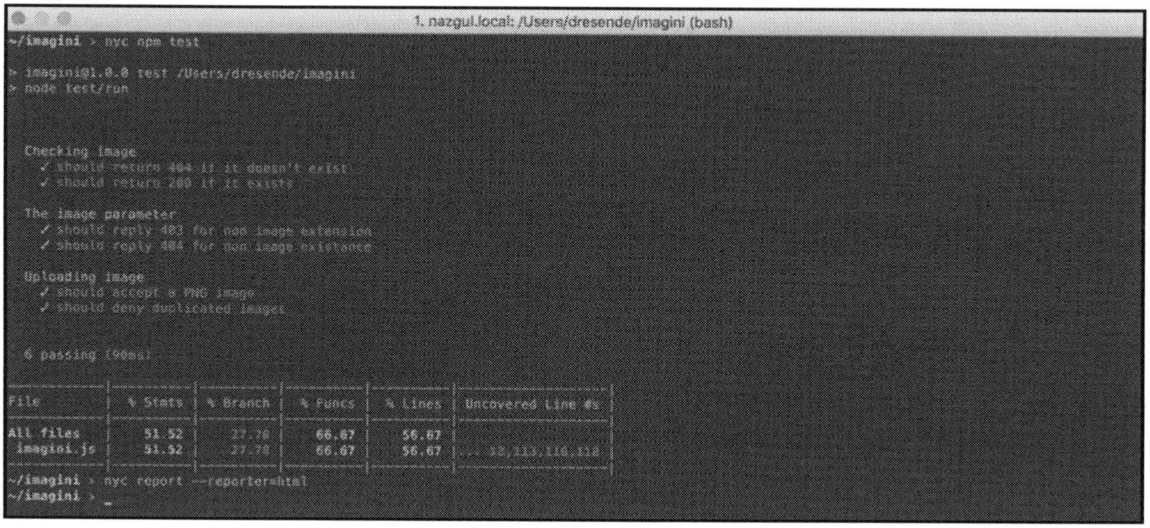


We can see our console report is getting bigger. As we're creating new integration test files and having a description for each one, `mocha` writes a nice tree view showing how the tests run. On the bottom, we can see the coverage report:

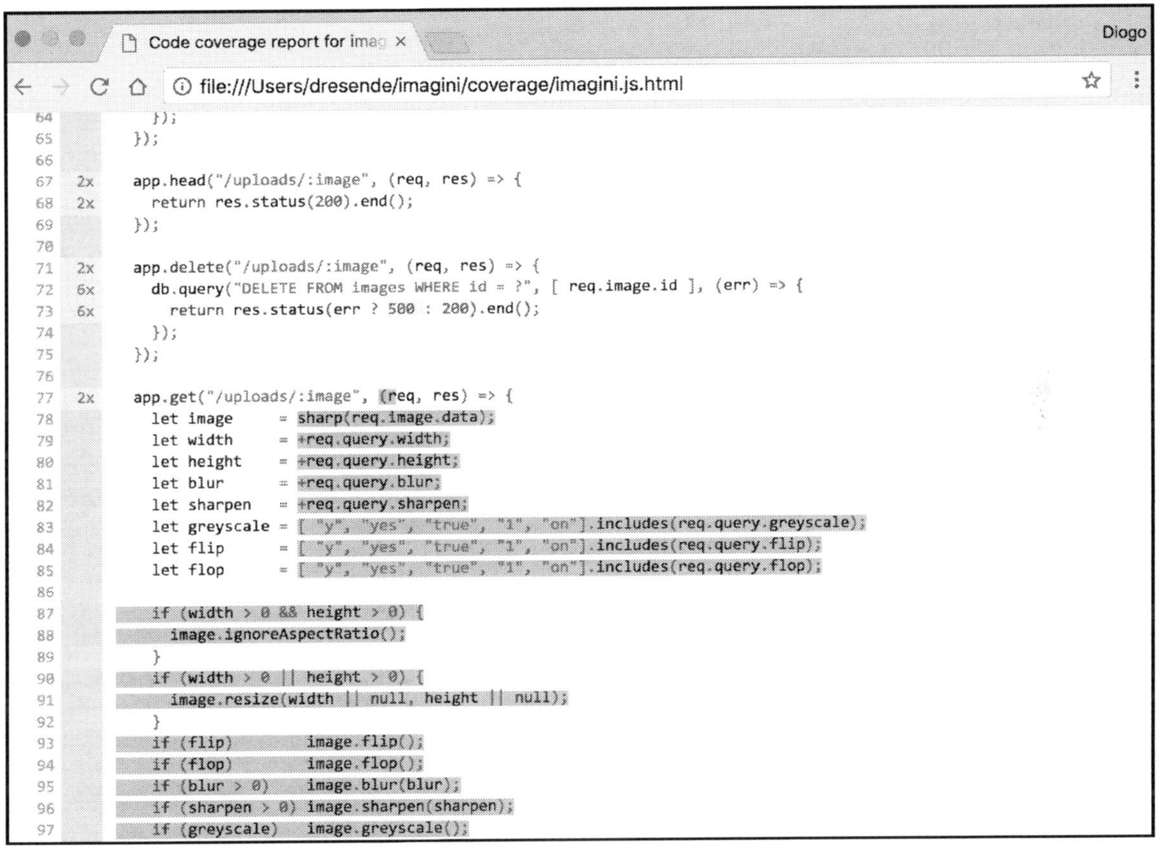


Looking at the check method, we see it's now fully covered. This one was very simple.

We're still in the middle of statement coverage as our top method; the image manipulation one is almost half of our code. This means that when we start covering it, the coverage will significantly rise.

Let's create an `integration` test for it:

```
const chai = require("chai");
const http = require("chai-http");
const tools = require("../tools");

chai.use(http);

describe("Downloading image", () => {
    beforeEach((done) => {
        chai
        .request(tools.service)
        .delete("/uploads/test_image_download.png")
        .end(() => {
            chai
            .request(tools.service)
            .post("/uploads/test_image_download.png")
            .set("Content-Type", "image/png")
            .send(tools.sample)
            .end((err, res) => {
                chai.expect(res).to.have.status(200);
                chai.expect(res.body).to.have.status("ok");

                return done();
            });
        });
    });

    it("should return the original image size if no parameters given",
    (done) => {
        chai
        .request(tools.service)
        .get("/uploads/test_image_download.png")
        .end((err, res) => {
            chai.expect(res).to.have.status(200);
            chai.expect(res.body).to.have.length(tools.sample.length);

            return done();
        });
    });
});
```

Before each test, we're deleting the image (if it exists) and then uploading a fresh sample one. Then, for each test, we'll download it and test the output according to what we asked for.

Let's try and run it:

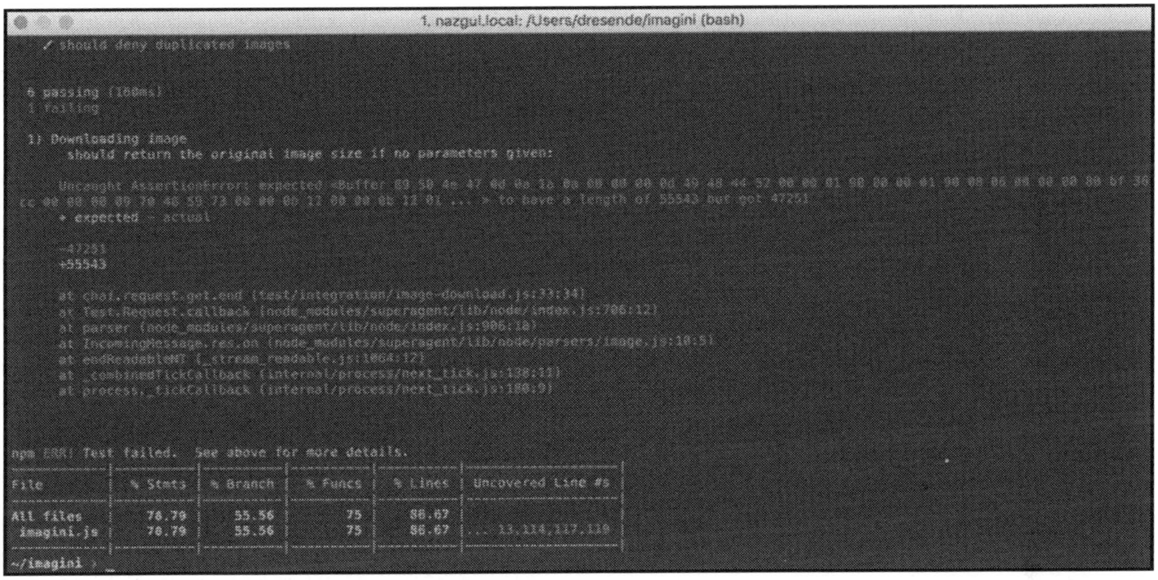


Well, that was unexpected. The test fails because our length check does not match. This is actually a good example of something we just notice when we start to execute testing.

What happens is that, when we request an image, we use the `sharp` module to make any manipulation on the image, according to query parameters. In this case, we're not asking for any manipulation, but when we output the image (through `sharp`), it actually returns the same image in size, but perhaps with a little bit less quality, or maybe it just knows how to better encode our image and remove data from the file that is not needed.

We don't know exactly, but let's assume we want the original image, untouched. We need to change our download method. Let's assume that if no query parameters are defined at all, we just return the original image. Let's add a condition to the top of our method:

```
if (Object.keys(req.query).length === 0) {
    db.query("UPDATE images " +
             "SET date_used = UTC_TIMESTAMP " +
             "WHERE id = ?",
             [ req.image.id ]);
```

```
        res.setHeader("Content-Type", "image/" +
        path.extname(req.image.name).substr(1));

        return res.end(req.image.data);
    }
```

If we run  it now, we should have no failures:

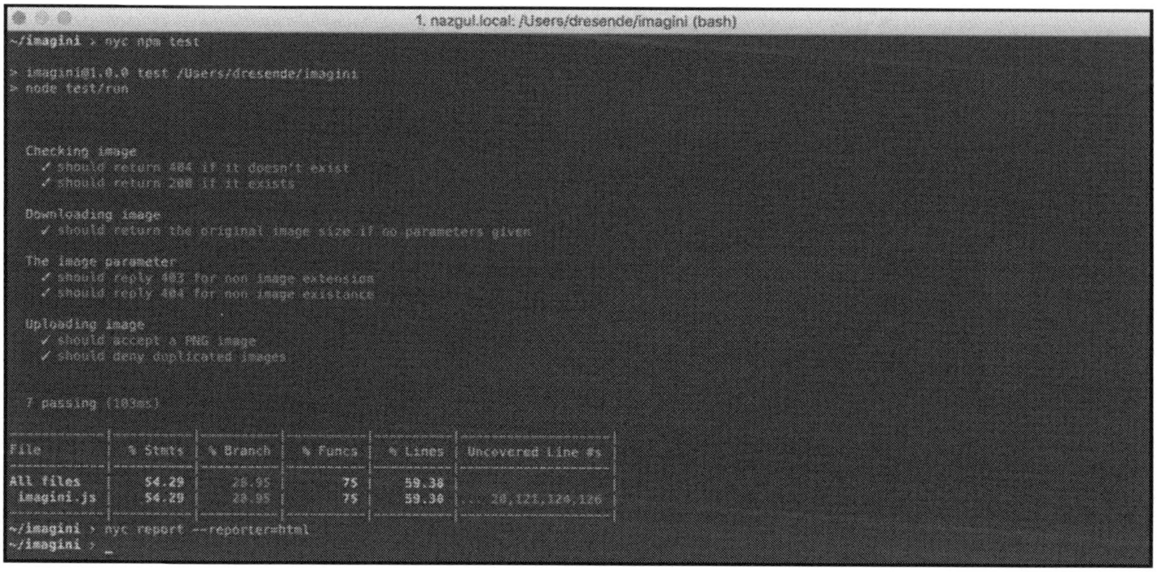


Our statement coverage did not rise much because we actually created a condition on top of the method and returned immediately, so our previous method is still untested:

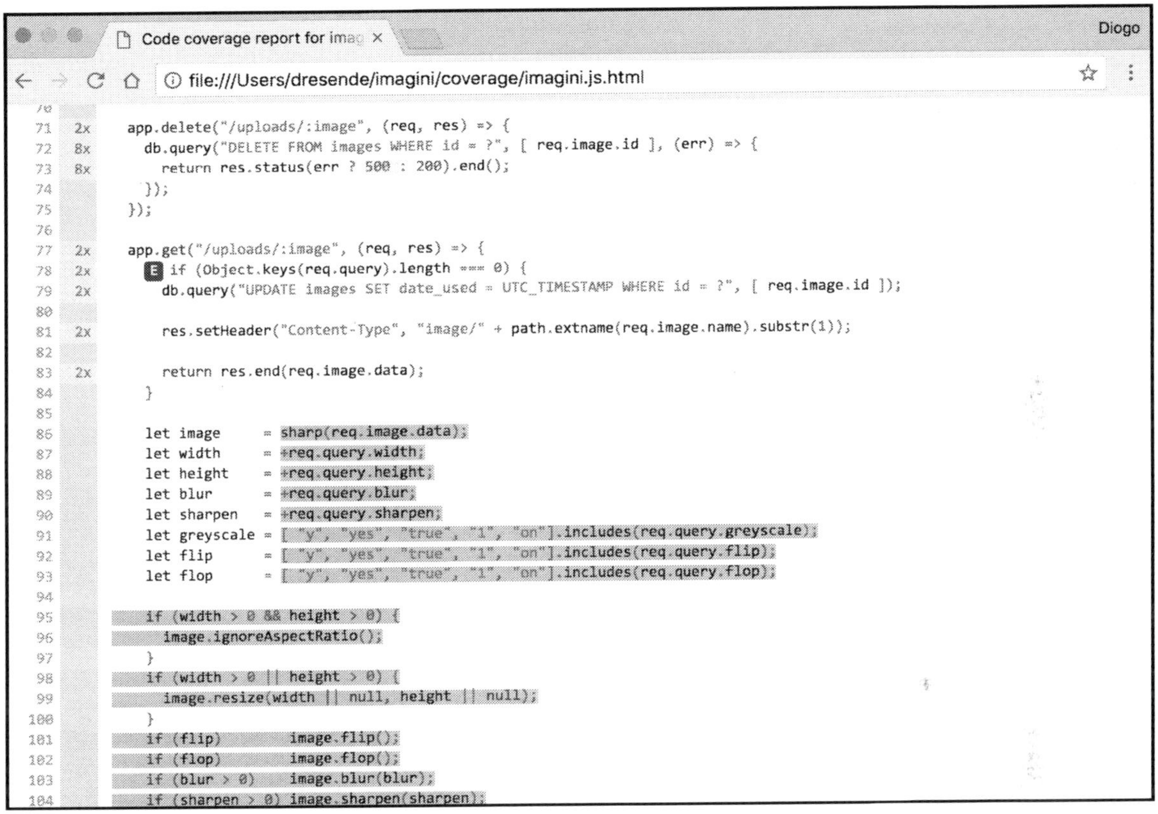

Looking at *line 78*, you should see a new mark, an `E` that means that the condition in that line never executed the `else` statement, which is the rest of our code. Let's add a test to this integration and resize our image.

We will need `sharp` to help us check whether the results are correct. Let's include it on the top of our file:

```
const sharp = require("sharp");
```

Then, add a resize test:

```
it("should be able to resize the image as we request", (done) => {
    chai
    .request(tools.service)
    .get("/uploads/test_image_download.png?width=200&height=100")
    .end((err, res) => {
        chai.expect(res).to.have.status(200);

        let image = sharp(res.body);

        image
        .metadata()
        .then((metadata) => {
            chai.expect(metadata).to.have.property("width", 200);
            chai.expect(metadata).to.have.property("height", 100);

            return done();
        });
    });
});
```

Let's run our test suite:

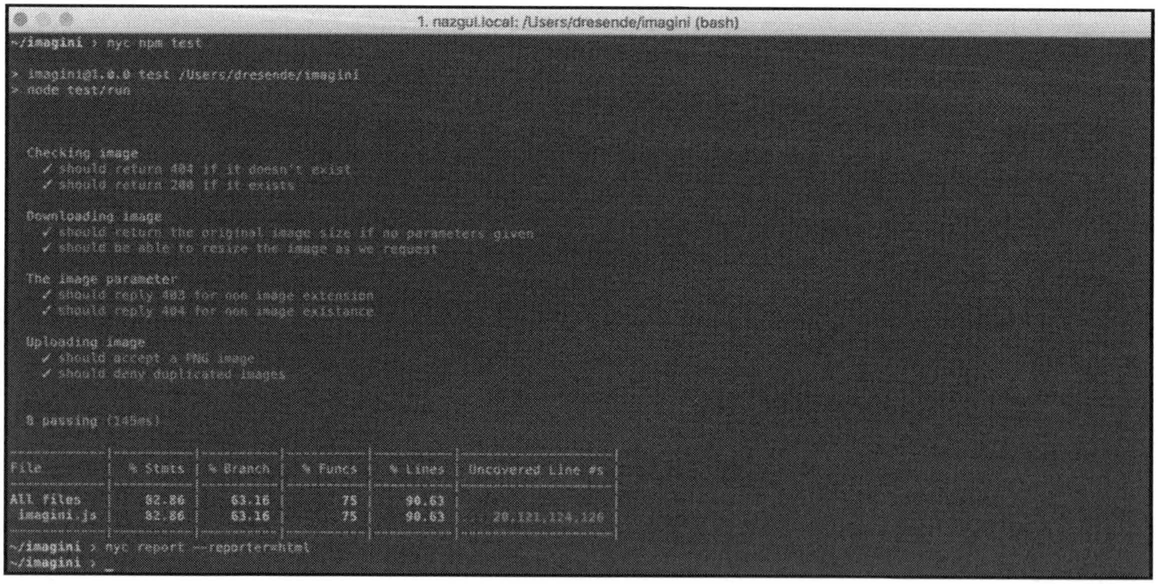

It now looks very good. From the console report, we can see some green. Let's look at the front page of the coverage report:

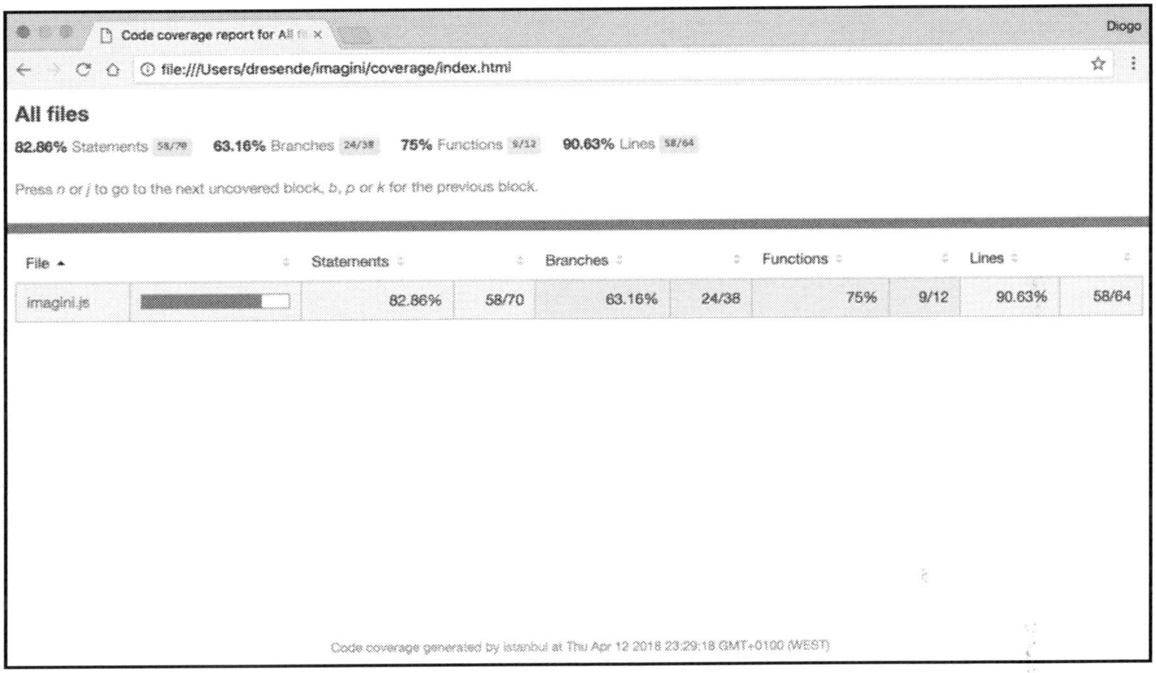

We see green here as well. Having more than *80%* coverage is good, but we can still go further. Let's see the file:

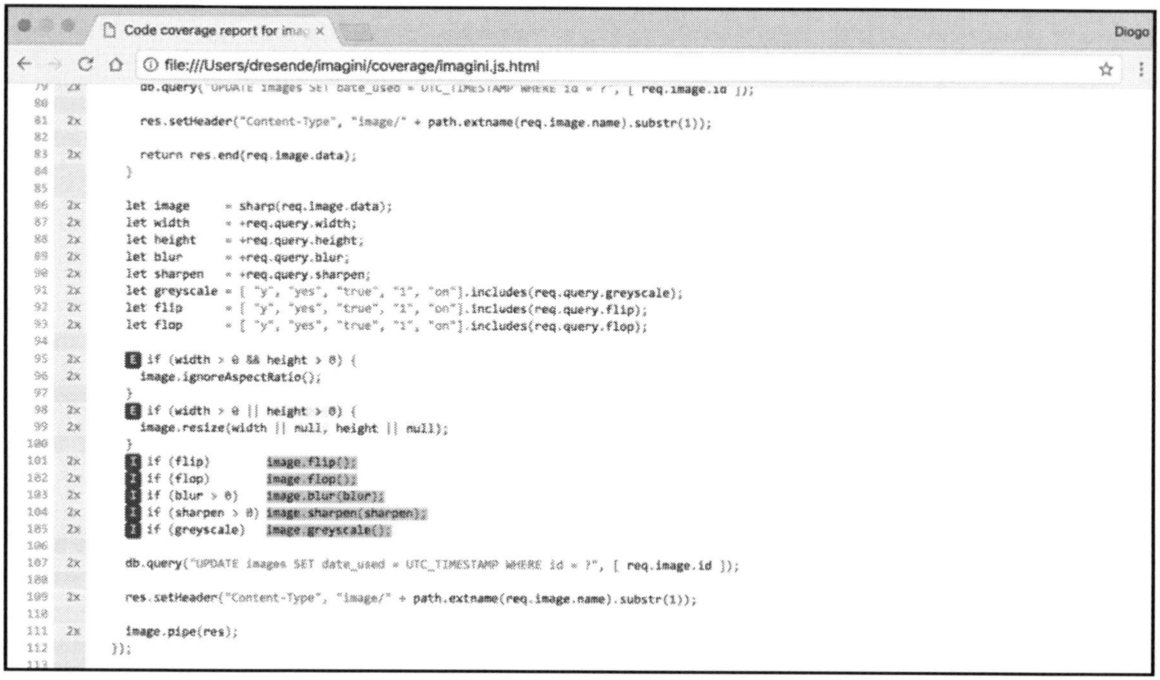

It's more or less covered. We still need to cover all the effects. We can actually run them all at once. The first two conditions also have an `E` marker, but that should disappear after adding a test without resizing. Let's add it:

```
it("should be able to add image effects as we request", (done) => {
    chai
    .request(tools.service)
    .get("/uploads/test_image_download.png?
    flip=y&flop=y&greyscale=y&blur=10&sharpen=10")
    .end((err, res) => {
        chai.expect(res).to.have.status(200);

        return done();
    });
});
```

Looking at our report now, we see the coverage is almost complete:

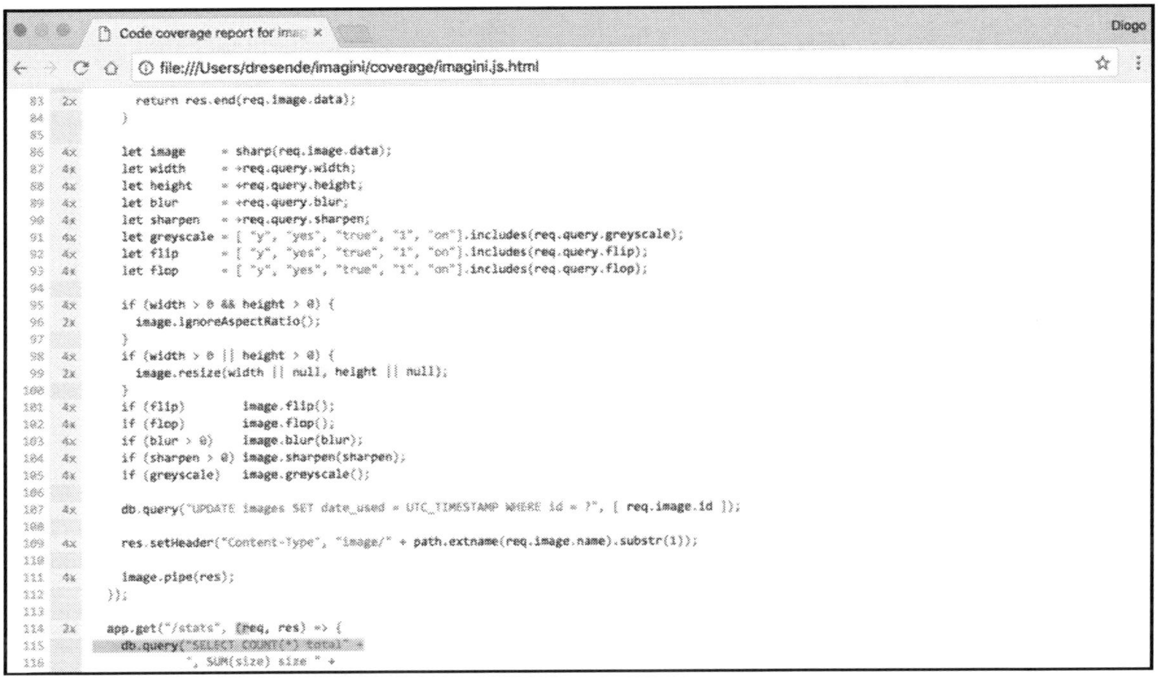

To cover those yellow nulls there, we need to resize the image with only `width` or `height`. We can add two tests for those:

```
it("should be able to resize the image width as we request", (done) => {
    chai
    .request(tools.service)
    .get("/uploads/test_image_download.png?width=200")
    .end((err, res) => {
        chai.expect(res).to.have.status(200);

        let image = sharp(res.body);

        image
        .metadata()
        .then((metadata) => {
            chai.expect(metadata).to.have.property("width", 200);

            return done();
        });
    });
});
```

Add a similar one for the `height`, and run the test suite. You should not see the statement coverage go up, only the branch coverage:

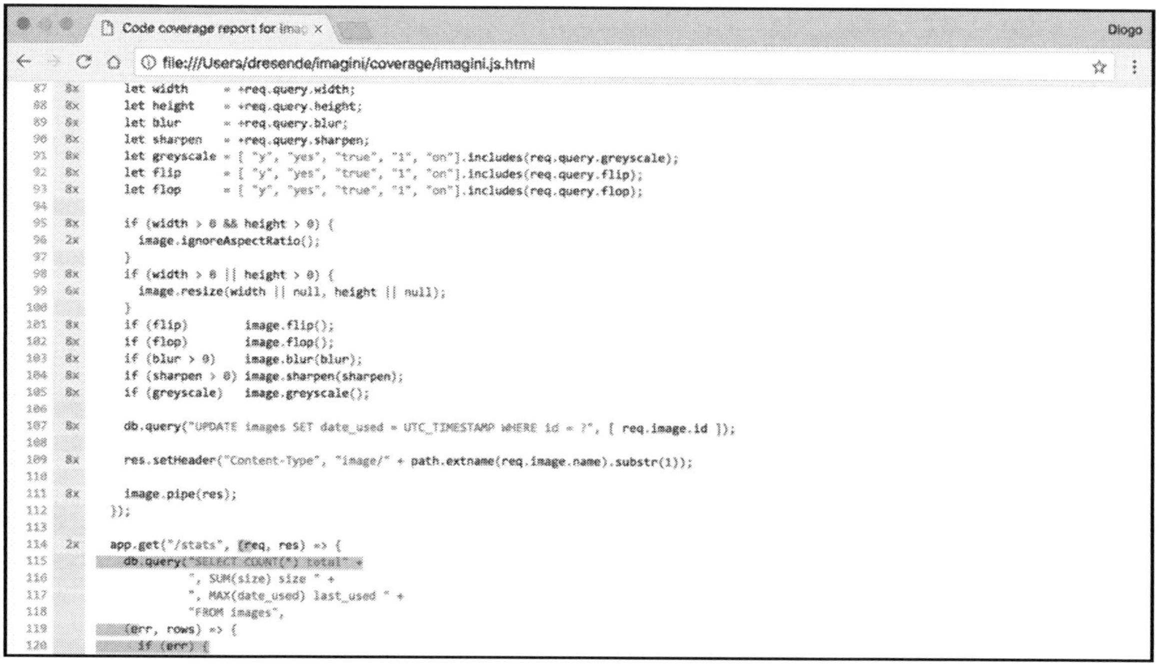


The only method missing is the statistics method. This one is simple. We could eventually run a more specific test, by asking statistics, making a change such as an upload, and asking for statistics again to compare. I'll leave that to you. Let's just add a simple request test:

```
const chai = require("chai");
const http = require("chai-http");
const tools = require("../tools");

chai.use(http);

describe("Statistics", () => {
    it("should return an object with total, size, last_used and
    uptime", (done) => {
        chai
        .request(tools.service)
        .get("/stats")
        .end((err, res) => {
            chai.expect(res).to.have.status(200);
            chai.expect(res.body).to.have.property("total");
            chai.expect(res.body).to.have.property("size");
```

```
            chai.expect(res.body).to.have.property("last_used");
            chai.expect(res.body).to.have.property("uptime");

            return done();
        });
    });
});
```

Now, running our test suite should give all green:

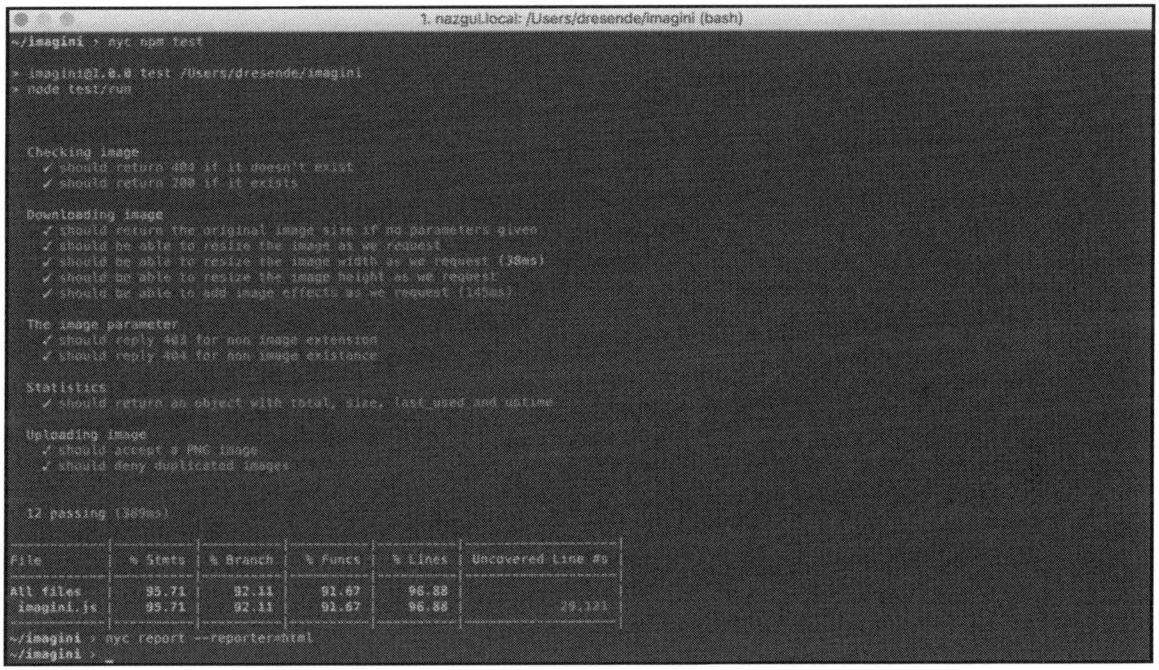

We see there are only two lines uncovered: `29.121`. The first one is our timer and the second one is on the statistics method. Let's refresh our HTML report:

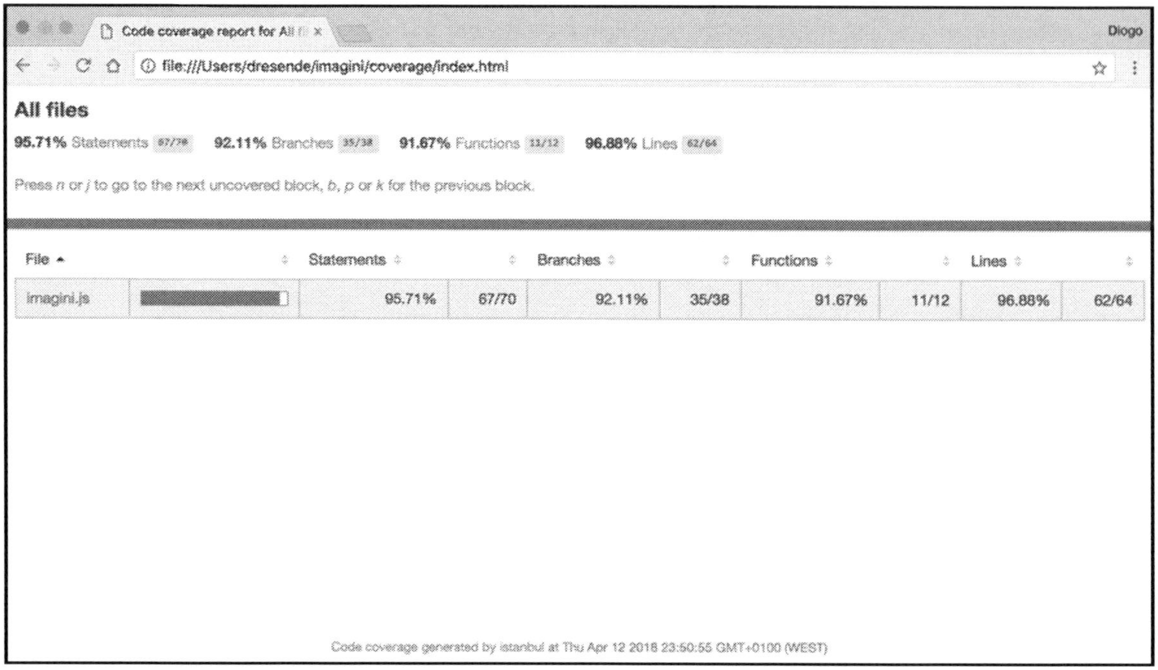


This is rewarding; we have almost *100%* coverage. There's only one function not covered, which is our timer. And, there are only tree statements, which also represent the three branches, that aren't covered, but those aren't actually that important.

What is important is to keep this high coverage mark during the course of our development.

# Mocking our services

It's not at all uncommon to have parts of your service that are harder to test. Some, or most, of those parts are error-related conditions, where it's hard to make an external service such as a database engine return an error that will rarely occur during normal execution.

To be able to test, or at least simulate these kinds of events, we need to mock our services. There are a couple of options around, and Sinon is the most commonly used one in the Node.js ecosystem. This framework provides more than mocking; it also provides the following:

- **Spies**: Which monitor function calls and record arguments passed, the returned value and other properties
- **Stubs**: Which are enhanced spies with a pre-programmed behavior, helping us drive the execution into a pre-determined path (allowing us to mock a behavior)

Sinon also allows us to bend time, by virtually changing the service perception of time, and to be able to test timed interval calls (remember our interval timer?). With this in mind, let's see if we can make our microservice reach *100%* test coverage.

Let's start by installing the framework, as we did with `chai`:

```
npm install --save-dev sinon
```

Now, let's add a test for the image deletion. This method is tested through the other tests and that's why we didn't need to add it before, but now that we want to fully test it, let's add a basic test file called `image-delete.js`, with the following content:

```
const chai = require("chai");
const sinon = require("sinon");
const http = require("chai-http");
const tools = require("../tools");

chai.use(http);

describe.only("Deleting image", () => {
    beforeEach((done) => {
        chai
        .request(tools.service)
        .delete("/uploads/test_image_delete.png")
        .end(() => {
            return done();
        });
    });

    it("should return 200 if it exists", (done) => {
        chai
        .request(tools.service)
        .post("/uploads/test_image_delete.png")
        .set("Content-Type", "image/png")
        .send(tools.sample)
        .end((err, res) => {
```

```
                chai.expect(res).to.have.status(200);
                chai.expect(res.body).to.have.status("ok");

                chai
                .request(tools.service)
                .delete("/uploads/test_image_delete.png")
                .end((err, res) => {
                    chai.expect(res).to.have.status(200);

                    return done();
                });
            });
        });
    });
```

Notice that I added the Sinon dependency on top, although I'm not using it just yet. You may run the tests again, but you shouldn't notice any difference.

We'll need to change the database behavior, so let's export a reference to it, so as to be able to access it from the tests. Add the following line in our microservice file before connecting to the database:

```
app.db = db;
```

Now, add another test to that file:

```
it("should return 500 if a database error happens", (done) => {
    chai
    .request(tools.service)
    .post("/uploads/test_image_delete.png")
    .set("Content-Type", "image/png")
    .send(tools.sample)
    .end((err, res) => {
        chai.expect(res).to.have.status(200);
        chai.expect(res.body).to.have.status("ok");

        let query = sinon.stub(tools.service.db, "query");

        query
        .withArgs("DELETE FROM images WHERE id = ?")
        .callsArgWithAsync(2, new Error("Fake"));

        query
        .callThrough();

        chai
        .request(tools.service)
```

```
            .delete("/uploads/test_image_delete.png")
            .end((err, res) => {
                chai.expect(res).to.have.status(500);

                query.restore();

                return done();
            });
        });
    });
```

What we're doing is uploading an image, but, before requesting to delete it, we create a `stub` on the `db.query` method. We then inform Sinon that when the `stub` is called with the first argument with `DELETE`, we want it to asynchronously call the third argument (counting starts at 0) with a fake error. For any other call, we want it to just pass through.

Then, after deleting the image, we check that we received an HTTP `500` error code and restore the `stub` to the original function, ensuring that the other tests pass.

We're able to test this because `mocha` runs tests in serial; otherwise, we would need to do some gymnastics to ensure that we wouldn't interfere with the other tests.

Now, open the previously created test file, `image-stats.js`, include Sinon on the top, and add the following test:

```
it("should return 500 if a database error happens", (done) => {
    let query = sinon.stub(tools.service.db, "query");

    query
    .withArgs("SELECT COUNT(*) total, SUM(size) size, MAX(date_used)
    last_used FROM images")
    .callsArgWithAsync(1, new Error("Fake"));

    query
    .callThrough();

    chai
    .request(tools.service)
    .get("/stats")
    .end((err, res) => {
        chai.expect(res).to.have.status(500);

        query.restore();

        return done();
    });
```

```
});
```

We're now over 97% coverage. Let's bend time and test our timer. Create a new test file called `image-delete-old.js`, and add the following content:

```
const chai = require("chai");
const sinon = require("sinon");
const http = require("chai-http");
const tools = require("../tools");

chai.use(http);

describe("Deleting older images", () => {
    let clock = sinon.useFakeTimers({ shouldAdvanceTime : true });

    it("should run every hour", (done) => {
        chai
        .request(tools.service)
        .get("/stats")
        .end((err, res) => {
            chai.expect(res).to.have.status(200);

            clock.tick(3600 * 1000);
            clock.restore();

            return done();
        });
    });
});
```

In this test, we're replacing the global timer functions (`setTimeout`and `setInterval`) with fake timers. We then make a simple call to statistics, and then advance time by one hour (the tick call), and then finish.

Now, run the tests and see the results:

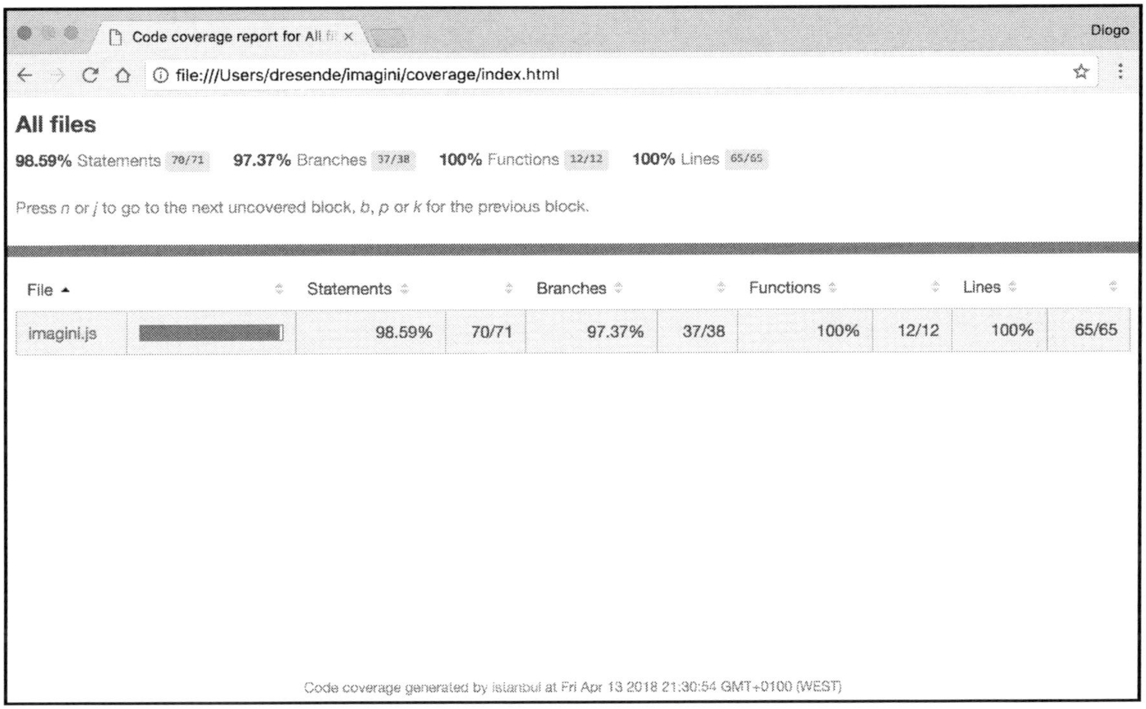

We now reach *100% coverage* on functions and lines. There's only one branch, with one statement missing. It's the possibility of a connection error:

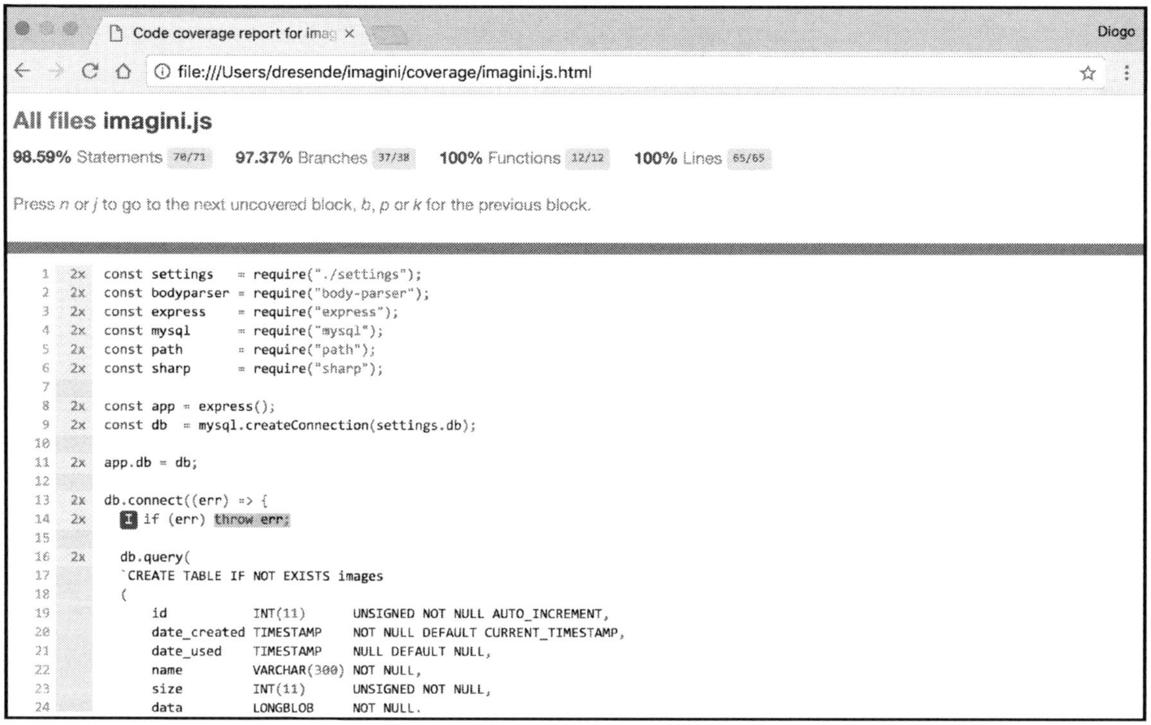


I'll leave it to you to figure it out how to mock that.

> Remember that if you successfully mock the `connect` method, you'll also need to handle the throw.

# Summary

Tests allow us to ensure a certain code quality level. It's very important to include tests from the very beginning, while the code is simple, to ensure that we keep tests updated and avoid regressions to the expected behavior.

It's very rewarding when we see that our code has a very high test coverage. This feeling forces you to keep that high mark and indirectly maintains good code quality.

Following on from this methodology of test coverage and continuous expected behavior, let's now look in the next chapter at how to deploy your code, be it for testing, staging, or production, while retaining the same expected behavior, no matter where you're deploying.

# 6
# Deploying Microservices

Now that we're able to test out our microservice, we can go a step further and test it in a controlled environment -- an environment that could, and should, be very similar to a production one.

Being able to develop and test a piece of code in an environment that is a replica of production ensures that you won't find yourself in a situation where your service works in your development environment, but not in production, and you don't know why.

This happens because your development environment is usually your laptop and you certainly use it for other activities. You eventually install tools and applications that change your environment. These tools may introduce you to libraries or interfaces that you then use in your microservice and forget to include those in production.

To ensure your different environments are the same, there are several alternative paths. Let's look at two of them, which are going to be virtual machines and containers. We'll then take the container path and deploy our microservice using Docker.

## Using virtual machines

One option is to use a virtual machine, a replica of production, that ensures that the environments are the same. There are a couple of drawbacks to this option:

- It's slow, as there's a complete virtualization guest operative system that you have to boot every time you want to develop
- It's resource consuming, as you need to store a complete base layout in your disk and you need to reserve RAM memory to start it

To make things worse, having a read-only machine with read-write code is not simple and will eventually make you frustrated. Virtual machines are the only option when you need an environment that you cannot have unless the entire machine is virtualized, for example, when you have a macOS laptop and you need a Windows environment.

Other than that, like when you're developing a microservice, the environment should be common to most operative systems. Node.js runs across platforms and, in this case, you're just exposing an HTTP interface.

# Using containers

Another option is to use a container. A container is an operative system-level virtualization mechanism, where you isolate an environment inside your operative system. You still need the space for a base layout, but there are container layouts under 5 MB.

The most common and widely used container environment is Docker, which uses Linux containers and cgroups to create a secure and isolated environment to run applications. What boosted Docker actually was was the centralized repository of base layouts, called Docker images, where people could define, build, and then share these images with others, so people wouldn't have to build them themselves. There are pre-built images for all major database services and programming languages, so it's easy to just choose one and run your microservice inside it in a couple of minutes.

To make things even better, there's a description file, called `Dockerfile`, which has all the instructions you need to build an image locally. This is a text file that you can store in your code repository that allows developers to build an image to run the environment.

Even more interesting is the fact that images can be built on top of other images. You can pick one, add your specifications, and publish it. This is one of the major advantages that drove Docker to be the most used container technology.

There are a couple of Docker idiosyncrasies that you must understand before using it:

- Docker images are like a read-only template for running your application. There are ways of saving changes to images, but usually you pick an image and run your application inside an environment that will get lost when the container is removed. This is actually great because it ensures that when you restart your environment, everything is back to a common environment and nothing is left over.
- A container should run only one command and nothing more. This command can, of course, spawn other commands, but the purpose of a container is not to run multiple commands in parallel. If you have a complex environment, each service should run in its own container. For example, if you have a database, the database service could run in one container and your application should run on another.
- Because an image is supposed to be read-only, you can mount or link folders from the outside of the container. These are called volumes and allow you to, for example, run a read-only MySQL image with the data folder mapped to a folder on your laptop, allowing you to avoid losing your data when you stop the container. Volumes can either be folders or files and they can also be mounted read-only from the inside of the container.
- A container runs in an isolated environment and you need to create network links from your interface ports to the container ports. There's also an option to create virtualized networks that work across hosts and give you the power to deploy more complex environments.

# Deploying using Docker

Before we start using Docker, you obviously need to install it. There are several installation channels to choose from. For many Linux distributions, there are packages available in their package manager. For Windows and macOS, you need to go to the Docker website and download the installer. This is actually the preferred one as the versions available from the package managers may not be up to date.

There are several graphical interfaces to manage Docker, but we'll keep it simple and just use the command-line interface. This gives you greater control and you get to know more of the internals of how everything is glued together.

So, let's open a console and type `docker info` to check whether everything is correct:

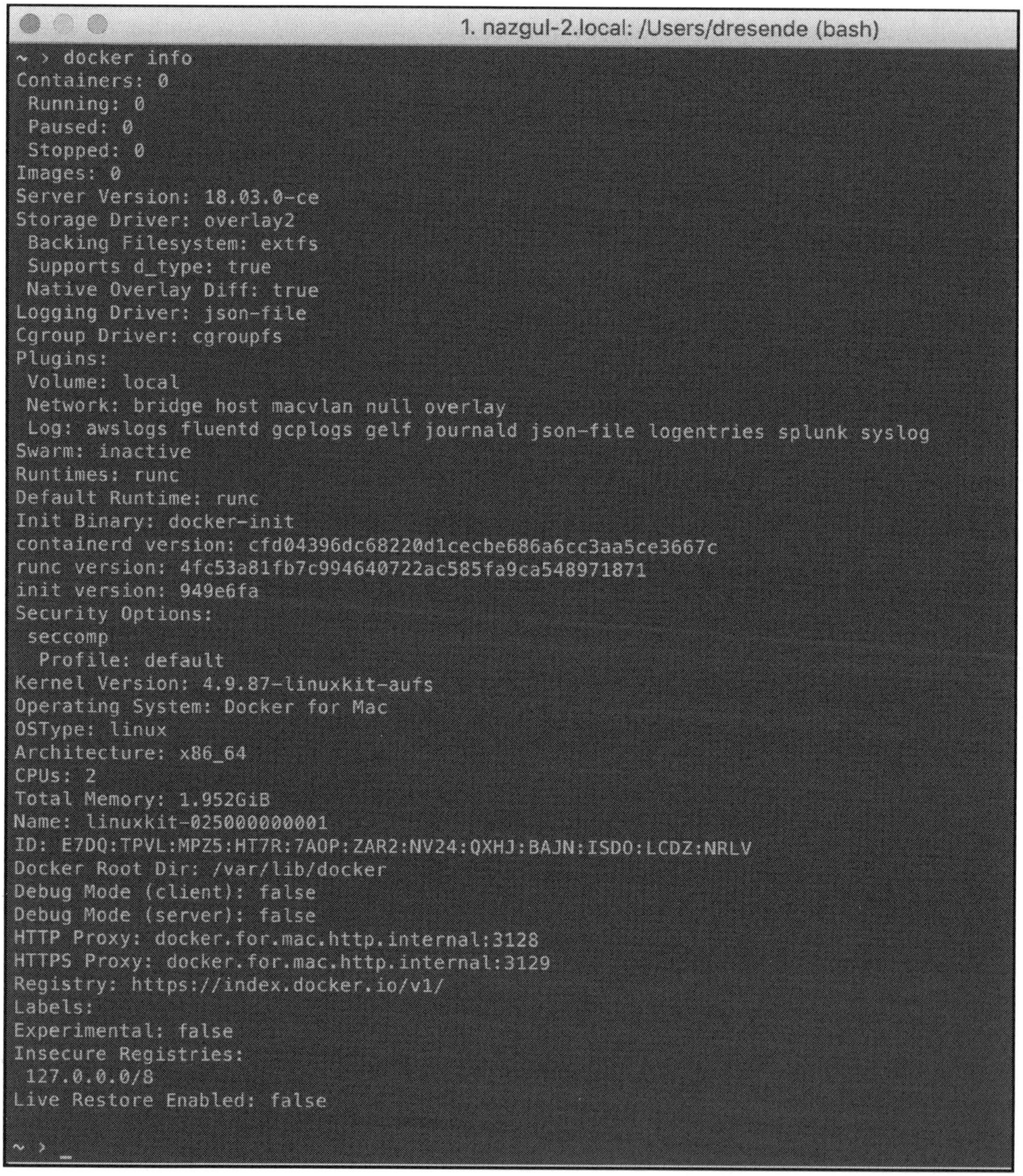

You can see that there are no containers or images running. There is other information, such as storage and network information. You may also figure out that Docker for Mac uses a virtual machine to enable Docker on a macOS laptop.

This means that the `docker` command is actually a proxy to the `docker` command inside that virtual machine. You don't have to worry about it, it will work just fine; you'll probably only notice some lag from time to time.

# Creating images

Before we deploy, we need to create an image for our service to run inside. Our service has no dependencies other than the ones defined on the top:

- `express` and `body-parser`: To handle our HTTP requests
- `mysql`: It enables us to use a MySQL database
- `sharp`: It enables us to manipulate images
- `path`: It is a core module to help working with directory paths

The core module is not a problem, and the first three are also not a problem since they're built completely in JavaScript. On the other hand, `sharp` is compiled, so our image needs to have at least a compiler.

To keep our image as slim as possible, we'll be using the Node.js Alpine version, which is a Node.js image based on Alpine Linux and it has a much smaller size than other distributions. You'll see what I mean in a moment. Let's download the image. Run the following:

```
docker pull node:alpine
```

If everything goes well, you should then have a new container image available, as the following screenshot shows:

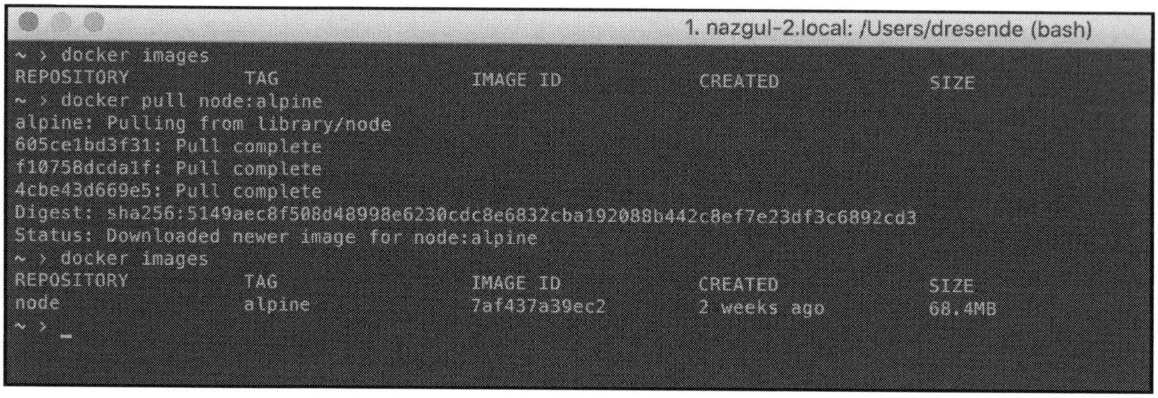


First, I just checked that we had no local images. Then, I requested that Docker pull the Alpine version of the Node.js official repository. Notice that I didn't specify the version, as I'm targeting the latest stable one. If you want a specific version, head to Docker Hub and search for Node official images.

We now have our image, but there are a couple of things to do before being able to start our microservice. First, we need to create our own image. What we downloaded is just a base image, which doesn't have our code. We need to add our code and dependencies. To do that, we need to create a `Dockerfile`.

# Defining a Dockerfile

This is a file specification with instructions for Docker to create an image. The instructions are clear and allow you to share that file on several servers so that Docker builds the image.

Our `Dockerfile` will have three parts:

- The header, which indicates the base image and author
- The instructions to build the image
- The instructions to run the image

There are many more instructions that we'll probably not cover. To get to know `Dockerfile` better, head over and read the documentation. This is an introduction that will actually help you go a long way. Here's our first `Dockerfile`:

```
FROM node:alpine
MAINTAINER Diogo Resende

ADD imagini /opt/app

WORKDIR /opt/app
RUN npm i

CMD [ "node", "/opt/app/imagini" ]
```

The empty lines were added for clarity only. The first two instructions define the base image (`FROM`) and the author (`MAINTAINER`). The next three add our `imagini` folder to the `/opt/app` folder inside the image. Then, we change directory to that folder and run `npm i` to install the required dependencies. Finally, the last instruction indicates how to run the image later on.

Save this to a file called `Dockerfile` and place it in an empty folder. Then, grab our microservice and place it inside a folder called `imagini`, inside this newly created folder:

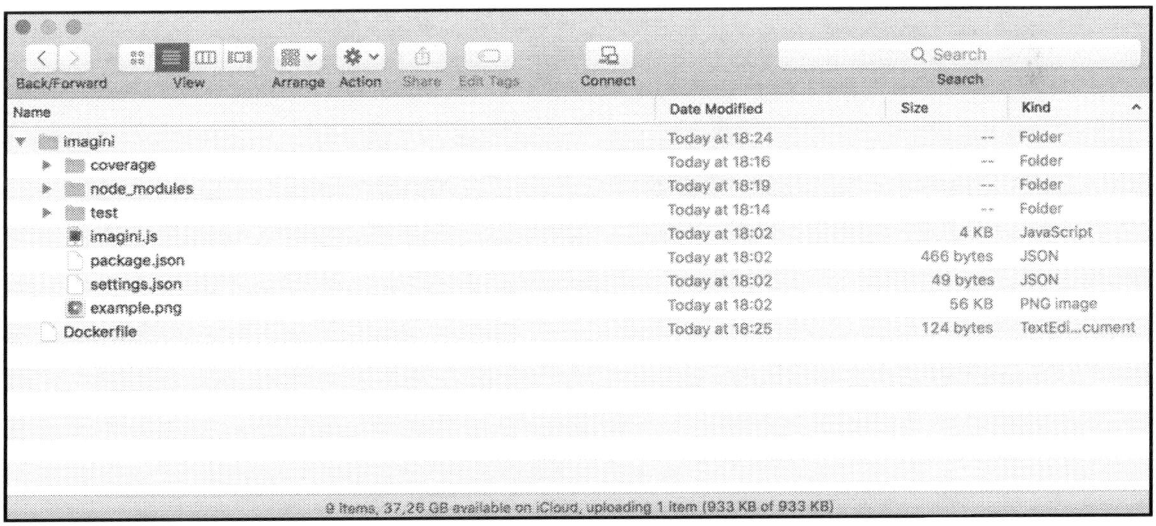

We can now try to build our image using the `docker build` command. Let's create the image, assign the name of our service, and indicate an initial version:

```
> docker build -t imagini:0.0.1 .
Sending build context to Docker daemon   43.4MB
Step 1/6 : FROM node:alpine
 ---> 7af437a39ec2
Step 2/6 : MAINTAINER Diogo Resende
 ---> Running in 009093d8c9d4
Removing intermediate container 009093d8c9d4
 ---> cdbe5185faf4
Step 3/6 : ADD imagini /opt/app
 ---> 9c062473535a
Step 4/6 : WORKDIR /opt/app
Removing intermediate container d734af3adba8
 ---> e39bdbfaf5ae
Step 5/6 : RUN npm i
 ---> Running in 3437fc2f74c9
npm notice created a lockfile as package-lock.json. You should commit this file.
npm WARN imagini@1.0.0 No description
npm WARN imagini@1.0.0 No repository field.

up to date in 0.613s
Removing intermediate container 3437fc2f74c9
 ---> 0b50046161f3
Step 6/6 : CMD [ "node", "/opt/app/imagini" ]
 ---> Running in 8d5786ea6ecf
Removing intermediate container 8d5786ea6ecf
 ---> a3e21d6fd379
Successfully built a3e21d6fd379
Successfully tagged imagini:0.0.1
> _
```

Let's check the list of images available:

```
> docker images
REPOSITORY          TAG                 IMAGE ID            CREATED             SIZE
imagini             0.0.1               a3e21d6fd379        22 seconds ago      110MB
node                alpine              7af437a39ec2        2 weeks ago         68.4MB
> _
```

Let's just start a container and see what happens. To do that, we use the `docker run` command and pass our image name and version. We don't need to specify what to run inside the image since we defined that on the `Dockerfile`, but we could change that:

```
1. base (bash)
> docker run imagini:0.0.1
internal/modules/cjs/loader.js:683
  return process.dlopen(module, path.toNamespacedPath(filename));
                 ^

Error: Error loading shared library /opt/app/node_modules/sharp/build/Release/sharp.node: Exec format error
    at Object.Module._extensions..node (internal/modules/cjs/loader.js:683:18)
    at Module.load (internal/modules/cjs/loader.js:566:32)
    at tryModuleLoad (internal/modules/cjs/loader.js:506:12)
    at Function.Module._load (internal/modules/cjs/loader.js:498:3)
    at Module.require (internal/modules/cjs/loader.js:598:17)
    at require (internal/modules/cjs/helpers.js:11:18)
    at Object.<anonymous> (/opt/app/node_modules/sharp/lib/constructor.js:10:15)
    at Module._compile (internal/modules/cjs/loader.js:654:30)
    at Object.Module._extensions..js (internal/modules/cjs/loader.js:665:10)
    at Module.load (internal/modules/cjs/loader.js:566:32)
> _
```

Well, I expected that to happen. I did this deliberately so that you never forget that dependencies should be held carefully. Just as you don't push dependencies to a git repository, you don't push dependencies to an image. Instead, you should install them inside the image. That's one of the reasons the image built so quickly because NPM assumed that everything was all right.

Let's change our `Dockerfile` and create a new image, but before that, let's go inside the image and look at it. To do that, let's run the container specifying another command to execute. We also need to specify a few more parameters, namely `-i` and `-t` for an interactive terminal. Let's run a console (we don't have bash in Alpine, so we'll stick with `sh`):

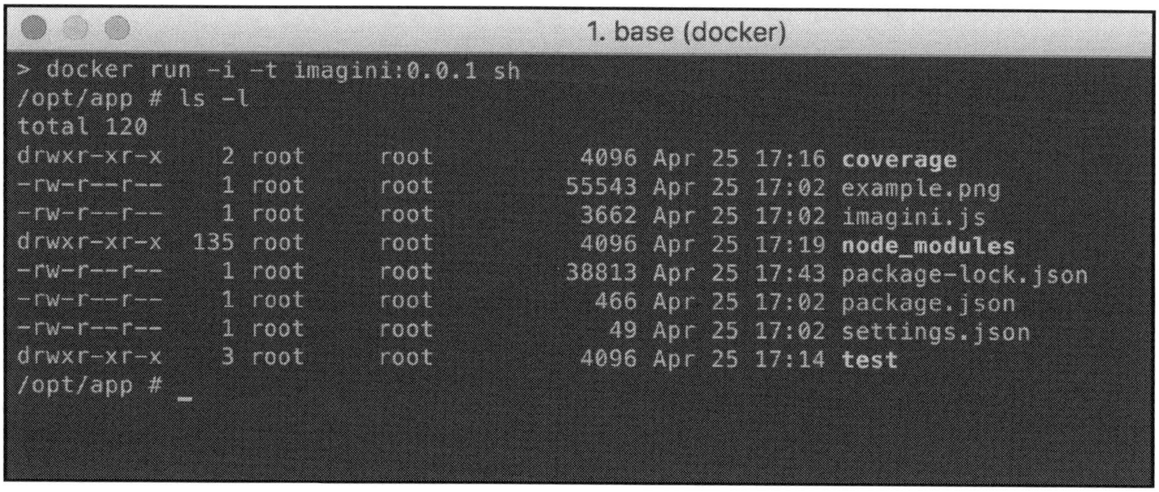


This is what's inside the `/opt/app` folder inside the image. There are a couple of things we don't need to add to, like the test and coverage folders. We can just stick to the microservice, the dependencies file, and the settings file:

```
FROM node:alpine
MAINTAINER Diogo Resende

ADD imagini/imagini.js /opt/app/imagini.js
ADD imagini/package.json /opt/app/package.json
ADD imagini/settings.json /opt/app/settings.json

WORKDIR /opt/app
RUN npm i

CMD [ "node", "/opt/app/imagini" ]
```

The `ADD` instruction can be used with files, not just folders. This will keep our image as slim as possible. Let's run it and assign a new version:

That looks better, despite the error. NPM tried to install `sharp` but our image is so slim it doesn't have Python installed. Actually, it's not only Python that will be missing; you'll find there are no build tools for you to compile anything. If you really need a very slim image, you can this way and see what other dependencies you'll need.

For demonstration purposes, let's switch our base image to the standard version:

```
FROM node
MAINTAINER Diogo Resende

ADD imagini/imagini.js /opt/app/imagini.js
ADD imagini/package.json /opt/app/package.json
ADD imagini/settings.json /opt/app/settings.json
```

```
WORKDIR /opt/app
RUN npm i

CMD [ "node", "/opt/app/imagini" ]
```

See how we change the first line to just `node`. If you now run the `docker build` command, Docker will download the standard image and build our image in a single operation:

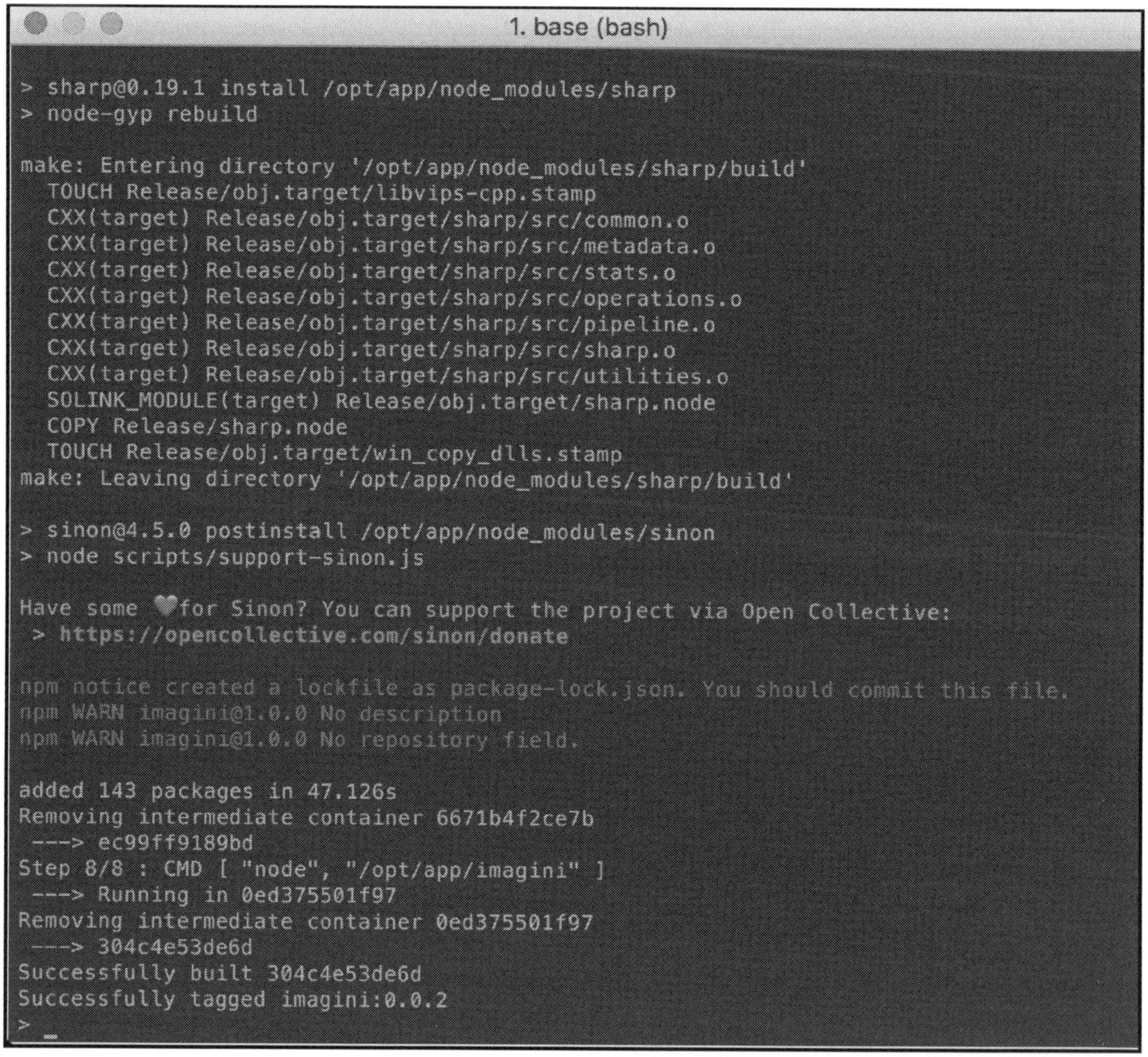

As we can see, NPM now compiled our sharp dependency.

> Note that if you only rely on simple dependencies, you can stick with the Alpine version.

Let's try to run our container again:

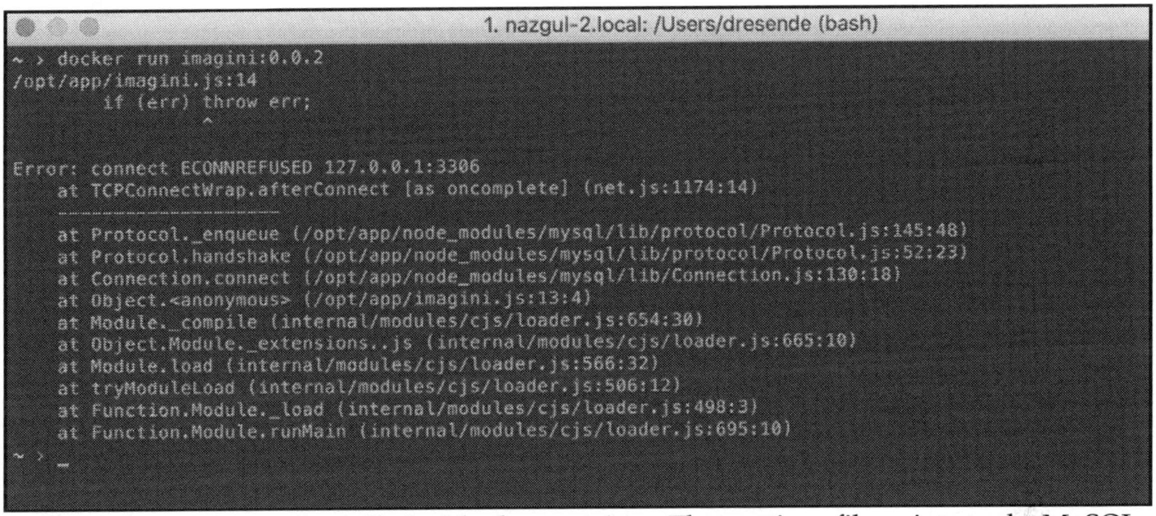


Well, we forgot our settings file inside the container. That settings file points to the MySQL server on the local address, which is actually wrong because the container has its own interface.

To make our image free of passwords and a little bit usable, we need to have our `settings` file outside the image, and every time we want to run the image, we indicate the `settings` file we want to use. This enables you to have different deployments with different settings sharing the same base image.

But, because of how Docker mounts, we need to have the file there already, even if it's empty, to avoid Docker mounting as a directory. So, let's move the `settings` file to the parent folder, and create an empty `settings` file where it was before. You should end up with a structure similar to the following screenshot:

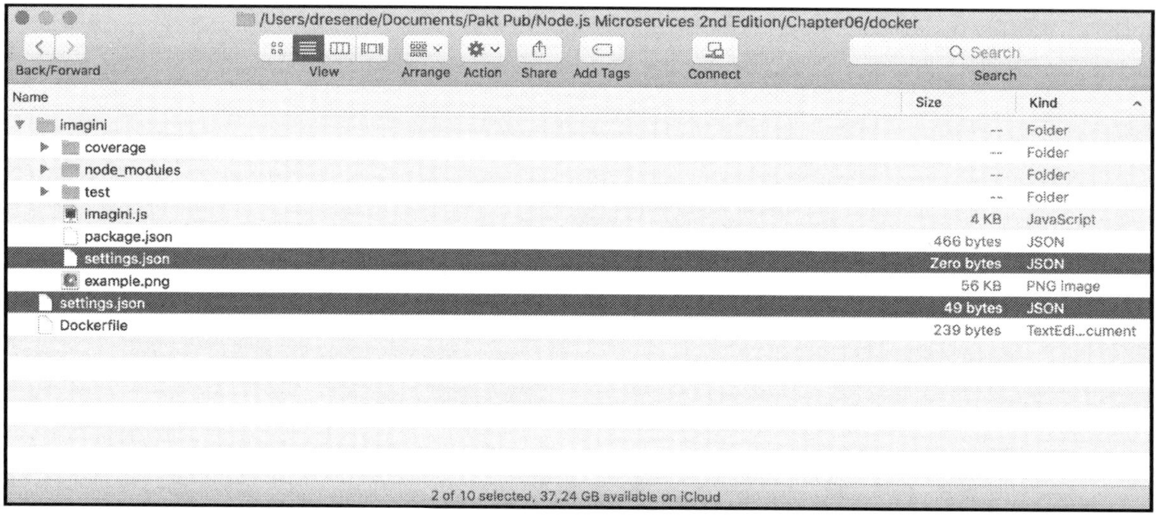


So, we should keep the same image instructions, but now with an empty settings file:

```
FROM node
MAINTAINER Diogo Resende

ADD imagini/imagini.js /opt/app/imagini.js
ADD imagini/package.json /opt/app/package.json
ADD imagini/settings.json /opt/app/settings.json

WORKDIR /opt/app
RUN npm i

CMD [ "node", "/opt/app/imagini" ]
```

Now, let's create a new version:

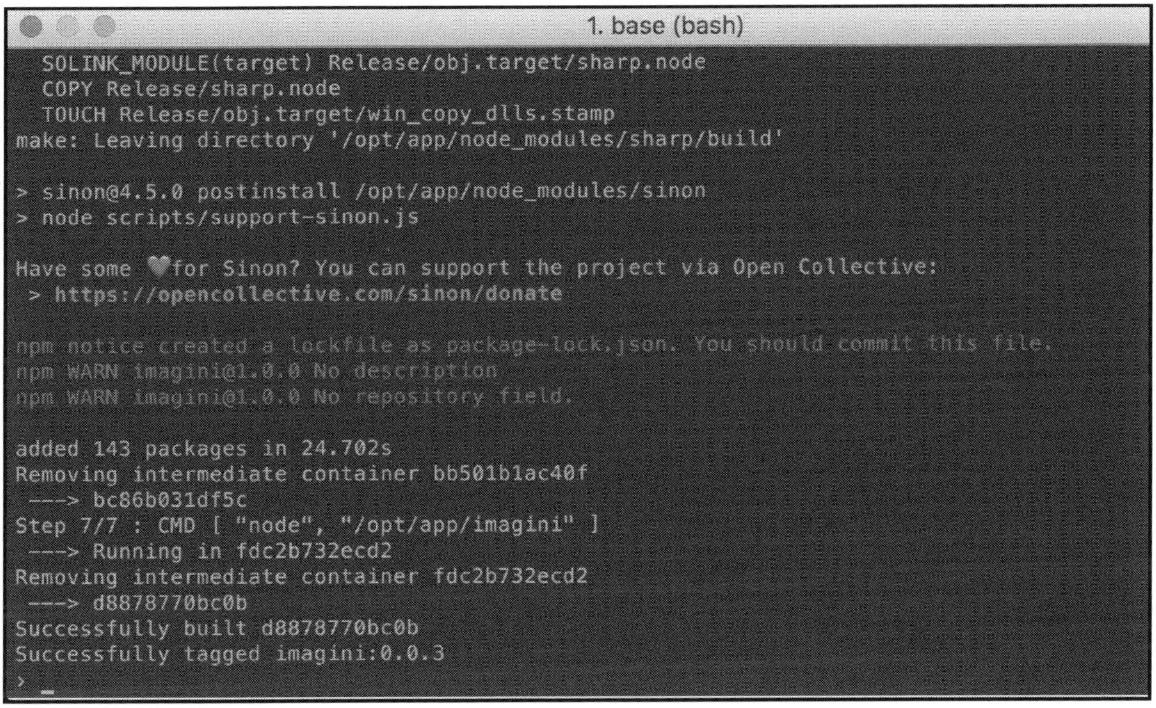


There are two things you should know about building an image:

- Since we haven't published the image to the public, and we're still testing, we could overwrite our image version and avoid incrementing the revision value. We're doing so just for you to see how the community usually adds new versions.
- If you read the log lines of the build, you'll notice some lines that contain `Using cache`, which indicate that Docker found that instruction step in a previous build and is using that instead of rebuilding. If we had the `ADD` instructions after the dependency installation, you would probably see that installation using cache and taking much less time to build.

To run our container with our image and our settings attached, we need to use the `-v`, which stands for volume, and allows us to mount a folder or a file from our local filesystem to the container filesystem. Assuming we're in a console on our root folder from the preceding screenshot, we should run the following command:

```
docker run -v $(pwd)/settings.json:/opt/app/settings.json imagini:0.0.3
```

Docker enforces us to use full paths, so I just added another bash interpolation to get the current working directory (`pwd`). Let's run it:

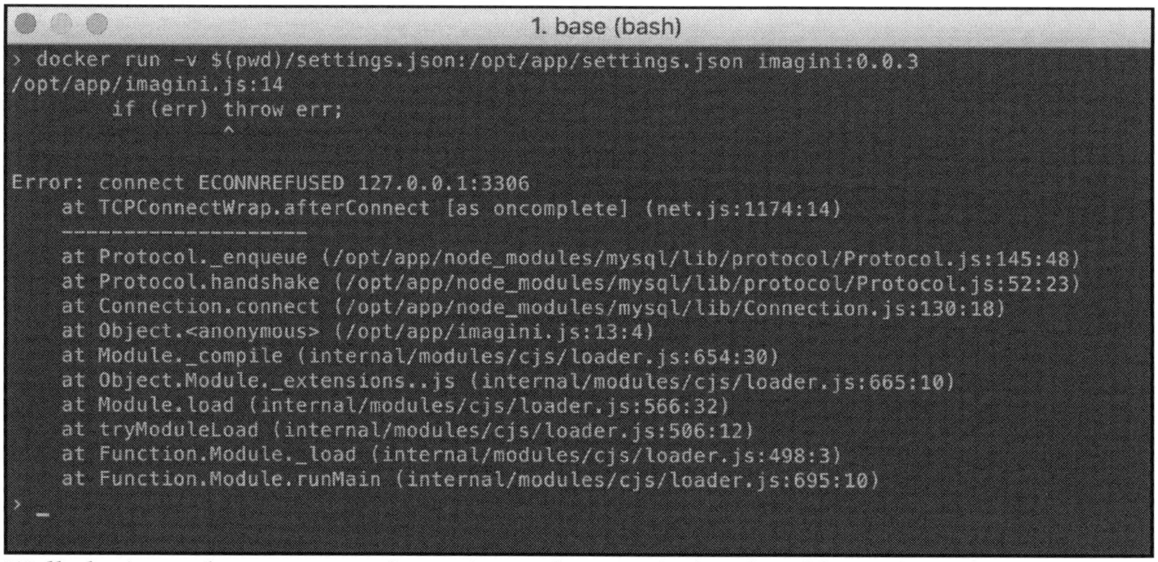


Well, that's another property of containers; they run isolated and have their own network interface. That interface is attached to a virtual switch created by Docker, which has no outside connectivity unless you say so.

We're using localhost as the database server hostname, which, in this case, points to the container itself. We need to change this to the local address of our system. Since our local system may have a changing IP address, Docker has a special DNS address, which is `host.docker.internal`, that points to our host.

I'm changing my `settings` file to something like the following lines. Change it according to your previous configuration:

```
{
    "db": "mysql://root:root@host.docker.internal/imagini"
}
```

If we run it again, we should be able to finally start our container:

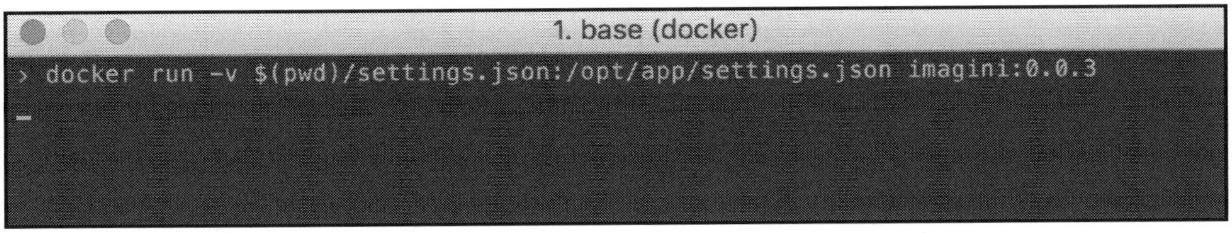


## Managing containers

You may notice that the container is running in the foreground, which is not very useful because your console will be blocked until the service ends. Because our service is supposed to never stop, we should try running the service in the background. If you open another console and list the running container processes, you'll see that it's running:

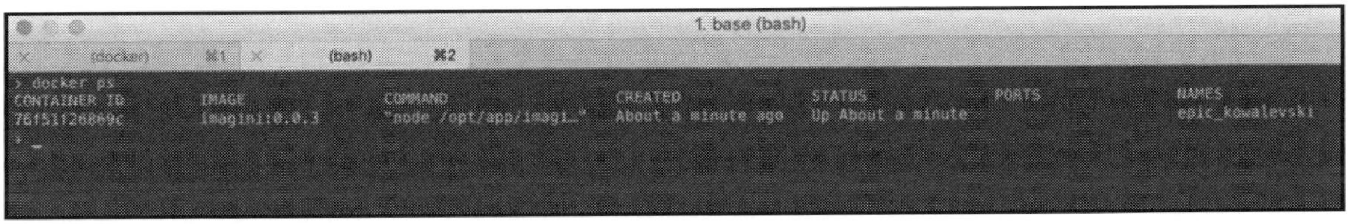


You can see the `CONTAINER ID`, which, along with the container name, can be used to perform several actions such as restarting and removing containers, as well as the image, and its status and uptime.

Let's stop our container and measure the time to stop it. You'll notice that it won't stop immediately:

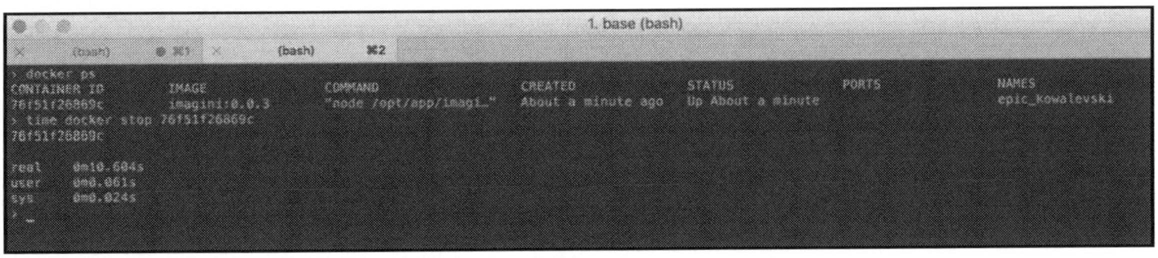


It took *10* seconds, which is a lot if you just made a change and want to restart it. This is because our service is ignoring any environment signals.

When trying to stop a container, Docker sends a `SIGTERM` signal and waits *10* seconds for it to stop. If it doesn't, Docker then sends a `SIGKILL`, which will escalate to the kernel and which, in turn, will immediately stop our service and the container will stop.

We can change this behavior and try to stop gracefully. Change our `app.listen` line to something along the following lines:

```
app.listen(3000, () => {
    console.log("ready");
});

process.on("SIGTERM", () => {
    db.end(() => {
        process.exit(0);
    });
});
```

This adds a `ready` line when starting the container and tries to close both the database connection and the HTTP server when receiving a `SIGTERM`. Let's build our image again (because we changed our service), this time as version `0.0.4`, and run it again:

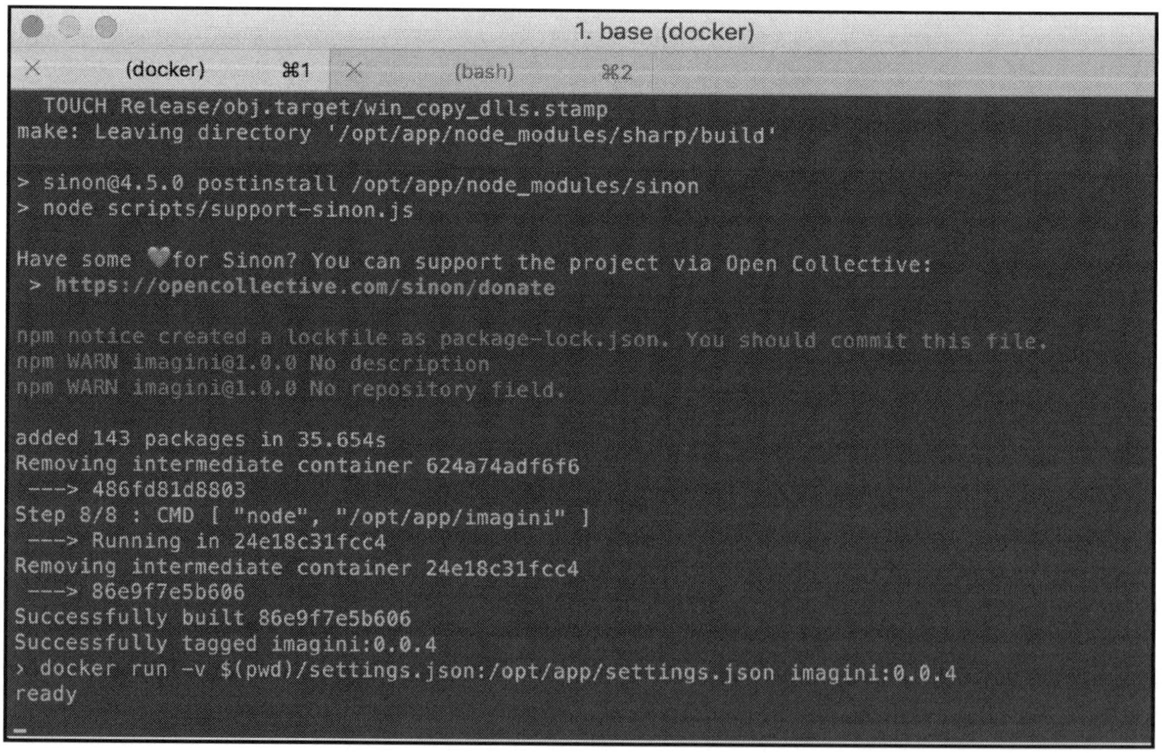

Head to the other console and try to stop the container again:

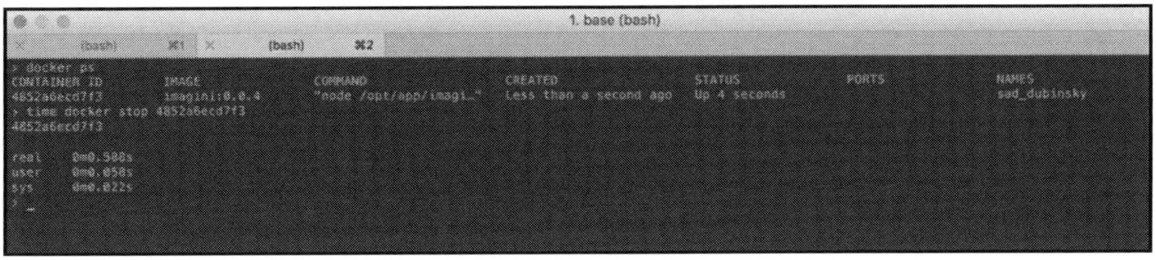


That was way faster. It could be even faster, but it's better to stop gracefully. We're just stopping the database connection, but you could also stop Express from accepting more connections and then wait some seconds while it handles the active connections before closing gracefully.

We can now continue to improve on our deployment by changing our container to run in the background instead of just blocking our console. This way, we don't need two consoles to deploy and manage our container. To run this in the background, we use the `-d` options, which enables detached mode.

Our updated command is now:

```
docker run -d -v $(pwd)/settings.json:/opt/app/settings.json imagini:0.0.4
```

If you try it out, Docker will inform you of the full `CONTAINER ID` and turn you back to the console:

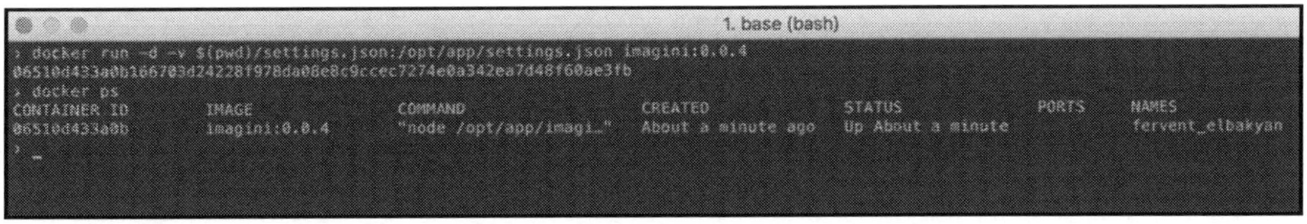


If you check the running containers, you'll see our container, with the short ID (which corresponds to the first *12* characters) and some more information. Something that is actually important and is empty is the `PORTS` column, which indicates the container ports that are linked to ports on our host.

That column being empty means you have no access to the container other than through Docker itself, which is actually useless. We can't access our HTTP interface.

We need to change our image again and expose a port. To do that, we must use the `EXPOSE` instruction and pass the port we want to expose. Our service listens on port `3000`, so we need to expose it:

```
FROM node
MAINTAINER Diogo Resende

ADD imagini/imagini.js /opt/app/imagini.js
ADD imagini/package.json /opt/app/package.json
ADD imagini/settings.json /opt/app/settings.json

WORKDIR /opt/app
RUN npm i

EXPOSE 3000

CMD [ "node", "/opt/app/imagini" ]
```

You can now build the image, but before using our new version, we need to change our run command. Just because we're exposing a port does not mean the person using our image wants those ports exposed. We need to specify what host ports we want to connect to the container ports. To accomplish that, we're going to use `-p`, which allows us to configure incoming ports. The syntax is similar to the previous `-v` but for ports:

```
docker run -d -p 80:3000 -v $(pwd)/settings.json:/opt/app/settings.json
imagini:0.0.5
```

In this case, we're exposing local port `80` to port `3000` of the container:

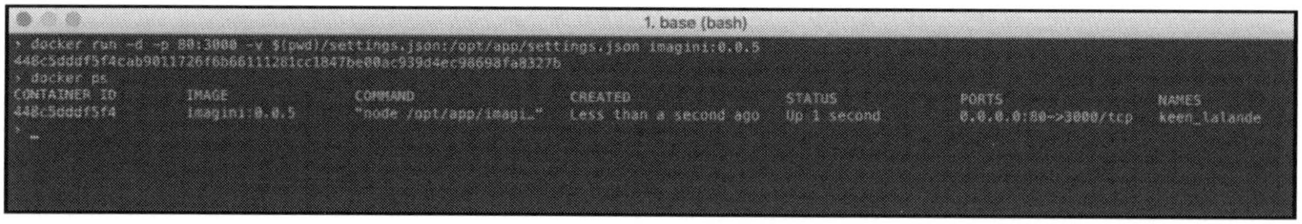


You can see that the container is running and that the address `0.0.0.0:80` (all our addresses at port `80`) point to the container port `3000`. We should be able to try it out and see if it's running correctly. Open a web browser and point it to the `stats` path:

We can now manage our container in a similar fashion to the service management on the current operative systems. You can start, stop, and restart it:

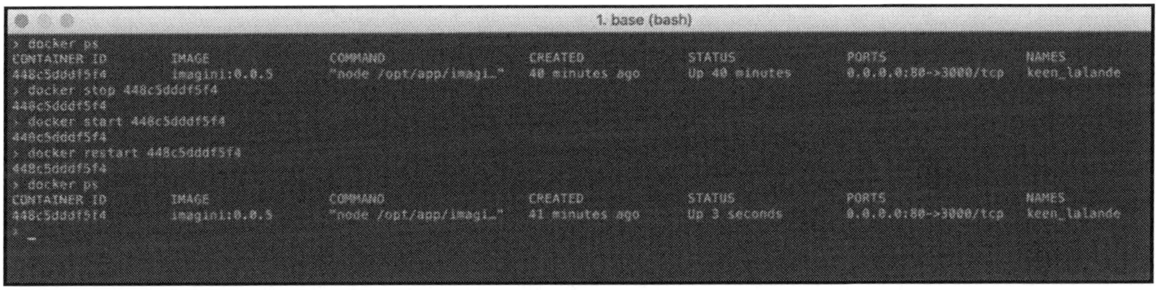


Every time you change one or more container's states, Docker returns the container IDs that have changed state. This allows you to, for example, to script actions and pipe the output of one command to the next.

# Cleaning containers

Containers, when stopped, are not removed by default. Let's stop our container and list the currently running containers:

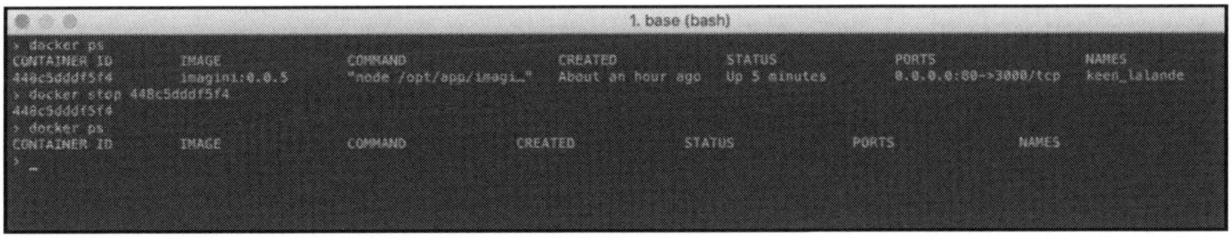

Nothing running now. So, where are they? Well, the container is stopped and, while it's not using your processor and memory right now, it's using space. And it's not just that container, either; it's all the containers we ran before.

To see all containers, use the `docker ps -a` command:

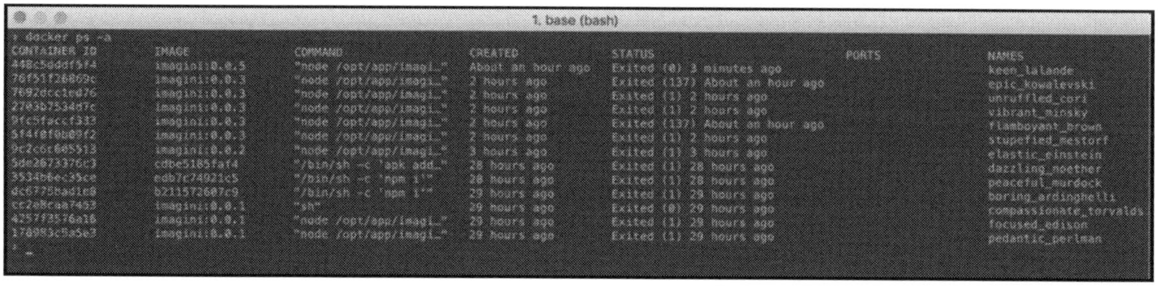


Wow, that's a lot of containers. We can see that we have containers for practically all the images we built, and that means the images are also available and using our disk space:

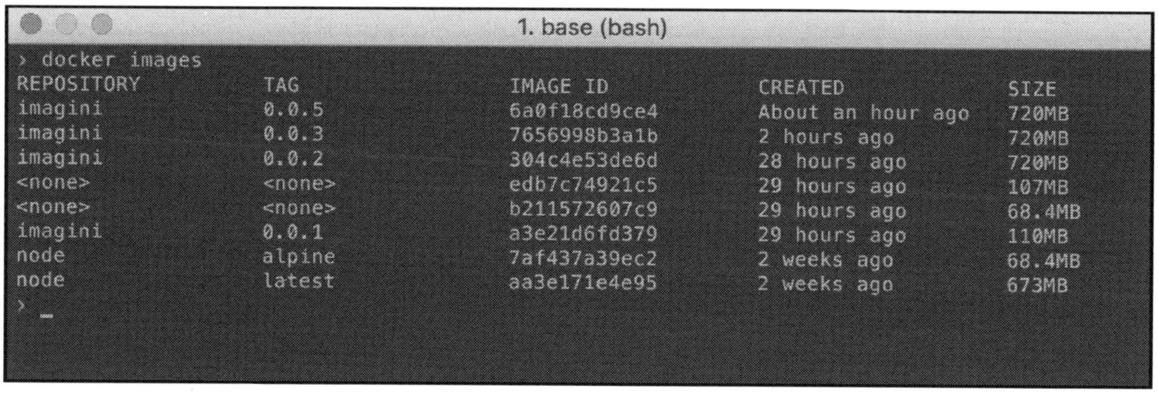

In the case of images, we can see the size they are occupying. Since we don't need them any more, as they were non-functioning experiences, we can remove them. To do that, we need to use the `rmi` command and pass the image IDs, or the name and version (the `TAG` column), as parameters.

But before removing the images, we need to remove the containers, or Docker will deny removing them as they're being used. As a dirty workaround, we can use a useful parameter from `docker ps`, which returns only the container IDs and passes those to the remove command. Docker won't remove any running containers, so it's safe to run.

Start our latest container (`docker start`) and then list the containers (`docker ps`):

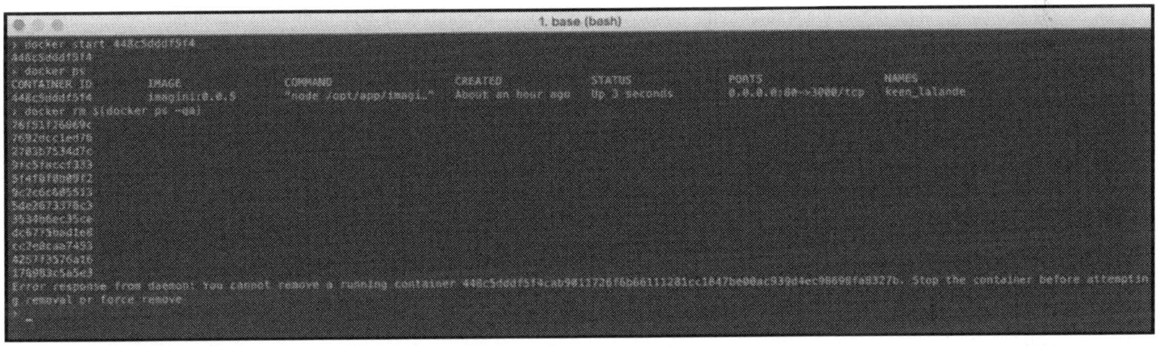


As described earlier, Docker will indicate each of the container IDs as it changes state (in this case, it removes them). The final error is our running container, which, as I explained earlier, Docker won't allow to be removed as it's running.

We can now do the exact same thing with the images. Those quickly occupy a lot of space and, when developing, it's easy to make changes to images and forget about non-functional images that we left behind:

The last two errors are expected. First, one of the images is from our running container. Second, the other image is the base image of our image.

You may also notice that there are way more lines than images from the previous list. They're not images; they're the layers of each image (remember the cached steps when building?). Docker stores images in layers, which means that a similar image may have layers in common, and, in turn, some disk space may be saved.

You should now have something like this:

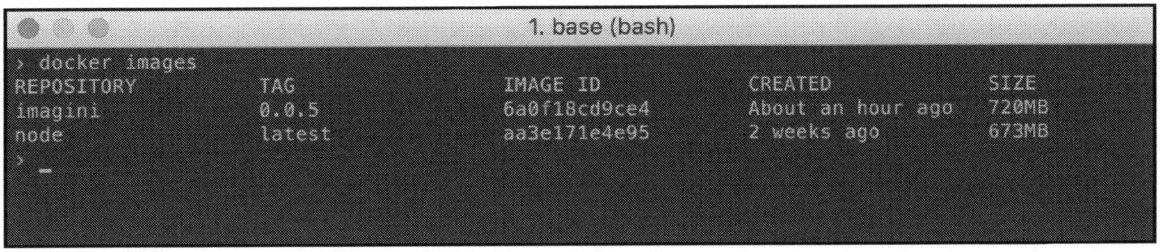


That looks much better; no more garbage from our previous development iterations. We can now move on and focus on another dependency of our service that we still rely on and is not on a container yet.

# Deploying MySQL

We now have our service running inside a container, with all its dependencies properly defined and installed inside. But we still need a database server and we're still relying on MySQL, which is on our host.

A single container was not meant to run many services at once. Similar to microservices, a container should do only one job. But containers can communicate with the outside, so this means they can communicate with each other.

We can deploy an additional container to run our database server. There are official MySQL container images, so it's as easy as a simple command to start running a database. But first, we need to take care of two things:

- The database server needs to store the database content on the host, or we'll lose the data when we remove our deployment
- Our initial container needs to know where the database server is, and this changes dynamically on each deploy, so we need to have a way of knowing this

Docker has a way of knowing what host port was associated to a container port. This is by using Docker port, and its syntax is simple; you indicate the container to get all port assignments or you indicate a specific port to get only that one:

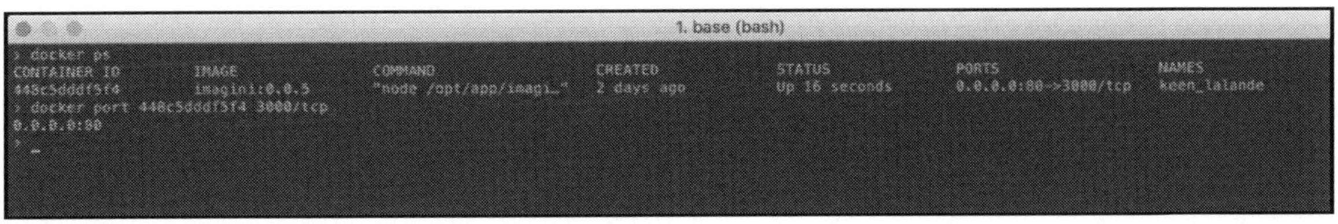

In the case of our original container, we know that we are associated with port `80`, and that's what the command indicates. In a production environment, you'll have several containers competing for the same ports. Docker has networks to help us isolate container groups easily and allow us to create custom networks of containers.

Let's just dive in and create a network for our service using `docker network`:

That's it. We have a network named imagini with the ID returned by the command. We can get a list of current Docker networks with the given command:

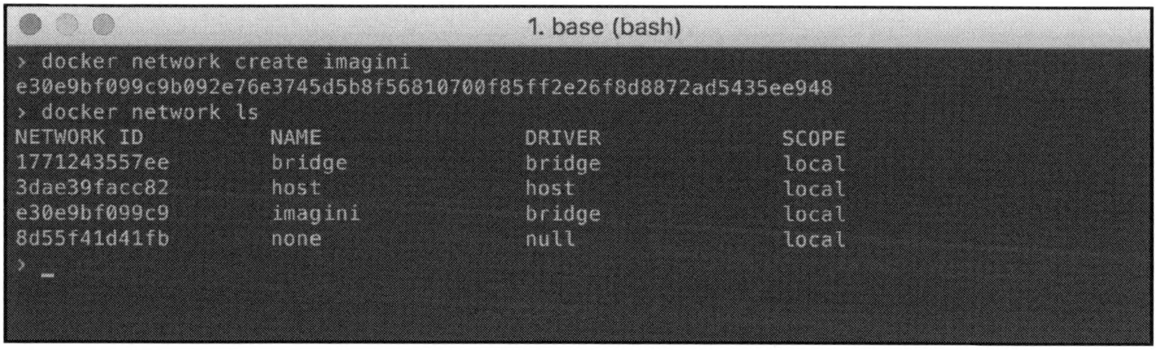


There are now four networks, one of which is the one we created. The other three are:

- **Bridge**: The default one for new containers
- **Host**: If you want to attach a container directly to the host network
- **None**: If you don't want a container to have a network at all

Now, let's remove our current deployment and make a few changes. First, let's remove and stop the container:

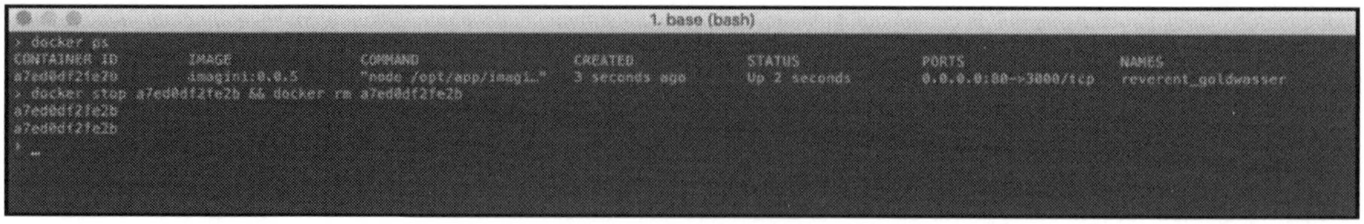

Second, let's deploy our new database server container on our new network. We'll use the official container image. We'll also create a `mysql` folder to store the database and anything else the server needs to operate between deployments without losing information.

I'll also introduce another option from Docker, which enables us to name a container. You might have noticed some funny names when you previously listed containers. We can avoid those random names and use our own:

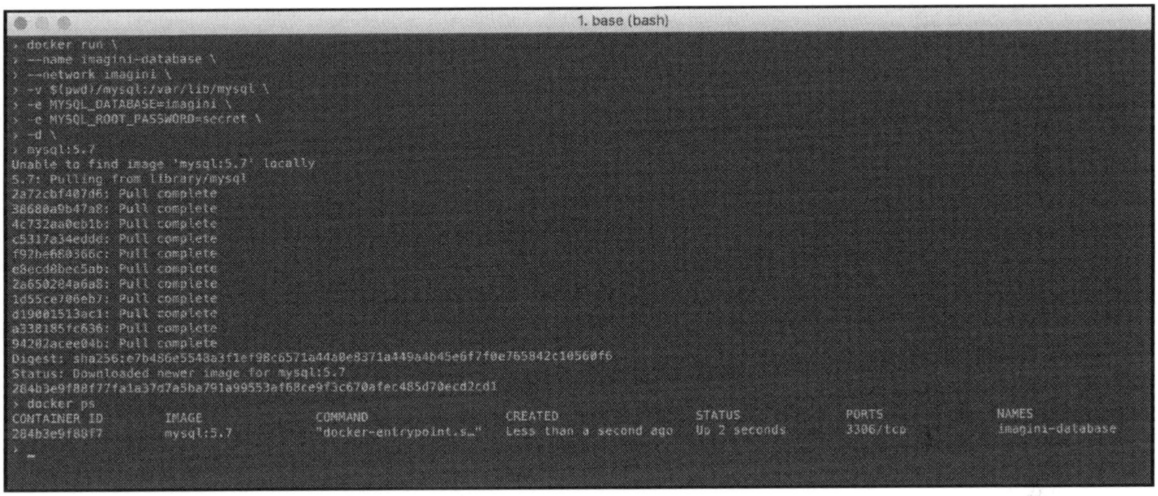


Docker automatically downloaded the latest MySQL version. We now have a database server called imagini-database running on our imagini network. Notice we didn't assign any of its ports to the host because we actually don't need to access it outside our custom network.

You can also see that I defined the database to be created initially, as well as the root password. We're specifying image `mysql:5.7`, which points to the latest revision of MySQL version 5.7.

> **TIP:** Always remember to use specific versions with containers. Never use the latest version as this may change between development and production, and you need to be certain of the versions you're running.

This is specific to this image and you can read more about it on the official Docker Hub page. We can confirm that the server is up and running using our local folder by just looking at its content:

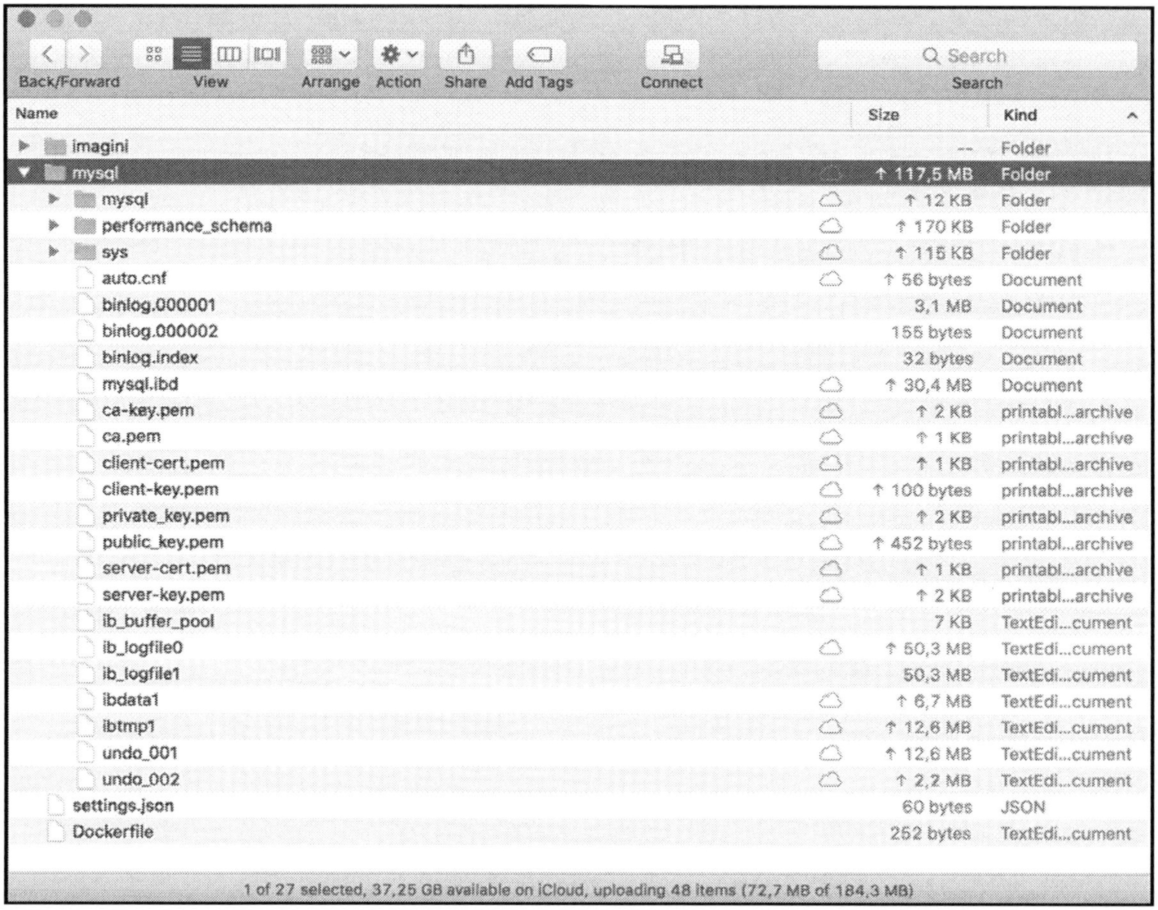

Before starting our main service container, we need to make just a few more changes. First, we need to change the `settings` file to point the configuration to our new database location.

One advantage of using a proper name for a container is that you can use that name just like it was a DNS name. We can confirm that our database server is reachable from another container we created on the same network.

Let's create a container to test this:

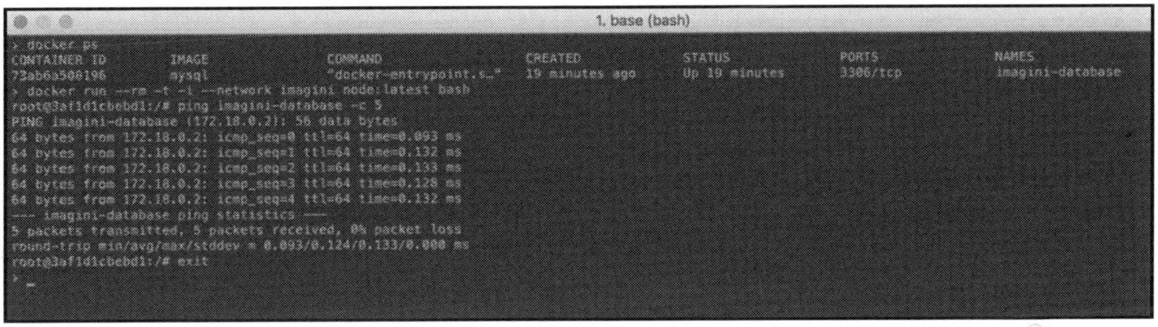


We just used an image that's already available and started the container with a bash console. We tried to ping our database server and it works. We then exited the container. Because we used the `--rm` command, the container is removed after the first stop.

Now, let's remove the `settings` file to point to the new location and to also change the root password:

```
{
    "db": "mysql://root:secret@imagini-database/imagini"
}
```

We can now deploy our container again. We'll just give this container a name, too:

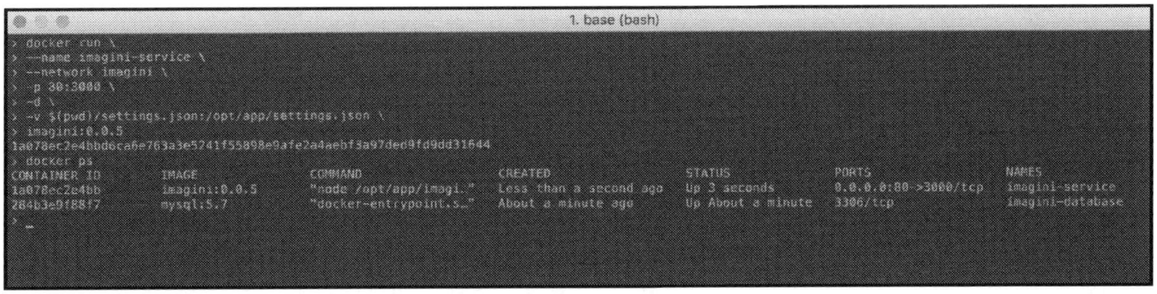

We can see that our service is running correctly, with connections to the new database server by just hitting the stats address and seeing that there are no images there, contrary to our previous version that we used to test this:

# Using Docker Compose

Wouldn't it be great if we could define all the containers we need for our service to work in a simple interface? Welcome to Docker Compose. This is an orchestration tool that enables us to do what we just did in a simpler way and, most importantly, in a distributed way.

We can define how our containers interact with each other and what they need in a simple file structure, and then we can transfer that to another host and just run Docker Compose, where it will deploy it all for us.

Docker Compose uses a YAML file, which is a human-readable data serialization language. It's easier to read and understand and at the same time, allows us to make complex configurations.

Let's migrate our two containers to this layout. The only step we need right now is to create a file called `docker-compose.yml`. Inside, we define our two containers, the network, the ports, and the volumes. Here's an example:

```
version: "3"
networks:
    imagini:
services:
    database:
        image: mysql:5.7
        networks:
```

```
        - imagini
        volumes:
        - ${PWD}/mysql:/var/lib/mysql
        environment:
            MYSQL_DATABASE: imagini
            MYSQL_ROOT_PASSWORD: secret
    service:
        image: imagini:0.0.5
        networks:
        - imagini
        volumes:
        - ${PWD}/settings.json:/opt/app/settings.json
        ports:
        - "80:3000"
        restart: on-failure
```

Let's do this step by step:

```
version: "3"
```

First, we indicate that we're defining our services in Docker Compose version 3 syntax and features:

```
services:
    database:
        image: mysql:5.7
        networks:
        - imagini
        volumes:
        - ${PWD}/mysql:/var/lib/mysql
        environment:
            MYSQL_DATABASE: imagini
            MYSQL_ROOT_PASSWORD: secret
```

Then, we define our database using image `mysql:5.7`, attach it to the `imagini` network, and then use the host `mysql` folder to store the database and define the two environment variables. This is exactly what we did in the previous command:

```
    service:
        image: imagini:0.0.5
        networks:
        - imagini
        volumes:
        - ${PWD}/settings.json:/opt/app/settings.json
        ports:
        - "80:3000"
        restart: on-failure
```

Finally, we do the same for our service, indicating the name, the `imagini:0.0.5` image, the network, the local `settings` file, and the port assignment. But there's something more, which is very important, and this is the restart policy. Because our database service does not load instantly, our service will most probably fail at first and stop. Docker will then lift it up again and then the database server will be ready, and everything will be up and running.

As we're composing a Docker Compose project, we can avoid using `imagini` on the service names, and so we need to once again change our `settings` file to something like this:

```
{
    "db": "mysql://root:secret@database/imagini"
}
```

We can now try it out by running `docker-compose up`. This will deploy our containers under the `imagini` project, which is the folder name:

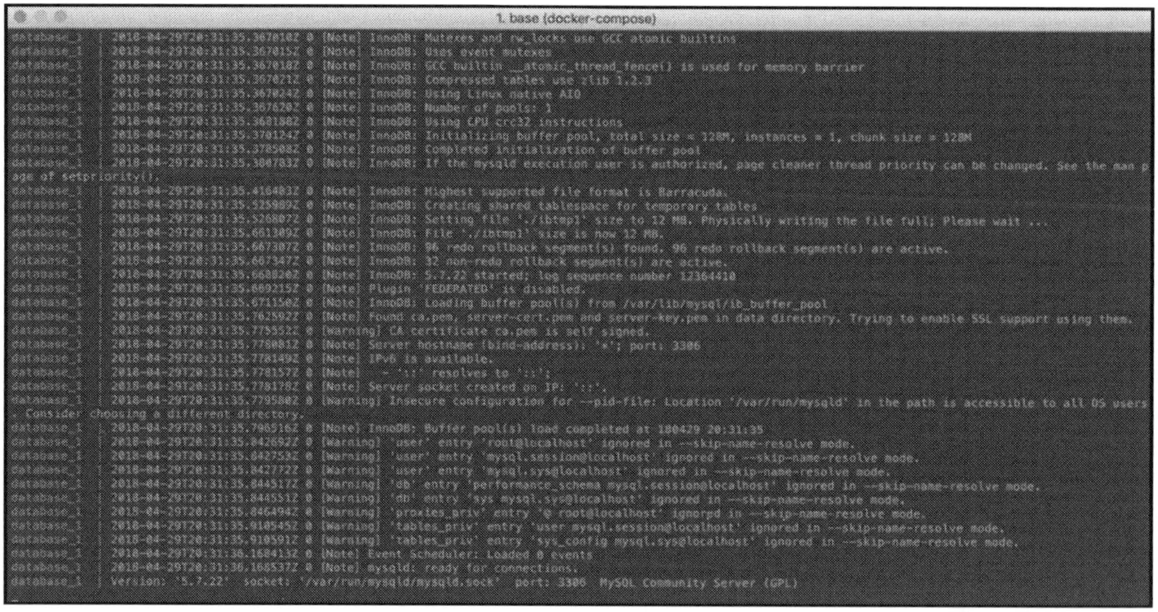


This will start the containers, but you'll notice that they didn't start detached. To do that, hit *Ctrl* + C to stop the containers:

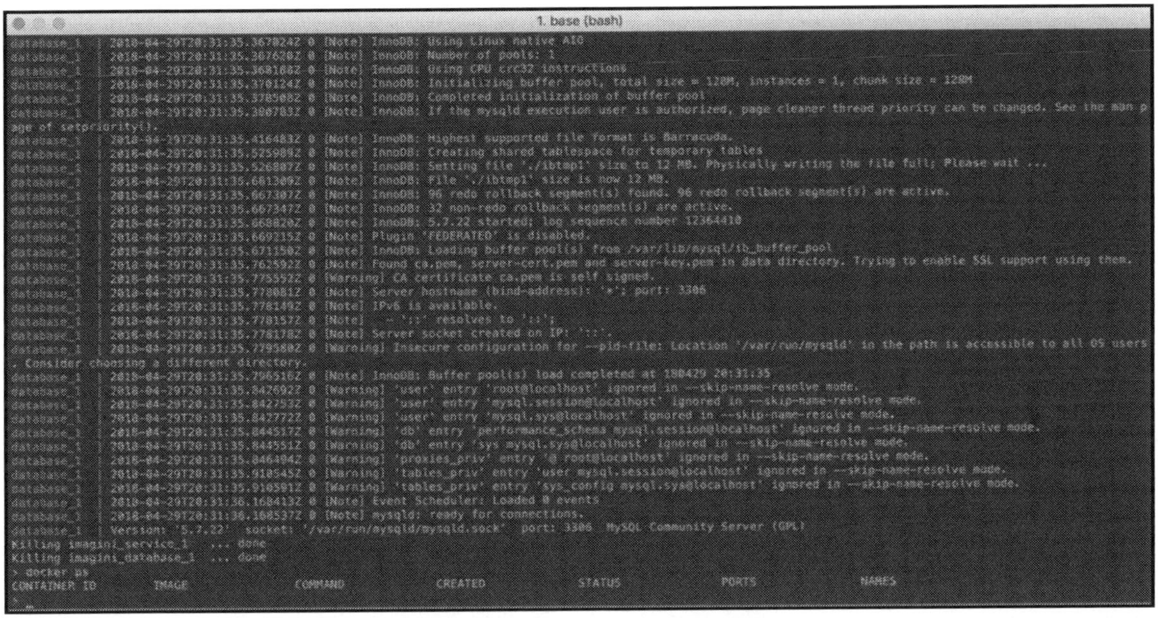

Now, let's run this again properly by using the `-d` parameter:

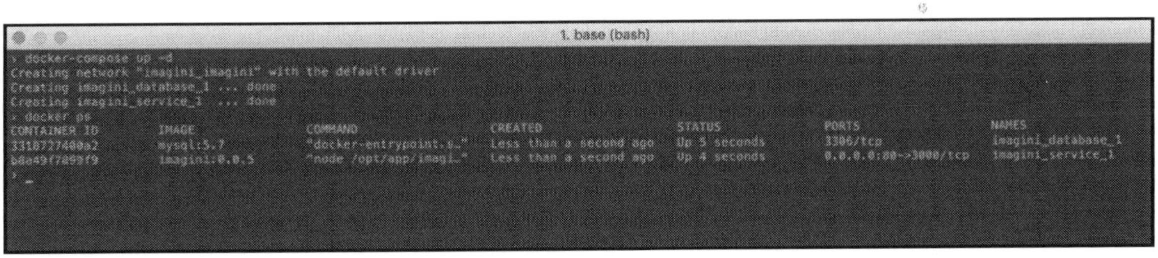

Great! We can start our service with everything it needs in a single command. You could just share this folder with a co-worker and he or she could have the service up and running in a matter of seconds.

# Mastering Docker Compose

Now that we have our services up and running, we need some more information to manage these services together, and more specifically, to control and monitor its state.

To look at a specific service, you just need its original name. In our case, there's only the service and database to choose from. Let's look at our service:

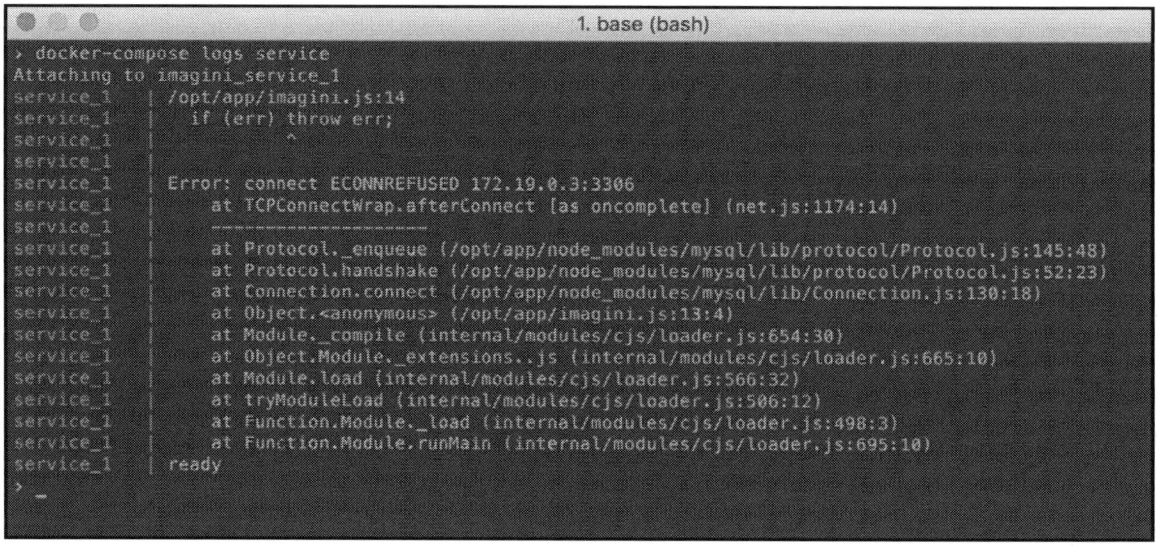


As I told you previously, the service will probably fail at first and then Docker will restart it before it finally becomes ready. We can see that in this log. If you want to see the logs of all of the services mixed together by date, you can just omit the service name.

Another important command to memorize is used to list the services that are running. This is the same as for Docker, but it only lists the ones from our configuration:

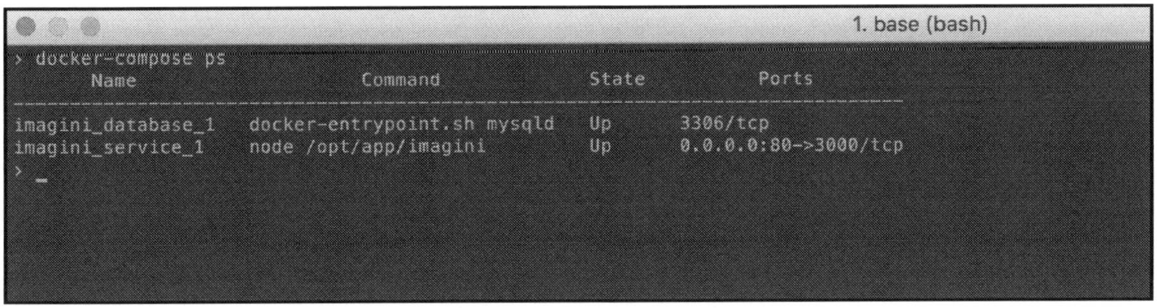


Finally, to stop and remove everything from our deployment, we can run `docker-compose down`. This will first stop the containers and then remove them completely. This ensures that we don't leave any garbage behind:

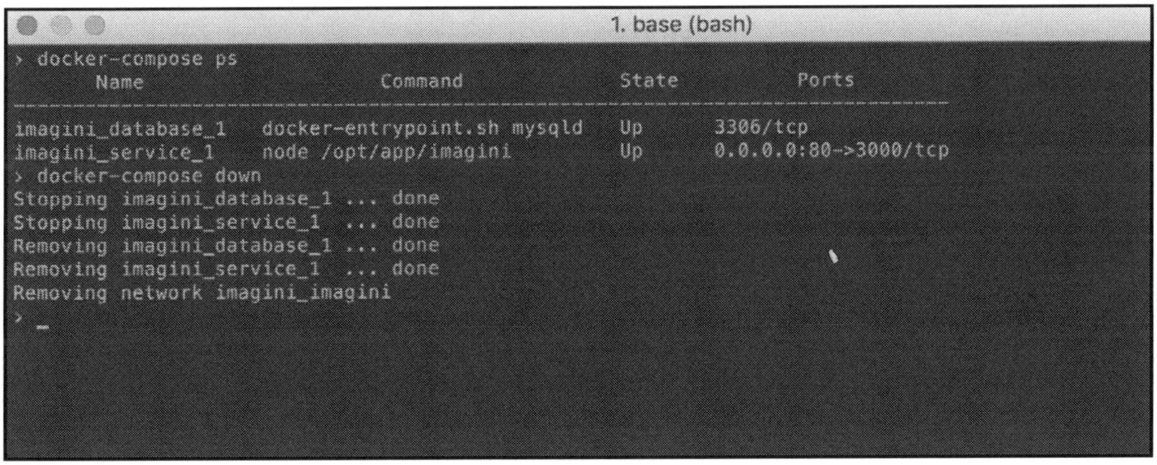

# Summary

We now have a tool to deploy our service in a consistent way across hosts. We're now able to orchestrate other services, like we did with the database server, in order to have as many dependencies as possible in a controllable state. This ensures that the transition from development to deployment is as smooth as possible.

Let's follow this path and see what else Docker and other tools can do to help us deploy our service. In the following chapter, we'll see how we can take advantage of Docker tools to scale our service by creating replicas. We will see how to distribute our service parts and monitor its state.

# 7
# Scaling, Sharding, and Replicating

We're now able to deploy our microservice almost anywhere with minimal effort. Let's take a look at how we can leverage this and scale our microservice to handle an intensive usage environment.

Before starting, let's see what each of the topics covered in this chapter mean. We'll start from the end. Replicating is the easiest one, and it means to replicate, or copy, your service. Basically, replicating a microservice means it is running multiple instances at the same time, usually on different locations.

Sharding is similar, but with a different purpose. When replicating, each replica can do the full service job. When sharing, each shard can do only part of the service and you need all shards to have your service online. This is a common practice on very large database servers.

Scaling is a common meaning to both replicating and sharding, as both of them allow you to scale your service. Scaling is the process of growing your microservice to handle more load or failure events.

Being able to deploy consistently is important. This gives you better confidence when developing and testing because you have a consistent base layout for your service to run on. Not just that, it also allows you to deploy to multiple locations faster.

This enables you to replicate your service across multiple locations. Replicating a microservice not only allows you to develop in parallel, enabling every developer to have an instance running on its own computer, but it also gives you several advantages in a production environment, such as:

- **Distribution**: When your service is spread across geographic locations, being closer to every customer, reducing latency from every location
- **Fault tolerance**: When your service has an outage or usage peak on specific instances and you're able to route customers to instances being less used
- **Zero downtime**: When your service has enough replicas that even if a substantial part of your infrastructure is affected by an external incident, your service is still generally available

Distributing your service geographically puts it near your customers. Usually, you want to distribute it in different continents to avoid inter-continental latency. If your service is broadly used, you may need to have several instances per continent, perhaps one in every country.

Fault tolerance and zero downtime are related to each other. Being able to operate when instances of your service are faulty gives users the perception of no downtime. This is also very important when you want to make an upgrade to your service without bringing all the instances down. You may phase-in each instance to upgrade while routing your customers to other instances, keeping your global service online in a virtual sense.

In this chapter, we'll see how we can use Docker tools to replicate our service using Swarm. Later on, we'll see how easy it is to migrate our microservice to Kubernetes locally.

# Scaling your network

Scaling a service by itself is not sufficient. Just because you create instances of your service doesn't mean they'll just work together. There are two important steps to enable a service scale:

- Making instances work together
- Making instances reachable

Instances don't need to communicate with each other, but an instance must be able to work without interfering with the others. An instance should be able to handle a request from a client that was previously served by another instance. In our case, this means an instance must be able to manipulate an image that was uploaded by another instance. This ensures that if an instance goes offline, others can take over its clients.

Instances need to be reachable, which means you need to be able to point your customers to the nearest instances that are live and operating normally. This means you need to be able to monitor your instances and distribute your customers to the online instances.

Services are usually reachable by a DNS address. You need to be able to control address name resolution, preferably by geography, to point your customers to the best instances. You can point directly to instances or have proxies monitor a couple of nearby instances and proxy the traffic based on policies.

There are many different kinds of policies. For example, if the proxy is able to monitor how busy an instance is, it can direct new requests to the less busier instances. Or, it can just distribute requests using a round-robin approach.

There's also another common policy that routes traffic according to the IP address. For example, if you have three instances, you use the remainder of the remainder of the devision of the IP address (as a 4-byte integer) by three to choose the instance (possible values would be *0*, *1*, and *2*).

# Replicating our microservice

Picking up from the previous chapter, we ended with a Docker Compose configuration that starts our two containers, one with our microservice and the other with the database server that stores our data:

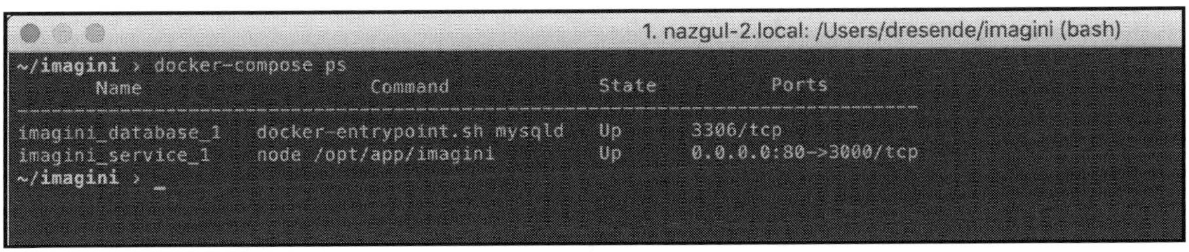

You may have noticed when deploying with Docker Compose that our two containers have a `_1` suffix on the name. This is because Docker Compose supports replicating our instance using Docker swarm.

Docker swarm is another component of the Docker engine that enables you to create a cluster of hosts to run your microservice instances while orchestrating all of this using a simple tool from any of the hosts in your cluster.

Swarm is the name Docker uses to reference a cluster of nodes. Let's create a new Swarm using our host as the manager of the swarm. Since I'm using Docker for Mac, I need to create another Docker virtual machine to be able to simulate a couple of hosts. If you're using a Linux machine, you can just test this with two different hosts.

If you're using macOS like me, follow these steps. We'll use Docker machine to create two virtual machines to run as Docker hosts. First, let's see what machines we have created by typing:

```
docker-machine ls
```

You should see an output as follows:

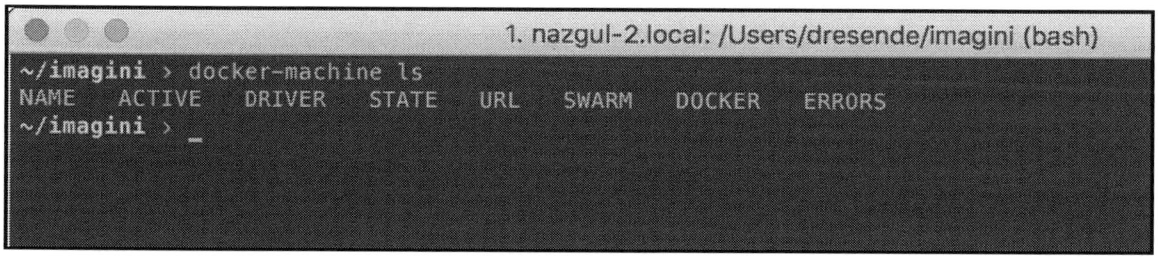


No machines. Let's create a manager node. To do that, run:

```
docker-machine create manager
```

Docker will create the new machine, assign a new IP address, and prepare the Docker engine inside the machine:

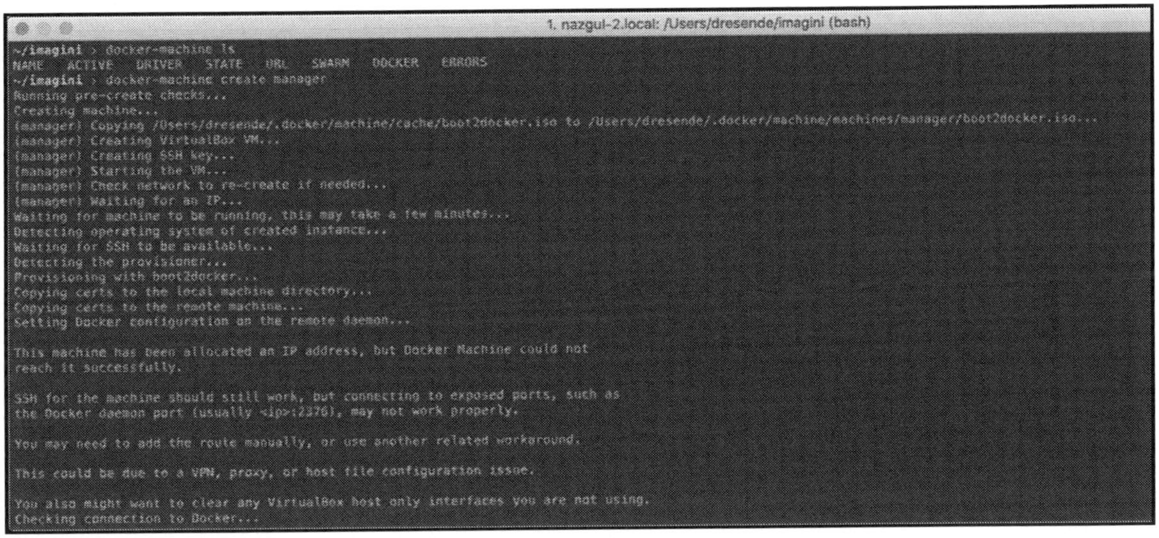


Now, run the following command:

```
docker-machine ls
```

You'll see that our new machine is ready to be used. You can see the IP address of the machine in the URL column:

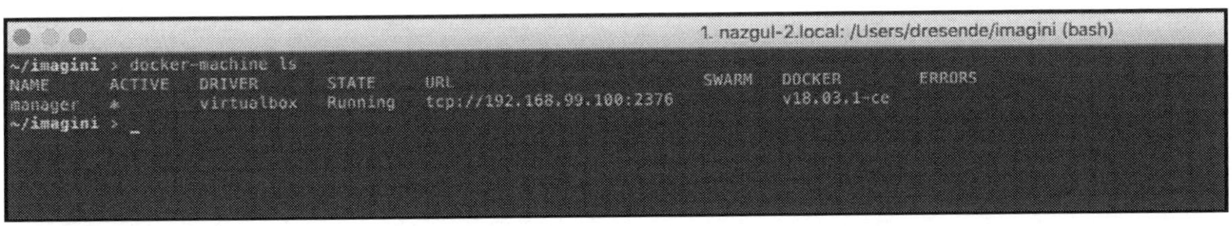


The Docker engine has an exposed API that enables you to manage a Docker host using the Docker commands from another host. The URL column indicates the API address to manage that specific host.

We can use a little helper command to configure our Docker command to manage this new host. Just type the following command:

```
docker-machine env manager
```

And follow the instructions:

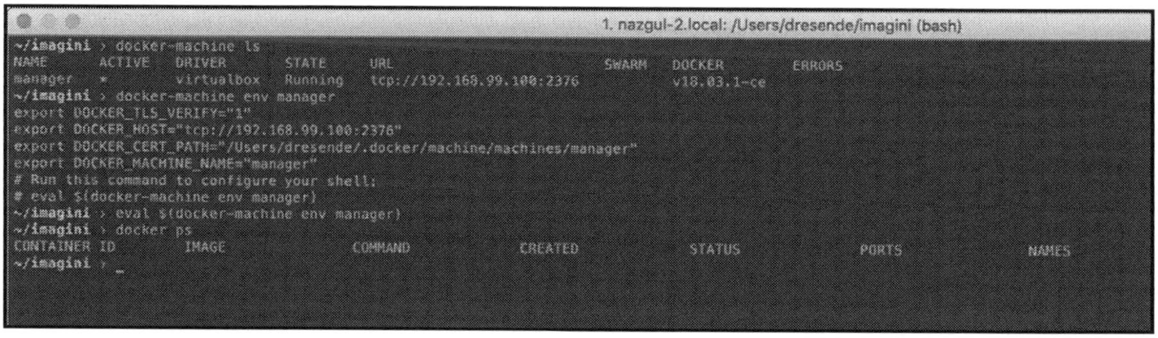


Now, let's keeps this Terminal untouched and open a new tab so that we can create a second machine. Let's call it replica, which will hold a second instance of our microservice:

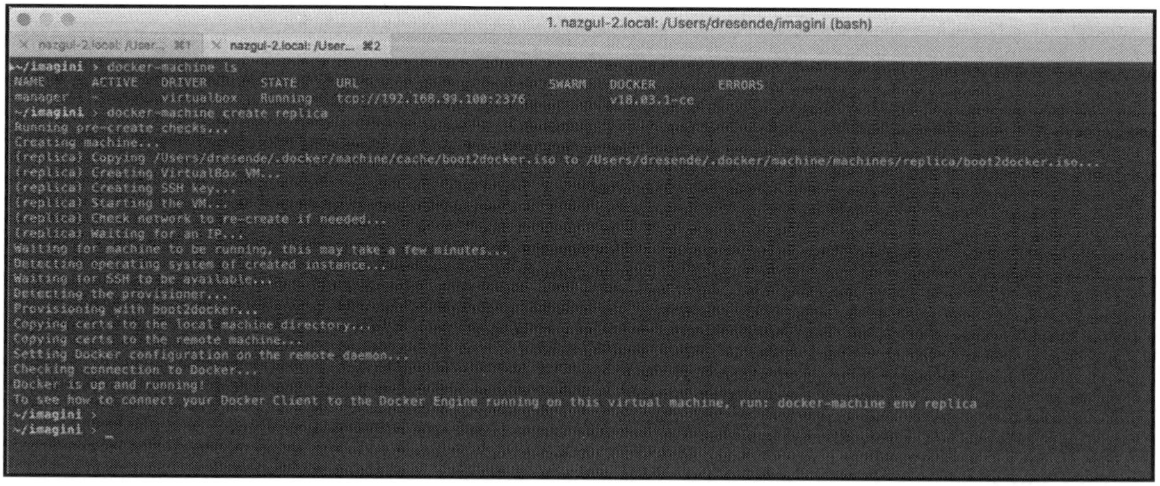

We can check that our new virtual machine is ready and running by checking the following output once more:

```
docker-machine ls
```

Both of our machines should be ready and running:

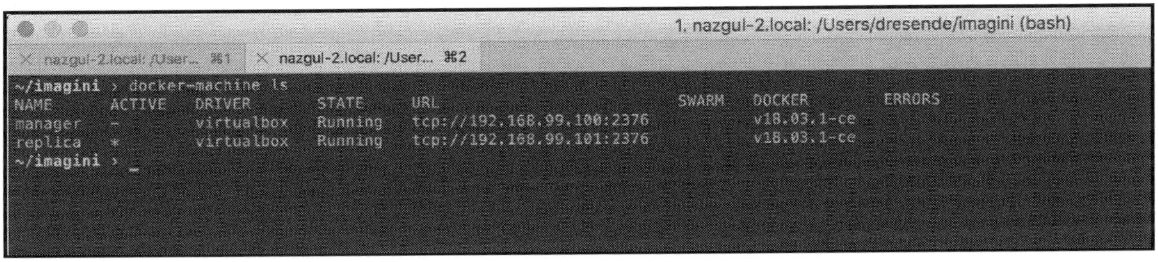


Using our initial tab, where we have the manager host, let's create a swarm. We're indicating the advertisement address because our virtual machines have more addresses, but we want the advertisement to be done on the network shown previously, so we're pointing out a specific IP address at the end:

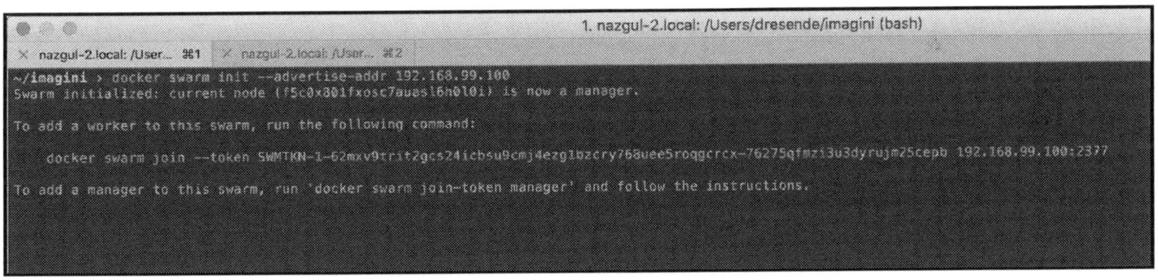


Docker created our swarm and gave us instructions on how to make other hosts join the swarm using a kind of secret token. If you want to add more nodes later on, save that command.

Now, head to the second tab and let's change our Docker command to manage our replica host and then join the swarm:

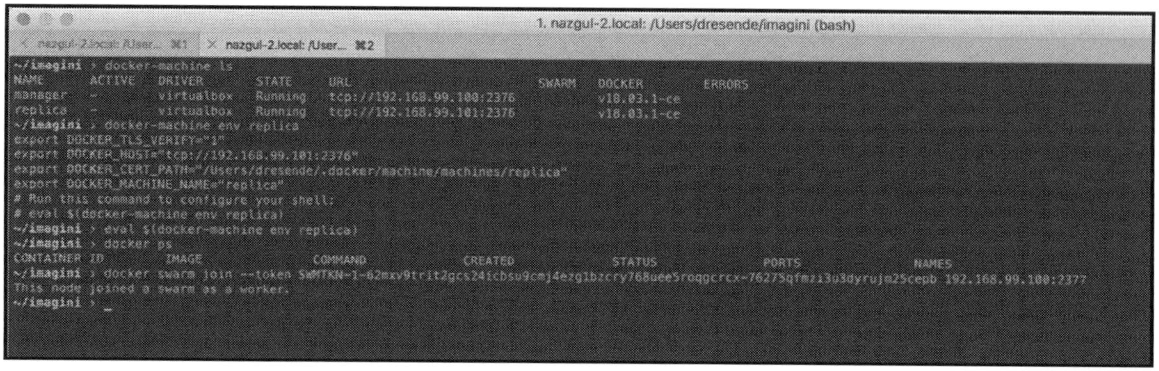


We now have two nodes on our swarm. From this point forward, assume that the first tab of our console is the manager host and that the second tab is our replica host.

We can check that the swarm has our two active nodes by using the `docker node ls` command from our manager:

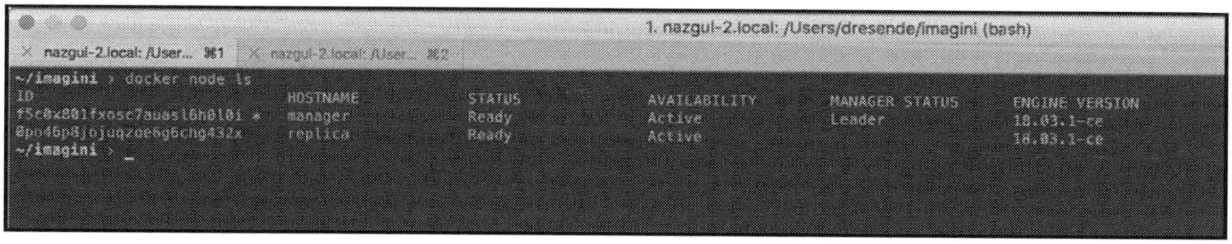


# Deploying to swarm

We have two clean nodes in our swarm. We need to go back a little bit and prepare our hosts for our service. More specifically, we need to create our image again.

Because we have our `Dockerfile`, this is an easy task. Just run:

```
docker build -t imagini:0.0.5 .
```

Do this on both hosts:

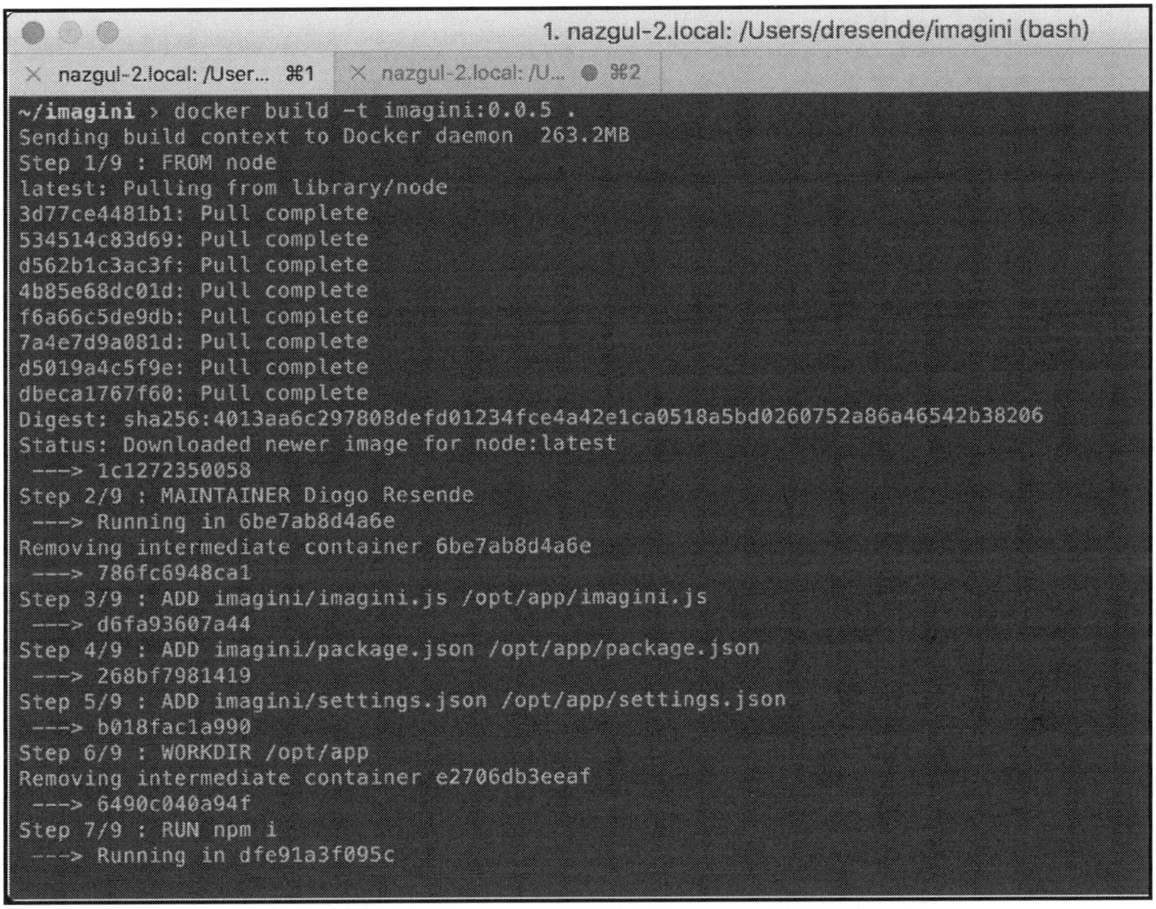


Finally, we'll have our image available on both nodes. Our database container also needs an image, but since that's an official, published image, we don't need to build it, as Docker will download it when it needs it.

We can now use the Docker stack tool to deploy our instances. It uses our previous Docker Compose configuration to know how to deploy our service. But before we do this, we need to make a couple of adjustments to the configuration.

For now, we'll enforce our database to only have one replica, as we're not yet prepared to distribute our database server just yet. We can do that by having this section on the configuration:

```
deploy:
    replicas: 1
    placement:
        constraints: [node.role == manager]
```

It indicates that we only want one replica and that the container should be placed (should run) in the manager node.

Another change we need to do is change the database volume because our containers are running on a virtual machine that is no longer local. Let's change the volume section to this:

```
volumes:
- /var/lib/mysql:/var/lib/mysql
```

We need to create the folder on the manager machine. To do that, run:

```
docker-machine ssh manager 'mkdir /var/lib/mysql'
```

To sum up, you should have a configuration as follows:

```
version: "3"
networks:
    imagini:
services:
    database:
        image: mysql:5.7
        networks:
        - imagini
        volumes:
        - /var/lib/mysql:/var/lib/mysql
        ports:
        - "3306:3306"
        environment:
            MYSQL_DATABASE: imagini
            MYSQL_ROOT_PASSWORD: secret
        deploy:
            replicas: 1
            placement:
                constraints: [node.role == manager]
    service:
        image: imagini:0.0.5
        networks:
        - imagini
```

```
        volumes:
        - ${PWD}/settings.json:/opt/app/settings.json
        ports:
        - "80:3000"
```

Head to the first tab, the one that controls the manager node, and run the following:

```
docker stack deploy --compose-file docker-compose.yml imagini
```

This should start the deployment. It will create the network on the swarm and then deploy the two services:

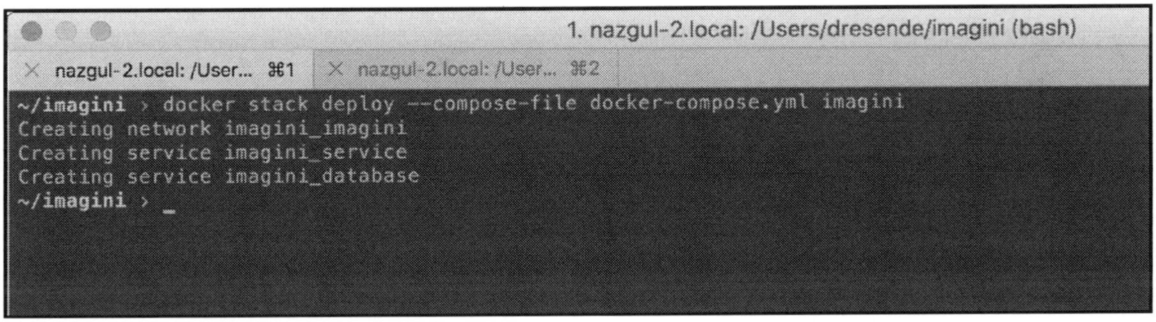


Wait a little bit and then run the following command:

```
docker stack ps imagini
```

This will do the same as `docker ps`, but just for our stack:

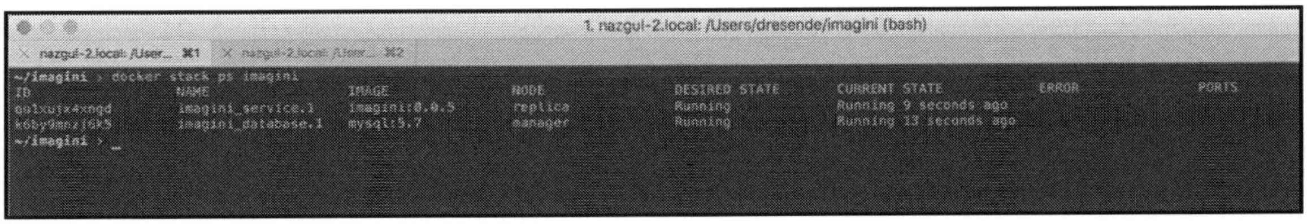


The only difference you may notice is that the name of the containers have a `.1` on the end of them and that a new `NODE` column indicates where it's running inside our swarm.

Because our containers are running in a swarm inside two virtual machines, we need to use the IP address of the node that has the service running on it. Looking at the previous screenshot, we can see that it's in the replica machine:

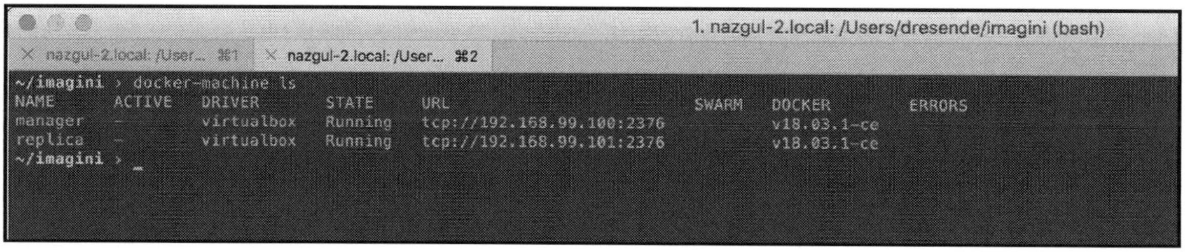


Its address is `192.168.99.101`. Head to the browser and see if our service is available or not:

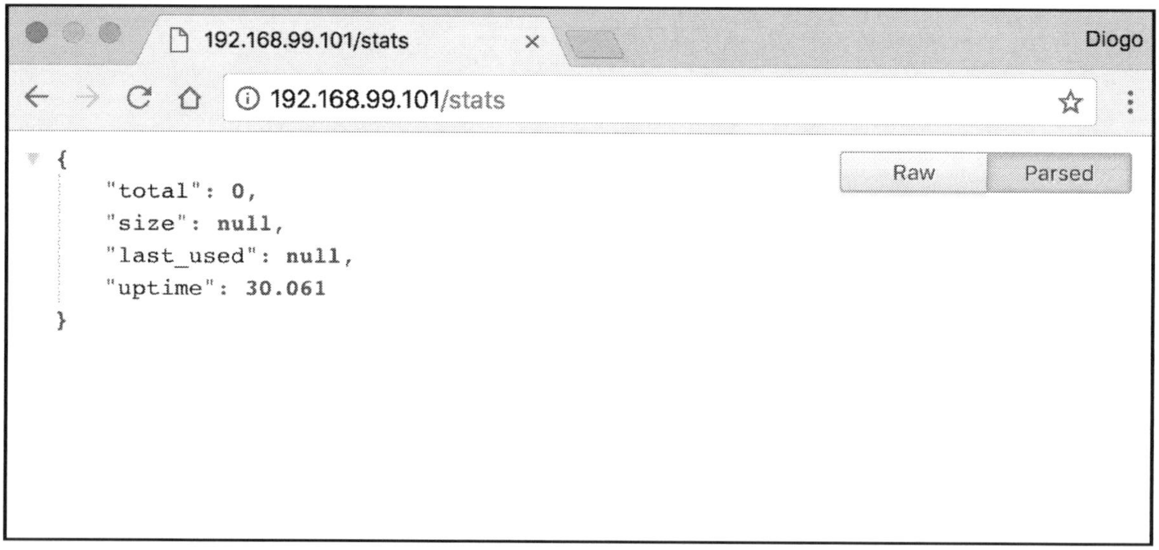


Great! It's working. But, if you think about it, if this is a swarm, shouldn't it be available from anywhere in the network? You're right, yes, it should be available. Let's check the other node address:

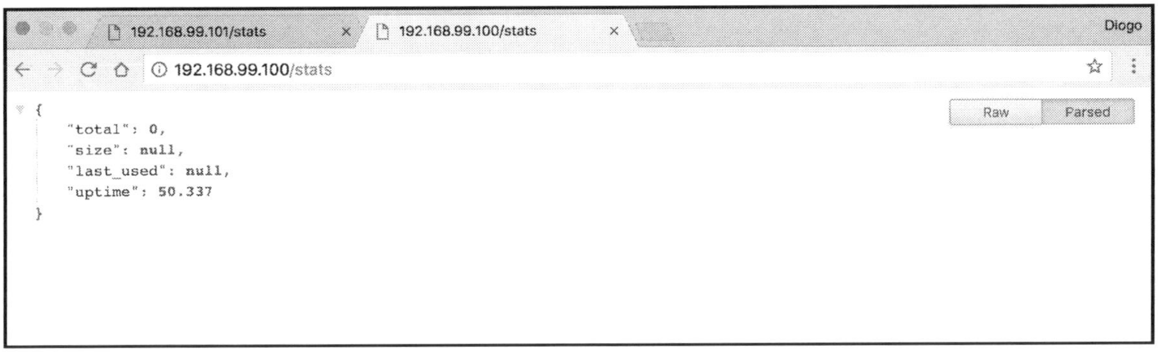


Now, this is something awesome. Notice that we only had one instance of each of our two services, and our `imagini` service was on the replica node. Although it's available from any of the swarm node addresses, if, for some reason, it fails, you wouldn't be able to reach it.

We can change this by scaling the number of instances, or replicas, in our swarm. To do that, just issue the following command to change the scale to two instances:

```
docker service scale imagini_service=2
```

Docker will handle the deployment and check if everything goes as planned:

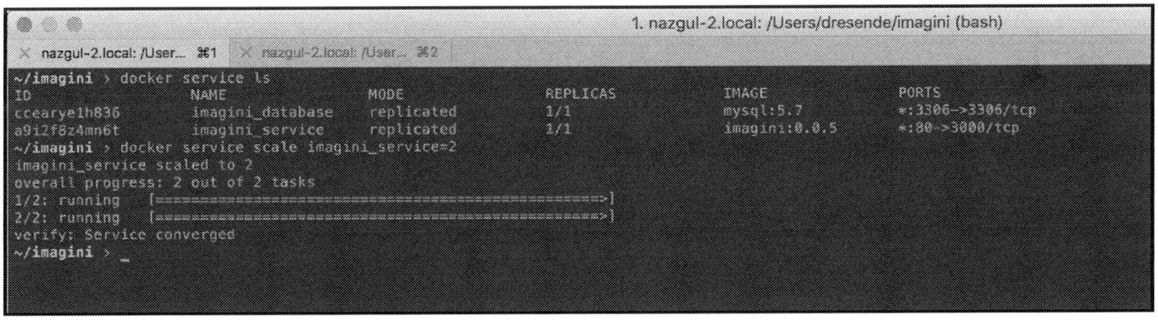


You can check the status of the services at any time using the following command:

```
docker service ls
```

Notice how our service 2/2 replicas are running:

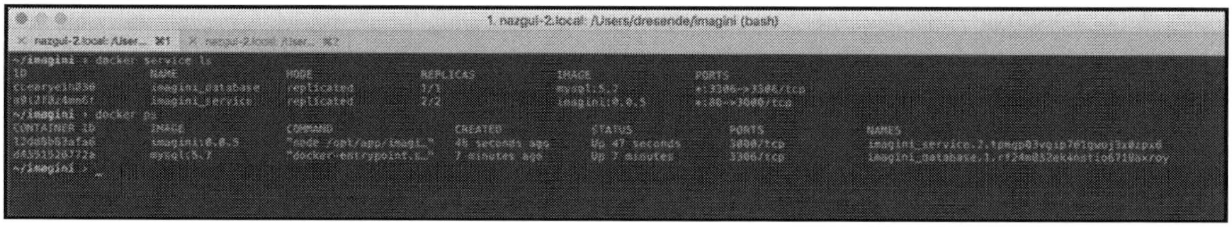

If you head to the browser, both addresses still work as expected, but in the background, we have two services running. You can notice this by looking at the `uptime` property.

If you run a little test, such as refreshing both addresses repeatedly, you'll notice that the uptime changes up and down. This is because we deployed both of the instances at different times, and although the statistics come from the database server, which is the same, the `uptime` is the process uptime:

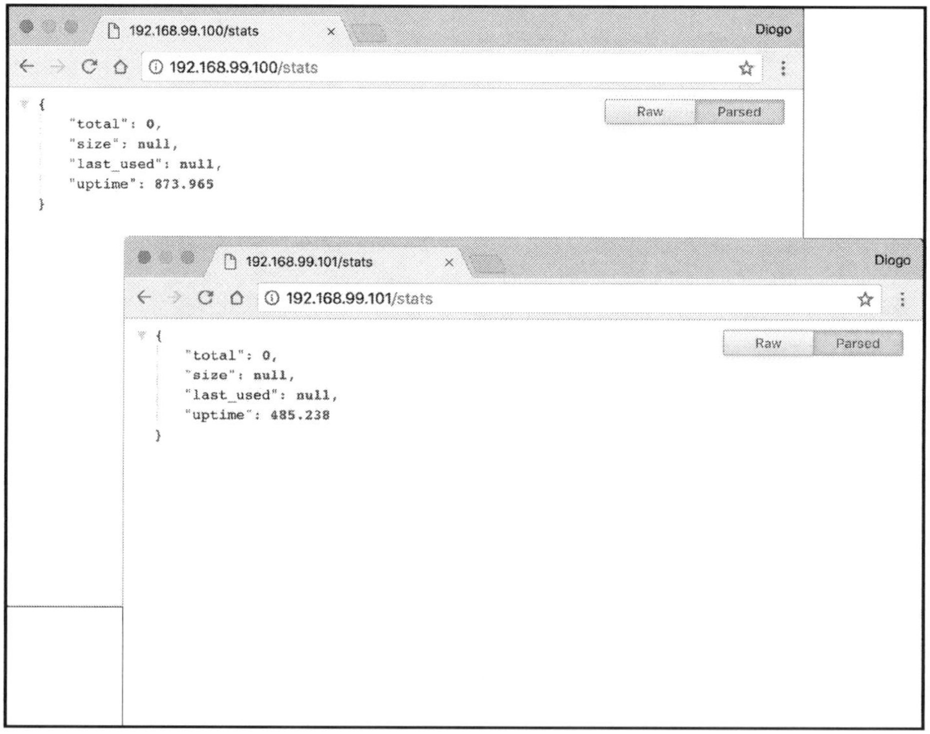

Notice how the swarm is not constant and does not give you the same instance for the same address. It keeps rotating it.

The swarm also monitors our container instances. For example, let's imagine you're working on a host and, by accident, stop a container:

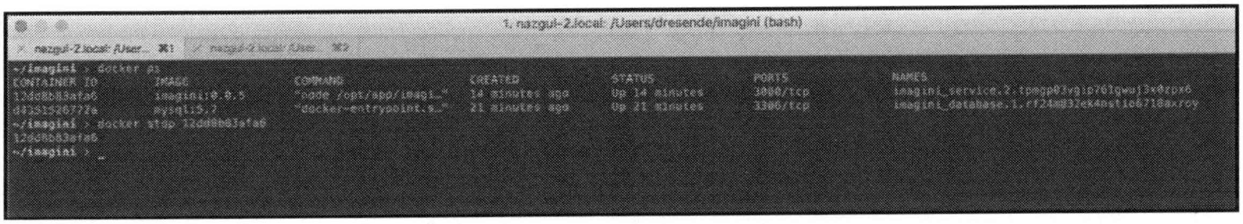


It's not very critical since we have two replicas running. But if you head to the browser and hit refresh, you may see something odd:

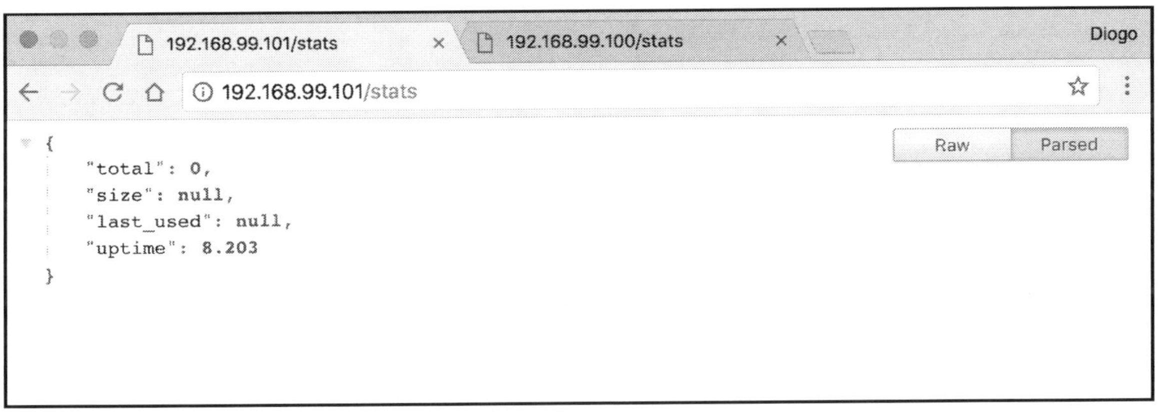


What happened to our `uptime`? It just went down to a few seconds. This is because the swarm just noticed our container stopping and restarted it. If you look at the Docker containers again, it's still running. Well, actually it restarted:

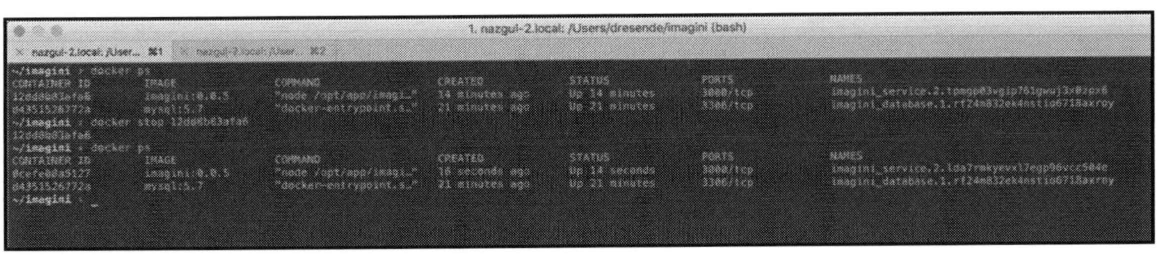

If you want to scale to more instances, you don't need to have more swarm nodes. There's no limitation on the number of instances of the same containers running on the same node. This is actually a good practice.

It enables you to test if your service is ready to be used in a scaled environment and also allows you to test a phased upgrade by stopping a container and upgrading one by one, while at least one other container is still serving your customers.

Let's just scale our service to five instances:

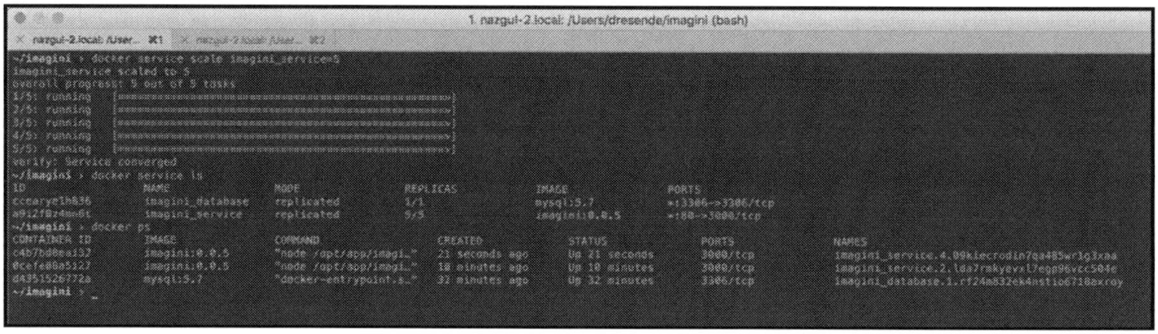

Notice how we have two of the five services running on this node, and also the database instance. The other three are in the replica node. This is known as swarm balancing the instances.

# Creating services

You may have noticed how we're using the Docker service command to scale our instances. This is a command that is similar to the basic Docker command, but with services and scaling in mind. We can use this command to create containers and scale them easily.

MySQL has no simple replication mechanism. There are only two ways of doing it and both have disadvantages:

- Creating a set of nodes as masters of each other, creating a complex mesh of connections that will eventually lead to chaos
- Creating a cluster, which involves more nodes and still leads to a complex deployment, which is easier to manage but resource-intensive to maintain

Looking back at our examples from previous chapters, we could change our service to use another database server. More specifically, RethinkDB has a much friendlier cluster mechanism.

So, just replace our `imagini` service with the one we used with RethinkDB. This time, let's use the Docker Service commands manually and deploy our microservice step by step.

To begin with, let's prepare a RethinkDB cluster. To make it resilient, we will do the following:

1. Create an instance called `db-primary`.
2. Create another instance called `db-secondary` and instruct it to join `db-primary`.
3. Scale `db-secondary` to two instances so that we have a proper three-node cluster.
4. Remove and recreate `db-primary` to instruct it to join `db-secondary` this time.
5. Scale `db-primary` to two instances.

This will give you four nodes, two of each kind, that are formatted to join the other kind when they fail, and swarm restarts them. This is the definition of *no single point of failure*.

Because we're doing everything manually, we need to start by creating a network. Let's create the network `imagini`:

```
docker network create --driver overlay imagini
```

Then, create `db-primary` with only `1` replica as we're removing it later on:

```
docker service create --name db-primary \
                      --network imagini \
                      --replicas 1 \
                      rethinkdb:latest \
                      rethinkdb --bind all --no-http-admin
```

Then, create the first `db-secondary` with only `1` replica and tell it to join `db-primary`:

```
docker service create --name db-secondary \
                      --network imagini \
                      --replicas 1 \
                      rethinkdb:latest \
                      rethinkdb --bind all --no-http-admin --join db-
primary
```

You should now have something like this:

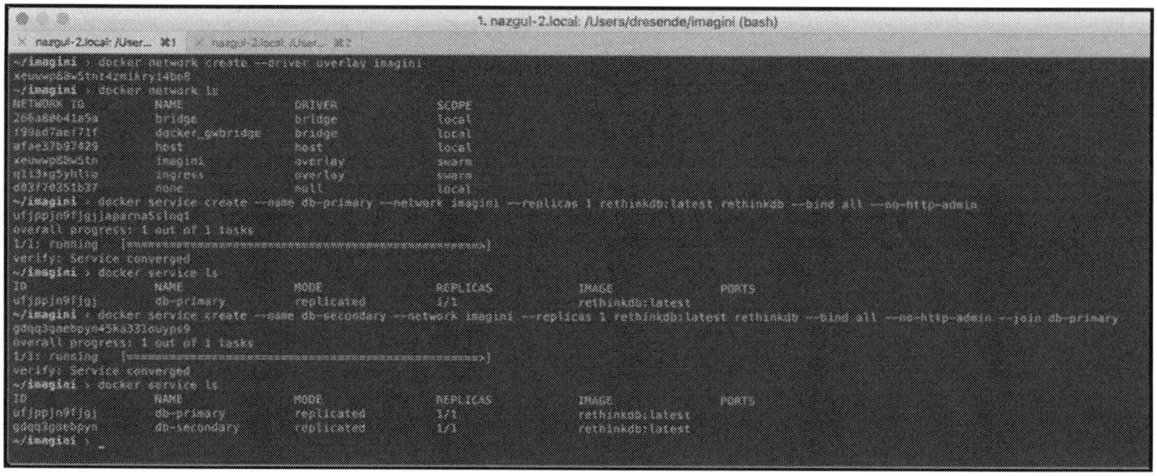

Similar to what we did before, let's scale `db-secondary` to two instances:

```
docker service scale db-secondary=2
```

Then, remove the `db-primary` and recreate it:

```
docker service create --name db-primary \
                      --network imagini \
                      --replicas 1 \
                      rethinkdb:latest \
                      rethinkdb --bind all --no-http-admin --join db-
secondary
```

Then, scale it to two instances:

```
docker service scale db-primary=2
```

You should now have four instances. List the services and you should see something like the following screenshot:

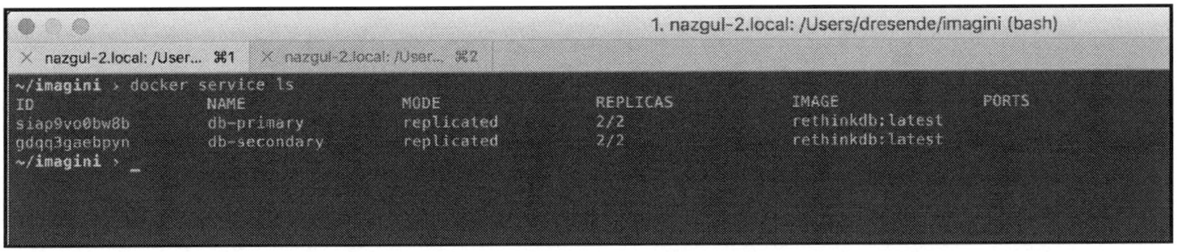


If you try to stop the containers, you'll notice that they will restart without you doing anything. Just give it a little time and they'll be up and running again:

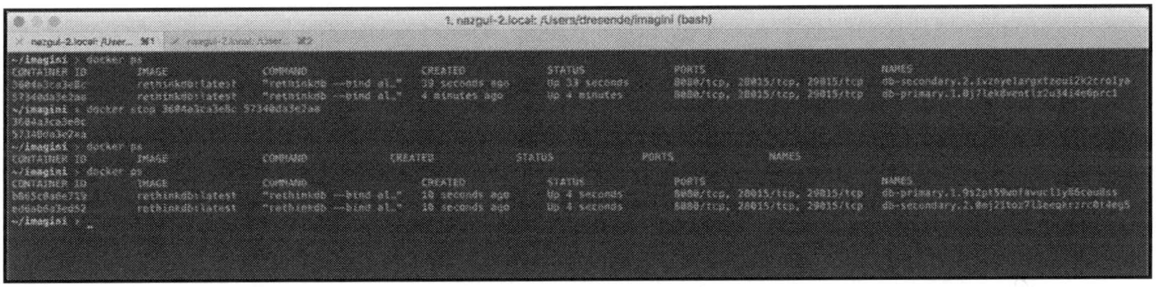


Now that we have our database cluster ready, we just need a proxy to be able to access the cluster:

```
docker service create --name database \
                      --network imagini \
                      --publish 8080:8080 \
                      --publish 28015:28015 \
                      rethinkdb:latest \
                      rethinkdb proxy --bind all --join db-primary
```

If we look at the services, we can now see that we have our four cluster nodes and a proxy called database, which we'll use to manage and access the data:

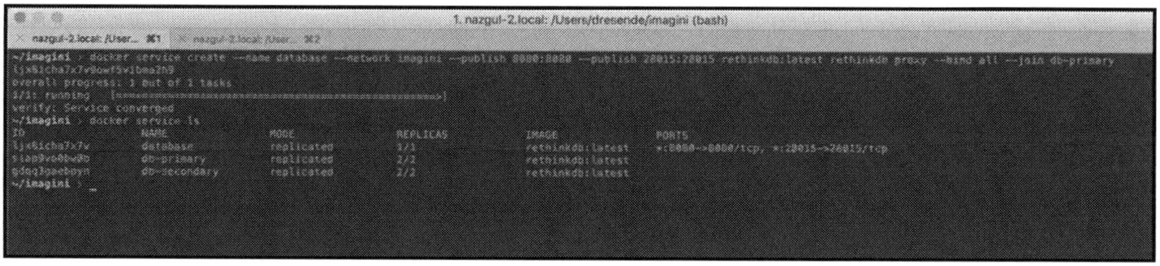


We can also see that we have the management port exposed, `8080`. Head to the browser at any of the swarm addresses on that port and see if you can see the RethinkDB management interface:

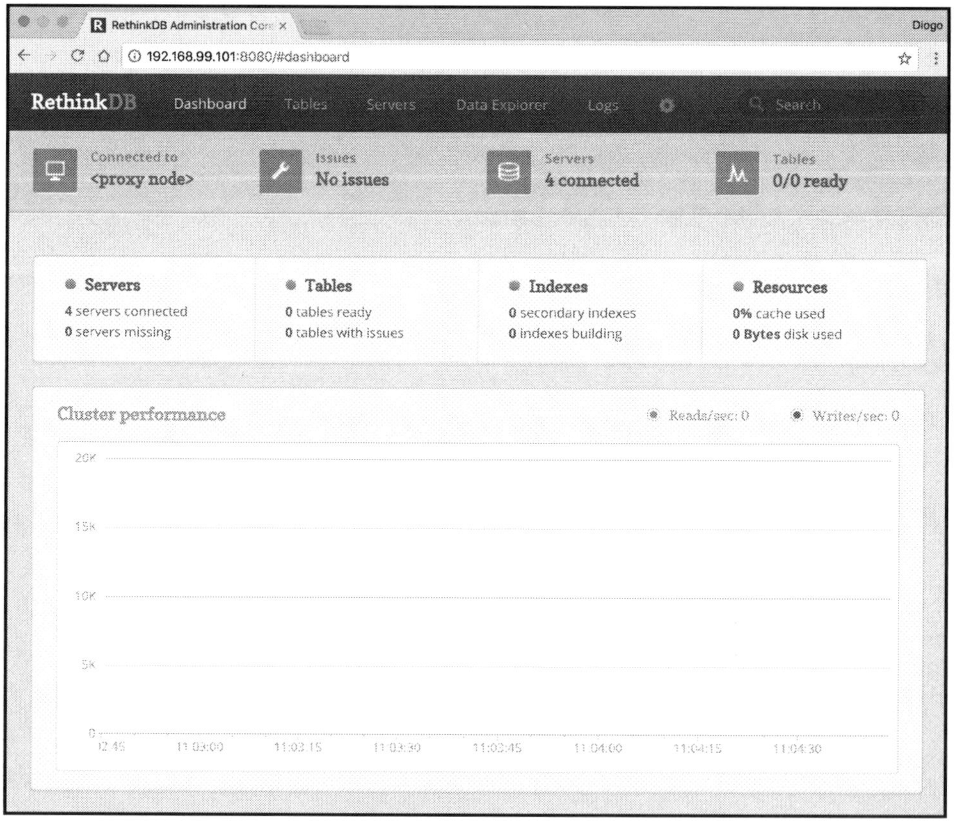

Great! We can see that there's a **4 servers connected** under the **Servers** label. On top, there's also a **Servers** section that you can look into and see that our instances are all there:

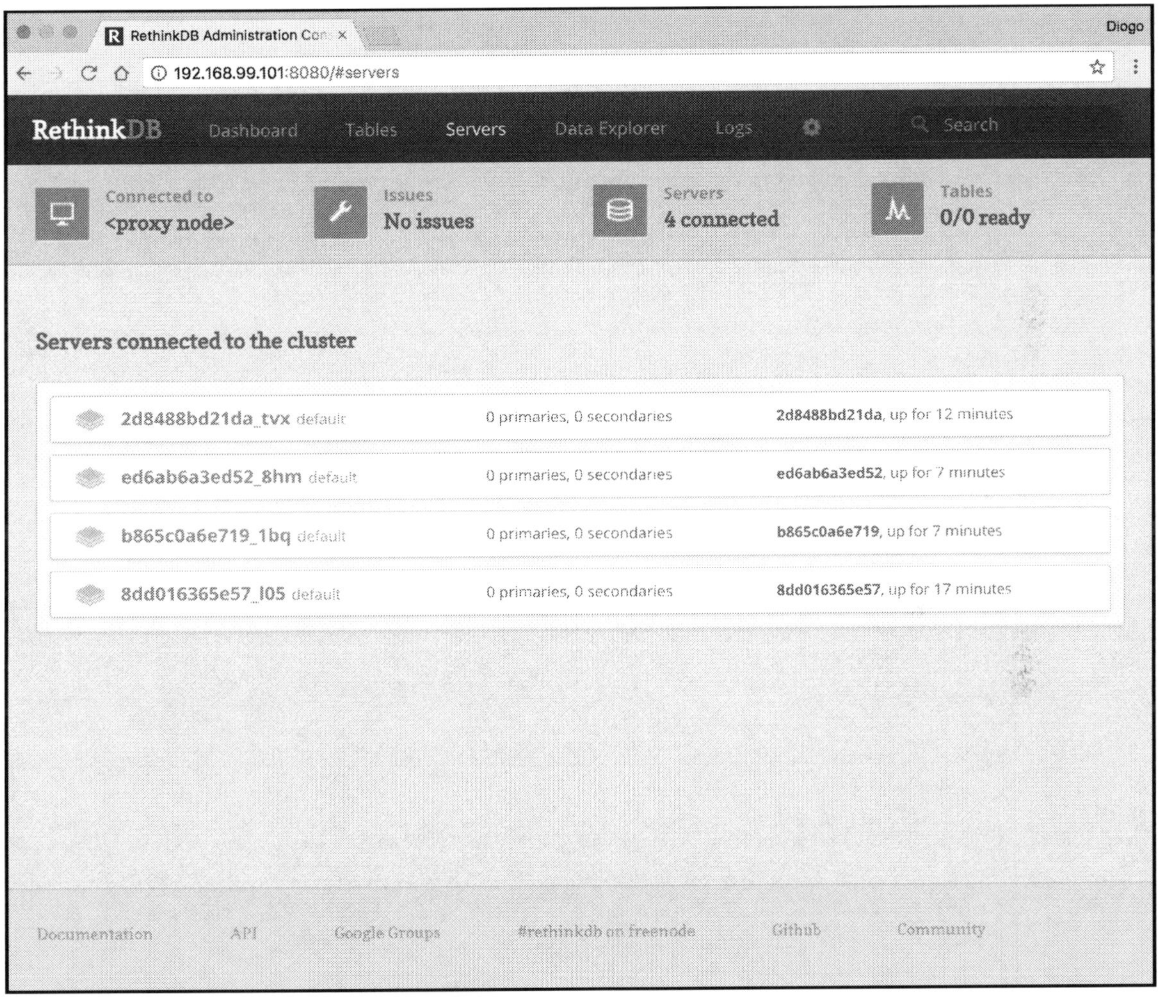


Use this interface and create a database called `imagini` in the **Tables** section.

# Running our service

The only part missing is our main service. We need to rebuild it again. If you change the source code to use RethinkDB again, you have to change the `package.json` file in order to have different dependencies. We need to rebuild this using our `Dockerfile`. To avoid introducing another theme, which is Docker Volumes, let's change our RethinkDB connection to not depend on the `settings` file:

```
rethinkdb.connect({ host: "database", db: "imagini" }, (err, db) => {
```

This way, we can avoid mounting a settings file altogether. Now, let's just increment the version and build it on both tabs:

```
docker build -t imagini:0.0.6 .
```

Now, the only thing missing is creating our service:

```
docker service create --name imagini --network imagini --publish 80:3000
imagini:0.0.6
```

In just a few seconds, we have our service running:

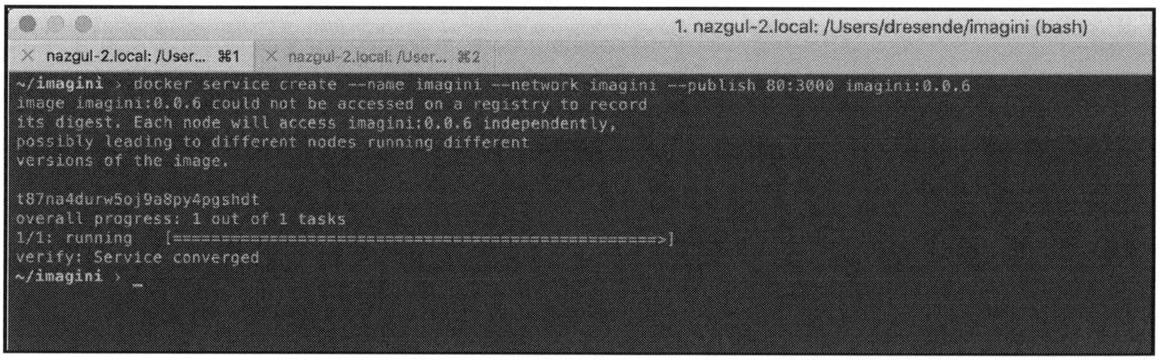

We can even scale it right away and have three instances:

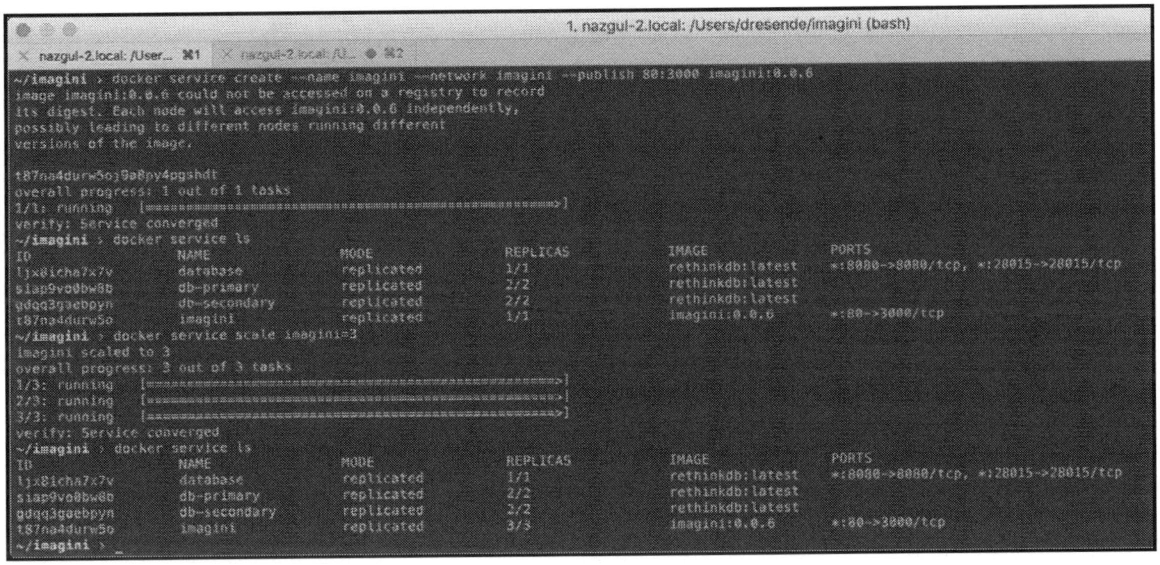


We can see that it's exposed on port `80`. As we did previously, we can see that the service is up and running. I'll just upload the example image again as this is a clean service and it has no images yet:

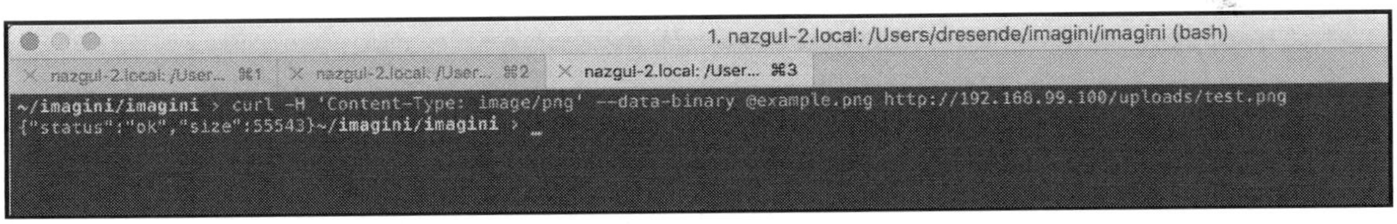

You can see it on the RethinkDB administration interface. And even if we use the other swarm address, we see that the image is now available to download:

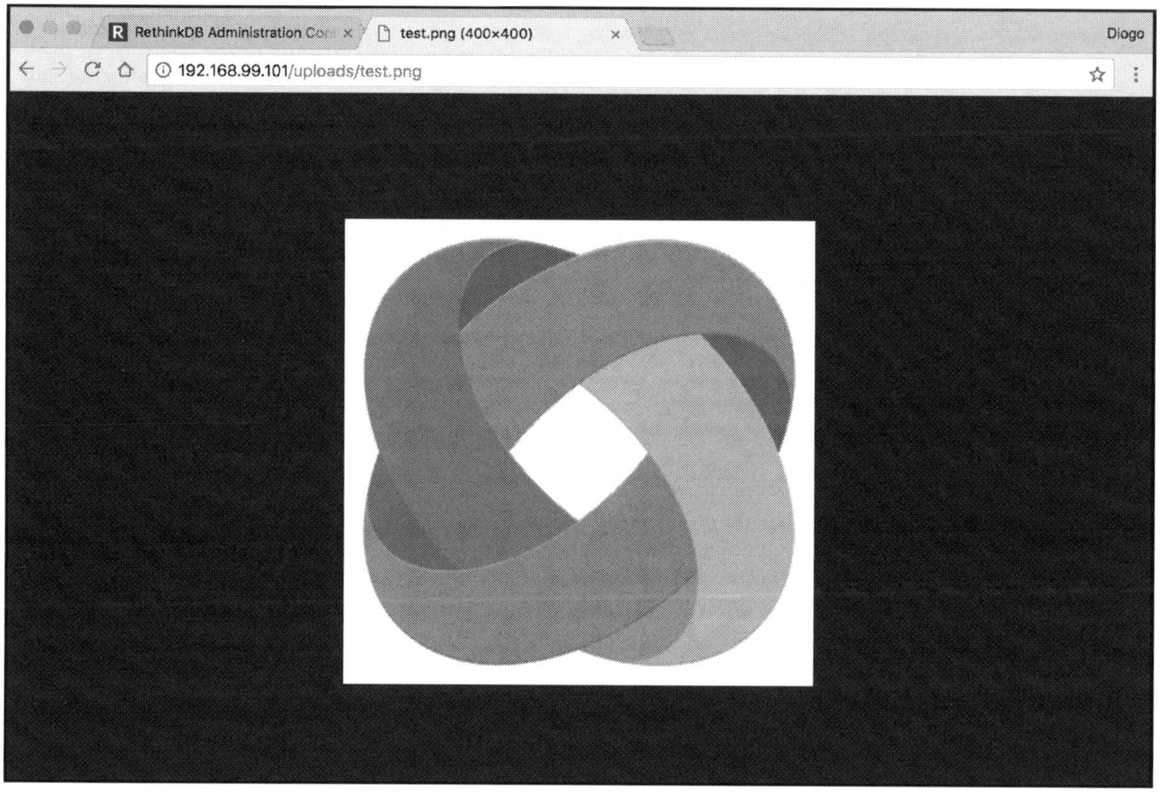

# Sharding approach

Sharding is the process of fragmenting the data across different locations. This enables us to split a large dataset into different servers, each one with a smaller set. This is comparable to a RAID 0 configuration, where, for example, you may need a 10 TB disk and do this by combining two 5 TB disks:

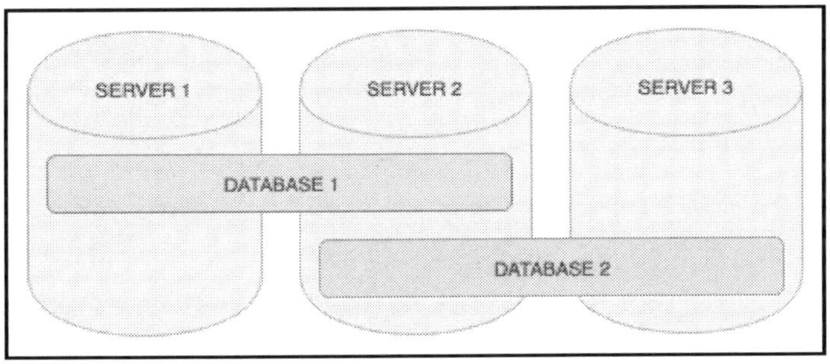


Doing so is considered scaling, but it comes at a cost. Each piece of data is important; it's not a copy, it's a fundamental part. Sharding adds complexity to your deployment but sometimes is inevitable if you have a very large dataset.

# Replicating approach

Replicating is the process of having copies of the data across different locations. This enables us to have a bigger throughput as we can have different services serving the same data. It also brings complexity, at least for the database servers, as they need to keep everything synchronized:

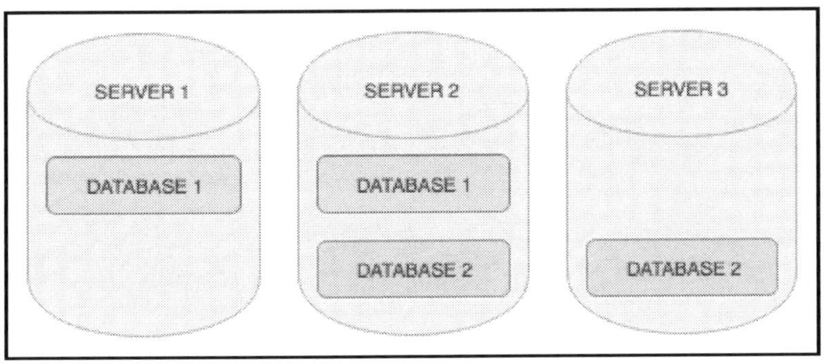

Doing replicas also gives you redundancy in case of any failures in regards to parts of the server nodes, depending on your configuration. If you use a database cluster for more than one application, you don't need to have replicas of a database in all cluster nodes; it all depends on your needs.

# Sharding and replicating

Looking at our service, now that it's using RethinkDB, we can have the best of both worlds and enable sharding and replication at the same time. Head to the Administration Console and click on the **Tables** tab at the top:

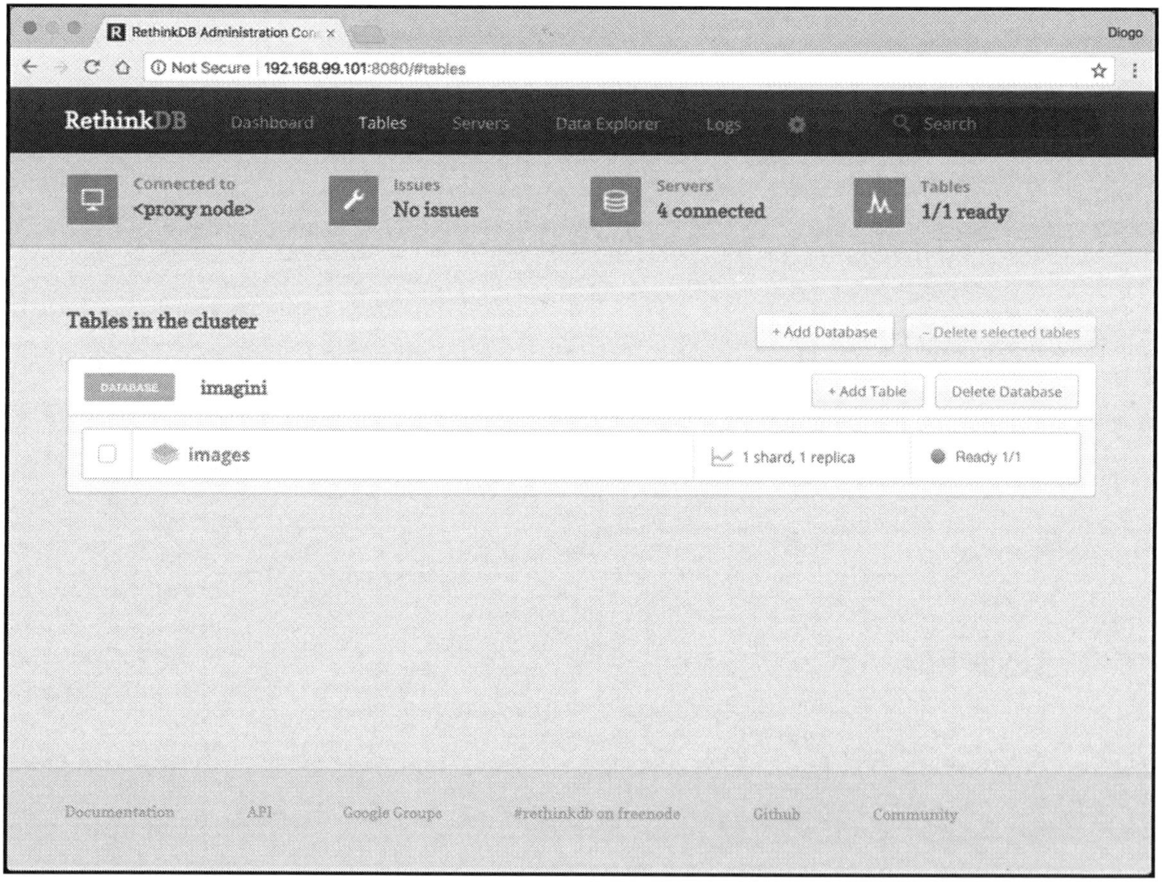

Click on our **images** table and scroll down:

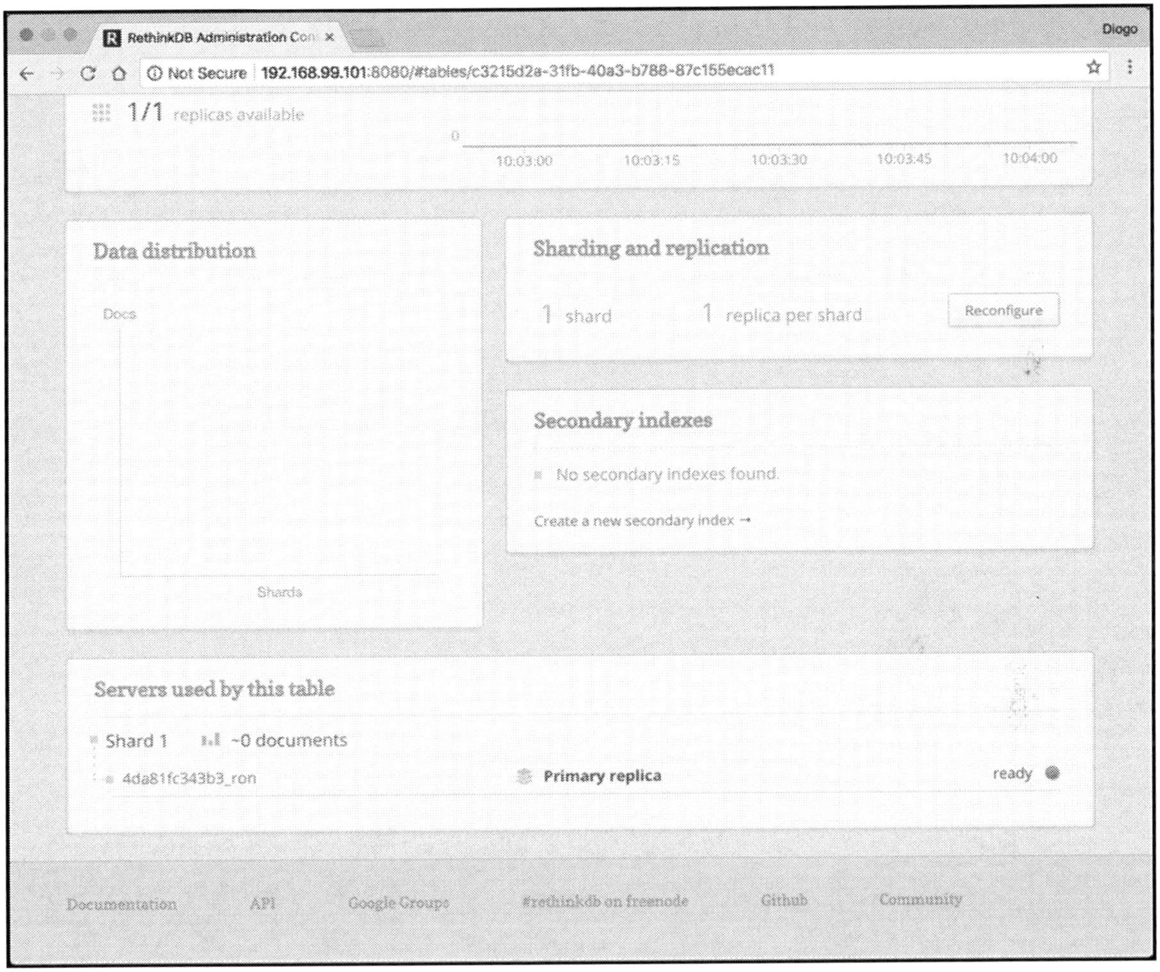

You can see that our table is on one shard (the default), with only one replica per shard. Down the bottom, you can see the server (blue link) on our cluster that is holding the table. Click on **Apply configuration**:

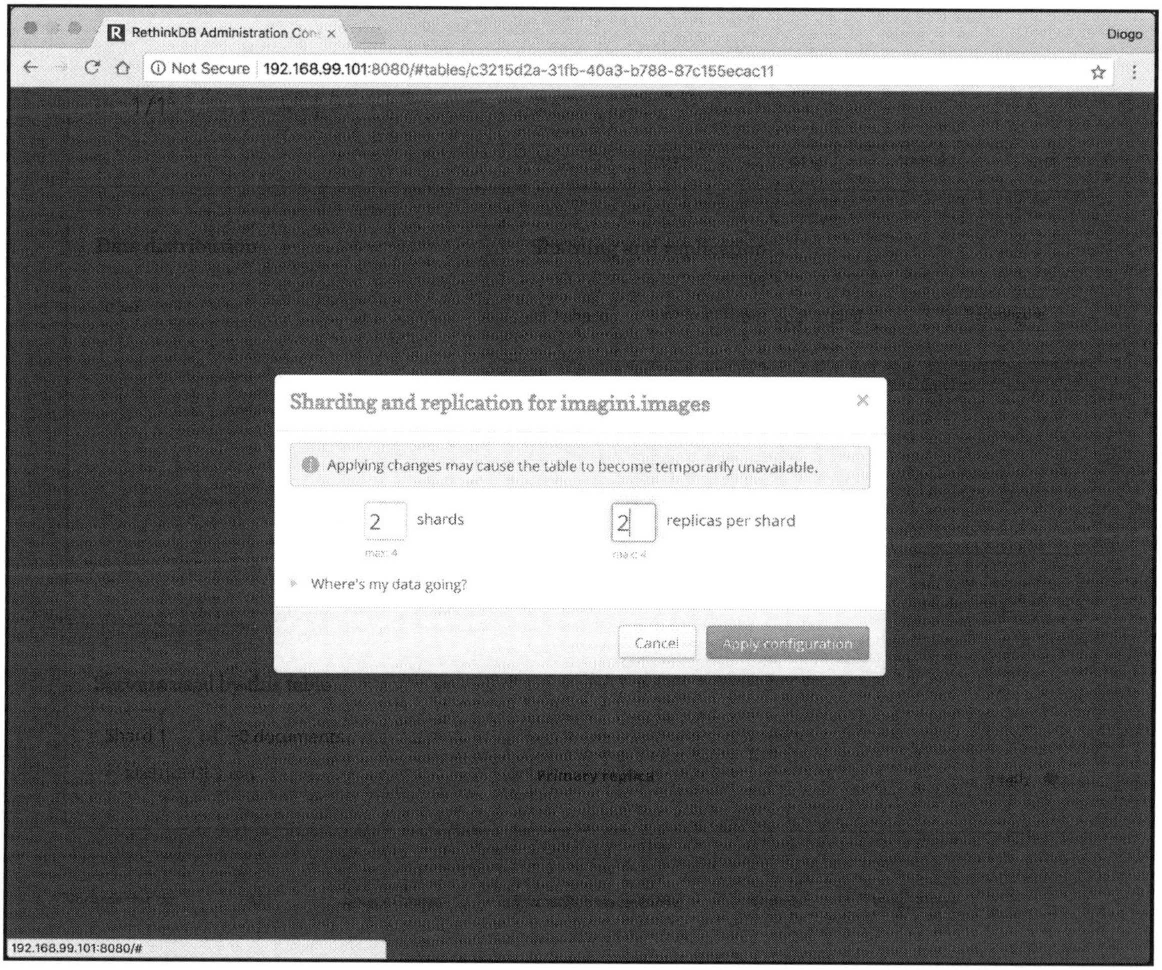


You can configure the number of shards and the number of replicas of every shard. The limitation on four shards and four replicas is because our cluster has only four nodes. Any number above that would not make sense.

Let's configure our table with two shards and two replicas per shard and apply the configuration. Wait a couple of seconds and look at how our table is distributed:

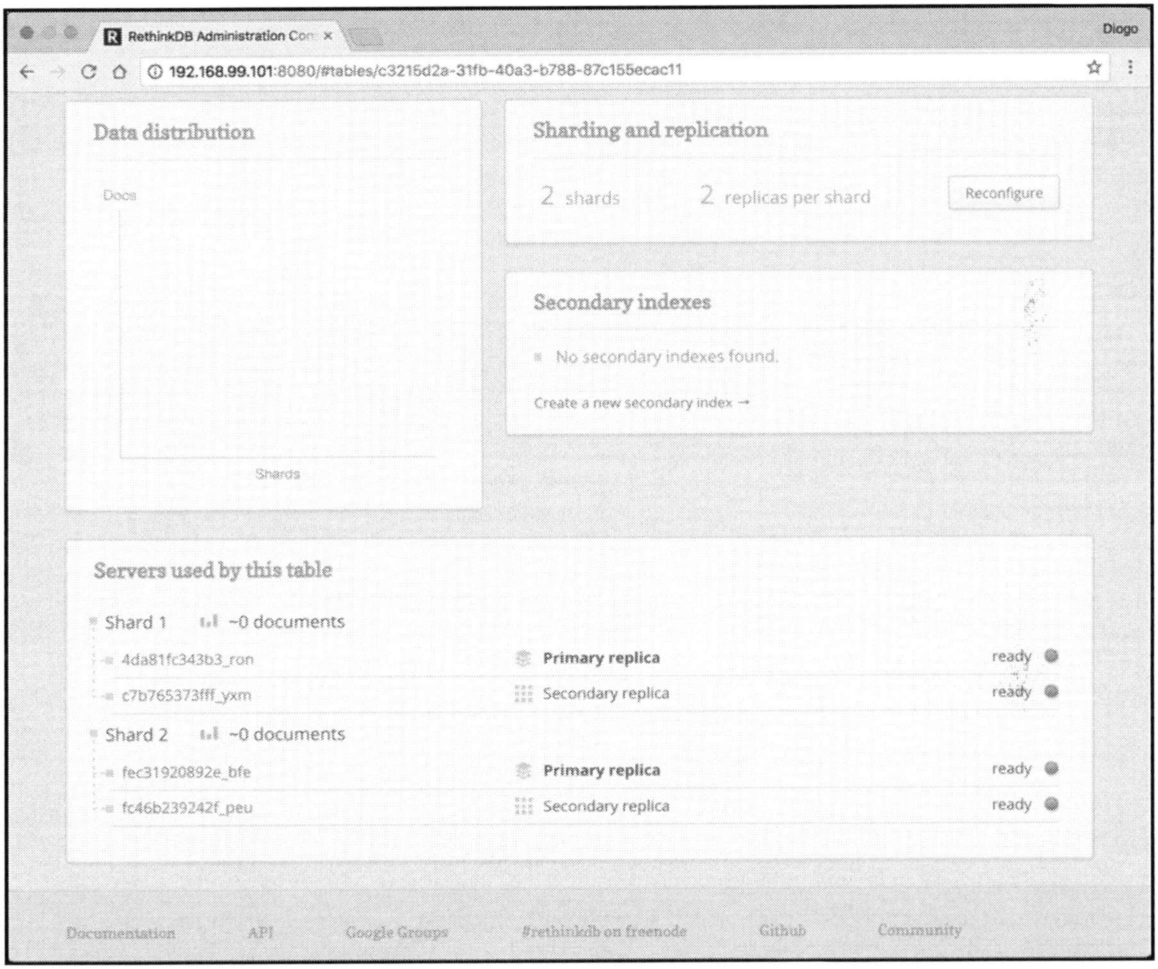


If one node restarts, the database keeps running without a problem. It will recover and synchronize everything when the node comes online again. Let's just try that. Head to a console of one of the Docker machines and restart one of the database containers.

If you keep the administration console open, you should see something like the following screenshot for just a few seconds:

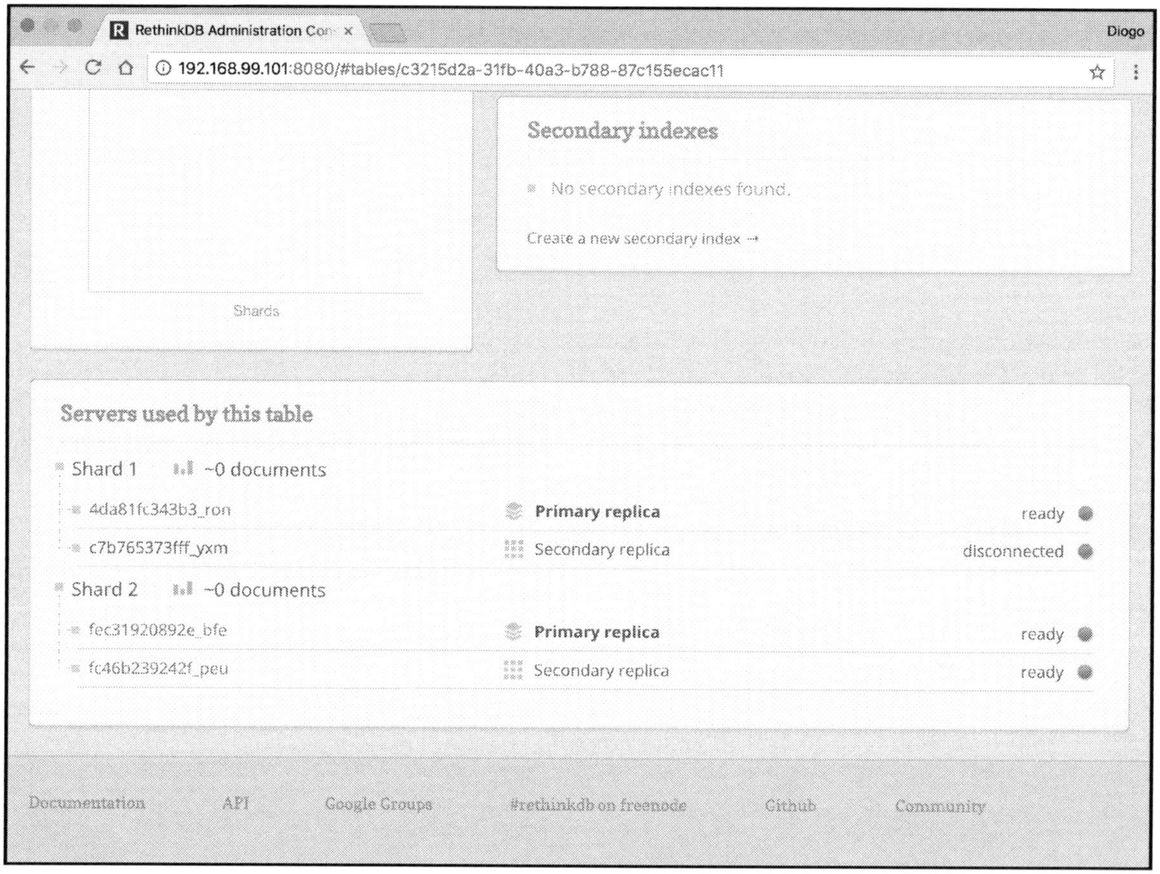


The server then reconnects, and everything recovers immediately. But this is a specific feature that will vary according to the database server and cluster type. Your operations' team should be comfortable with the database server chosen to run in production.

We now have a production-ready environment that we can tweak and scale to our needs.

# Moving to Kubernetes

Kubernetes began with a group of Google developers from a previous Google system called Borg. Its goal was, and is, to help in the deployment, scaling, and maintenance of applications. When it was first announced in 2014, there was no open source alternative. At the time, there was no Docker swarm, Docker networks, or Docker services.

Let's see what changes we need to make to our microservice in order to successfully run it using Kubernetes. But first, we need to clarify some of the concepts that are used in Kubernetes:

- **Pods**: A Pod consists of one or more containers that share some resources, and because of that, need to be located on the same host. A Pod is assigned a unique network address to avoid port collision. Note that several Pods of your deployment may be created, each with a different address.
- **Labels**: Kubernetes allows us to assign several labels to Pods in order to create groups of different kinds of components, such as frontend and backend, production and staging.
- **Services**: A Service is a group of Pods that work together, like our microservice and the database server. You can create a Service by defining a Label of Pods.

# Deploying with Kubernetes

That's not all of the concepts needed, but you may see some similarities and differences between Docker and Kubernetes. Actually, Kubernetes uses Docker and adds a few tools to enhance the deployment, scaling, and monitoring of containers.

The best way to start with Kubernetes is to install `minikube`. This is a tool to run Kubernetes locally on a single virtual machine:

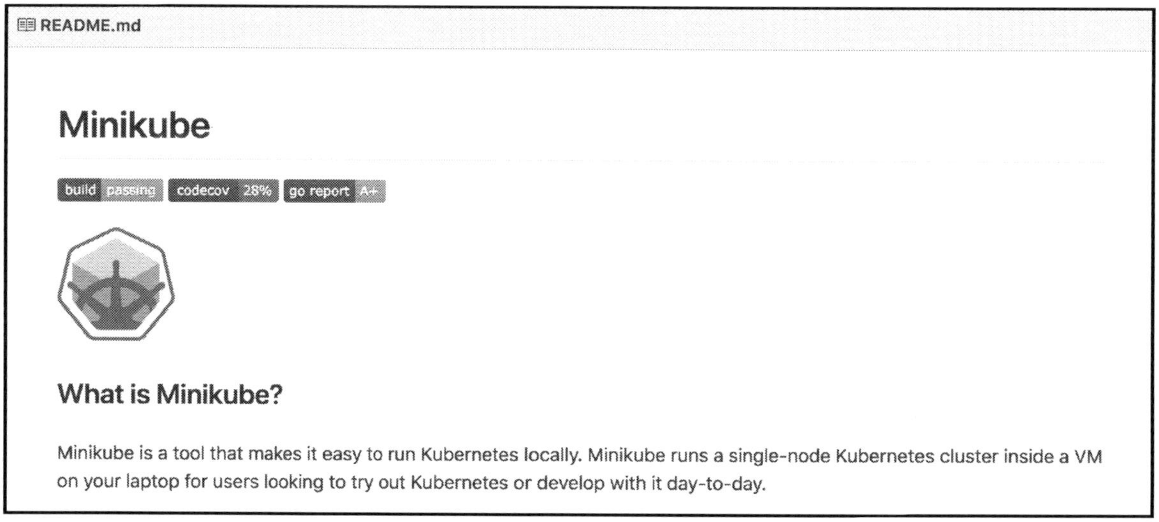


Follow the installation instructions. If you're on macOS and have `homebrew` installed, you just need to run:

```
brew cask install minikube
```

After installing `minikube`, you have to start it by running:

```
minikube start
```

You have to wait a minute or two before everything is set up:

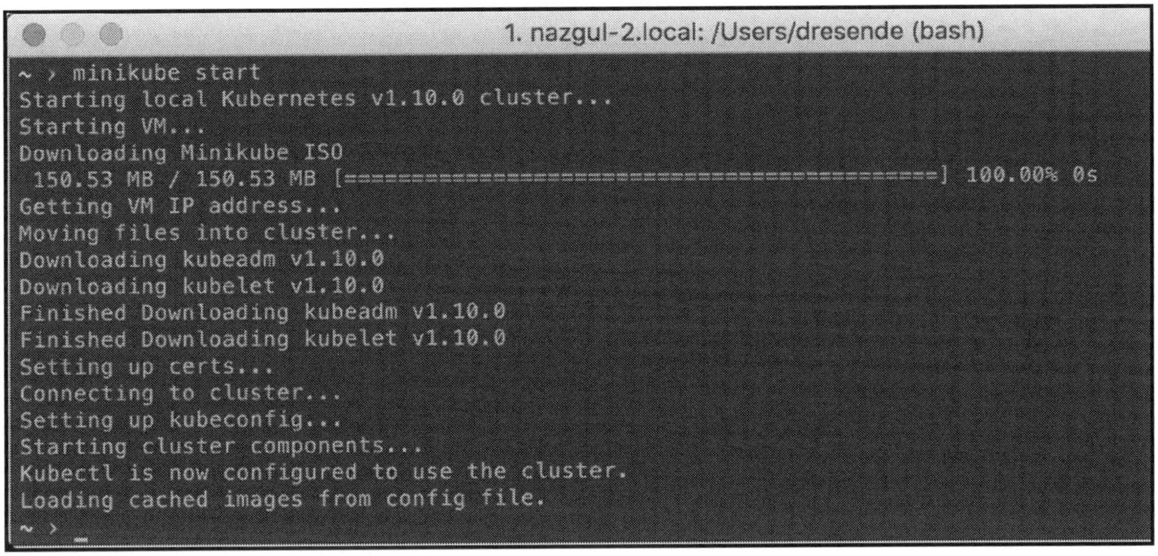


We can see that our Kubernetes cluster is up and running by running:

```
kubectl cluster-info
```

This is a cluster of nodes that run containers, similar to Docker swarm. You should get a positive response as follows:

You're now able to access the Kubernetes dashboard by running:

```
minikube dashboard
```

Your browser should open something along the following lines:

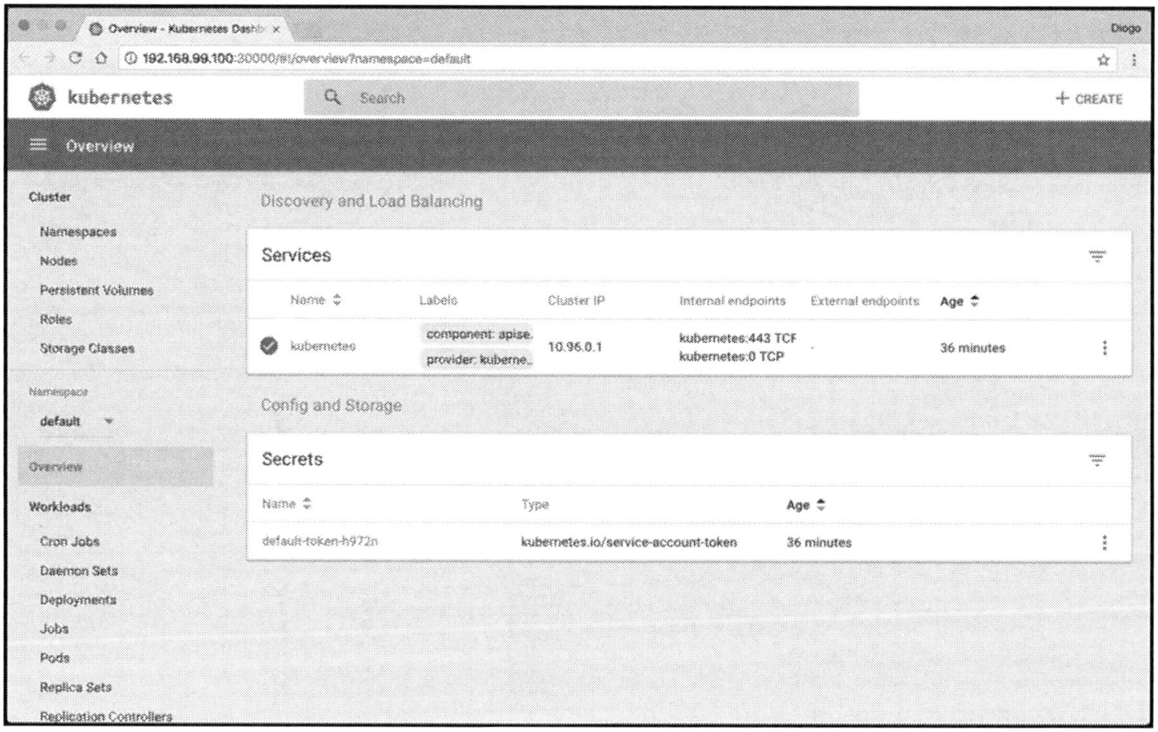


You can use the interface to monitor all of Kubernetes, but also to create services and deployments. Since our service depends on RethinkDB right now, we first need to ensure we have that up and running.

To begin, hit the **Create** button in the top right-hand corner of the page. On the text input that shows appears, write the following YAML configuration:

```
apiVersion: apps/v1beta1
kind: StatefulSet
metadata:
  name: rethinkdb-master
spec:
  serviceName: rethinkdb-master
  replicas: 1
  template:
    metadata:
      labels:
        app: rethinkdb-master
```

```
    spec:
      hostname: rethinkdb-master
      containers:
      - name: rethinkdb
        image: rethinkdb:2.3.6
        command: ["rethinkdb"]
        args:
        - --bind
        - "all"
        - --canonical-address
        - "rethinkdb-master:29015"
        - --canonical-address
        - "$(MY_POD_IP):29015"
        volumeMounts:
        - name: rdb-local-data
          mountPath: /data
        env:
        - name: MY_POD_NAME
          valueFrom:
            fieldRef:
              fieldPath: metadata.name
        - name: MY_POD_IP
          valueFrom:
            fieldRef:
              fieldPath: status.podIP
      volumes:
      - name: rdb-local-data
        hostPath:
          path: /var/data/rethinkdb

---
apiVersion: v1
kind: Service
metadata:
  name: rethinkdb-master
  labels:
    app: rethinkdb-master
spec:
  ports:
  - port: 28015
    name: rdb-api
  - port: 29015
    name: rdb-cluster-api
  selector:
    app: rethinkdb-master
```

Hit **Upload** and wait a few seconds. You should have a running RethinkDB database in no time:

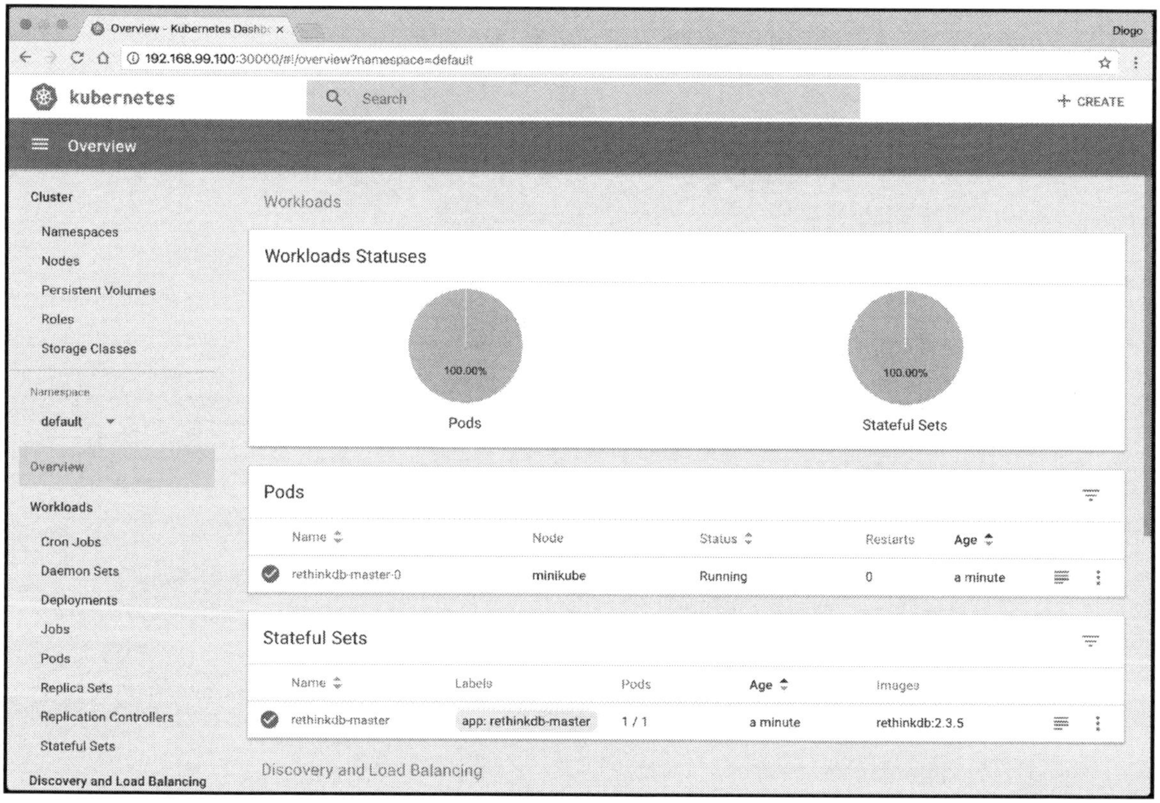


To check that our RethinkDB server is running correctly, we can add port forwarding from the outside of the cluster. First, let's list our services:

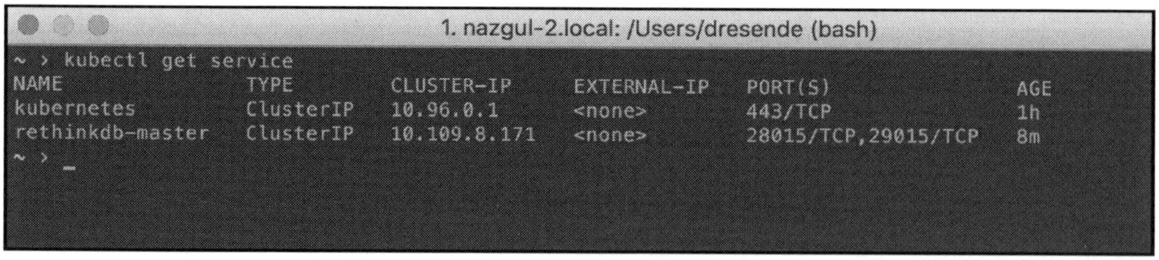

Our service is there. There are some endpoints, but the Administration Console isn't actually there. Let's forward that local port, which is 5000, to port `8080`:

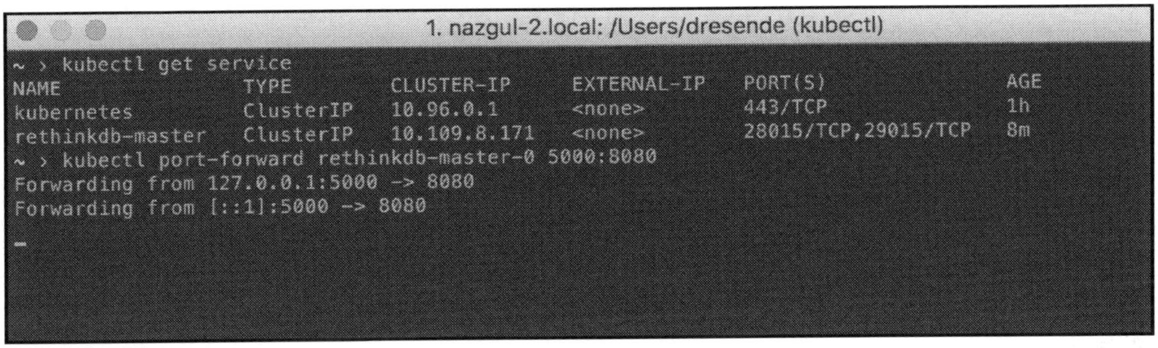


While keeping the command running, open a new browser tab and head to port `5000` of the localhost. You should see the RethinkDB Administration Console:

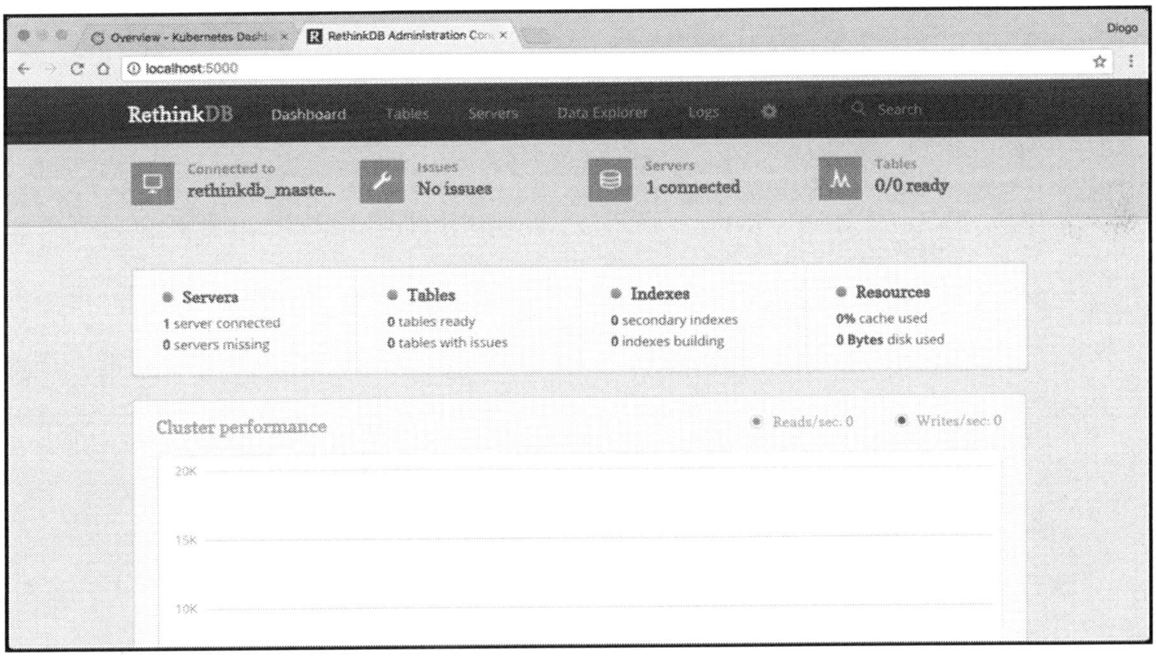

We can now head to our microservice and try to deploy it, similar to what we did previously with Docker. First, create the `imagini` database on the Administration Console:

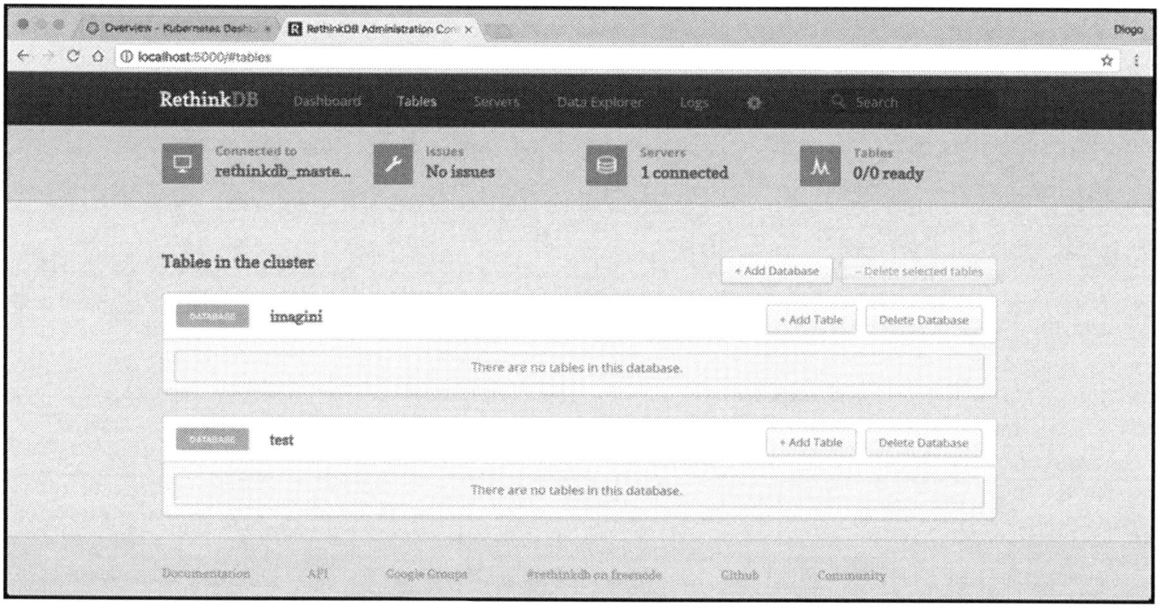


To keep it simple, we're keeping the RethinkDB connection hardcoded on our code. I'll leave it up to you to try it out later on with Kubernetes to see how you can have a persistent volume, have your settings there, and the database.

We just have to change our line to:

```
rethinkdb.connect({ host: "rethinkdb-master", db: "imagini" }, (err, db) =>
{
```

Since we have a local image, we need to build it just like we did before. Let's build it inside our `minikube`. First, let's make sure that we're going to push our commands to `minikube` and not our Docker base:

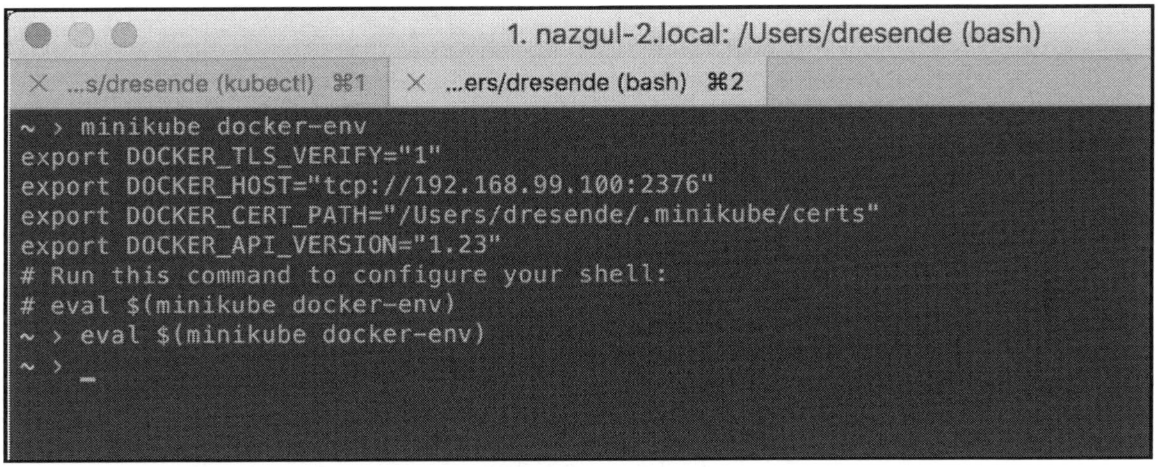


Then, let's build our image using the same Docker command:

```
docker build -t imagini:0.0.6 .
```

After building it, let's begin the deployment:

```
kubectl run imagini --image=imagini:0.0.6 --port=3000
```

If everything runs smoothly, you should see a message like the following:

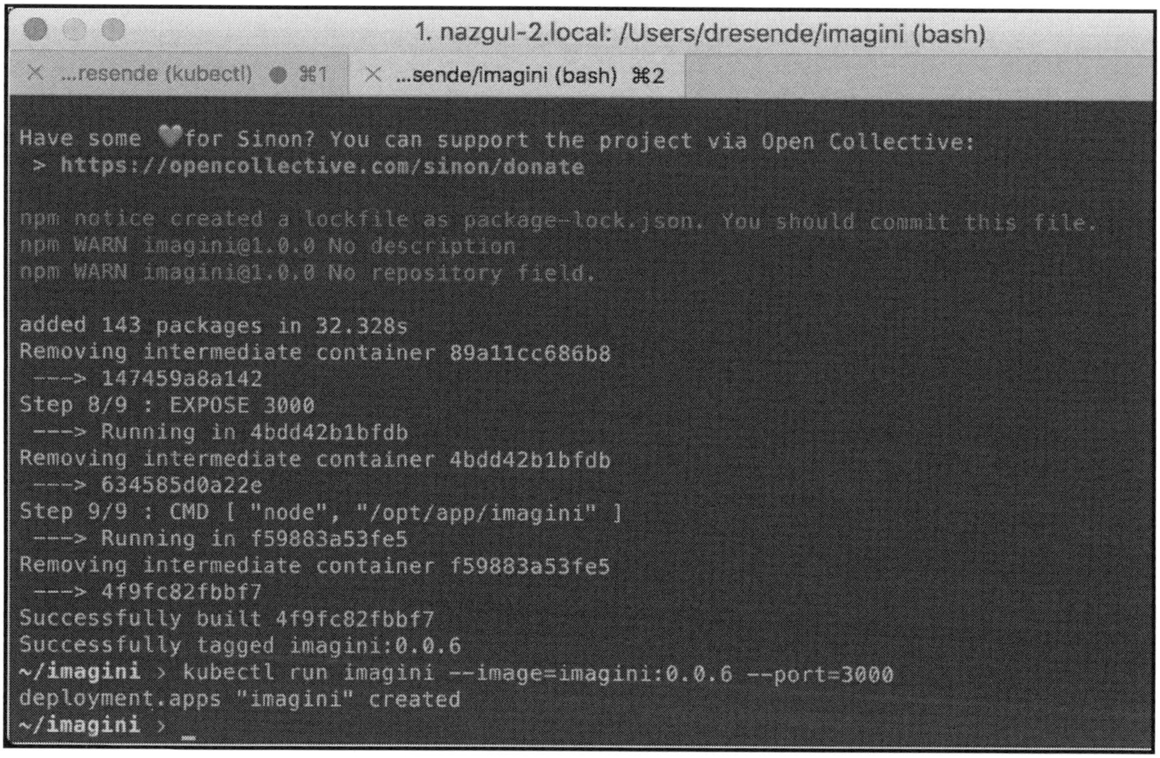

If you refresh the Administration Console, you now have **Deployments** and a new Pod:

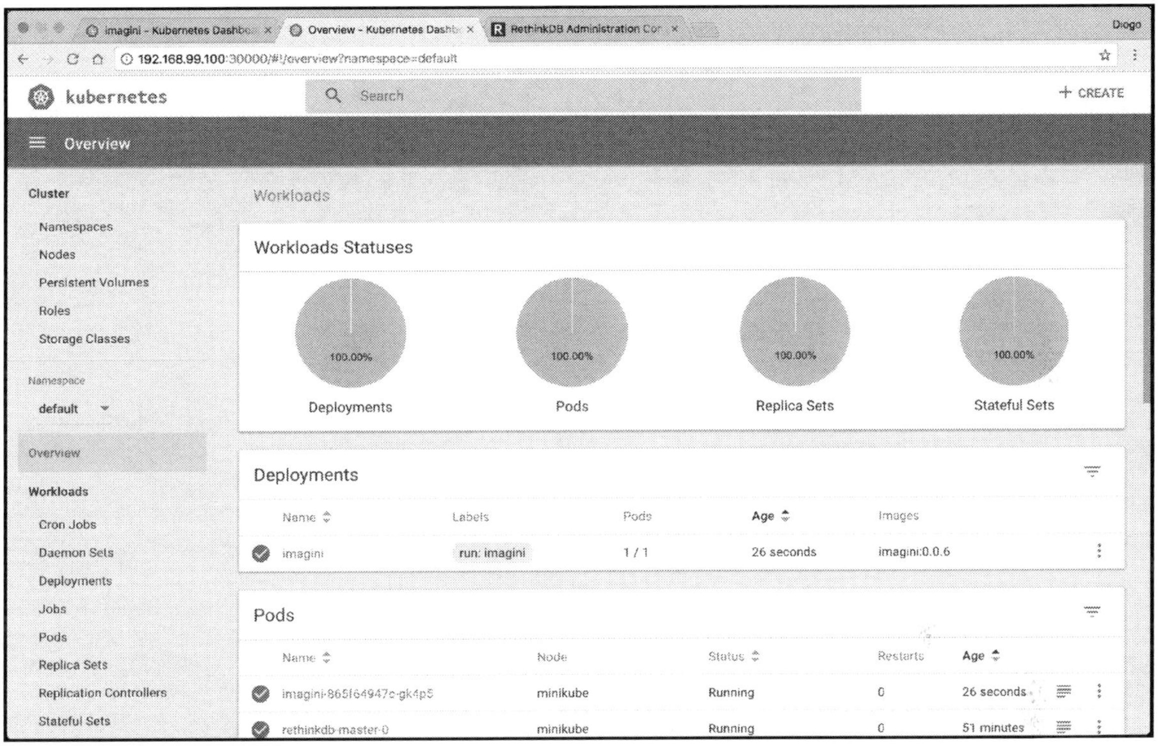


But Pods are, by default, only visible on the internal network. We need to expose our `imagini` to the exterior. Do this by running:

```
kubectl expose deployment imagini --type=LoadBalancer
```

If you check the services, you'll see that our service will expose on port `3000`, but it's currently pending. This is because we're using `minikube` and it has no `LoadBalancer`. For example, on a cloud provider, this would launch a real load balancer with an external address and would route traffic to the inside:

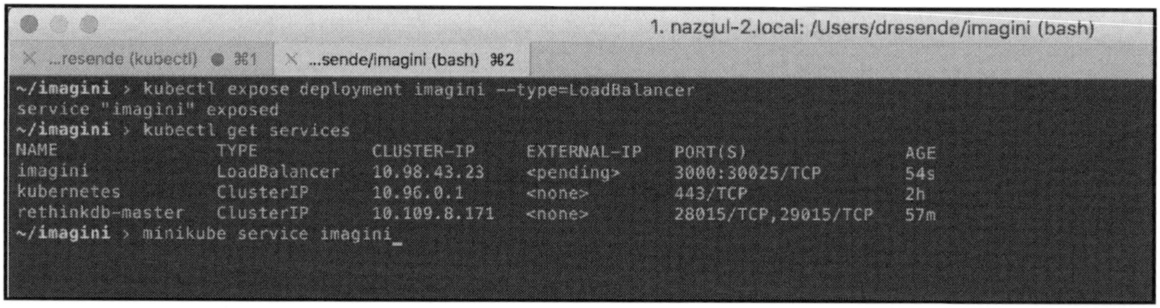


In our case, we can use the direct port, `30025`, which was assigned randomly. We can use the last command you see in the preceding screenshot in order to launch a browser window and point to our service.

You could do all of this using the administration tools from the browser or from the console. Some may be easier on the console, but it's up to you.

This is not an extensive introduction to Kubernetes. The objective was actually to see how easy it was to just make a few changes to our service and get it up and running on a new environment. That's one of the powers of containers.

# Summary

Scaling an application used to be hard and complex. Today, with more information passing through our applications, and with a constantly increasing number of connected users, scaling is now imperative.

Thankfully, containers showed up a couple of years ago and helped solve this problem in a simpler way. There are still obstacles, but with the tools provided by Docker, Kubernetes, and others, replicating our applications and microservices became something that you can do almost without changing your code.

In the next chapter, we'll see what we need to do to have our service be cloud native while deploying our microservice to the **Google Cloud Platform** (**GCP**).

# 8
# Cloud-Native Microservices

Let's recap what we have done so far. We started by looking at the advantages of building applications based on microservices. Then, we looked at several tools that can help us start building our microservices. We stood with Express and embarked on building a simple microservice.

We learned the basics of state and security by interconnecting our microservice and a database server. We've chosen a test suite and added tests until we had a very good code coverage.

Finally, we learned how to deploy our microservice using containers. We then explored how we could scale our microservice using replicas across different sites.

When we deploy our microservice inside a container, we're opening a new world of possibilities. There are plenty of cloud providers that support containers. This means that as soon as we have our microservice running on a local container, we can replicate and do the same on many of these providers in no time.

You might have found that developing using containers gives you consistent and predictable behavior with the application. This also extends to the operations when they need to deploy.

Containers give them a much simpler and faster method to deploy any application. It's almost like your application is already native to the cloud environment, and they just need to specify a few details and that's it, it's deployed.

In this chapter, to make our microservice cloud-native, we're going to use the **Google Cloud Platform** (**GCP**), and:

- Create a new project
- Deploy a database service
- Create a Kubernetes cluster
- Create our microservice files on the cluster
- Deploy our microservice to the cluster

# Preparing for cloud-native

But what is cloud-native? What makes an application cloud-native? We say an application runs in the cloud when it's running outside our premises. More than that, it denotes when an application is supposedly running and spread across different locations and is resilient to failures.

A cloud-native application or microservice is designed from scratch to run in the cloud and take advantage of that computing model. It is able to scale and operate even if parts of its infrastructure fail. Being cloud-native is about how we deploy our microservice, not where.

And, we're already doing that! Since we first deployed using Docker, we have already started and restarted our microservice, and rebuilt new images and replicated without the worry of where, but instead, how.

Thinking generically, there are a few points to take into account when designing our microservice, or anything that will be cloud-native, for that matter:

- Understand what data your microservice will handle, and what kind of structures and relations will there be. Does a relational database such as MySQL or PostgreSQL suffice? Do you need a more loose database server that can handle documents with different information structures, such as MongoDB or RethinkDB?
  These questions must be answered to narrow the options. There are plenty of other types of databases. After narrowing your choices, you should pick the one that gives you more resilience and that can be replicated the same way as your microservice, to handle some degree of failure.
- Find out what other dependencies you might need. If you have choices, go for the ones that are not dependent on a specific operative system. Below the cloud servers, there are different operative systems and you don't want to be forced to choose any type.
- Avoid going non-standard. More specifically, try to take the most out of current standard protocols. Because you can deploy to geographically distant hosts, connectivity and policy rules may introduce restrictions to traffic, so keep with standards such as HTTP in order to communicate between microservices.
- Design your microservices to be able to scale horizontally. It's not uncommon for microservices to not scale linearly just by adding replicas, but try to design them to be able to distribute loads more evenly. One easy path is to have a layer of proxies on top.

# Going cloud-native

Now that we're able to deploy using containers, and we have used Kubernetes already on a local virtual machine, let's see how we can do the same on a cloud environment. You can choose any type of cloud provider, as long as you follow the considerations we just discussed in the previous section.

We're going to use GCP. There's a one-year trial with free credit available, so you can try it out while you read this. Head to the website and register if you haven't done it before. You'll probably be asked to enter a payment method, but don't worry, they won't charge unless you exceed the free credit:

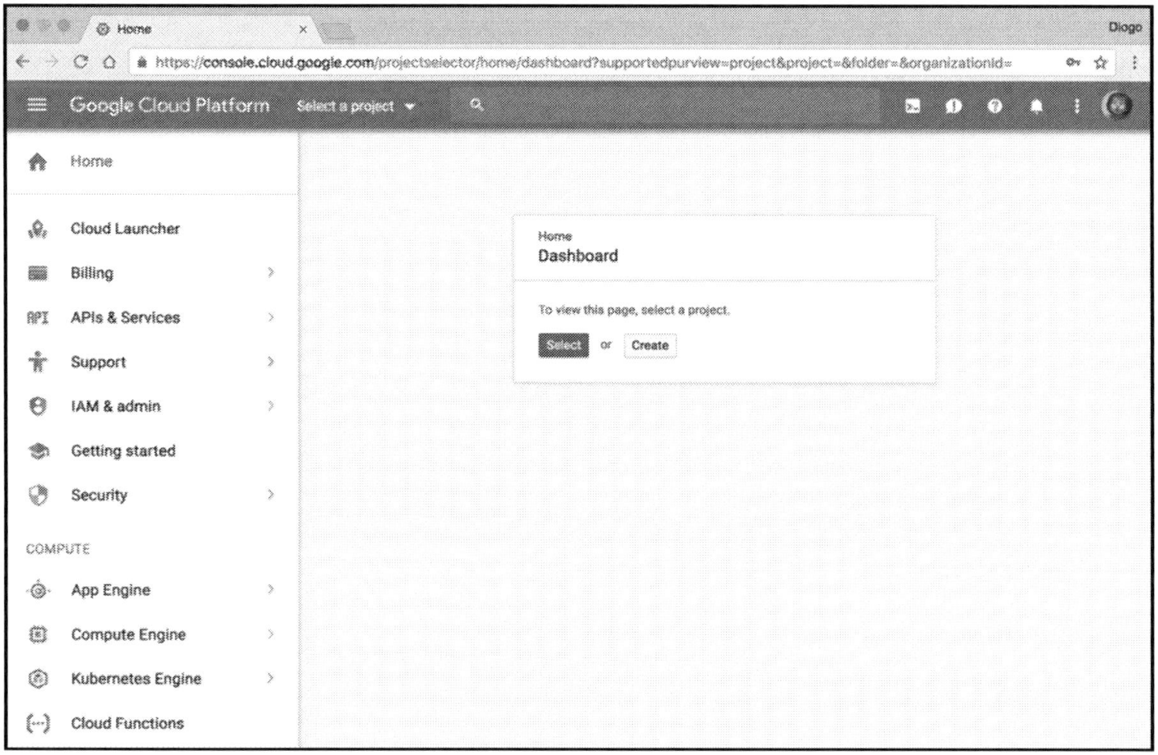


## Creating a new project

You now need to create a project. Just follow the instructions, set a name, and hit the **Create** button:

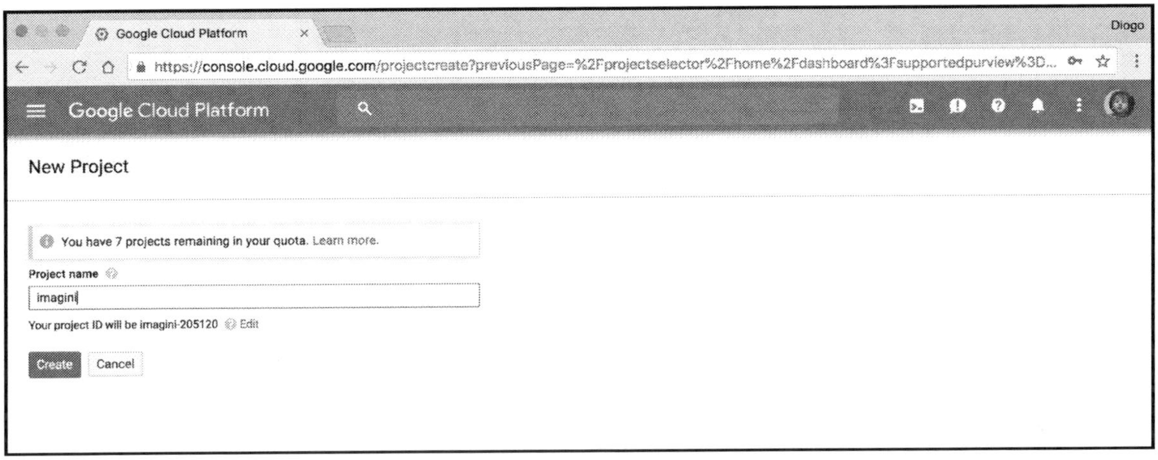

You'll then have access to the project dashboard. You can check resource usage and project status, as well as billing information:

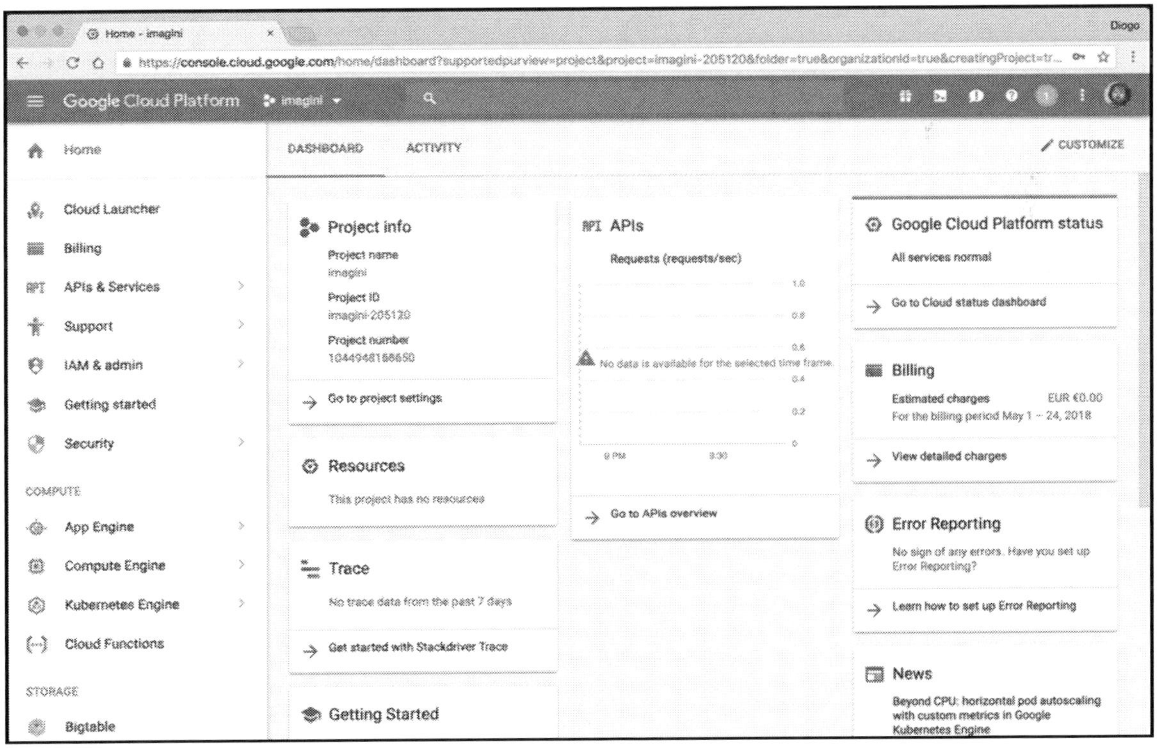

# Deploying a database service

On the left-hand side, there are the main navigation options, one of which, Cloud Launcher, lets us easily set up services that we need. Since we used RethinkDB in the previous chapter, let's now try MySQL again. We need a database server, so let's head to Cloud Launcher:

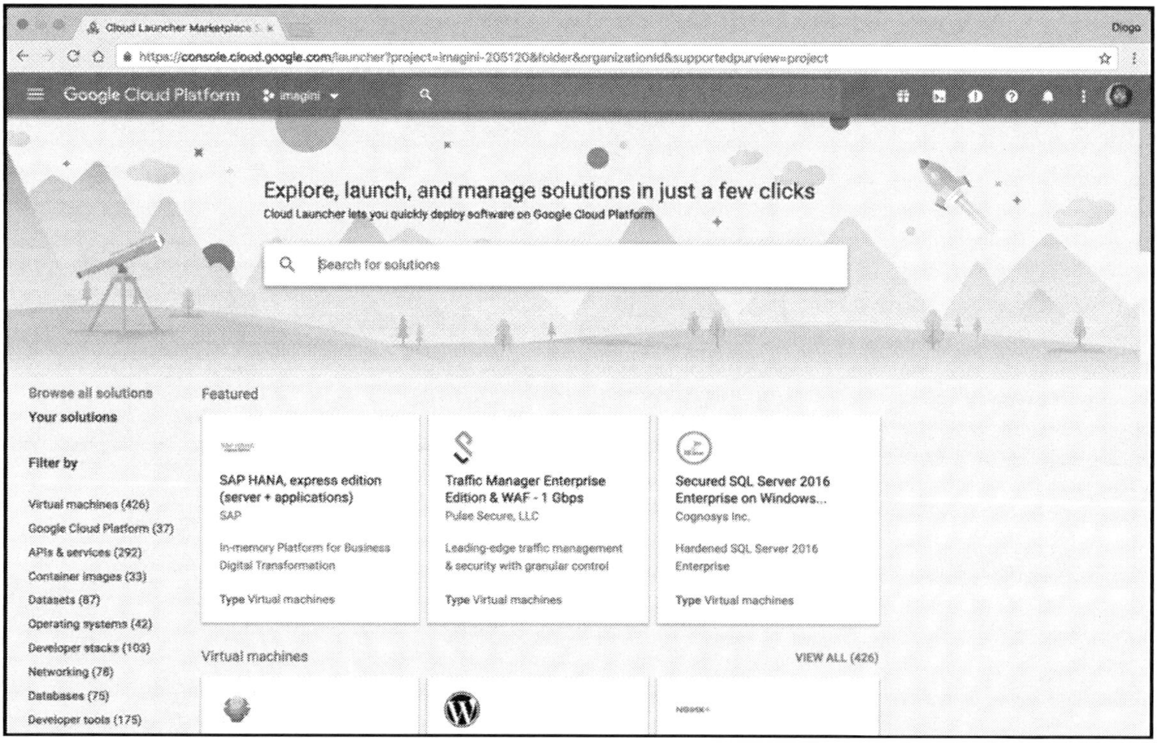

On the sidebar, there are a couple of service categories to choose from. Let's use the filter on top to search for **mysql**:

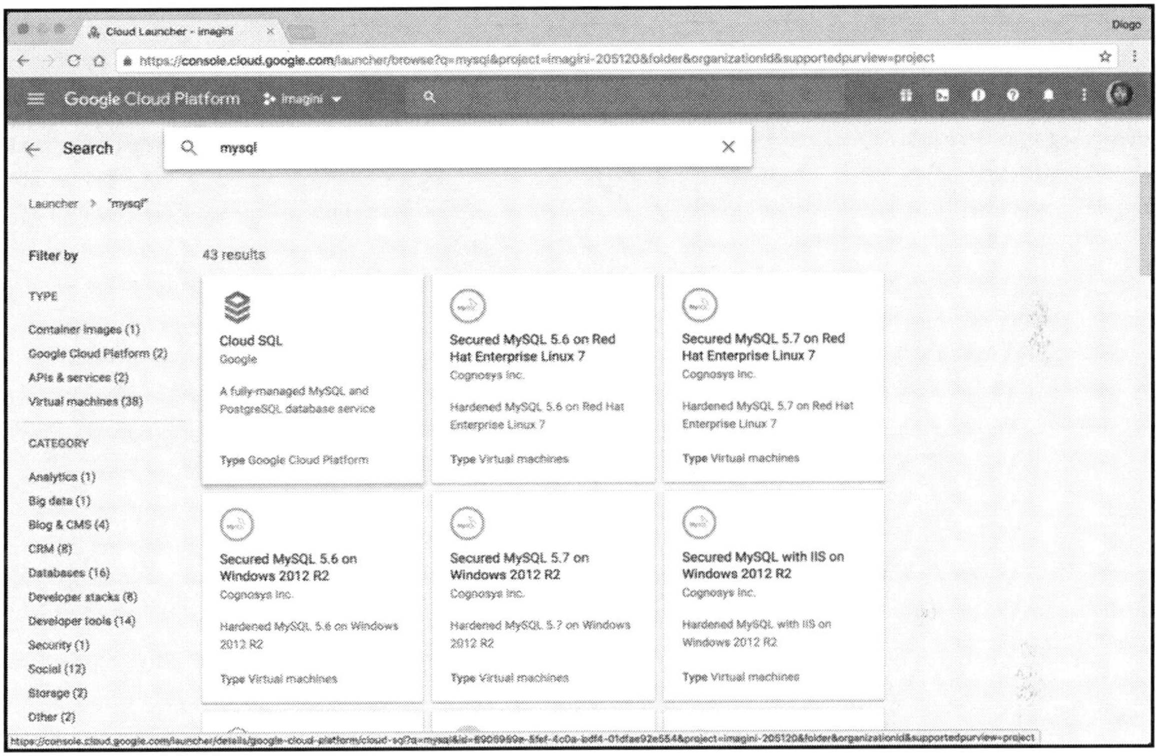

One of the options, in my case the first, is **Cloud SQL**, which is a Google service used to run a fully-managed MySQL or PostgreSQL database service. It alleviates the burden of configuration and maintenance. Click on that option:

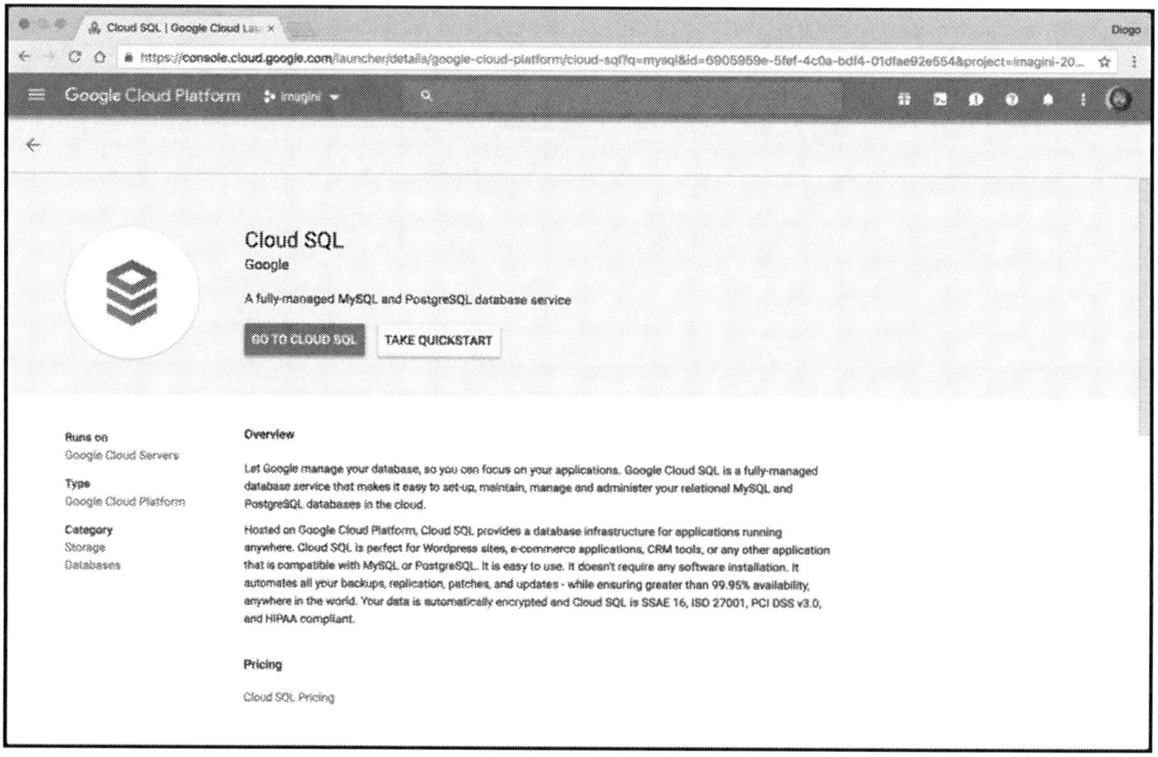

There's an overview with an explanation of the service, as well as pricing if you want to consult it. Because we're using free credit, that is not a concern for now. Click on **GO TO CLOUD SQL**:

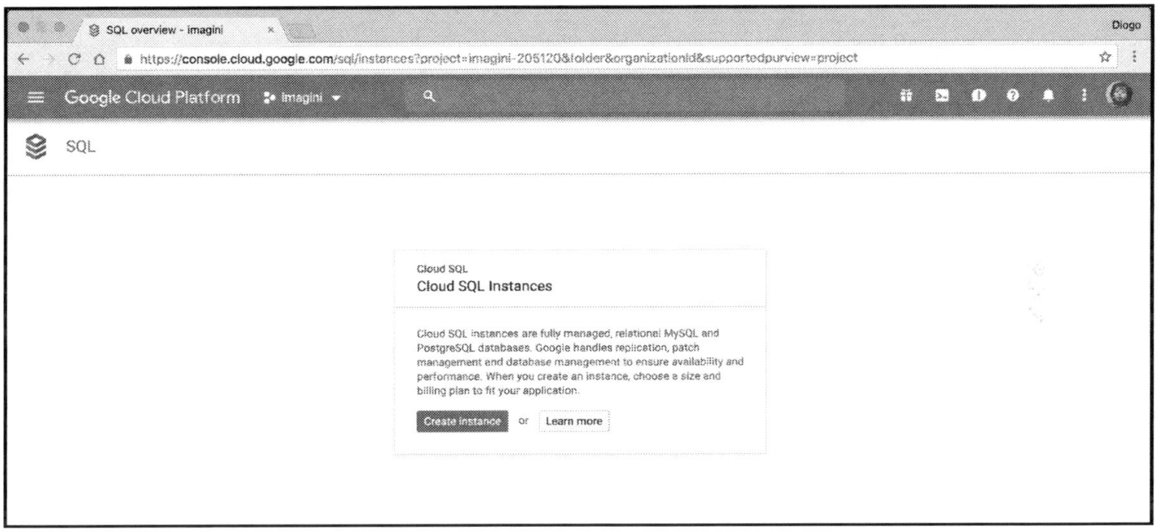


Because we're using the service for the first time, there's no service instance. Click on "Create Instance" to create a new one, follow the instructions, and create the instance. You'll be asked for a password for the default root account; don't forget it. At the end, you should see an instance list. Wait until your instance is fully up and running:

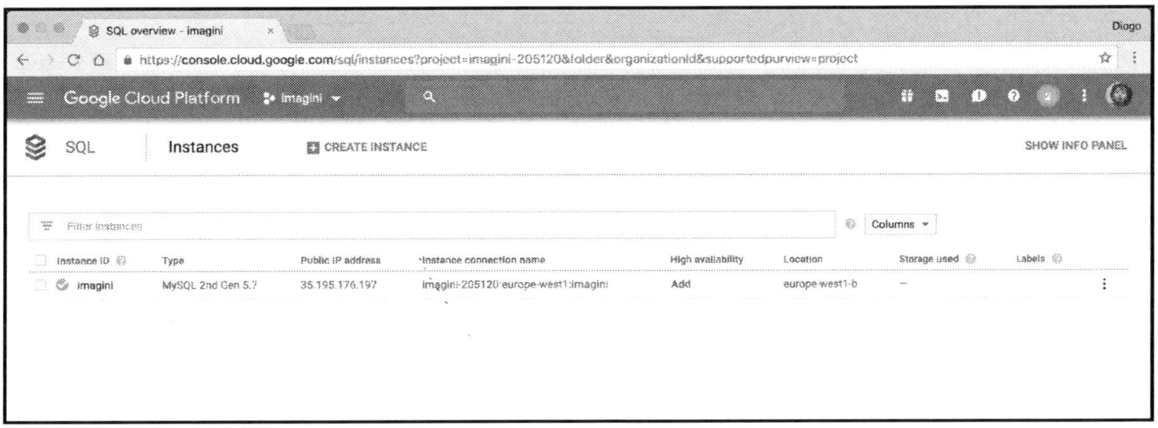

You can click on the instance ID and see more information about it. You'll have access to a service dashboard, as well as be able to import and export:

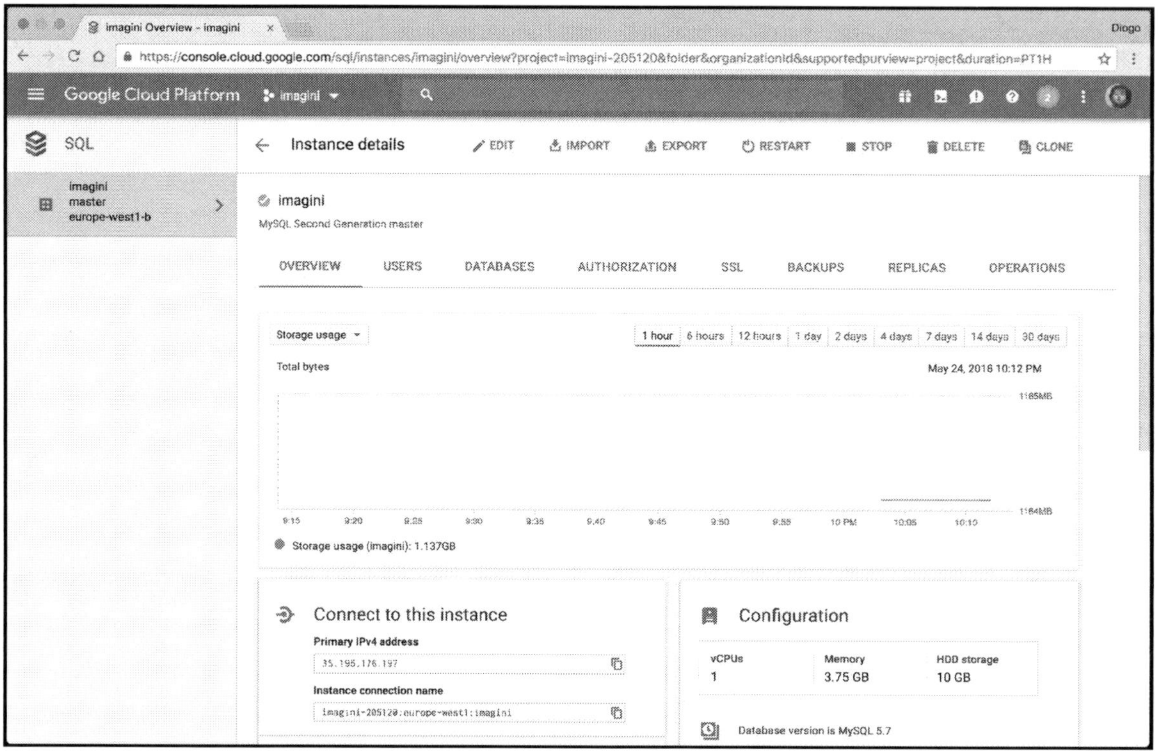

There's a **DATABASES** tab where we can create our microservice database. Head there and create it. Retain defaults on the character set and collation:

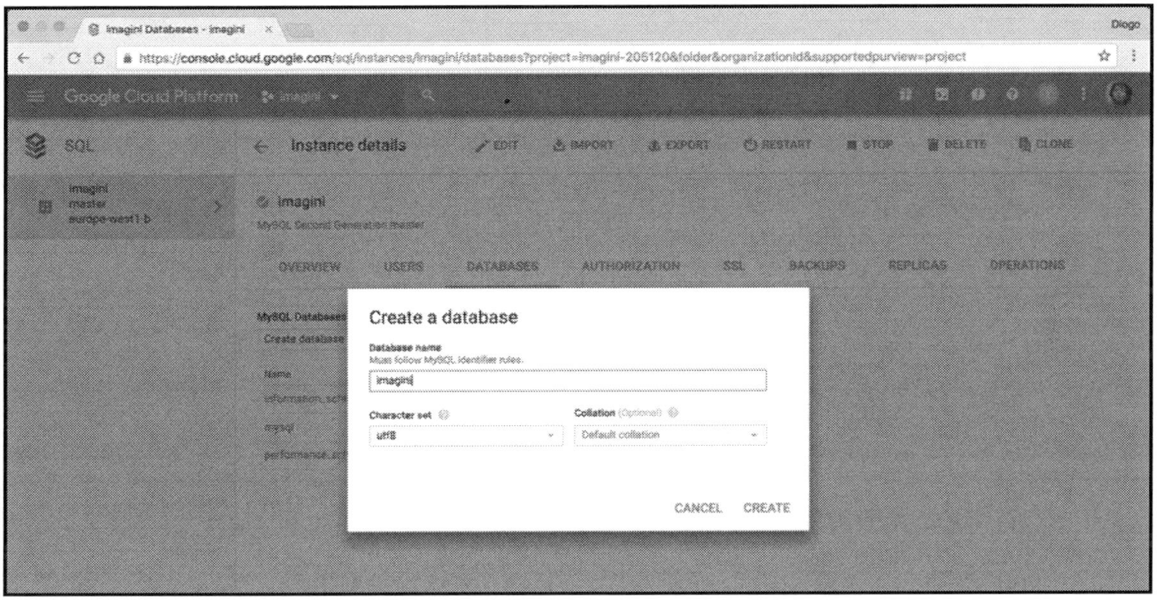

Our database is now ready. Let's head back to the project dashboard. Click on **Google Cloud Platform** in the top-left corner of the screen:

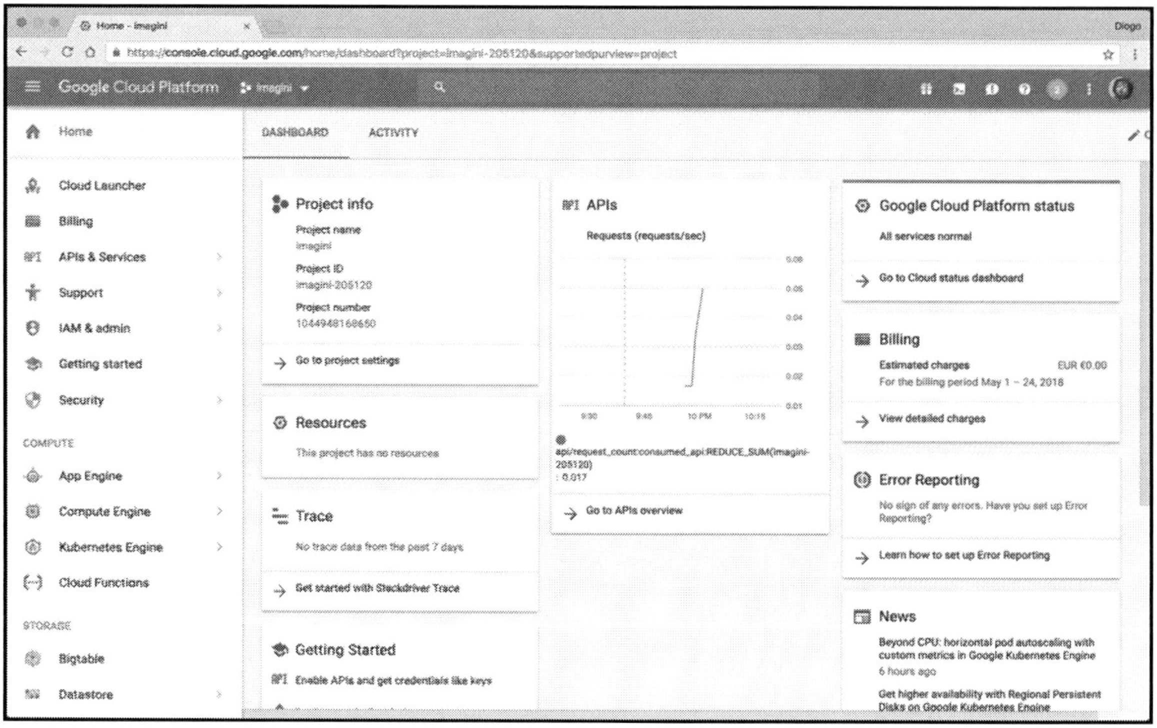

You'll notice that the **APIs** block on the middle column now has a line showing some activity. APIs are part of the infrastructure and, since we just created a service instance, there's some activity going on. Click on **Go to APIs overview**:

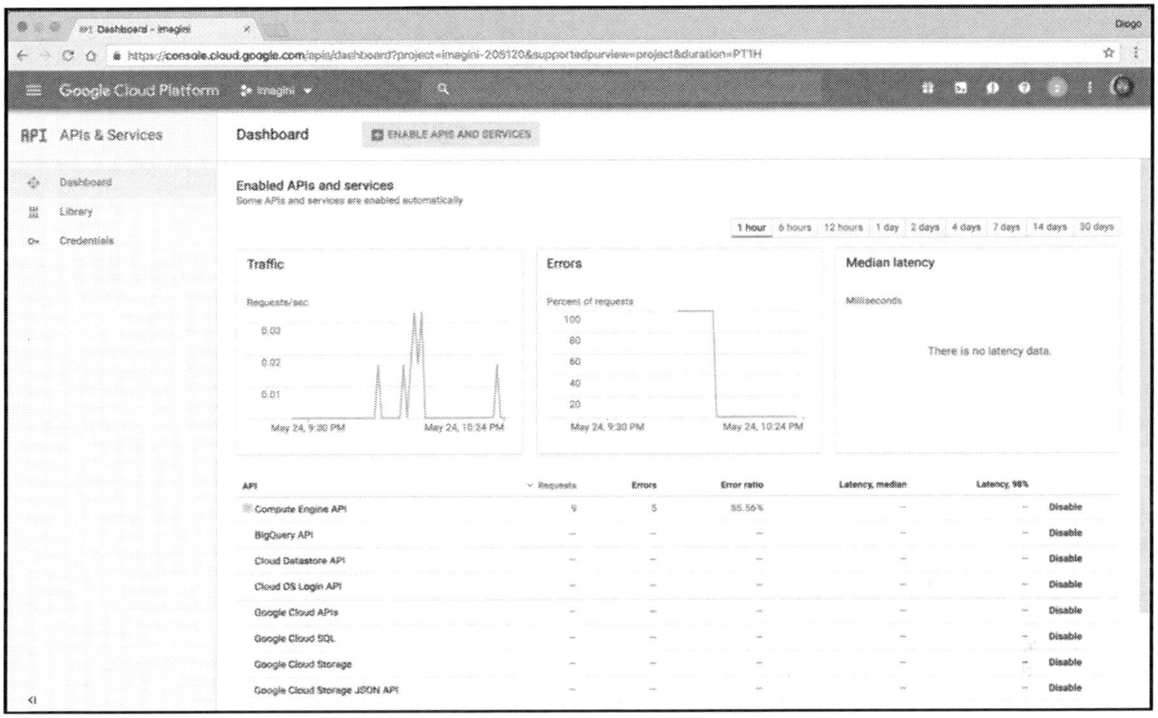


Here, you can monitor activity, traffic, and errors of all enabled and used APIs. Heading back to our project dashboard, and looking at the sidebar, you'll notice there are plenty of options available.

Scrolling down a bit, you'll find an **SQL** section, where you can find our previously created instance. If you need to go there in the future, this is how you find it:

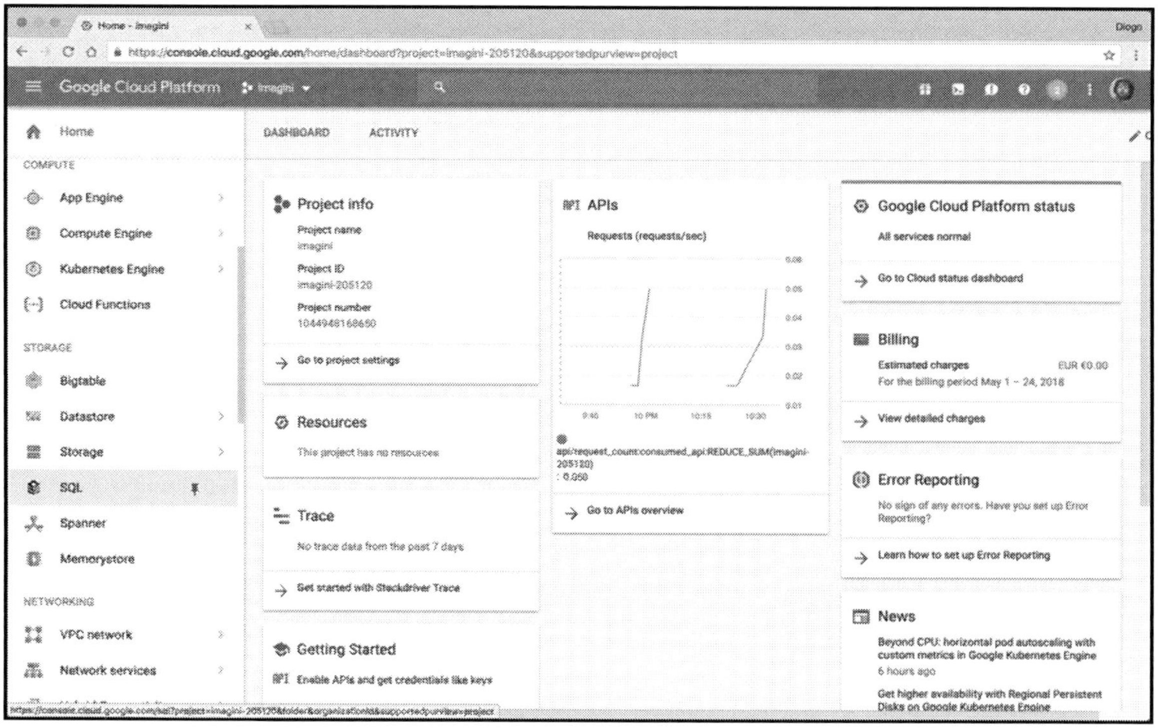

# Creating a Kubernetes cluster

Previously, for a few items, you may have noticed the **Kubernetes Engine** option. That's where we're heading to prepare our cluster:

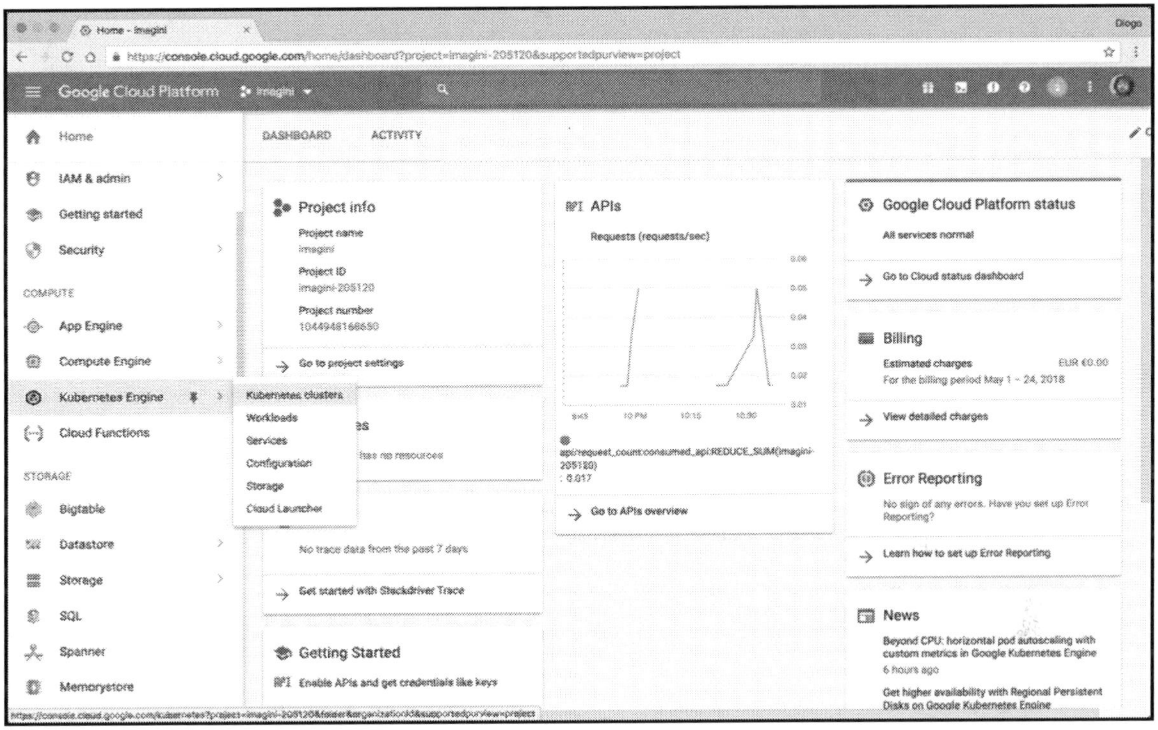

You'll be asked to create a new cluster. Choose the default options, or change the ones you want to try out, and create a cluster for our microservice to run on:

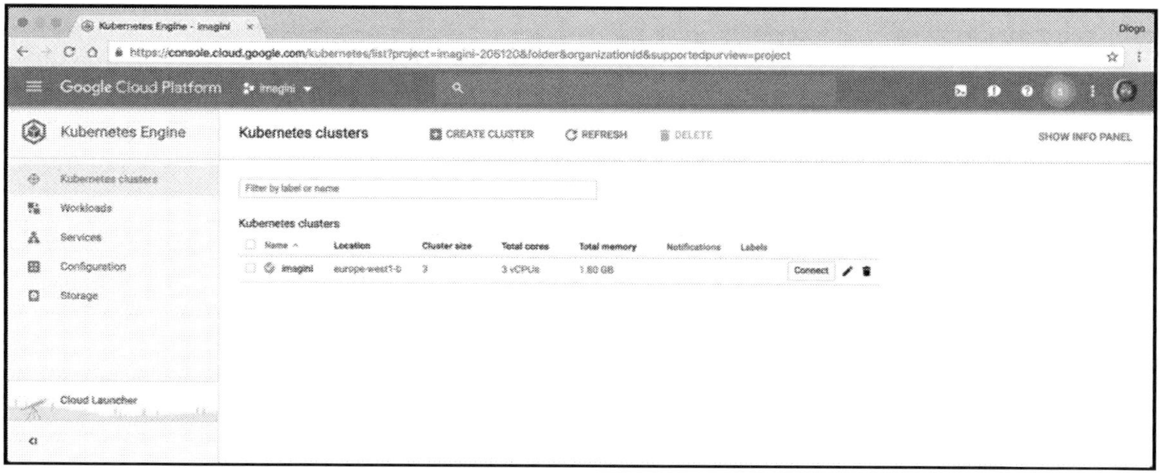


We now have a Kubernetes cluster of three nodes to run our microservice. In the top-right corner of the screen, you'll find one important icon, which is the **Google Cloud Shell icon**:

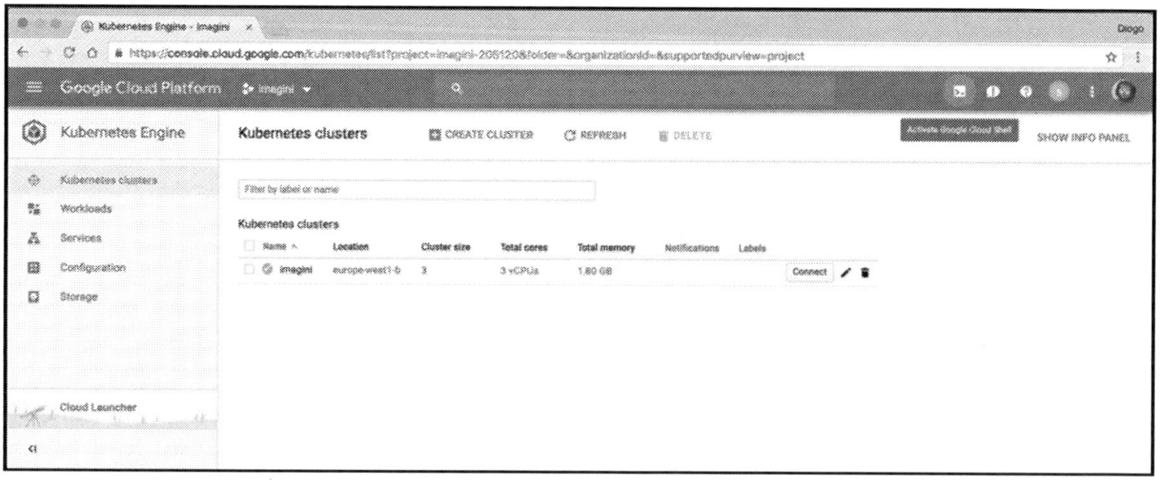

If you click on it, a console will open that gives you access to your platform using a terminal. You can do all kinds of stuff, such as monitoring containers, and checking connectivity:

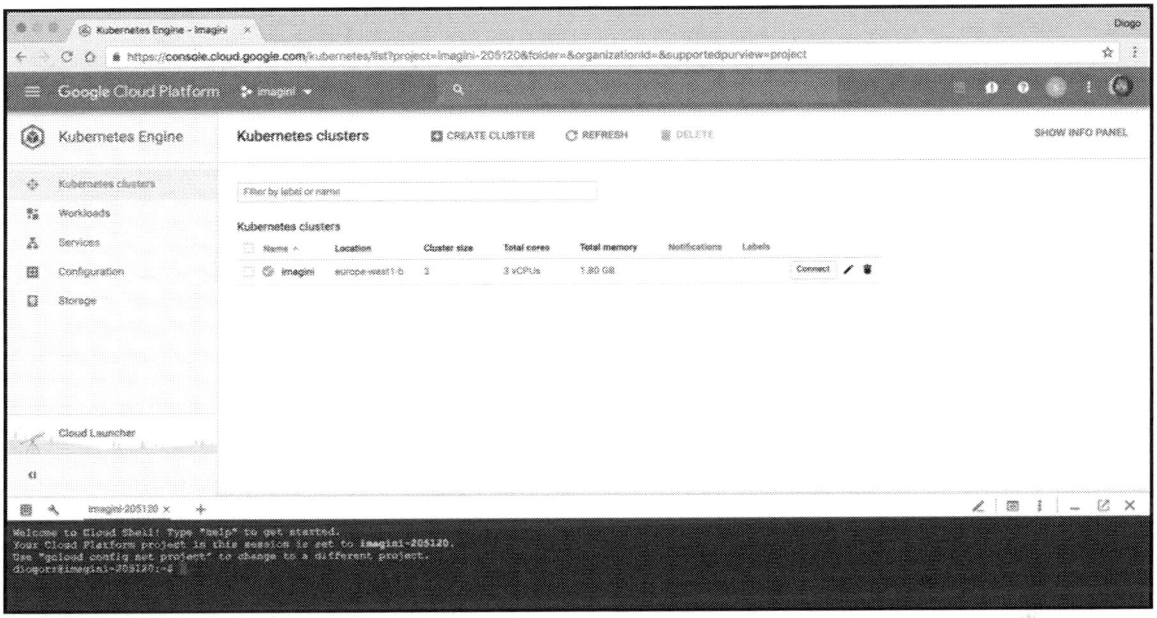


This is a normal console, but with the `gcloud` and `kubectl` commands already installed. You can have those installed locally and manage your clusters remotely, or just access this console to make a quick change or checkup.

# Creating our microservice

Similar to what we did before, these are the steps we need to perform before successfully deploying to our new cluster:

1. Create our docker image that will use our MySQL instance.
2. Create credentials to access the instance.
3. Create the configuration for our service.
4. Deploy it.

First, notice the pencil icon in the top-right corner of the console. It's an online editor we can use to create the files we need:

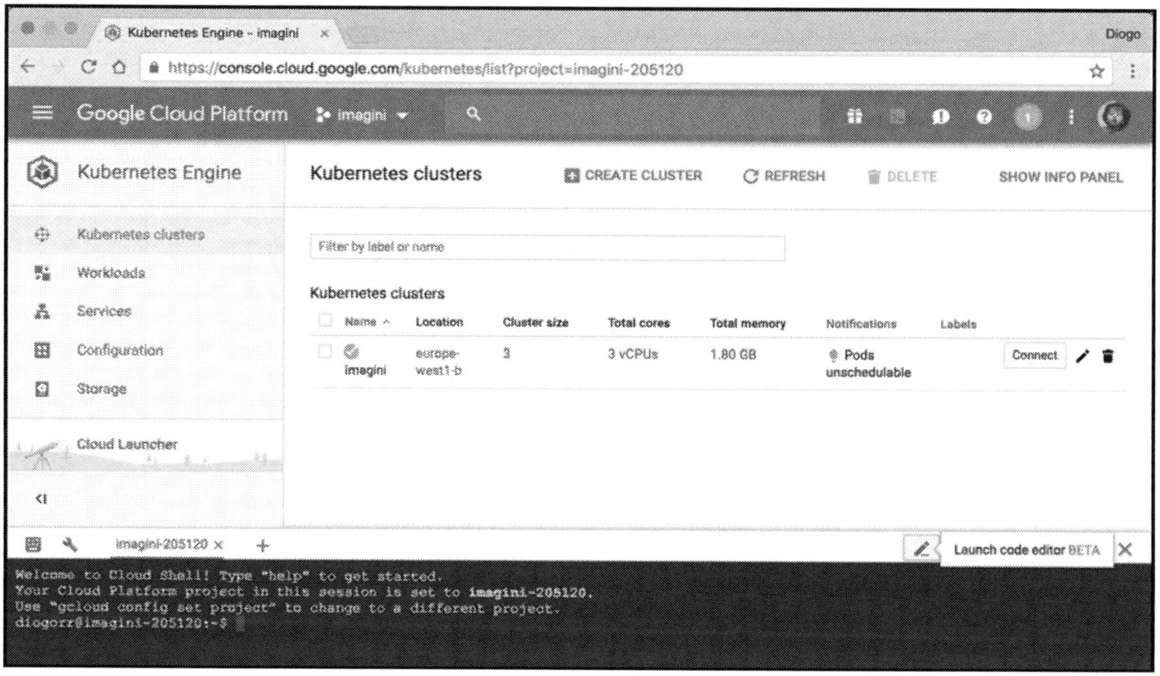

Click on it. It should open a new tab with an empty editor. This represents the root folder of the console you have on the bottom:

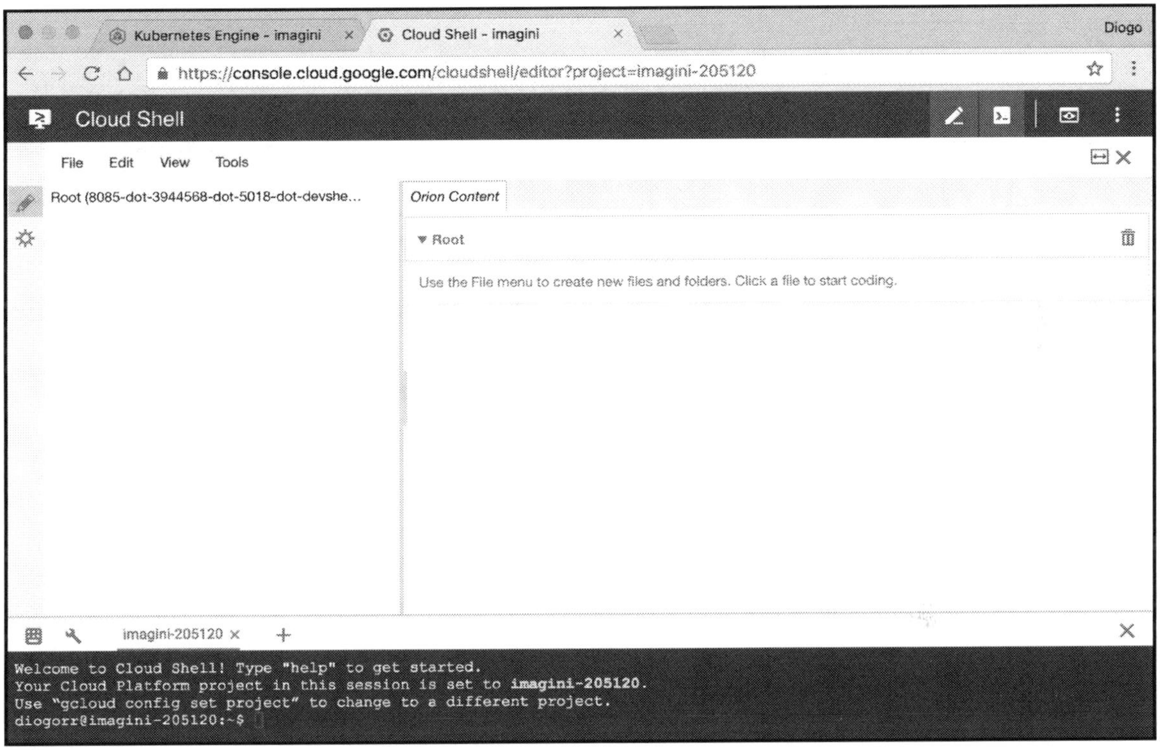

Let's start by creating our `package.json` file. Go to **File** and click **New**, and then **File**. Type `package.json` and insert our dependencies. Remember, we're using MySQL this time:

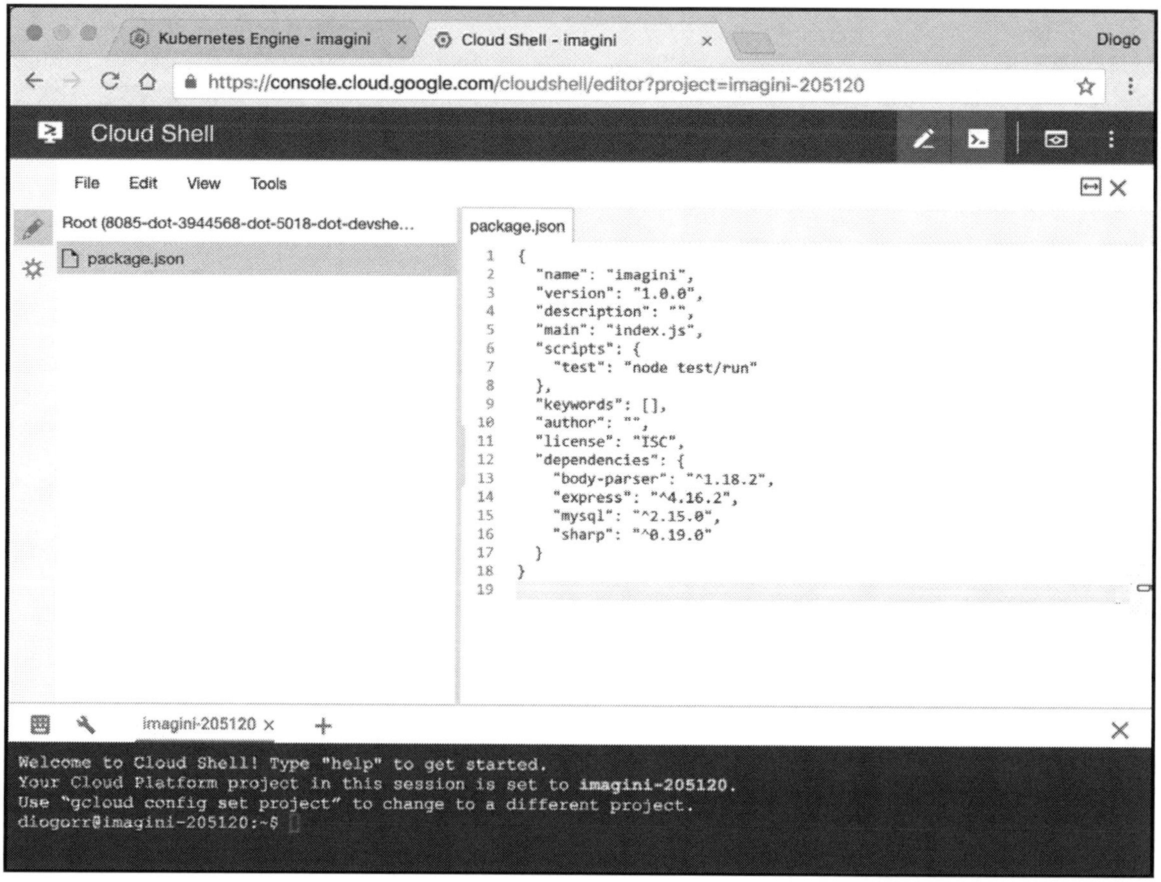

Then, create our service file. We're not using a `settings.json` file; we're going to use credentials passed to the container using an environment variable:

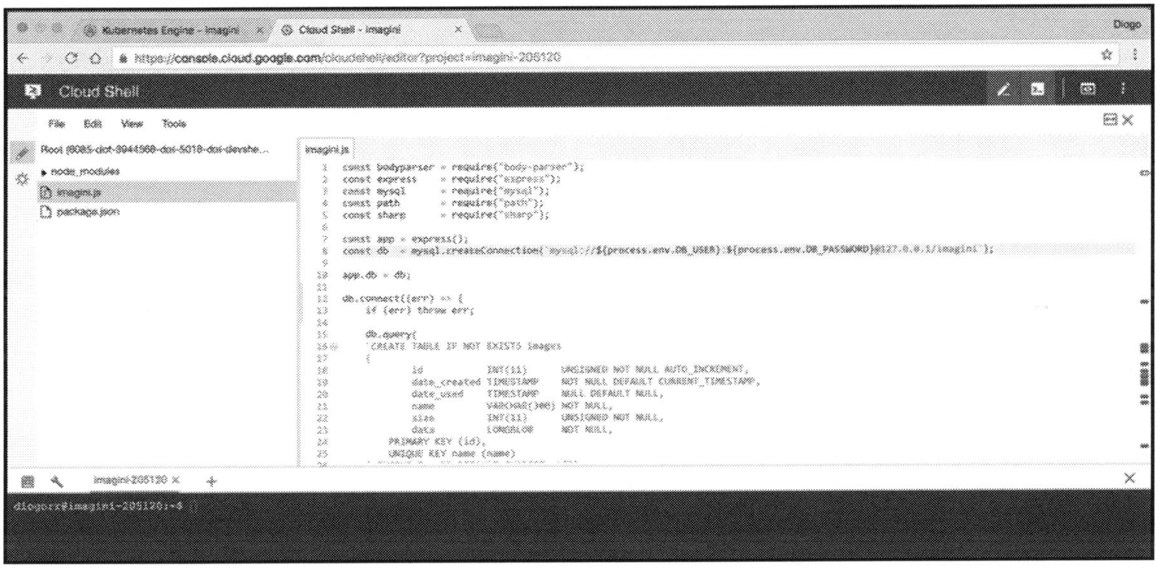

Then, create the `Dockerfile` for our service:

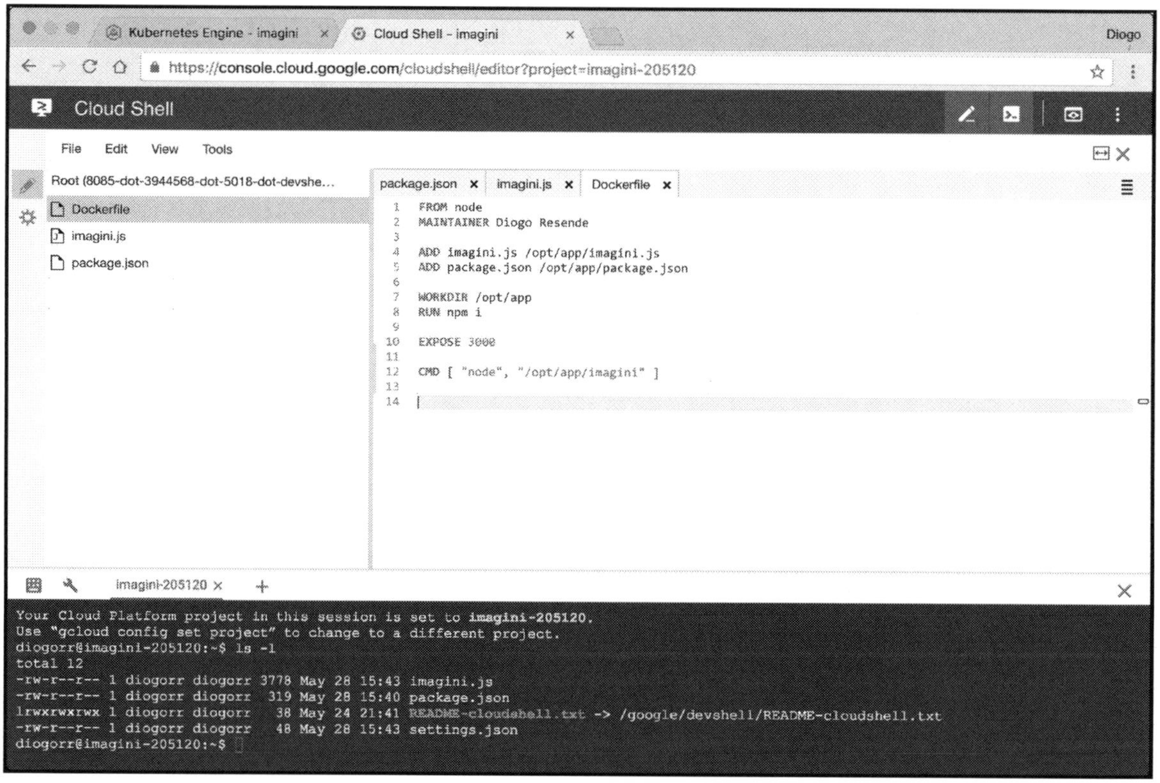


You can see on the bottom console that we're creating the files in the root folder. We're now going to use the console to create our container image. Type the following command:

```
docker build . -t gcr.io/imagini-205120/imagini
```

We're using a more composed name because we're publishing to the **Google Container Registry** (**GCR**), and so it's good practice to use the project ID (as I did) and then the name of the service:

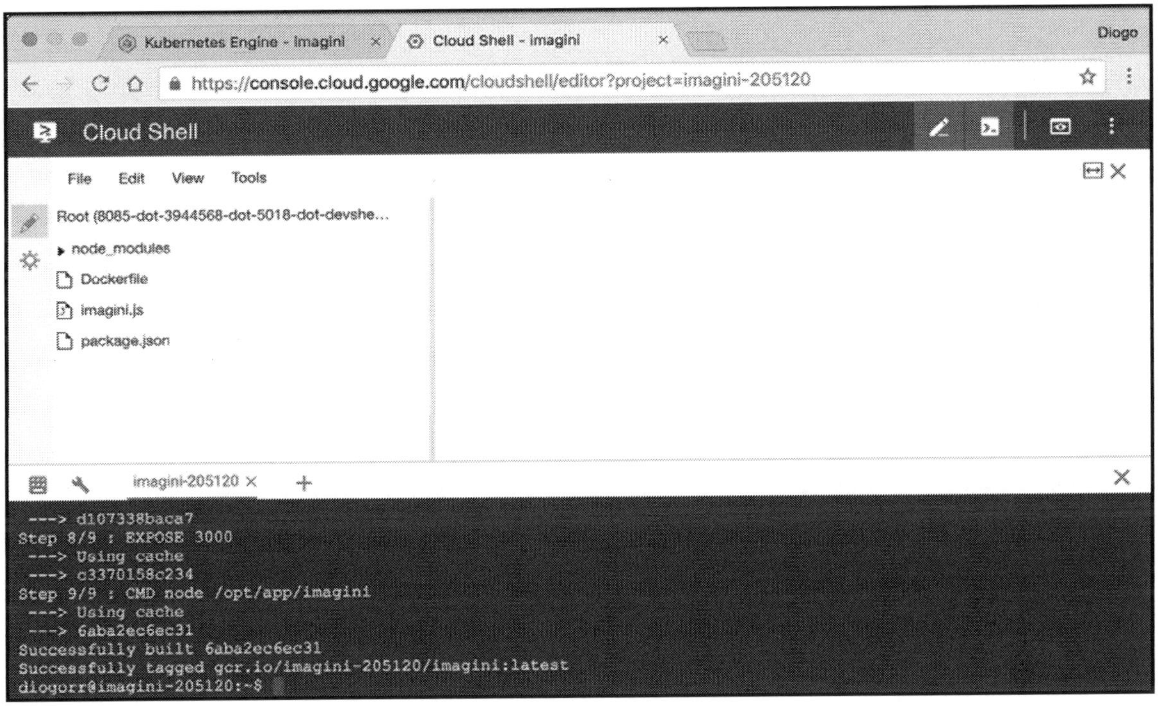


Then, let's push it to the registry using the following command:

```
gcloud docker -- push gcr.io/imagini-205120/imagini
```

If everything goes right, you should see a list of layers of the image being pushed (published to the registry) and, in the end, a digest and the size of the image, as shown here:

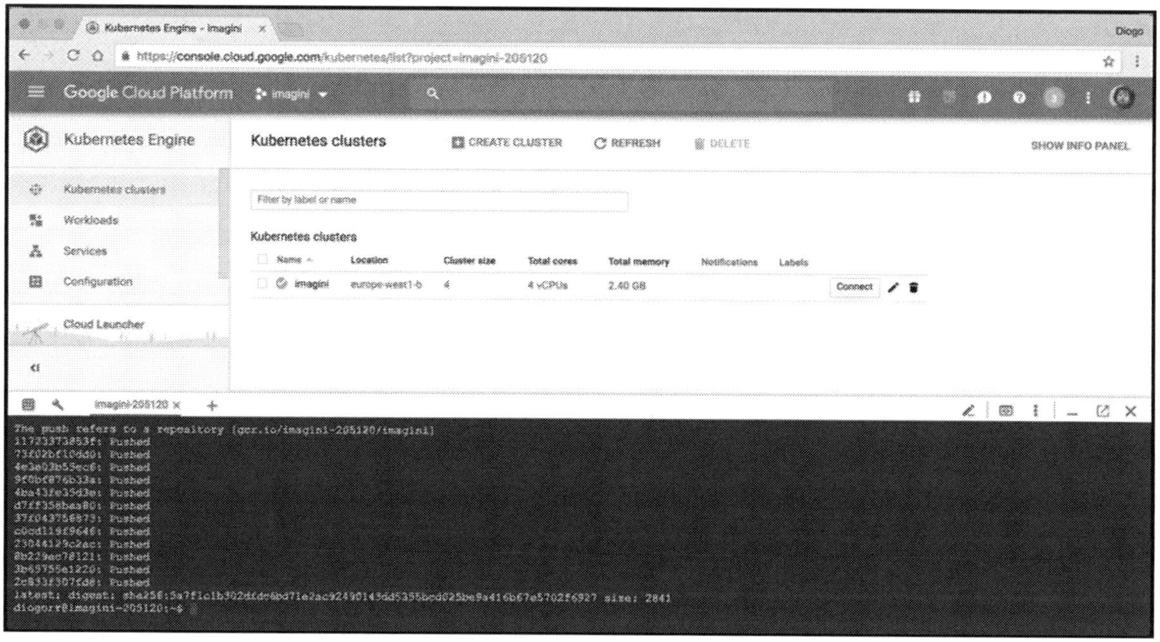


You may notice that I closed the editor between commands. You can use any console, and can even have more than one open.

We now need to create the credentials. We're not going to have passwords on text files. We're going to use an SQL proxy, and we'll expose credentials when the containers are executed, using an environment variable.

First, close the console and click the **Connect** button that is located on the right-hand side of the cluster name:

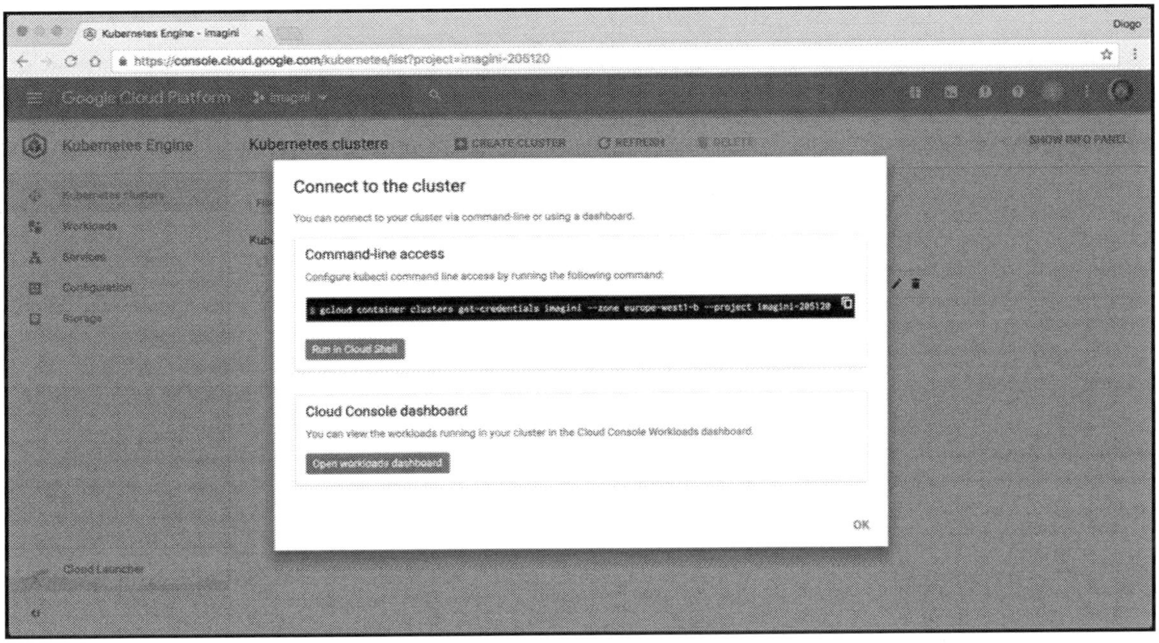


Click **Run in Cloud Shell**. This will reopen the console, but will type in the command to connect to our cluster:

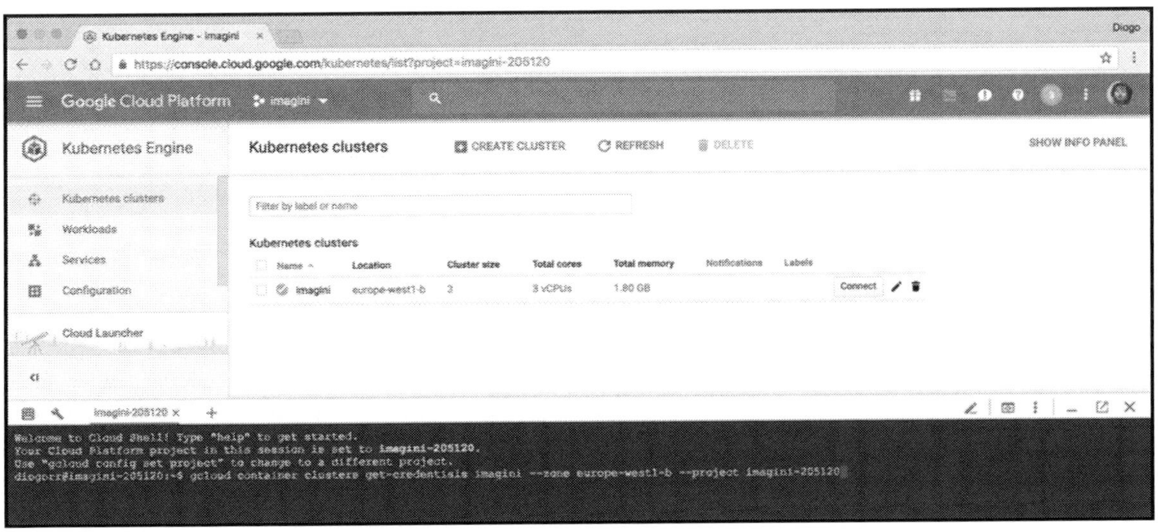

Just hit the *Enter* key in order to have access to the cluster:

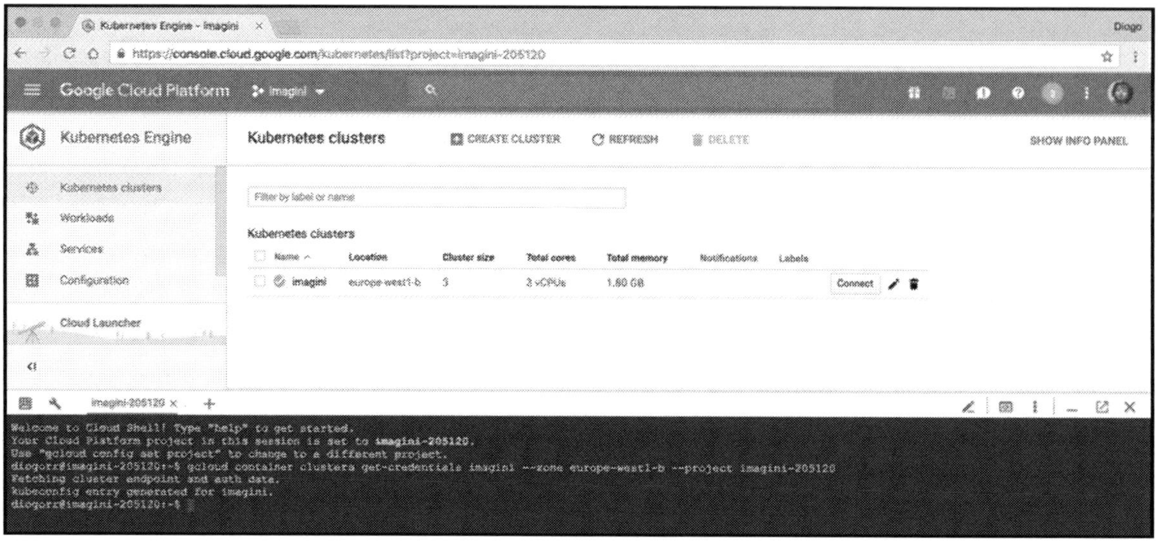

Then, we'll use the `gcloud` command to create the proxy user account that will be used by the SQL proxy to access our Cloud SQL instance:

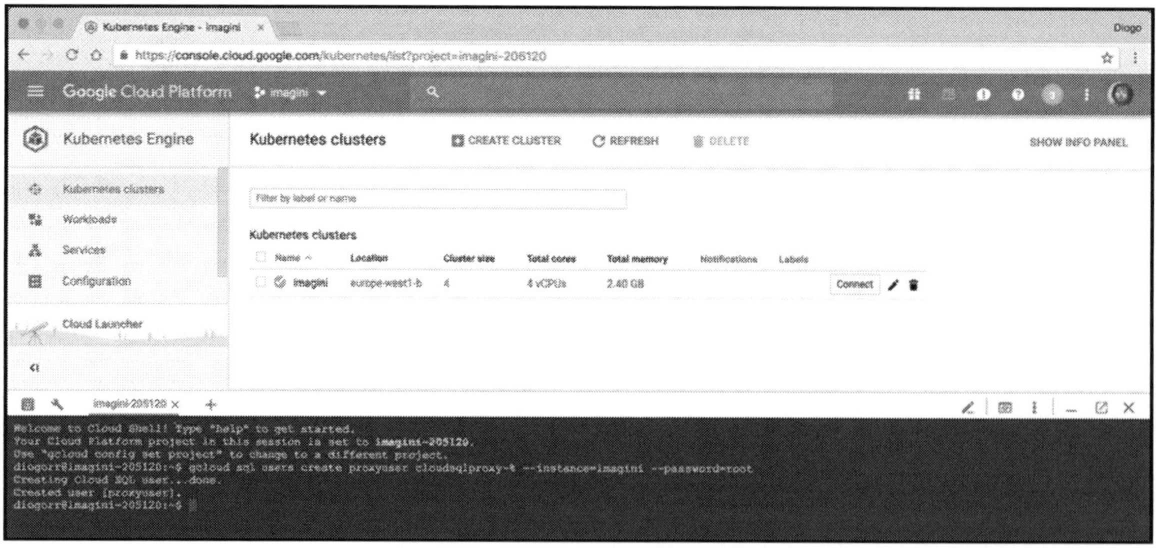

Now, type the following command:

```
gcloud sql instances describe imagini
```

Scroll up the console log until you see a line that starts with **connectionName**:. Take a look at the following screenshot and note the highlighted text in the console.

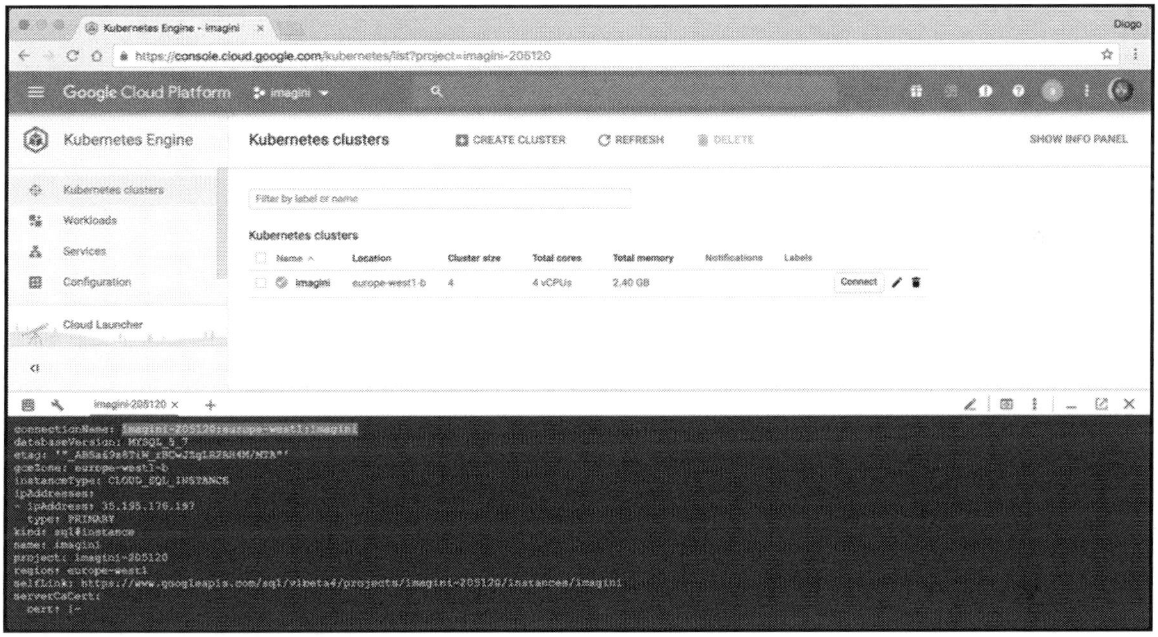


Copy the name down and save it for later. We'll need it when we create our deployment configuration.

Now, let's create a service account that is able to access our Cloud SQL instance. Head to **IAM & admin** and click **Service accounts**:

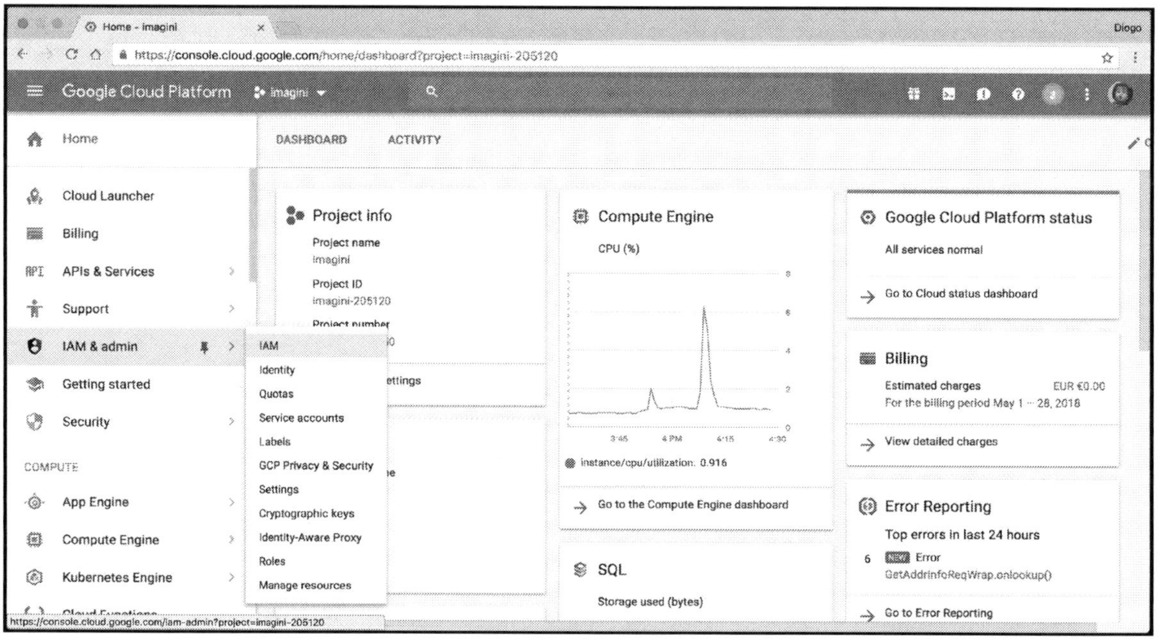

Create a service account with the **Cloud SQL Client** role, and check **Furnish a new private key**:

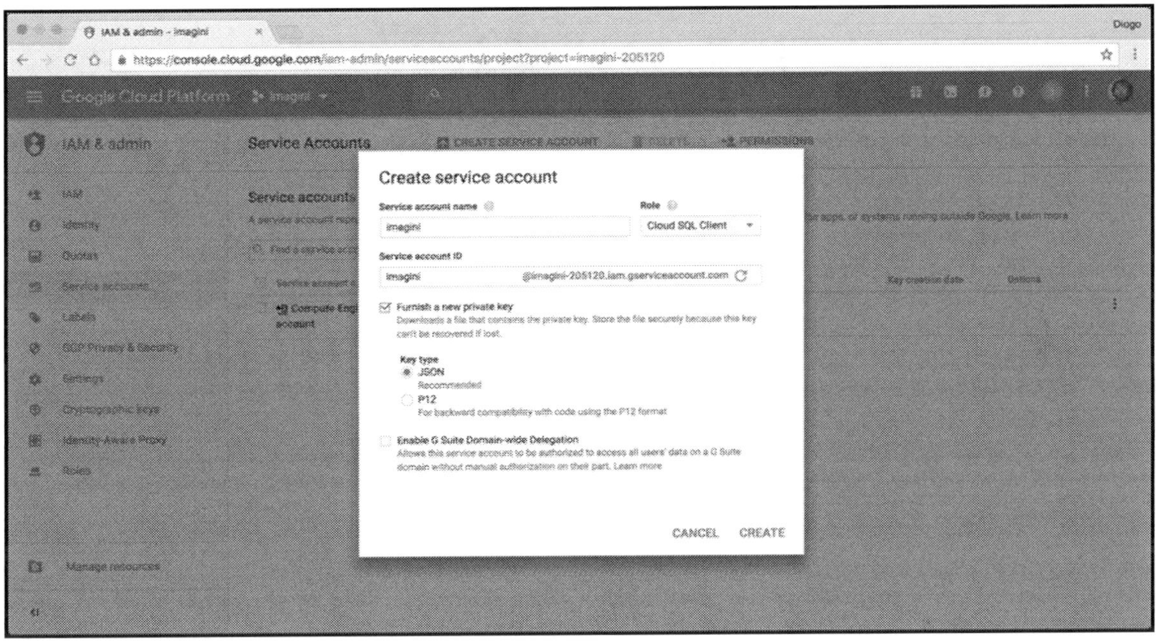

After hitting **Create**, the account will be created and a JSON file will be given to you to save in your local disk. Head back to the cluster, open the console, and then click to open the editor again.

You'll notice that there's a menu with several options in the top-right corner, one of which is **Upload file**:

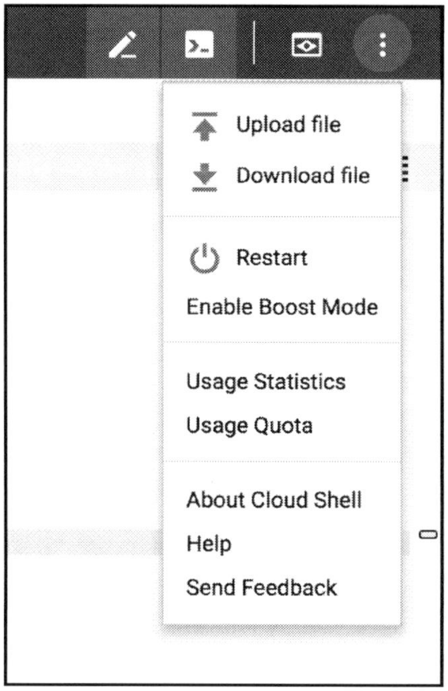


Pick the JSON file you just saved and upload it using that option:

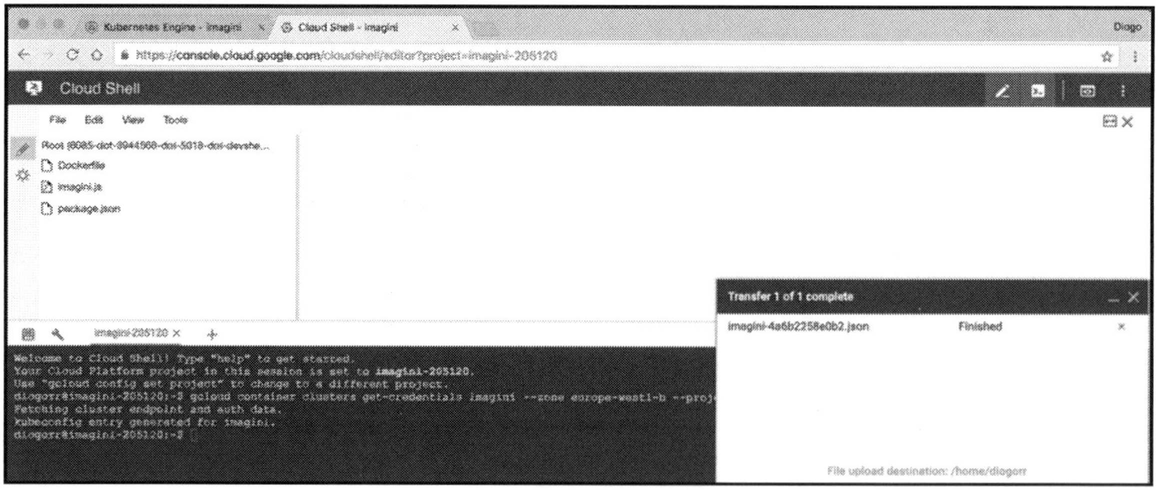

Now, let's use the console to create the instance secret using that credentials file. Use the following command (change the name to your JSON file):

```
kubectl create secret generic cloudsql-instance-credentials --from-
file=credentials.json=imagini-4a6b2258e0b2.json
```

The following screenshot shows the result of the preceding command executed in the console. You should see something like **secret "cloudsql-instance-credentials" created**.

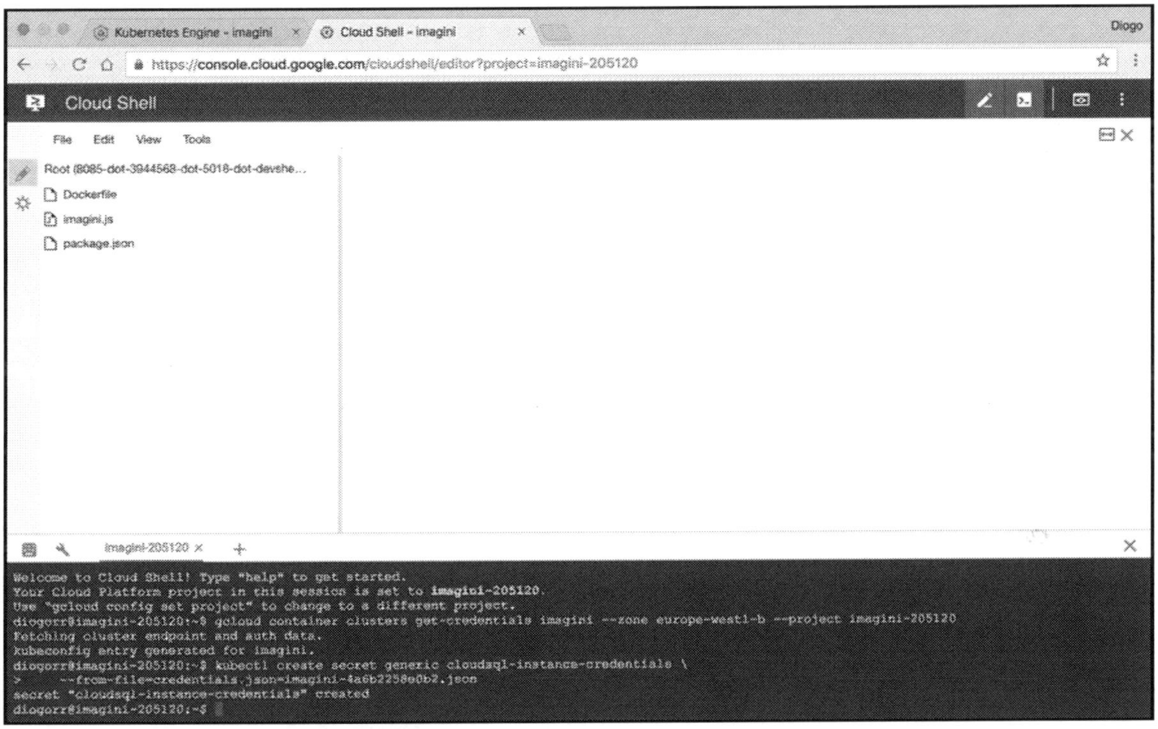

Now, let's create the database credentials secret:

```
kubectl create secret generic cloudsql-db-credentials --from-
literal=username=proxyuser --from-literal=password=root
```

The following screenshot shows the result of the preceding command executed in the console. You should see something like **secret "cloudsql-db-credentials" created**.

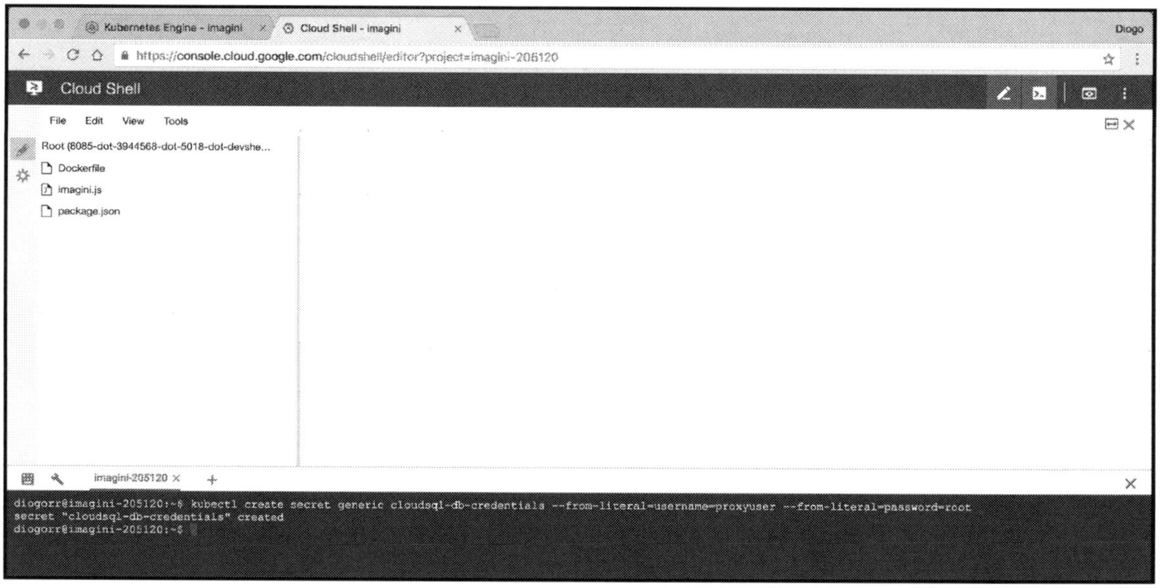


We now have everything ready to deploy our service. This is the configuration we'll be using:

```
apiVersion: extensions/v1beta1
kind: Deployment
metadata:
  name: imagini-frontend
  labels:
    app: imagini
spec:
  replicas: 3
  template:
    metadata:
      labels:
        app: imagini
        tier: frontend
    spec:
      containers:
      - name: imagini-app
        image: gcr.io/imagini-205120/imagini
        imagePullPolicy: Always
        ports:
        - name: http-server
          containerPort: 3000
        env:
          - name: DB_USER
```

```
          valueFrom:
            secretKeyRef:
              name: cloudsql-db-credentials
              key: username
        - name: DB_PASSWORD
          valueFrom:
            secretKeyRef:
              name: cloudsql-db-credentials
              key: password
    - name: cloudsql-proxy
      image: gcr.io/cloudsql-docker/gce-proxy:1.11
      command: ["/cloud_sql_proxy",
                "-instances=imagini-205120:europe-
                west1:imagini=tcp:3306",
                "-credential_file=/secrets/cloudsql/credentials.json"]
      volumeMounts:
        - name: cloudsql-instance-credentials
          mountPath: /secrets/cloudsql
          readOnly: true
    volumes:
      - name: cloudsql-instance-credentials
        secret:
          secretName: cloudsql-instance-credentials
```

Summing up, we're defining the following:

- The service name and same meta information
- The number of replicas we want
- The service, using our container image that we published earlier
- Two environment variables, based on the secrets we created earlier
- The SQL proxy that will enable our service to securely connect to our Cloud SQL

The secrets ensure that we have no confidential information spread on clear text files. Notice the instance name there. Replace it with the instance in **connectionName** that we saw before.

```
-instances=INSTANCE_ID=tcp:3306
```

# Deploying our microservice

We can now create our deployment. Head to the editor and create a deployment file called `imagini.yml` with the content I just described:

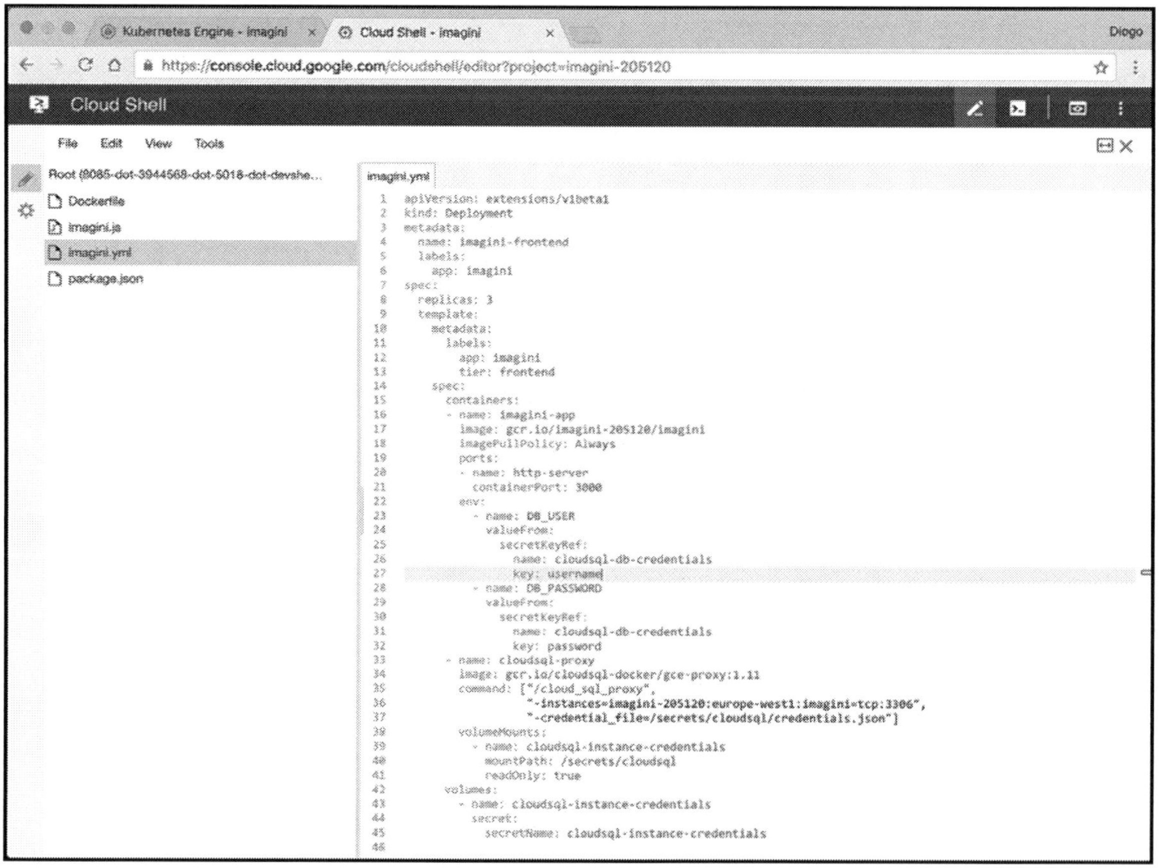


Then, use the console and type the following:

```
kubectl create -f imagini.yml
```

If nothing wrong happens, you should see a line along the lines of **deployment "imagini-frontend" created**, as shown in the console in the following screenshot:

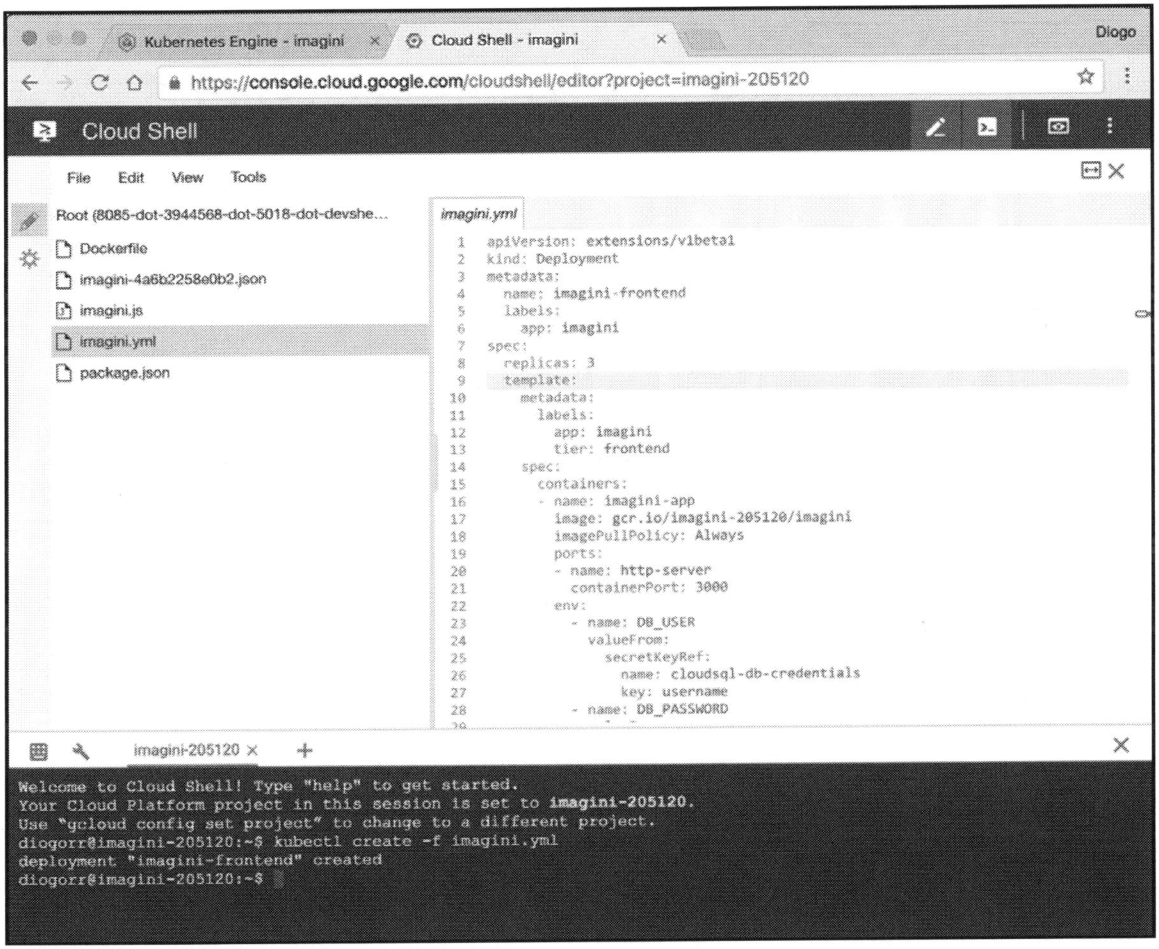

Our service is now deployed. It will take some time until it is fully running. Go back to the **Kubernetes Engine** and click on **Workloads**:

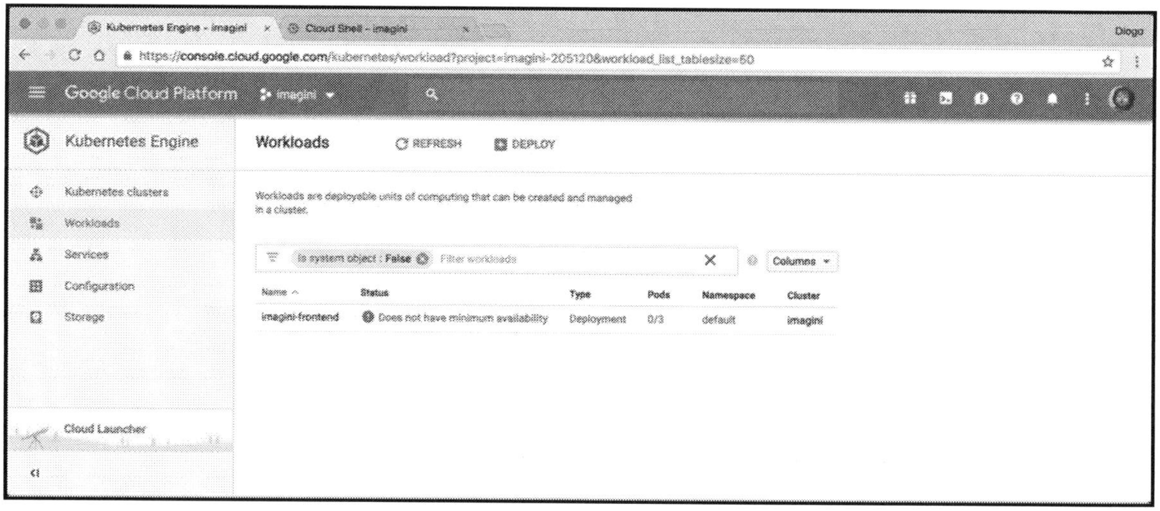

Click on **imagini-frontend** to see how deployment is proceeding:

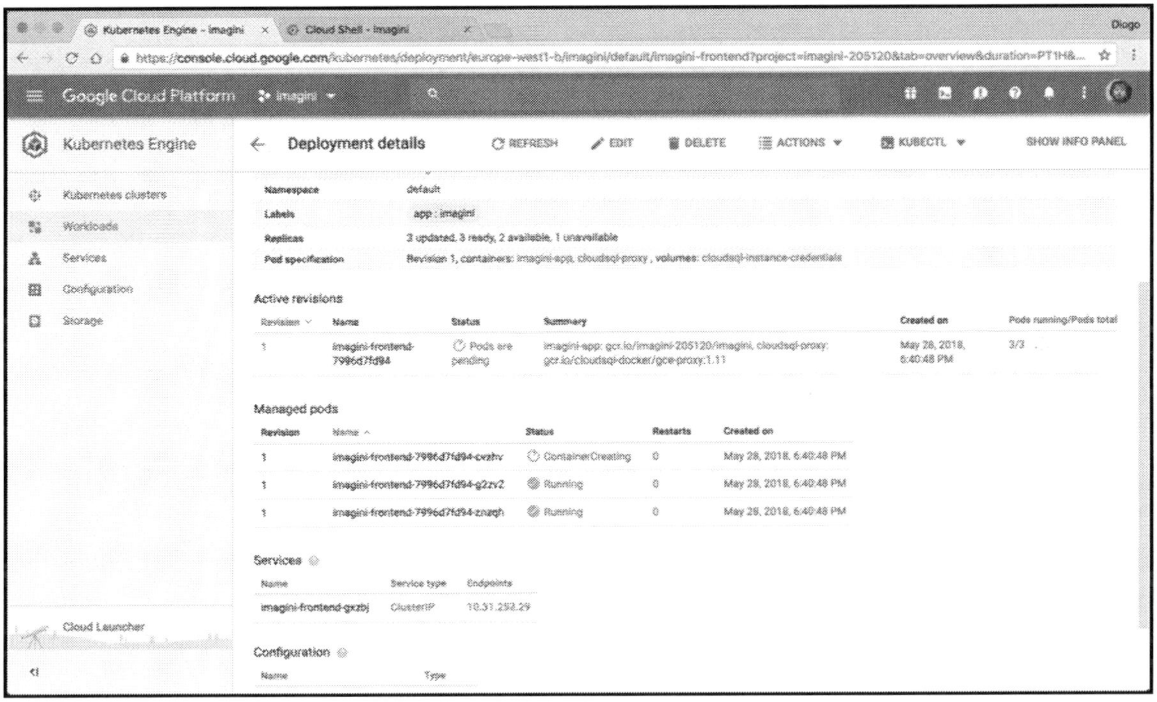

We see that some of the replicas are not running yet. You can hit **REFRESH** at the top to find out when all are ready. When they are, you'll see an **OK** on the previous page:

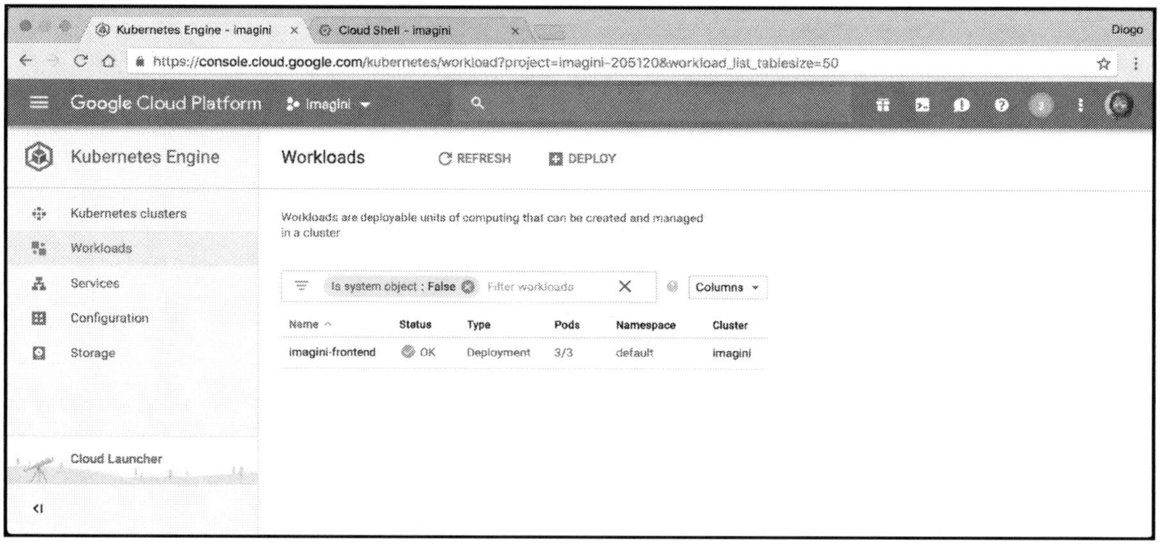

Inside the workload, you can change or destroy it, as well as scale it:

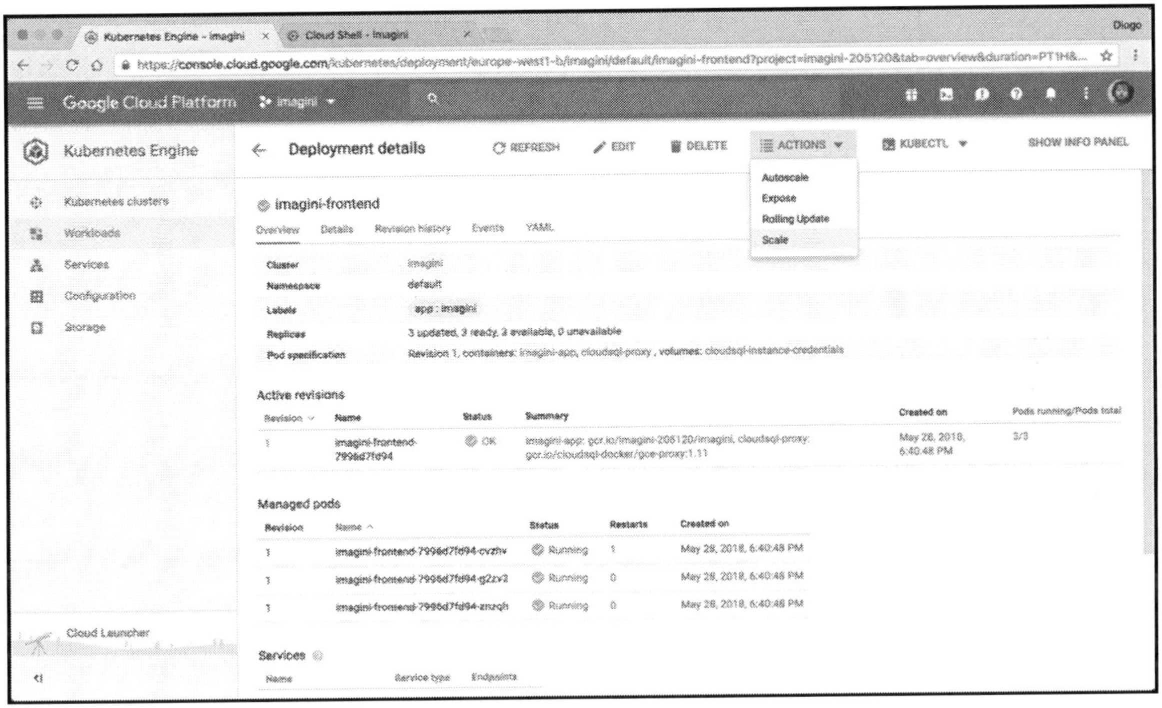

Try changing to five replicas. After a few seconds, you should now have five instances running:

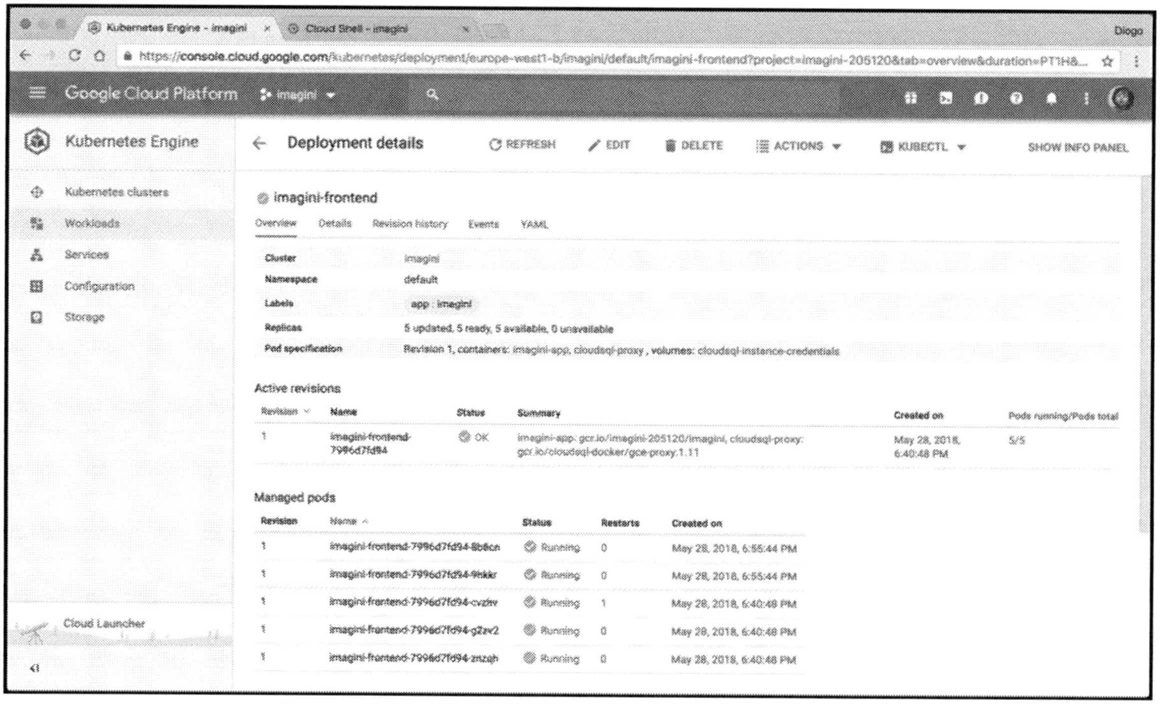

On the left sidebar, click on **Services**:

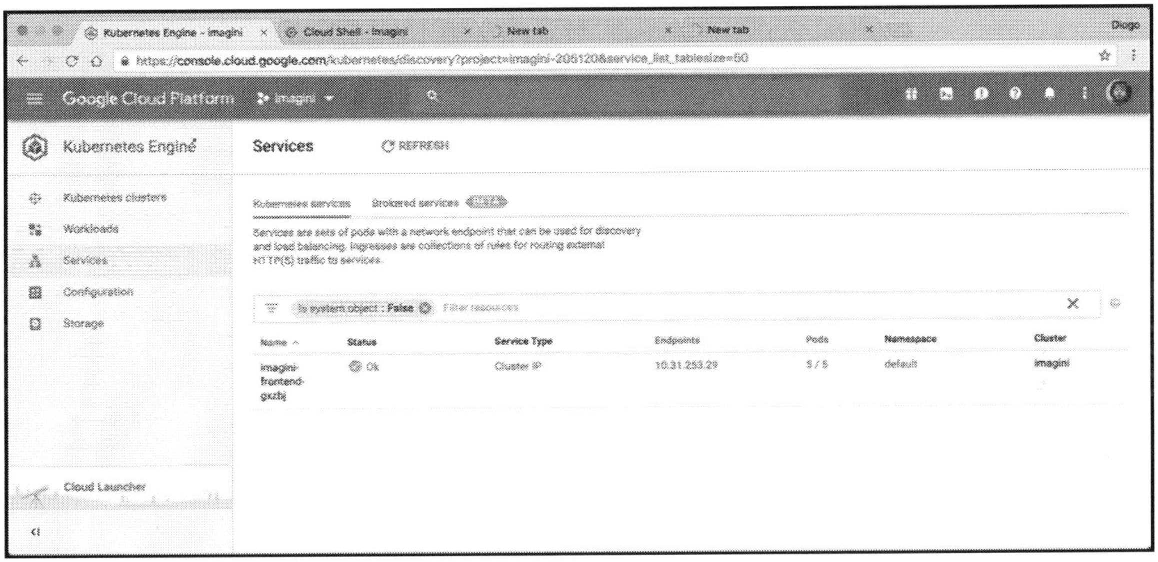

Our service is listed, using the cluster IP endpoint. You can click on the name for more details:

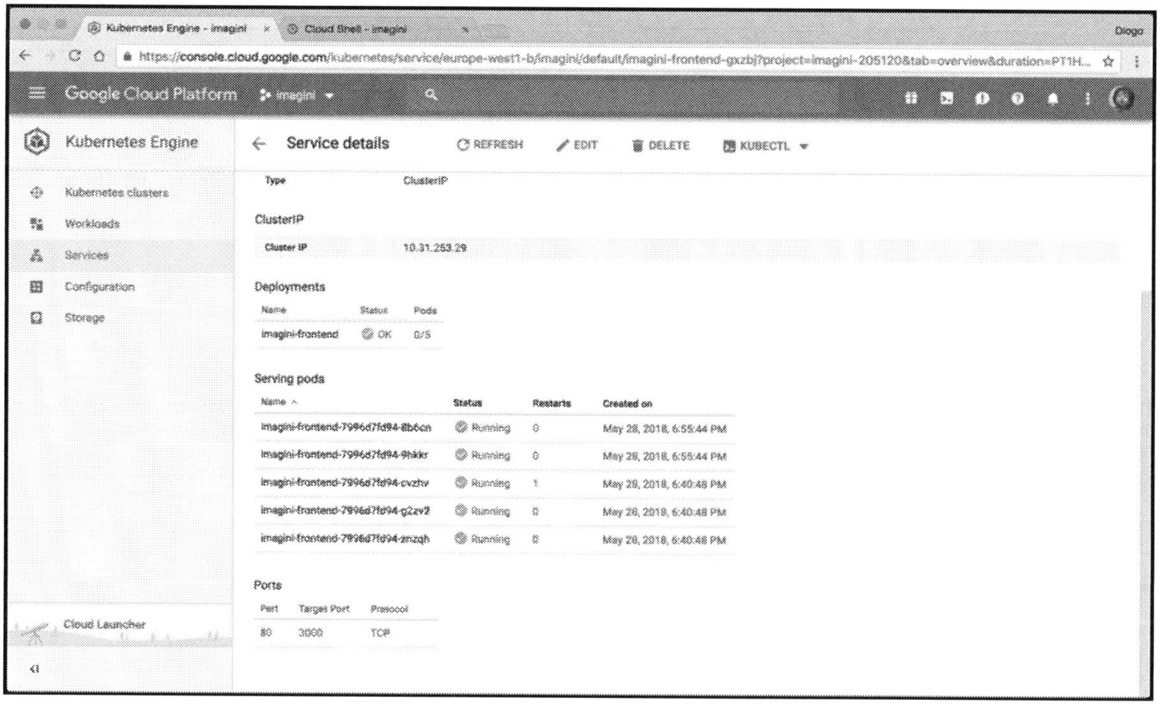


Scrolling down, you'll see the service port **3000** was exported to port **80**. And that's it!

# Summary

As I mentioned earlier, being cloud-native is about how we deploy our microservice, not where. If you design it from scratch to not depend on where it's deployed, moving it to the cloud is as simple as getting around any cloud provider.

If you keep yourself out of provider lock-ins, you'll be able to migrate your microservice from provider to provider, or even deploy to multiple providers with little to no effort. We will look at some design patterns and best practices in the next chapter before you're fully ready to create your own microservice.

# 9
# Design Patterns

In the previous chapter, we successfully deployed our service to a cloud provider without having to fundamentally change our code. We used a database to store our data, and the only thing we needed to do was to point to the new location.

It's common, during the specification and development process, to have challenging problems with one or more ways of solving them. The ways, or paths, you choose throughout the development are called design patterns, as they're part of your design.

Some design patterns are more common than others. Some are well-known, others, not so much. Some are good design patterns and you should follow them. Others are bad because of the disadvantages they bring in the short or long term.

In this chapter, we're going to take a look at the importance of choosing good patterns; we will look at some common architectural patterns and review the continuous integration we followed through the entire book until we successfully deployed to the cloud.

## Choosing patterns

Patterns are not libraries or classes, they're concepts, reusable solutions to common programming problems, tested and optimized for specific use cases. As they're just concepts to solve specific problems, they have to be implemented in every language.

Every pattern has its advantages and disadvantages, and choosing a wrong pattern for a problem can cause you a big headache.

Patterns can speed up the development process because they provide well-tested and well-proven development paradigms. Reusing patterns helps prevent issues and improves code readability between developers that are familiar with the patterns.

Patterns have major importance in high-performance applications. Sometimes, in order to achieve some flexibility, patterns introduce a new level of indirection in the code, which may reduce performance. You should choose when to introduce a pattern or when that introduction will hurt the performance metric you're targeting.

Knowing good patterns is essential for avoiding the opposite: anti-patterns. An anti-pattern is something that looks good in the beginning but later on turns out to look like the worst decision you ever made. Anti-patterns are not specific patterns but are more like common errors, seen by the majority as strategies you shouldn't use. Some of the most common and frequent anti-patterns seen out there are:

- **Repeating yourself**: Don't repeat excessive parts of the code. Lean back, look at the big picture and refactor it. Some developers tend to look at this refactoring as a complexity of the application, but it can actually turn your application simpler. If you think you won't be able to understand the simplicity of your refactoring, don't forget to add a couple of introductory comments to the code.
- **Golden hammer or silver bullet**: Don't think your favorite language or framework is universally applicable. Most of the languages can actually do practically anything, at least the mature ones, and with a huge community. That doesn't mean a language performs some tasks well. If your goal is performance, try to have a couple of hammers in your belt.
- **Coding by exception**: Don't add new code to handle new cases as they appear. By new cases, I don't mean new features; I mean behavior your code was not expecting. For example, when you're making a file upload feature of some kind, remember an error might happen during transfer, the file can be empty, have weird content, be huge, and so on.
- **Programming by accident**: Don't program by trial and error until you succeed. This is something you should really avoid. Programming by accident can sometimes make your code work in some cases (by accident) and produce erroneous behaviors in others.

# Architectural patterns

When developing microservices and, more specifically, an ecosystem of microservices, some patterns become very obvious, and you'll use them without knowing. Just looking at the architectural patterns, here are some that you might find interesting. Perhaps you have already used them before.

## Front Controller

The **Front Controller** pattern is when all requests go for a single point in your architecture, called the handler, which then processes and dispatches the requests to other handlers. This is the pattern used by, for example, load balancers and reverses proxies:

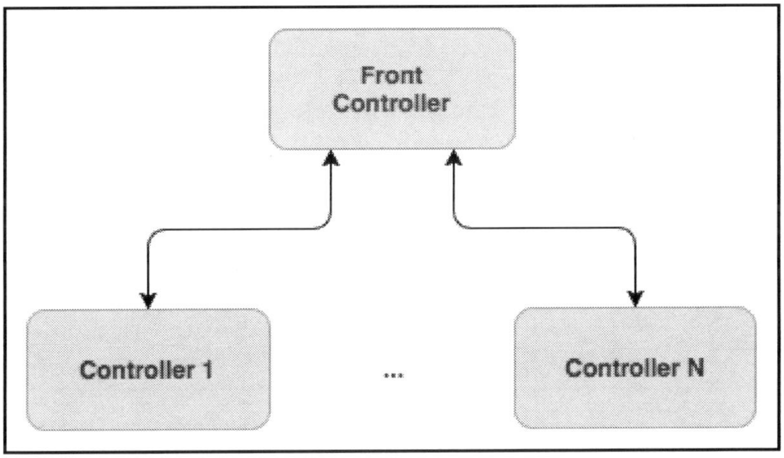


It's useful to scale horizontally, especially when the **Front Controller** is just routing requests, so it can handle a lot more requests than each separate controller, which need, some time to actually process each request.

This pattern is also very useful in helping other services not having to know where the controllers are and choosing the one with the lowest load that should handle the request faster.

# Layered

The layered pattern is common in filesystems and operative systems (and virtual machines for that matter). This pattern consists of creating different layers that go from the raw data through to the data seen by a user:

The idea is to separate the complexity of the different layers, each one not having to know how the others do their tasks:

- Handling the data structures and storing them in a fast and secure way
- Manipulating the data structures and adding business logic to them
- Handling user requests and showing the data in a localised format

# Service Locator

The **Service Locator** pattern is actually an anti-pattern. It's not considered a good practice because it adds much more complexity to an ecosystem. The pattern consists of a central registry, called a **Service Locator**, where services register their abilities, and other services can consult the registry and know where the services they need are located:

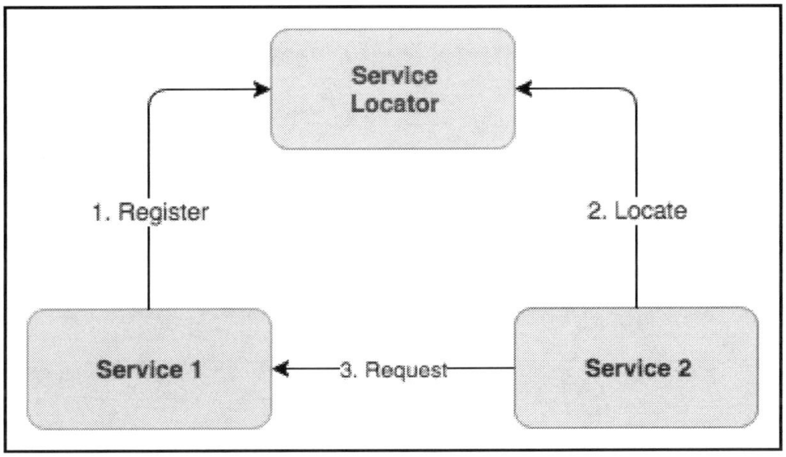


The **Service Locator** is similar to the Front Controller, but with added complexity, as you need to contact the Service Locator and the service you need, instead of just making a simple request to a Front Controller.

## Observer

The Observer pattern is used every day in Node.js. It consists of a **Subject**, which maintains a list of dependents, called Observers, which get notified of any state change happening on the **Subject**:

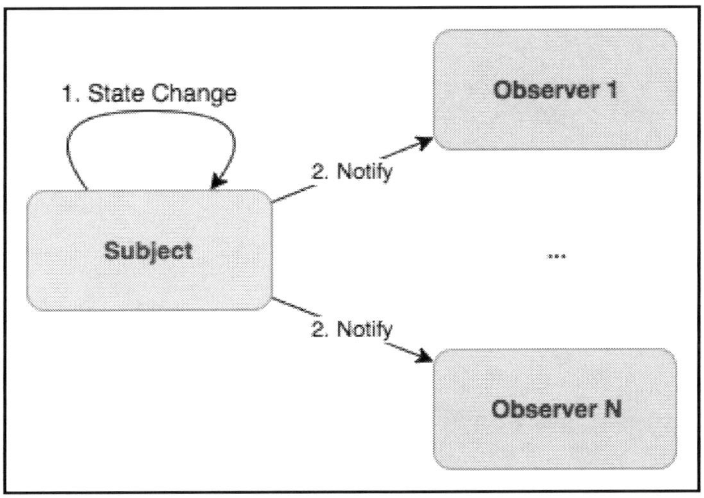

You can see this happening every time in your web browser when some code (**Observer**) attaches an event listener to an object or interface element (**Subject**).

## Publish-Subscribe

Another very similar pattern is the Publish-Subscribe pattern, usually abbreviated as **Pub-Sub**. This pattern is almost exactly the same as the previous one. You have Subscribers that, as the name implies, subscribe to a specific event, or topic, or whatever you want to call it, and then you have Publishers that emit those events or send information to those topics:

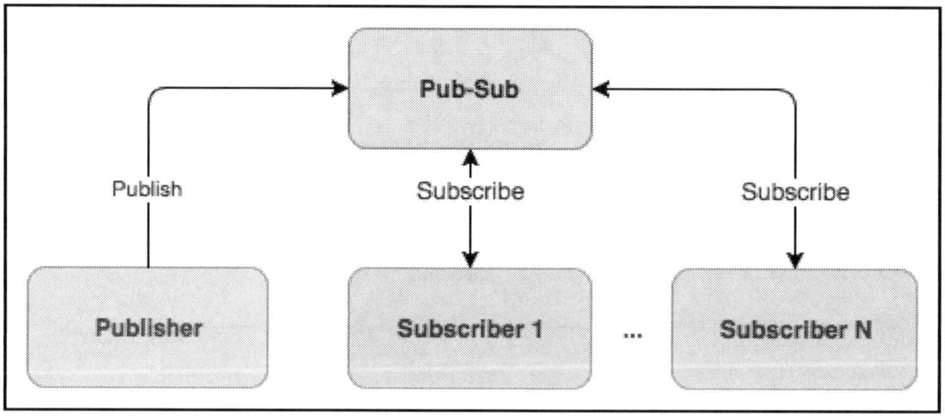


The difference to the previous pattern may look very thin but is actually very important. The **Pub-Sub** pattern involves a third-party service and, unlike the Observer pattern, the Publishers have no knowledge of the Subscribers. This removes the need to handle and directly notify the Subscribers, thereby simplifying your code.

This pattern is quite useful for microservice communication. It involves a third party that abstracts the state change notification. Also, Publishers and Subscribers have no knowledge of each other.

# Using patterns

Choosing good design patterns is essentially choosing best practices. Not all design patterns fit every purpose, but for many scenarios, they'll make your life easier. Perhaps you may not notice any difference in the beginning, but you should in the long-term.

Good design patterns also have indirect advantages. You'll find more documentation and examples online, as well as a broader set of options to choose from, for example, when using the Publish-Subscribe pattern, where you'll find many types of implementations to integrate with your services.

Choosing the pattern that fits your needs also involves planning and knowing what you need and what you'll need in the future. Think of the edge cases and see if the pattern is capable of handling them.

# Planning your microservice

Developing a microservice may look like a simple task. As the name implies, it is a micro service. But that is not necessarily true, as sometimes we tend to complexify something that should be simple.

This does not mean a service should be simple, it can be quite complex. What should be simple is the goal and the properties of the service. There shouldn't be any doubt regarding what it does and what it shouldn't do.

Before writing any line of code, you should start by knowing a couple of what I call characteristics of the service, such as:

- What is it for? What tasks will it do?
- What other services will use it? What protocol will it speak?
- Will it replace another service? Will it cover the same tasks?

This can be summed in one word—purpose. If you don't clearly define its purpose and just start developing tasks it can handle, you'll end up having a mixed service that deviates from the main goal of a microservice.

After having a proper purpose, you can then choose the best pattern and plan the individual tasks. The first task will probably take longer to develop, as you're creating the base layout for the service.

Don't forget to add tests, coverage, and documentation as soon as possible. I know this is something most developers tend to ignore, but it will bite you later. It's easier to add a simple test for a first simple task. Code coverage is easier at this point. Adding documentation should also be easier if you're planning the individual tasks.

After having your first task, with a proper test, you should set your first deploy. This will end your first development cycle and bring you back to planning. If you keep this loop going, with small tasks, you'll develop faster, and deploy faster:

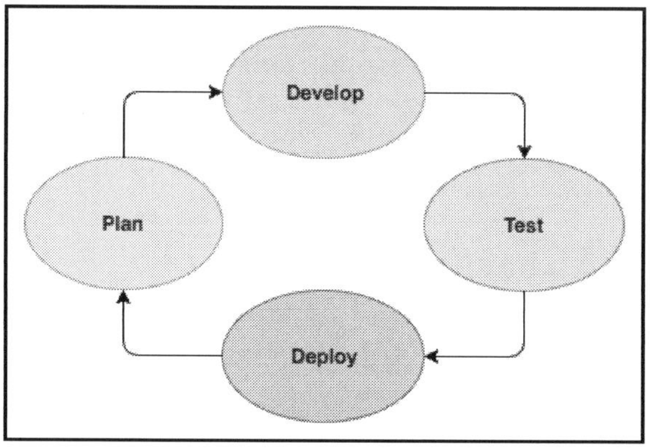


This type of simple loop with small tasks will allow you to do what is called **continuous integration** and **continuous deployment**, where you're able to develop and deploy to a testing cluster. The change can be automatically tested and deployed if everything passes the tests.

# Obstacles when developing

As we saw previously, a microservice architecture has many advantages, such as splitting code into smaller isolated projects, where it becomes easier to develop or even delegate responsibility.

These advantages come at a cost, which is the build of a more complex system or application. Because of how microservices are supposed to work, an information barrier is intrinsic. A microservice responsible for a type of information should be the only one manipulating it, forcing any other service to communicate with it to have access to information.

This gives you a finer control over the information because you know the service responsible for it, and you can force service or user authentication, with authorization or even rate-access limits. But, this means that a complex application will tend to penalize the network as there will be significant inter-service messaging.

Inter-service messaging means network traffic and latency. If the services are not on the same local network, this will eventually create noticeable latency. Adding some kind of cache service to accelerate access will also add more complexity.

Although testing and development for each microservice should be easier than a monolith application, looking at the microservice test frameworks all together, and having two or more services test together, is more complicated.

Finally, avoid something called a nanoservice. This is considered an anti-pattern, and it's when you exaggerate on fine-graining your architecture and create overly small services, complexifying your development to the extreme.

Find a good balance between the number of microservices and what each will do. Think of them as a person that will handle a specific task. Is the task too simple to have one person allocated to do just that? Shouldn't the person have a broader set of tasks from the same context?

# Summary

Today's applications have space for microservices. Applications are no longer monolith and left the traditional computer architecture long ago. Users constantly demand integrations and interoperability between applications.

Microservices help developers to reduce the complexity of applications by separating different contexts, such as frontend, backend, mobile, or a simple API. They're a concept, or a pattern, that, when used well, can give you great power, and split complexity and responsibility.

But, microservices are more than that. Microservices help you scale horizontally by just replicating the services you need and not a complete monolith application, saving resources and, ultimately, money.

There's a lot to explore out there; we have just scratched the surface. There are plenty of cloud providers and tools for you to experiment with and choose what fits you best. Remember, practice makes perfect, so head to your work desk, and good luck!

# Other Books You May Enjoy

If you enjoyed this book, you may be interested in these other books by Packt:

**Node.js Web Development - Fourth Edition**
David Herron

ISBN: 9781788626859

- Install and use Node.js 10 for both development and deployment
- Use the Express 4.16 application framework
- Work with REST service development using the Restify framework
- Use data storage engines such as MySQL, SQLITE3, and MongoDB
- Use User authentication methods with OAuth2
- Perform Real-time communication with the front-end using Socket.IO
- Implement Docker microservices in development, testing and deployment
- Perform unit testing with Mocha 5.x, and functional testing with Puppeteer 1.1.x
- Work with HTTPS using Let's Encrypt, and application security with Helmet

**Mastering Node.js - Second Edition**
Sandro Pasquali

ISBN: 9781785888960

- Build an Electron desktop app using Node that manages a filesystem
- Explore Streams and understand how they apply to building networked services
- Develop and deploy an SMS-driven customer service application
- Use WebSockets for rapid bi-directional communication
- Construct serverless applications with Amazon Lambda
- Test and debug with headless browsers, CPU profiling, Mocha, Sinon, and more
- Scale applications vertically and horizontally across multiple cores and web services

# Leave a review - let other readers know what you think

Please share your thoughts on this book with others by leaving a review on the site that you bought it from. If you purchased the book from Amazon, please leave us an honest review on this book's Amazon page. This is vital so that other potential readers can see and use your unbiased opinion to make purchasing decisions, we can understand what our customers think about our products, and our authors can see your feedback on the title that they have worked with Packt to create. It will only take a few minutes of your time, but is valuable to other potential customers, our authors, and Packt. Thank you!

# Index

## S



## T



## V



## W